Georgetown's Retail Past

Georgetown's Retail Past

Generations of Shops and Restaurants in
One of America's Great Historic Neighborhoods

KENNETH G. PETERS

Essex, Connecticut

An imprint of The Globe Pequot Publishing Group, Inc.
64 South Main St.
Essex, CT 06426
www.globepequot.com

Copyright © 2026 by Kenneth G. Peters

All rights reserved. No part of this book may be reproduced in any form or by any electronic or mechanical means, including information storage and retrieval systems, without written permission from the publisher, except by a reviewer who may quote passages in a review.

British Library Cataloguing in Publication Information available

Library of Congress Cataloging-in-Publication Data available

ISBN 9781493093625 (paperback) | ISBN 9781493093755 (epub)

CONTENTS

Introduction vii

CHAPTER 1: A Brief History of Georgetown 1
CHAPTER 2: Farm Supply and Feed Stores 15
CHAPTER 3: The Horse-Based Economy 22
CHAPTER 4: Horses Exit; Cars Arrive 29
CHAPTER 5: Clothing Stores: From Immigrant Families to Boutiques . . .36
CHAPTER 6: Shoe Stores and Shoe Repair 61
CHAPTER 7: Barbershops and Hair Salons 67
CHAPTER 8: Jewelers 77
CHAPTER 9: Laundries: The Evolution of Cleaning Clothes 87
CHAPTER 10: Grocery Stores: Corner Store to Supermarket 96
CHAPTER 11: Drugstores 114
CHAPTER 12: Candy Stores, Ice Cream Shops, and a Factory 128
CHAPTER 13: Tobacco Shops 138
CHAPTER 14: Florists 143
CHAPTER 15: Furniture and Home Furnishings Stores 148
CHAPTER 16: Antique Dealers 168
CHAPTER 17: Hardware Stores 181
CHAPTER 18: Paint and Glass Stores 193
CHAPTER 19: Appliance Stores: Keeping Up with Innovations 202
CHAPTER 20: Staying Overnight: Early Taverns to Hotels 207
CHAPTER 21: Restaurants 227
CHAPTER 22: Prohibition in Georgetown 248
CHAPTER 23: Bars and Bar Wars 253
CHAPTER 24: Movie Theaters 290
CHAPTER 25: Bowling Alleys and Pool Halls 299

GEORGETOWN'S RETAIL PAST

CHAPTER 26: Bicycle Shops 309
CHAPTER 27: Bookstores and Record Stores 313
CHAPTER 28: Toy Stores 323
CHAPTER 29: Sporting Goods Stores 327
CHAPTER 30: Georgetown's Own Banks 330
CHAPTER 31: Herring Hill Neighborhood Shops 340
CHAPTER 32: Changes in the 1980s: Georgetown Park
 and New Immigrant Entrepreneurs 349

Acknowledgments 361
Notes 363
Bibliography 401
Index 404

INTRODUCTION

Since the mid-twentieth century, Georgetown has been a place to find stores selling the stylish, the interesting, and the unusual, serving affluent neighborhood customers, shoppers from around the Washington area, and visitors from around the world. However, Georgetown was a retail center long before that, serving a different clientele.

The history of Georgetown retail stores often reflects larger forces: changes in the national economy and in the neighborhood's economy, changes in retailing practices, and technological changes that created new businesses and caused other businesses to disappear. As cars replaced horses, car dealers and garages replaced stables, blacksmiths, and carriage makers. The advent of home electrical appliances created a new category of stores, whose owners raced to keep up with innovations in their industry. Ubiquitous small grocers were replaced by chains of still-small grocery stores, which supermarkets in turn replaced later. In the mid-twentieth century, the restoration of Georgetown's historic houses and its growing reputation as a shopping destination gave rise to boutiques, antique shops, gourmet food stores, and restaurants offering fine dining, as well as noisy bars that irritated neighborhood residents.

A small business long has been an upward path for immigrants, and that was true in Georgetown, where immigrants owned many of the businesses. Washington is not often thought of as an immigrant destination; it lacks the vibrant ethnic neighborhoods of cities like New York, Chicago, Boston, and Baltimore. But it was the destination for thousands of immigrants, some of whom found their way into Georgetown's business community. In 1920, for example, when there were 289 stores on Wisconsin Avenue and M Street in Georgetown, the owners of at least 83 of them were born outside the United

States. The most frequent countries of origin among those 83 were Russia, Poland, Germany, and Italy.

It is conventional wisdom that District of Columbia natives are rare, but D.C. was the most common birthplace among U.S.-born Georgetown business owners in the early twentieth century. In 1920 again, of the owners whose birthplaces could be determined from the census, more than half were born in the District.

African Americans owned a few of the businesses, some along P Street in the Herring Hill neighborhood and a few others in the main shopping area on Wisconsin Avenue and M Street.

Over the generations, there have been hundreds of owners of Georgetown retail stores. It is possible here to tell the stories of only a selected few, focusing on those who seem typical of owners of stores like theirs, those whose businesses or personal stories are particularly interesting, and those whose stores were long lived and earned the description "Georgetown institution."

These are stories of ordinary people. Small business owners by and large did not make public speeches, keep diaries, or leave behind extensive records. The principal sources for this research have been city directories, census records, government property records, and the press. Oral history interviews recorded by the Georgetown Citizens Association have been a fruitful source as well.

At the same time, these seemingly ordinary people were extraordinary. One marvels at the entrepreneurial instinct of many. They started out in businesses where they had little experience, they shifted from one line of wares to another in response to perceived changes in customer preferences, they seized on the opportunity to buy the buildings where their stores were located, and they invested in other real estate. Several of them owned portfolios of Georgetown buildings. Some of them ended their lives in prosperous suburbs like Bethesda, Chevy Chase, Silver Spring, and Arlington. Some businesses were passed down through the founder's family, run by two, three, or even four successive generations.

It sometimes has been easy to learn about the proprietors of a business but hard to learn about the business itself. Until the mid-twentieth century, city directories tell us the name of a business's owner and the type of business—clothing store, restaurant, or hardware store, for example. Yet that

INTRODUCTION

often leaves us in the dark about the actual name of the store, its business model, and its stock in trade. For example, where a store is listed as selling "clothing," was it men's or women's or children's clothing? Was it clothing for average people or luxury goods? Was it sold at discount prices? Advertising sometimes fills the void and answers these questions, but many owners of small stores did not advertise.

Although the book touches on businesses in other parts of the neighborhood, it focuses primarily on stores on Wisconsin Avenue and M Street. When Georgetown's streets were renamed in the early 1880s, Bridge Street and High Street became M Street and Wisconsin Avenue, respectively, and the numbering of buildings was changed. To avoid confusing the reader with old addresses, pre-1880 business locations are identified by the post-1880 Wisconsin Avenue or M Street addresses of the same buildings, where the location of the old address can be identified with at least some confidence. Where that confidence is lacking, the original addresses are used.

In the preparation of this book, city directories and the census were referred to so frequently that it is not possible to cite each such reference in the notes. Where the text says that an event occurred in a specific year without citing a source, the reader can presume that the source was a city directory or, in a decennial year, that the source was either the directory or that year's census.

City directories were generally published in the first half of the year. Publishers collected information about city residents and businesses by door-to-door surveys, leaving cards to be mailed in by residents who were not at home when the surveyor visited.[1] In later years, publishers relied on mail surveys and telephone company records. Because each directory covered at most half of its year of publication and because of the lead time required by the collection process, we have presumed in this book that a business first opened in the year preceding its first directory listing, unless there is evidence from another source confirming that the store opened in the same year as the first listing. This assumption is imperfect, but it should yield the right opening year more often than the wrong one.

This book does not pretend to be a definitive study of Georgetown's retail history. Rather, it is a first effort to understand Georgetown's retail past, on which I hope others will build in the future.

CHAPTER 1
A Brief History of Georgetown

UNTIL THE 1830S, GEORGETOWN WAS A PORT FOR SHIPPING TOBACCO. It later became a canal terminal and a port for coastal shipping, with related industries. By the early twentieth century, it no longer was a port, and it had become a working-class urban neighborhood with an industrial district on its waterfront and a retail district serving farmers and suburbanites as well as local residents. Beginning in World War I and accelerating after World War II, new residents restored homes and changed the cultural and physical character of the neighborhood, creating the affluent enclave we know today but displacing lower-income residents.

Georgetown, Maryland, located at the most upstream navigable point on the Potomac River, was a natural place for deep water vessels to connect with inland planters seeking to get their tobacco crop to market. Georgetown's growth was spurred in 1747 when the Maryland legislature passed legislation that made it unlawful to ship tobacco from a Maryland port unless the tobacco had been inspected by a government inspector at an official inspection warehouse. This compelled planters to bring their tobacco to those few communities that had official inspection warehouses. The 1747 law specified George Gordon's existing warehouse in Georgetown as the official inspection station for Prince George's County, which at that time included Georgetown.[1] Later versions of the inspection law let each county decide where its inspection station would be, but by then the inspection function was firmly established in Georgetown, and there it stayed.

GEORGETOWN'S RETAIL PAST

In 1751, the Maryland legislature authorized five commissioners to formally establish the town and to purchase and subdivide sixty acres of land to accomplish that. In 1789, the legislature incorporated the town.[2]

One of Georgetown's earliest retail merchants was Robert Peter, who was an agent for British tobacco firm John Glassford & Co. Besides his tobacco trading activities, Peter was proprietor of the "Rock Creek Store," where customers could trade tobacco for European luxury goods. Peter later became the first mayor of Georgetown after the town's incorporation in 1789 and was one of the original donors of land for the creation of the District of Columbia. His descendants built and resided in the Tudor Place estate in Georgetown.[3]

The earliest map showing development in Georgetown is a hand-drawn 1799 map of the part of town south of Dumbarton Street.[4]

Looking at the map, we see that some lots are vacant, and many buildings do not use all of their lots' street frontage. Only two buildings clearly are businesses: a bank and a tavern next door to it on the southwest corner of High and Bridge Streets. Other buildings are identified with last names, many recognizable as names of longtime Georgetown families, but there is nothing to indicate whether those buildings were homes or businesses or perhaps both.

The tobacco trade declined in the late 1820s and the 1830s, when prices fell. The last tobacco firm in town closed when its owner, John Laird, died in 1833.[5]

In 1830, when the tobacco trade was declining though not yet gone, a Georgetown directory shows the retail core on High and Bridge Streets (today's Wisconsin Avenue and M Street) was firmly established, indeed thriving. There were 132 businesses on the two streets, including twelve dry goods stores, five clothiers, ten tailors, nine shoemakers, and two jewelers. Food was available from thirty-five grocery stores, five bakeries, six meat markets, and a candy store. There were two blacksmiths, four saddlers, and five tanners. There were two drugstores and three bookstores, as well as five bars and a tobacco store.

The town's businessmen, seeing its economy threatened by uncertain tobacco prices and increasing competition from other ports, joined other local leaders in promoting the construction of the Chesapeake & Ohio

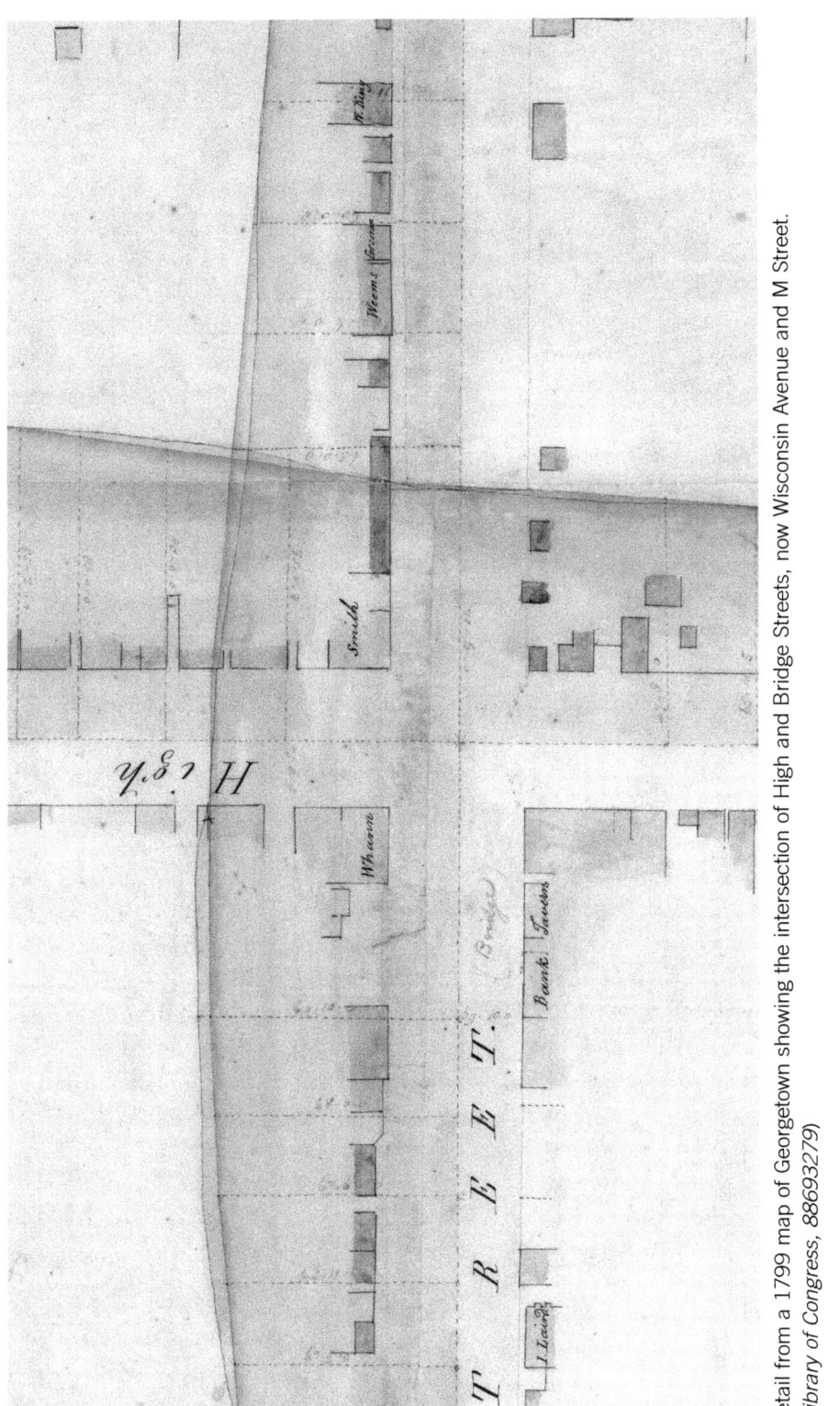

Detail from a 1799 map of Georgetown showing the intersection of High and Bridge Streets, now Wisconsin Avenue and M Street. (*Library of Congress, 88693279*)

(C&O) Canal, one of the largest public works projects in the country's history up to then. The vision was that the canal would bring inland goods to Georgetown's port, from which they could be shipped to domestic ports and overseas. Ground was broken in 1828, and the first phase of the canal opened in 1831. The first canal shipment to arrive in Georgetown was a load of coal from western Maryland, and coal would comprise a big part of canal cargo for decades to come—a single canal boat carried one hundred tons of it.[6]

The canal never lived up to expectations. Ironically, the day of the canal's groundbreaking also was the day ground was broken for the Baltimore & Ohio Railroad, which was tough competition throughout the life of the canal. Floods in 1836, 1843, 1847, 1852, and 1889 each damaged the canal, resulting in long closures.[7] In 1845, the Alexandria Canal Company completed construction of the Aqueduct Bridge between Georgetown and Virginia. The bridge carried a canal across the river, so that boats from the C&O Canal could reach the port of Alexandria, bypassing Georgetown's port.

Georgetown had a growing African American population during the decades before the Civil War. In 1776, about a third of the town's people were free African Americans, a combination of descendants of indentured servants, formerly enslaved people who had been freed by (or bought freedom from) their owners, and fugitive slaves pretending to be free. In 1830, 1,204 of the town's 8,441 citizens were free African American (14 percent). In 1860, the proportion had grown to 22 percent (1,935 out of 8,733). Some 200 African American families settled in Herring Hill in the northeast part of town, named for the herring that were plentiful in nearby Rock Creek. A concentration of businesses owned by African Americans would develop there.[8] (See chapter 31 for more about Herring Hill.)

By 1860, there were 164 businesses on the two main streets. The next year, A. Boschke published a map of Washington based on surveys conducted in 1856–1859, showing the locations of buildings throughout the city. Boschke's map shows us that buildings along Bridge Street (now M Street) now were continuous from 30th Street to 33rd Street and along High Street (now Wisconsin Avenue) all the way to P Street.

Georgetown began to decline as the Civil War approached. Construction of the Long Bridge (today's 14th Street bridge) had caused Georgetown's harbor to accumulate silt, reducing port traffic. The Panic of 1857 bankrupted

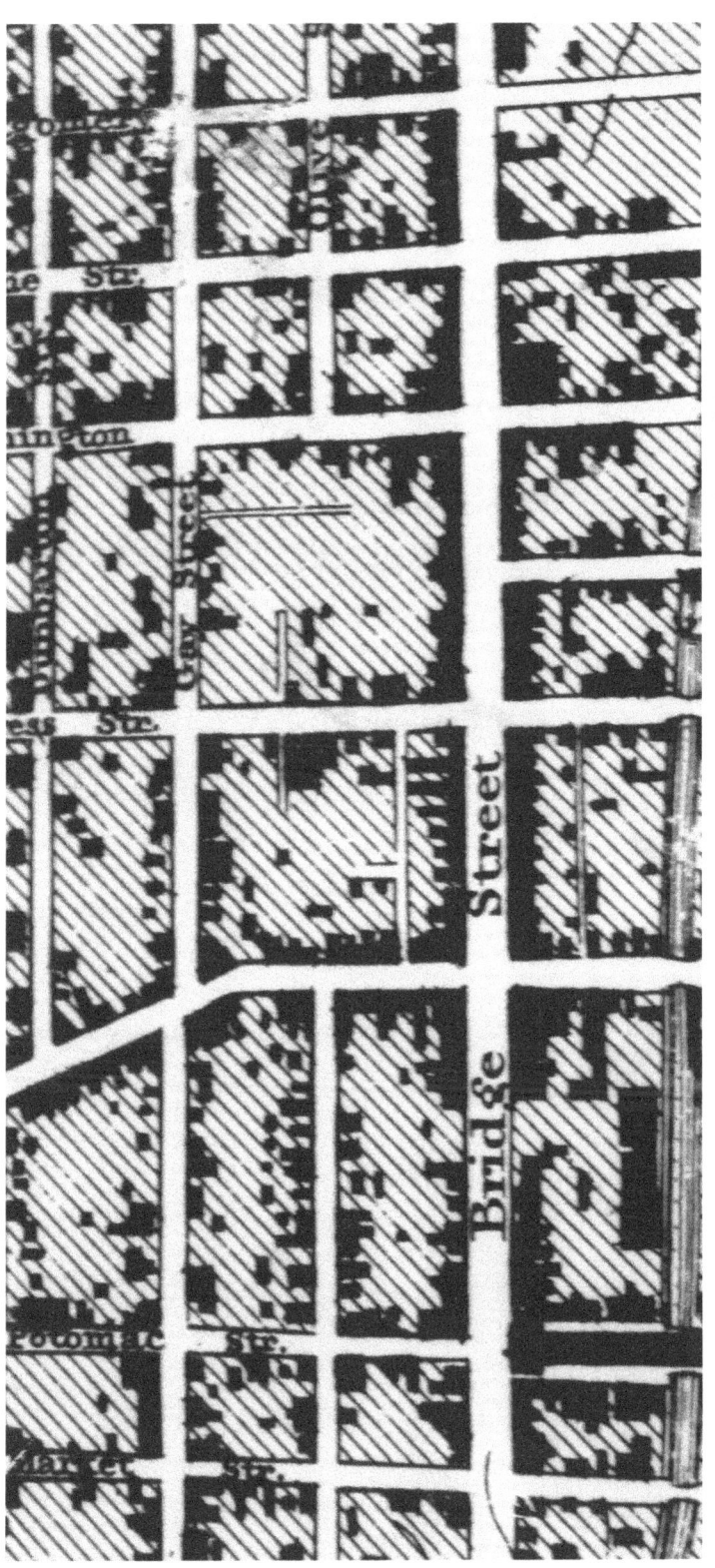

Detail from Boschke's map of Georgetown based on surveys from 1856 to 1859. (*Library of Congress, 88690673*)

several warehouses. The decline continued after the war, and fewer and fewer oceangoing vessels called at Georgetown. By the 1870s, silt had reduced the channel's depth to only ten feet at low tide. In 1881, after a major flood inundated parts of downtown Washington, the Army Corps of Engineers constructed the Tidal Basin and Haines Point, which improved the City of Washington's port and made it a stronger competitor.[9]

Georgetown suffered from a lack of control over its own affairs. It had its own municipal government until 1871, but that government lacked the authority to develop a much-needed rail line to Georgetown.[10] The Aqueduct Bridge was run by a consortium from the rival port of Alexandria, which seldom had Georgetown's interests in mind. The Army Corps of Engineers was more focused on the port of Washington than on Georgetown.

In 1871, Congress created a consolidated D.C. government, ending Georgetown's existence as a separate municipality.[11] After that consolidation, the city government tended to focus more on the city, and to not trouble itself too much with Georgetown's needs. For a while there even was a push to rename the neighborhood "West Washington."

Also in 1871, the newly created D.C. Board of Public Works under Alexander "Boss" Shepherd began an extensive campaign to improve the District's infrastructure, including a major regrading of Georgetown streets to moderate some of their steep slopes. The construction disrupted the Georgetown retail area for two years. One observer said, "so many foot pavements were torn up that Georgetowners came to be known by their walk, the 'gait of a horse with a spring-halt.'"[12] Lowering of the grade of some residential streets forced construction of the high front steps now found on some blocks.[13] The market house, built in 1865 on today's M Street at Potomac Street, measured 246 feet by 40 feet. That large structure had to be raised to the new, higher-grade level of M Street.[14]

All this construction, coming right after Congress eliminated Georgetown's separate municipal government and consolidated it with the City of Washington, added to residents' resentment and suspicion about the consolidated government. The cost of Shepherd's program drove the D.C. government into bankruptcy in 1873 and resulted in the end of Home Rule.[15] Georgetown did benefit from the paving of major streets for the first time:

M Street west of 31st and Wisconsin Avenue up to P Street with granite and trap block, and M Street east of 31st with asphalt.[16]

In 1880, the commissioners who headed the D.C. government ordered that street names in Georgetown be changed to conform to the street system in the City of Washington. Before this change, what is now M Street was called Bridge Street east of Wisconsin Avenue and Falls Street west of it, and Wisconsin Avenue was called High Street. Today's numbered streets had names like Frederick, Congress, and Washington. The house numbering system changed as well, creating some challenges today when identifying the existing building that a pre-1880 business occupied.[17]

By now Georgetown's industry was obsolete. It was powered by water from the canal and its raw materials came by canal boat, while modern industry elsewhere was supplied by railroads (which Georgetown lacked) and powered by steam and later electricity. Whenever floods damaged the canal, there was no power for the mills. Five of the seven flour mills along the waterfront closed by 1890. After that, the waterfront increasingly contained a concentration of industrial uses: lumber yards, blacksmith shops, foundries, tinsmiths, coal yards, construction contractors, sellers of gravel and paving, an ice company, and so on. The canal finally closed after yet another flood in 1924.[18]

Despite the industrial decline, two transportation developments late in the nineteenth century were boons for retailers. One was the federal government's purchase and renovation of the Aqueduct Bridge, as well as elimination of the bridge's high tolls.[19] The other was the construction of multiple streetcar lines that converged on Georgetown from rural areas to the north, from downtown Washington, and from Arlington, Virginia.[20]

The improved transportation brought residents of new suburbs and many more farmers into Georgetown. Shoe store owner Bernard Nordlinger (about whom there will be more in chapter 5) said years later that he had customers from Tenallytown in D.C. and Rosslyn, Vienna, and Herndon in Virginia. Liquor merchant Milton Kronheim recalled Georgetown being a marketplace for farmers from Montgomery County, Maryland.[21]

Georgetown thus became a regional retail marketplace, but the neighborhood otherwise stagnated. Rents in Georgetown were low, and some housing deteriorated or was converted to boardinghouses. Mary Mitchell described the state of affairs:

> *Despite its proximity to the central city, Georgetown in the first part of the 20th century had become a somewhat old-fashioned, second-class district, although people living today and growing up in those years say they were unaware of this kind of change.*[22]

In 1915, the wife of the secretary of war was overheard lamenting to a friend that, in order to find a house with a yard suitable for her children, she might have to go to Virginia. The wife's friend said, "Too bad! You will have to pass through Georgetown."[23]

M Street and Wisconsin Avenue in the nineteenth century were not solely retail. Merchants' families and other people lived above stores and in residential buildings next door to commercial ones. In 1880, 614 people lived on the three blocks of M Street between 30th and 33rd. In 1910, there still were 522 in those same three blocks.[24] In the ensuing decades, many residential buildings would be converted to retail use or replaced, or have their ground floors converted to retail use. Apartments would remain on the upper floors. As homes were converted to stores, many proprietors added store windows. Professional offices also occupied the ground floors of some buildings, including doctors, lawyers, insurance agents, real estate brokers, and undertakers.

In the nineteenth and early twentieth centuries, advertising billboards often were painted on building walls. Remnants of two such billboards remain in Georgetown today. One of them is partially visible on the east wall of the building at 3112 M Street. Partly obscured by buildings constructed since, it says "Quaker Oats. The World's Breakfast." That phrase appears in newspaper advertising by the Quaker Oats Company in 1912 and 1913, which must be when the billboard was painted.[25]

Georgetowners were wisely skeptical of big projects sponsored by outsiders. One example came in 1928, shortly after the Key Bridge was completed. The office of the DC Municipal Architect proposed that M Street be replaced with a grand boulevard 350 feet wide. All buildings between M and Prospect Streets from the Key Bridge to Rock Creek would be demolished to make way for the Francis Scott Key Parkway, as the proposed boulevard was to be called.[26]

A BRIEF HISTORY OF GEORGETOWN

Quaker Oats billboard on the east wall of 3112 M Street. (*Photo by the author*)

Had the proposed parkway been built, the entire M Street retail district would have been obliterated. Fortunately, the idea died quickly. There was no more mention of the idea in the newspapers, suggesting that it was an unsuccessful trial balloon floated by the Municipal Architect's office.

Though located next to and later within the City of Washington, Georgetown long had the look and feel of a small town. Recollections of residents consistently recall that flavor with nostalgia.

Kathryn Schneider Smith, author of *Port Town to Urban Neighborhood: The Georgetown Waterfront of Washington, D.C., 1880–1920*, described the thread running through her interviews of residents as she did her research:

All those interviewed shared some common lore about the place. All remembered the gathering of all kinds of people on M Street on Saturday night. They all were eager to describe the dramatic daily fire drills at the firehouse, though the stories

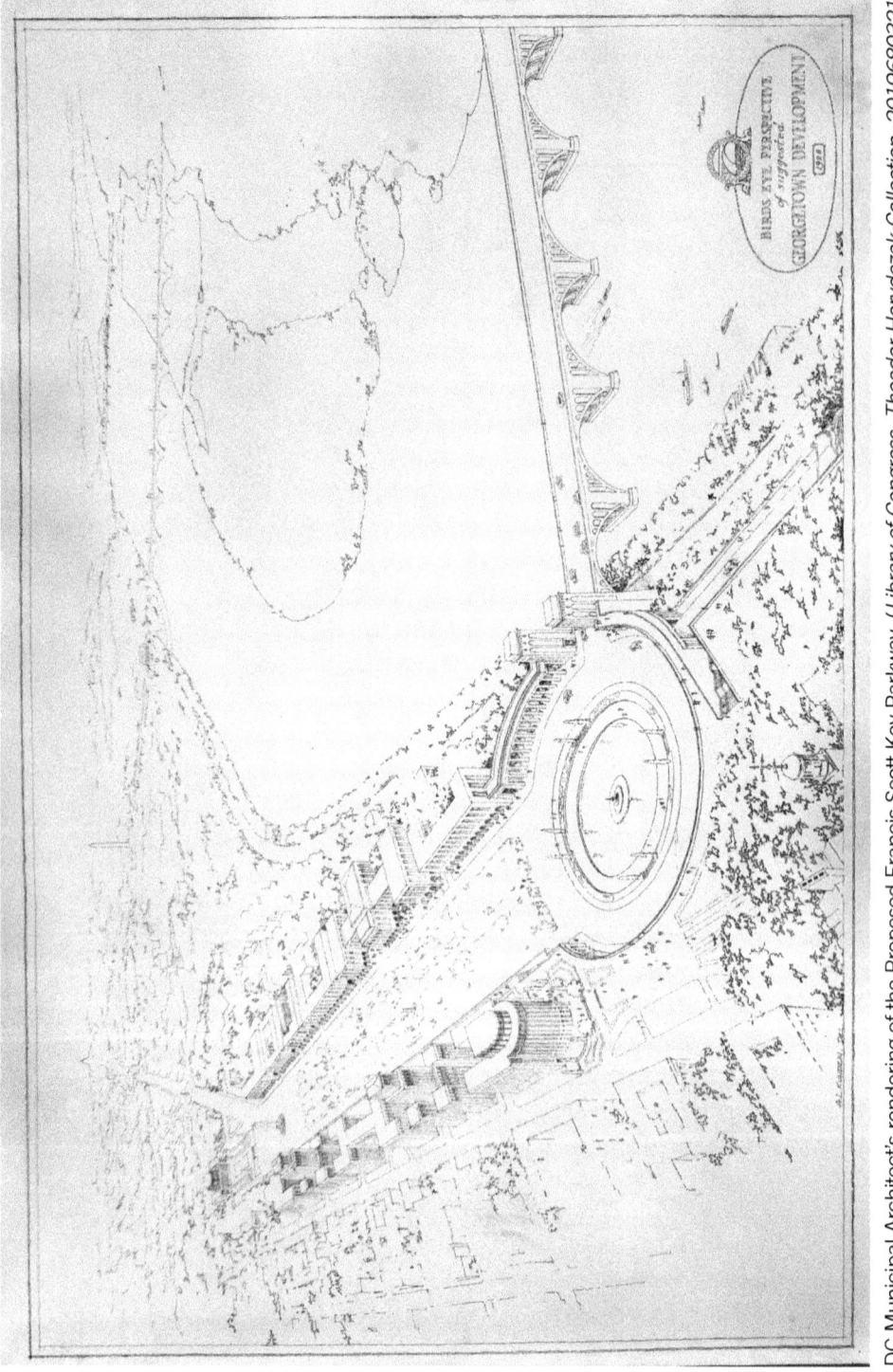

DC Municipal Architect's rendering of the Proposed Francis Scott Key Parkway. (*Library of Congress, Theodor Horydczak Collection, 2019680321*)

differed in detail. . . . Former residents remembered the three-masted schooners at the Georgetown docks and the crash of the Ice as it was unloaded down long chutes from the ships into the American Ice Company warehouse at the foot of 31st Street. They recalled with a sense of romance the canalboats and their residents who lived such different lives from their own. They remembered the open air movie house run by Inky Davis at Bank and M Streets, the wonderful candies and ice cream from the Chaconas Family's confectionery, and the military funeral parades that came down M Street on their way to Arlington Cemetery by way of the Aqueduct Bridge.[27]

Scott Hart, in his history of Washington during World War I, describes what a Georgetown streetcar passenger would have seen during those years:

Through the front windows of the [Wisconsin Avenue] streetcars could be seen stores and shops, some four or five stories high, dabs or pastel or merely time-worn brick. "This is not a street," a wartime visiting New Yorker exclaimed upon his first sight of the avenue. "This is a painting of a nineteenth-century small town main street."[28]

Surprisingly little has been written about the process by which Georgetown changed into the historically restored, affluent enclave we know today. Most histories of Washington just observe in passing that the catalyst for restoration was pioneering civil servants and government officials who took up residence in the neighborhood during the New Deal.

In his more comprehensive study of the subject, Dennis Gale observed that, as was the case with other historic neighborhoods, Georgetown's decline actually helped to preserve its historic character because, except for the waterfront, industrialization and development passed it by.[29] He traces the first forces of restoration as coming during World War I, when growth in the federal workforce created housing scarcity. Many of the newcomers were in Washington only temporarily and were unaware of what Gale calls "the déclassé image of Georgetown living."[30]

The 1937 *WPA Guide to Washington* suggested the restoration process was well under way by that time, describing an updated commercial section with new shop fronts and saying that "in recent years, the smaller homes have been bought by artists, newspapermen, moderately well-to-do government employees and others who appreciated the charm that lay beneath dilapidation."[31] Between 1929 and 1945, five times as many building permits for improvements and repairs were issued in the east central part of Georgetown as had been in the period 1915–1928, even though the years 1929–1945 included the Depression and wartime restrictions on building materials.[32] In July 1940, *House and Garden* devoted its entire issue to Georgetown.

Restoration accelerated after World War II. Higher demand for Georgetown housing caused prices and rents to rise, which in turn caused the neighborhood to become more of an upper-income district.[33] The higher prices forced less affluent residents to go elsewhere. The African American population shrank drastically.

Longtime residents Richard and Philip Levy said that when John F. Kennedy was elected president in 1960, it was "like somebody flipped a switch" and Georgetown became fashionable, but in fact Georgetown already had acquired social cachet by then.[34] *Holiday* magazine in 1952 said, "Today, Georgetown is to Washington what Russian and Telegraph Hills are to San Francisco, Beacon Hill to Boston, Mayfair to London and The Faubourg St.-Germain to Paris." Clearly Georgetown's days of being perceived as a backwater urban neighborhood were over. Gale observed that "from the New Deal onward, Georgetown's prestige was conferred as much *on* those who moved there as *by* those who did so."[35] Retailers found new customers among increasingly affluent residents and visitors attracted to the neighborhood's historic charm.

In 1950, improvements to retail buildings became regulated in a whole new way when Congress sought to safeguard Georgetown's historic architecture by passing the Old Georgetown Act. The act, which still is in effect, requires that the federal Commission of Fine Arts approve any plans for construction or exterior alteration of buildings in Georgetown. The Old Georgetown Board, composed of three architects, reviews plans for the commission.[36] Georgetown citizen groups pushed for the act, fearing that the reawakening historic neighborhood would be overwhelmed by apartment buildings.

There was much debate about the legislation before it passed. Proponents were inspired by Williamsburg, Virginia, and suggested that using colonial designs and materials instead of neon and plate glass could achieve a desirable historical atmosphere. Opponents among merchants wanted to modernize, not seek quaintness.[37]

Sally Peters (not related to the author) was one of the first merchants to seek a permit after the act went into effect. She wanted to move her florist shop to new quarters on Wisconsin Avenue but her plans were rejected the first two times she submitted them because they included a plate glass store window. Objections to plate glass store windows had been a topic of debate when the Old Georgetown Act was being considered, and the commission insisted that her window be a collection of small panes with an eighteenth-century flavor even though it would not be as good for displaying flowers as a full window would have been. A competitor only three doors away could keep a plate glass window constructed before the act was passed.[38]

The review process at times led to discussions that bordered on the metaphysical. In 1958, a dry cleaning business known as the London Cleaners sought approval for "a baroque-style sign with Old English lettering." When the commissioners who then governed the District of Columbia met to consider the application, a debate ensued as to whether *baroque* was the right word to describe old English lettering. The Fine Arts Commission opined that Old English was inappropriate in Georgetown. The head of the Department of Licenses and Inspections said the letters of the sign would be out of place because they were "crooked and cockeyed." One of the D.C. commissioners expressed concern that if the commissioners approved the application they would be "subject to learned criticism." Afterward the designer of the sign lamented that, having tried to do the right thing by creating a sign in keeping with the neighborhood, shop owners now were asked by the commissioners to do a modern rectangular sign instead.[39]

Merchants and residents like Sally Peters had to navigate the act's shakedown period, but a look around Georgetown today shows that the Old Georgetown Board, while still demanding that the neighborhood's architectural heritage be preserved, has become more pragmatic—plate glass windows abound, for example, and Sally Peters's paned store window has long since been replaced with plate glass. While the Old Georgetown Act helped preserve the neighborhood's historic appearance and atmosphere, it also contributed to the displacement of lower-income residents, many of them

African American, because complying with its requirements drove the cost of home repairs and maintenance above what those residents could afford.[40]

The streetcars that served Georgetown for decades were replaced by buses in the early 1960s. A few years later came another potential transportation development: the Metro rapid transit system. A widely held impression is that no Metro station was built in Georgetown because of neighborhood opposition. In fact, although some Georgetown residents were vocally fearful about who the system might bring to Georgetown, there were three other, bigger obstacles. Because M Street is far above the Potomac River, and trains would run in tunnels below the river, a Georgetown station would have been even farther below street level than today's Rosslyn station. To enable trains to turn east toward downtown, it would have been necessary to dig tunnels under historic homes and buildings in Georgetown. Finally, the focus of the system's planners was on getting commuters in and out of Washington, and in the 1960s few people commuted to Georgetown.[41]

The Georgetown retail district has continued to thrive despite the absence of a subway station. One can only speculate as to how different things would have been had there been a Georgetown station.

CHAPTER 2

Farm Supply and Feed Stores

Farmers long were customers of Georgetown retailers. Parts of the District of Columbia outside the old city boundary of Florida Avenue (formerly called Boundary Street) did not really start to urbanize until the 1870s, and rural areas remained in nearby Maryland and Northern Virginia long after that. The suburban shopping areas that now surround Washington did not exist, and people from the surrounding rural areas came to Washington and to Georgetown to shop. Stores in Georgetown served farmers' needs, selling "agricultural implements" and feed for livestock and horses.

CROPLEY, BOTELER, AND CRAMPTON

Charles B. Cropley, born in 1852, was the youngest son of Samuel Cropley, whose family also ran grocery stores and drugstores in Georgetown (see chapters 10 and 11). In the early 1880s, Charles worked as a retail clerk in his brother George's drugstore. In 1882, when he was thirty years old, he and two other retail clerks, George Boteler and John Crampton, joined forces to start an agricultural implements business.

Although they listed themselves in city directories as dealers in agricultural implements, an ad they purchased in an 1884 business directory tells us they also were in the fertilizer manufacturing business, and sheds light on what "agricultural implements" were:

> *[Cropley, Boteler and Crampton] are agents for various agricultural implements and outfits, among which we mention Deering & Co.'s harvesters, Tennessee Wagon Co.'s wagons, Greencastle grain drills, Remington ploughs,*

and Baldwin's patent reversible slip share. . . . They are all young, industrious and enterprising men who, by their commercial ability, have achieved a prominence accorded only to those whose transactions have been based on the strictest principles of mercantile honor.[1]

The same ad said that Cropley, Boteler, and Crampton manufactured fertilizer, specializing in the "Acme" and "ammoniated" bone superphosphate and "Bone and Potash" fertilizers. Manufacturing fertilizer can be a noxious process, so the warehouse/factory may have been somewhere other than M Street. The ad said that they had a five-thousand-square-foot warehouse in addition to the eighteen-hundred-square-foot store.

The business lasted about ten years. In 1903, Charles Cropley began selling seed from a store of his own on M Street, but that venture soon ended in bankruptcy. Charles went on to become a partner in Cropley and Paschal, "merchandise brokers and manufacturers' agents," at the same address as his failed seed store.[2]

MAYFIELD & BROWN

Frederick L. Moore was in the agricultural implements business starting around 1867. After its startup years, his business was located at 3147 M Street, in a building since demolished.

At some point, probably in the late 1880s, Moore developed a business relationship with William P. Mayfield and William T. Brown. Mayfield and Brown both were born in Georgetown. Their fathers, Benjamin R. Mayfield and Stephen T. Brown, were brothers-in-law who ran a dry goods store on M Street from 1852 to 1869 (see chapter 5) and later became officers of the Farmers and Mechanics' Bank in Georgetown. The elder Brown continued in the dry goods business until 1896.

In 1891, Mayfield and Brown opened an agricultural implements store on M Street in the space formerly occupied by Frederick L. Moore's milling business, in which Mayfield and Brown had been partners.

Mayfield and Brown's store continued in business for another thirty years. Farmers of course were the customer base. Among other promotional activities to reach that base, the store was a regular exhibitor at each year's Montgomery County Fair.[3] It was the last agricultural goods store in the neighborhood, closing in 1920. The weakness of the post–World War I economy had combined with the increasing urbanization of Arlington County, Virginia, and rural D.C. to spell the end for agricultural implements businesses.

There was a court-ordered sale of the goods in Mayfield and Brown's store. The published notice of the sale provides a vivid picture of their inventory and a further lesson in just what "agricultural implements" were:

> *Farming Implements and Parts, consisting of a large stock of Plowshares, Cultivator and Harrow Points, No. 2 Simplex Corn Planter, Plows, Harrows, Cultivators, Double Roller, Corn Shellers, Garden Tools, Chicken and Hog Wire, Horse Collars and Pads, Hardware, Rope, Chain, Wheelbarrows, Lanterns, Whips, Iron Gates, Pumps, 2-Horsepower International Gas Engine, Poultry and Animal Medicine, Seed, etc.*[4]

The fact that in the early twentieth century this equipment was being sold at the corner of Wisconsin Avenue and M Street underscores how much Georgetown changed during the remainder of that century.

THE LEE FAMILY

Alfred Lee and his descendants were one of Georgetown's most successful African American families, running a feed business in Georgetown for one hundred years. Alfred Lee was born in 1806 and, by 1830, was living in Georgetown. A newspaper advertisement, possibly his first, tells us that he was in the feed business in Georgetown by 1845.[5] His store was located at the eastern end of the 2900 block of M Street.

In 1848, Lee opened a second feed store on 12th Street in downtown Washington. A newspaper ad announced the new store and also revealed that Lee's practice of extending credit had created some challenges: "[Lee] earnestly solicits those who have not settled up their bills for the last eighteen months to do so without further notice."[6]

By 1858, Lee's Georgetown store was in quarters at what now is 2902–8 M Street.[7] Although it is not possible to determine the store's exact construction date because the District of Columbia did not require building permits before 1876, it seems certain that Lee was the builder.

> **SEED OATS, SEED OATS!**—The subscriber tenders his sincere thanks to the public, and specially to his punctual customers for past favors, and respectfully solicits a continuance of their favor. He has in store, selected from the best lots offered from the upper parts of Virginia and Maryland, about—
>   500 bushels of good heavy Seed Oats
>   Also, a good stock of common do
>   1,000 bushels of Corn, in the ear and shelled
>   6,000   do   Shipstuff, a part of which is a superior article
>   8,000   do   Brownstuff and Shorts
>   100   do   pure Rye Chop
>   100   do   Rye, in grain
>   400   do   Corn Meal, and a portion of cut Hay and Straw.
> All of which he will sell on very reasonable terms for cash or to punctual customers.
>   He would thank those who are indebted to him prior to this year to settle up their bills without further notice.
>   ALFRED LEE,
>   Wholesale and retail dealer in Produce, Grain, &c.
>   South side Bridge street, Georgetown, D. C.
>   mar 16—ep3t

An 1847 ad provides a partial picture of what Lee sold. (National Intelligencer, March 16, 1847, 3)

The new building, which still stands, was large, with sixty feet of frontage on M Street, and another twenty feet on 29th Street. Most stores in Georgetown had frontage of twenty-five feet or less.[8] The Lees lived at 2908 and leased 2902 to residential tenants until they expanded the store into that space in 1930.

Lee and his wife Margaret were both classified by census takers as "mulatto," meaning mixed race. Although they may have been born into slavery, from 1830 on they were listed in the census as "free colored." They had a large family—the 1850 census shows the two of them living in Georgetown, with nine children ages two to twenty-one. Three of those children later would become part of the business. The same census shows that Alfred owned real estate that he said was worth $4,300, a sign that he had started on the road to success.

FARM SUPPLY AND FEED STORES

After Alfred Lee's death in 1868, an obituary in the *Freedman's Press* said that Alfred was the half brother of Robert E. Lee. Enslaved status passed through the mother, so if what the obituary says is true, Alfred's father would have been "Light Horse" Harry Lee, and his mother would have been enslaved by the Lee family. The obituary made much of the contrast between Alfred's loyalty to the Union during the Civil War and Robert E. Lee's participation in the rebellion. Did Alfred Lee himself claim this relationship? We do not know. Birth records for enslaved individuals were nonexistent, making it impossible to substantiate the claim. Some suggest that Alfred Lee's father was Aloysius Lee, who owned property that Alfred later came to own.[9]

The obituary also says that Alfred "bought his time as a slave," which seems to mean he bought his freedom. Since he was free by 1830, he would have purchased his freedom by the time he was twenty-four, no small accomplishment.

When Alfred Lee died in 1868, he left behind an estate worth $300,000, considerable wealth for any man to have accumulated in the mid-nineteenth century, much less an African American.[10]

Building at 2902–8 M Street that was home to the Lee Feed store for eighty years. (*Photo by the author*)

GEORGETOWN'S RETAIL PAST

In his will, Alfred said "it is my express desire and wish that [sons John T., Samuel, and William H. Lee] continue to carry on the same business as feed dealers, peaceably and in a brotherly manner." They did so. They initially changed the name of the store to "J. T. Lee & Co.," but a few years later changed it back to "William H. Lee, feed," and that is the name under which the business continued for another seventy years. When William H. Lee died in 1893, his own son, also named William H., took over the business.

Today the term *feed store* suggests food for horses and cattle, but the Lees sold food for other creatures as well. Armistead Peter Jr., who owned Georgetown's Tudor Place estate, raised pigeons as a hobby. He regularly bought enormous quantities of pigeon feed from the Lee store, including five hundred pounds in a single $18 transaction on January 8, 1935.[11]

The business finally closed in the mid-1940s.

In this photo, the handwritten notation is incorrect—D. B. Jackson ran this feed store on Wisconsin Avenue at Dumbarton Street from 1877 to 1885. (*Peabody Room, D.C. Public Library*)

PATRICK MORAN

Patrick T. Moran ran the other long-running feed store, which he started in 1913 at 3259 M Street, near the stables at the west end of M Street. This was late to be getting into the feed business. Although farmers would always need feed, the Washington area was already rapidly urbanizing, and the transition to the automobile would soon reduce the demand for feed for urban horses. Despite these challenges, Moran's store was the last Georgetown feed store to close, in the late 1950s.

Moran was born in Ireland, and his parents brought him to the United States in 1878, when he was twelve. Besides running the feed business, he was active in the business community, serving as president of the Chamber of Commerce and vice president of the Lincoln National Bank. He also was active in the Knights of Columbus.[12]

Unlike the Lees, none of Moran's sons took over the business after his death. Someone else did (we do not know who), because the store in Georgetown remained open from Moran's death in 1923 until the late 1950s. The business continued even after that, in suburban locations.

As the demand for feed in Georgetown diminished, the business broadened its product market and opened other locations in Vienna and Arlington, Virginia. Moran's also began selling food for pets and other smaller animals.[13]

In the early 1990s, new owners Michael and Mary Claire Molony had turned Moran's into a small chain of pet food superstores that included two twenty-thousand-square-foot locations as well as smaller ones. They won the 1993 Pet Retailer of the Year award from the industry publication *Pet Products News*.[14]

CHAPTER 3

The Horse-Based Economy

IN THE EARLY TWENTIETH CENTURY, AUTOMOBILES AND TRUCKS RAPIDLY replaced horses and wagons as the means of transporting people and goods within cities. In the process, businesses and occupations that had supported horse-drawn transportation were supplanted by new ones supporting the automobile. Developments in Georgetown mirrored these trends.

It is hard today for us to comprehend how ubiquitous the horse was. In 1900, Manhattan Island, in its twenty-three square miles, contained 1.8 million people and 130,000 horses (about 5,600 horses per square mile). All those horses needed food—three tons of hay and one ton of oats per year for a working draft horse. They also produced waste products—four million pounds a day in New York City. Support businesses provided stables, tack (reins, etc.), feed, and blacksmith services, among other things.[1]

Automobile use grew rapidly after the turn of the century. The number of registered motor vehicles in the United States grew from 8,000 in 1900 to 1.7 million in 1914. By 1912, cars outnumbered horses in New York City.[2] People using cars to move around and transport goods were no longer using horses, and the demand for horse-related goods and services dropped.

In 1900, there were 289 horse-related businesses (stables, carriage makers, blacksmiths, and harness makers) in the District of Columbia. By 1920, that total had shrunk to 91. The same decline in the horse-related economy was visible on Georgetown's main commercial streets.

Horse-Related Businesses on Wisconsin Avenue and M Street by Year

	1860	1881	1914	1920	1930
Stables	3	2	4	2	0
Carriage makers	1	2	4	2	0
Blacksmiths	4	7	0	0	0
Harness makers	2	4	2	1	1
Feed stores	1	6	3	3	2
Total horse-related businesses	11	21	13	8	3

By 1930, the horse-related economy essentially was gone. Some blacksmiths remained, but they were probably doing mostly general ironwork, such as repairing the cast iron front steps that are common in Georgetown and elsewhere in the city.

In Georgetown, a few owners of horse-related businesses anticipated the change and transitioned to car-related businesses, but most did not.

STABLES

Georgetown stables were located in three places: at the east end of town, on Wisconsin Avenue or Pennsylvania Avenue next to Rock Creek Park; farther west, around 33rd and M Street near the Georgetown Market; and between those extremes, on Wisconsin Avenue just south of M Street. Stables both rented and sold horses.

At the east end, Richard Cruit and his son Richard Cruit Jr. ran a livery stable on M Street near Rock Creek from 1860 to 1871, when they closed their Georgetown location and opened a stable in downtown Washington.[3] George W. Wise, a Georgetown entrepreneur who also was in the grocery and funeral home businesses, ran a stable from 1914 through 1920 at 28th and Pennsylvania Avenue, where the Four Seasons Hotel is located today. James H. Johnson then took over Wise's location and ran Georgetown's last stable there until 1927.

Richard Darne

Near the market, Richard H. Darne (possibly known as Harry) opened in 1853 what was to be Georgetown's longest-running stable, on M Street near

In this photo taken in 1905, horse-related businesses are clustered together near the Georgetown Market. Richard Darne's Arlington Livery Stable is on the right, a carriage maker is in the middle, and Timothy Shugrue's blacksmith shop is on the left. (*DC History Center*)

the corner with 33rd Street, across M Street from the Georgetown Market. At some point before 1890, he started calling it the Arlington Livery Stable. (Curiously, the Cruits used the same name for their downtown location, though there was no apparent connection between them and Darne.)

Mary Mitchell, writing in the 1980s, described what she thought the atmosphere must have been like near Darne's stable:

> *This was the market space intersection with M Street where a rowdy atmosphere spiked with blarney and southern lingo flourished. Here were three saloons run by the convivial men of Erin, two livery stables, one owned by R. H. Darne from Virginia who always had a highbred stallion to show off, and a barbershop. Horse talk, deals in the marketplace or a saloon when a stallion was at stud, fast talk in the barbershops, a mingling of smells emanating from stable and bierstube.*[4]

The third stable to which Mitchell refers probably was the place where one of the city's horse-drawn streetcar lines kept its horses, on the future site of the Georgetown Park shopping mall.[5]

Richard Darne and his twin brother Fayette Darne were born in Virginia in 1827. Richard lived in Georgetown until the 1870s, but after that preferred to live on his farm in Fairfax County, Virginia. Among his other activities, Darne was one of the bodyguards at Abraham Lincoln's inauguration. He also was a skilled horseman, winning the $500 stakes of a trotting race from Washington to Leesburg, Virginia.[6]

Between 1887 and 1892, Darne leased the stable, first to William McFarland and later to Benjamin Bridges Jr. and Thomas L. Presgraves. This is an excerpt from McFarland's paid listing in an 1881 business directory:

> *A fine lot of horses, carriages, buggies, barouches, phaetons, and road wagons, saddle horses &c are kept for hire. Horses are taken by single feed or boarded by the week or month and employment is given to 4 hands. His facilities for furnishing first-class turnouts to individuals or parties are unsurpassed. Horses are bought and sold on commission and prompt returns made, his personal attention being given to the sales department, he being a thorough judge of horseflesh.*[7]

In 1893, Darne decided to make major improvements. He tore down the stable and invested $6,000 to construct a new 40-by-120-foot brick stable building.[8] In 1895, he was back in the stable business himself, in the new quarters.

Shortly after 1900, when he was seventy-three years old, Darne turned the stable business over to his twin brother's son, Fayette T. Darne, a blacksmith, who ran the business for a few more years, with partners.[9] After 1908, the property ceased to be a stable.

Richard Darne died in 1910 of injuries sustained in a fall. His dying request was to be buried under an apple tree on his farm. An obituary called him "Dean of Liverymen."[10]

John Dugan

From 1880 to 1920, John Dugan, born in Ireland, ran a stable just a couple of doors from Darne's, at 3301 M Street. In 1890, like Darne, Dugan made improvements. He spent $4,000 to construct a brick stable building 42 feet wide by 120 feet deep, a few doors away at 3307 M Street.[11] This was the year before Darne built his new stable, which was the same size as Dugan's—perhaps Darne was keeping up with the nearby competition.

Dugan and Darne did not make the business transition from the horse to the automobile, but the large, solid brick buildings they constructed did make that transition (see chapter 4).

In the middle of town, Parkway Livery's stable did business at 1065 Wisconsin Avenue, south of M Street, from 1904 to 1914. Its owner, Ellsworth T. Simpson, did make the transition to the automobile, as we will also see in chapter 4.

HARNESS MAKERS AND BLACKSMITHS

Many harness makers congregated in the nineteenth century on Wisconsin Avenue between M and Dumbarton Streets. While most blacksmiths were located near the stables on M Street west of the Georgetown Market, others were near the waterfront, and three were located near Wisconsin Avenue and Q Street. For blacksmiths, shoeing horses was not the only activity. They also made a variety of iron tools and implements, as well as metal parts like hinges.

Georgetown's longest-standing harness maker was William Stombock. Born in Virginia in 1878, Stombock followed in the footsteps of his father, also a harness maker. He came to Washington around 1902 at age twenty-four and worked as a harness maker for several years before opening his own shop on M Street in 1910. The store moved among different locations until 1917 when it settled at 3278 M Street, next door to the Georgetown Market. Stombock and his wife Ollie (probably short for Olivia) never lived far from the business, residing for a while on 33rd Street just north of M and finally settling on Dent Place near 33rd.

Stombock experimented with diversification and hedged his bets when the automobile came along. In the 1920s, he not only sold and made harnesses but also sold automobile accessories, a business his brother later took over and moved around the corner as Stombock's Auto Top and Body Shop. In the 1930s, Stombock listed himself in a city directory as a source of "horse goods, English saddler, leather goods repairing, dog accessories."

THE HORSE-BASED ECONOMY

A 1959 photo of the building that was the home of Stombock's Saddlery for more than fifty years. (*DC History Center*)

Specialized items one could buy at Stombock's included jowl hoods, breast plates, bits and bridles, snaffles, crowns, skull caps, girth tubes, and hoof dressing. The store supplied the Washington Polo Club and Rosecroft Raceway, and it had prominent people among its clientele. General George Patton bought his boots there and had Stombock make the cartridge belt and holsters for his two pearl-handled revolvers. During World War II, Patton ordered custom-made leather goods from Stombock's that his wife mailed to him. The shop made a special harness for President Franklin D. Roosevelt that enabled him to pull himself up to review parades, and made a pony harness for David Eisenhower when he was a boy. John F. Kennedy came to the store to have his riding boots custom-dyed.

A fifteen-foot-high plaster of Paris horse on wheels stood in front of the store. One day in the late 1930s, a group of Georgetown students hitched the horse to an eastbound streetcar. The police found it at Washington Circle.

William Stombock died in 1940, and his son Earl (nicknamed Bud) continued the business, which had been renamed "William H. Stombock &

Son" in the late 1930s. When Earl died in 1960, he willed the business to an employee, Danny Durham, who had begun working for the store in the 1930s as an after-school sweeper for $2 a week.[12] In 1970, Durham moved the store to Potomac, Maryland, where he had opened a branch some time before, and later moved it to Gaithersburg, Maryland, finally closing it in 1990. The plaster of Paris horse, which had moved with the business and had been christened "Old Georgetown," was sold to the Clyde's restaurant chain to decorate their new location in Reston, Virginia.[13] The Georgetown store space is occupied in 2025 by a J. McLaughlin clothing store.

CHAPTER 4

Horses Exit; Cars Arrive

As automobile use grew, Georgetown became a center for car-related businesses of all kinds—new and used car dealers, repair shops, tire stores, auto parts dealers, and service stations. This table shows the growth of such uses on Wisconsin Avenue and M Street.

Car-Related Businesses on Wisconsin Avenue and M Street by Year

	1860	1881	1914	1920	1930
Auto dealers	0	0	1	1	10
Auto repairs	0	0	1	1	10
Auto parts	0	0	0	6	4
Gas stations	0	0	0	1	8
Total car-related businesses	0	0	2	9	32

What accounted for this concentration? One factor may have been the highway system. Until the Memorial Bridge opened in 1932, there were only two bridges from Virginia into downtown Washington. The 14th Street Bridge led to the Mall, but the Aqueduct Bridge and its later replacement, the Key Bridge, led motorists into an existing commercial district (Georgetown) where businesses to serve the passing cars could locate. Motorists crossing the Chain Bridge also were routed into Georgetown by Canal Road. Georgetown before 1950 was not a particularly prosperous neighborhood, and rents for commercial space were not high.

As noted in chapter 3, only a handful of proprietors of horse-related businesses successfully made the transition into an automobile-dominated marketplace.

The number of auto-related businesses began to decline in the 1960s, when Georgetown's rise as a retail and entertainment district created more lucrative uses for properties on the two main commercial streets.

CAR DEALERS
Probey-Haynes

The first car dealer to open for business in Georgetown was Probey-Haynes Motor Company in 1914, on Wisconsin Avenue just north of M Street. James K. Probey was a carriage maker, in business since the 1890s, who, by the early twentieth century, saw demand for carriages dropping and saw cars as an opportunity.

When Probey started selling Haynes electric cars, he added "Haynes" to his own business's name. Newspaper ads run by Probey-Haynes boasted that "every function of the Haynes is controlled by electricity," and said the car could reach speeds as high as sixty miles per hour. To counter the stereotype that electric cars were only for women, ads assured readers that "the Haynes is a man's car in every way, but any woman may drive it."[1]

Electric cars were quickly eclipsed by those with internal combustion engines, probably explaining the disappearance of Probey-Haynes after 1916.

Parkway Motors

Parkway Motor Company, later renamed Parkway Motors, was the successor to Parkway Livery, a stable located at 1065 Wisconsin Avenue. Ellsworth T. Simpson owned Parkway Livery and, like Probey, saw the handwriting on the wall and moved from selling and boarding horses to selling and servicing cars.

In October 1916, the *Evening Star* ran announcements of an auction of all the equipment of Parkway Livery, including thirty horses, multiple wagons, and harnesses.[2] We do not know whether this liquidation was voluntary, but we do know that Simpson already had gone into the car business a few months before the auction, in March 1916. The *Evening Star* of March 12 included an ad for "Parkway Motor Truck Company," a distributor for Federal Trucks and Commerce Trucks with a "service station and salesroom" at

HORSES EXIT; CARS ARRIVE

This photo was taken in 1925 in front of Parkway Motors' Wisconsin Avenue showroom. (*Library of Congress National Photo Co. Collection LC-DIG-npcc-13384*)

1065 Wisconsin Avenue—the same address as Parkway Livery.[3] By 1918, Parkway was known as Parkway Motor Co. and was a Ford dealer.

In the mid-1920s, Simpson got out of both the car business and the feed business and went into real estate. He sold Parkway Motor Co. to four brothers, Robert, Fred, Walter, and William Carter.[4]

The Carters set out to expand and, in 1929, announced that they had acquired four lots on the southwest corner of M and Thomas Jefferson Streets, where they intended to build "a three-story building to provide the most up-to-date construction in garage and salesroom arrangement," including a wash stand for three cars, a paint and body shop, and "specialized equipment for Ford repairs." Instead of elevators, the building would have ramps for moving cars around, and the roof would provide additional parking.[5] The new building, at 3040 M Street, still stands in 2025.

GEORGETOWN'S RETAIL PAST

This 1964 photo shows the building Parkway Motors constructed at 3040 M Street in 1929–1930. (*DC History Center*)

With the scarcity of land in Georgetown, later expansion was a challenge. In the early 1940s, Parkway Motors (as it was known by then) opened a used car lot across M Street on the grounds of the historic Old Stone House, which is the oldest house in Georgetown. By the mid-1950s, Georgetown civic groups had begun raising objections to the presence of a used car lot on a historic property, and in February 1956 the Interior Department, which had acquired the property, made Parkway vacate. Another challenge came in 1954, when Parkway proposed to build a garage on a vacant lot between Thirtieth and Thomas Jefferson Streets just south of M Street. A dispute with nearby residents ensued. Parkway apparently lost, because the lot remains vacant in 2025.[6]

Parkway Motors ceased doing business in Georgetown in the late 1960s. Their building, which was uniquely large for Georgetown, became in succession a multi-screen movie theater (see chapter 24), a Barnes & Noble bookstore, and a Nike sporting goods store. Barnes & Noble returned to the space in November 2024.

HORSES EXIT; CARS ARRIVE

Stohlman Chevrolet

Stohlman Chevrolet opened for business in 1930 at 3307 M Street, in the brick building that John Dugan had built for his stable forty years before. After Dugan closed his stable in 1920, the space had been home to the Potomac Garage and later the Georgetown Rent A Car Company. The Stohlman dealership would do business in Georgetown for forty years, selling both new and used cars.

Edwin L. Stohlman, who started the business, was one of nine children of John W. Stohlman, the proprietor of Stohlman's Bakery, a Georgetown institution (see chapter 12). Edwin apparently inherited his father's entrepreneurial spirit and opened Potomac Tire Co. in 1925, when he was thirty. America's entry into World War II brought rubber rationing and hard times

The stable building that John Dugan built in 1890. This photo was taken between 1921 and 1926. In 1930, Stohlman Chevrolet would open for business in the building. (*Library of Congress National Photo Co. Collection LC-DIG-npcc-30274*)

Stohlman Chevrolet is on the left side of M Street in this photo taken between 1958 and 1960. By now the stable building had been replaced by a more modern one.
(*D.C. Department of Transportation*)

for tire dealers, and by 1943 Potomac Tire was gone, as were several other Georgetown tire dealers. By this time, Stohlman Chevrolet had been open for more than ten years.

In the 1950s, Stohlman needed space for the used car part of his dealership, for which he took over another former stable, this time the brick stable building that Richard Darne had built sixty years before at 3289 M Street.

Stohlman was prominent in the local auto industry, serving as the president of the local association of auto dealers from 1953 to 1956. In 1972, he sold the Georgetown dealership and retired. He died that December. Automobiles were in the family's blood, however; at the time of his death, his sons owned Volkswagen, Oldsmobile, and Datsun dealerships in Northern Virginia. As of this writing in 2025, the Volkswagen dealership still is in business.

AUTO REPAIRS

In 1915, Bernard Buscher opened the first auto repair business in Georgetown, again in the area where there formerly had been a concentration of stables, near 33rd and M Street. He was gone by 1920, but by 1926 there were many more cars on the road, and someone had to repair them. In that year, there were fourteen auto repair shops on Wisconsin Avenue and M Street. Many of the new shops were located in the 2700 and 2800 blocks of M Street, also near where there had been stables in past years.

AUTO PARTS

The first auto parts store appeared in Georgetown around 1918. By 1920, there were a half dozen such stores on Wisconsin Avenue and M Street, and the number peaked at eight in 1943. After 1960, there were only a handful. The historic Georgetown Market was home to an auto parts store from 1956 to 1980 (see the photograph in chapter 10). It was the last auto parts store in the neighborhood to close.

SERVICE STATIONS

In 1938, the number of gas stations on Wisconsin Avenue and M Street peaked at thirteen. All have been replaced by newer commercial buildings, except for two at Wisconsin Avenue and Q Street. Gas stations have been in those two locations since the 1930s.

CHAPTER 5

Clothing Stores

From Immigrant Families to Boutiques

In the mid-nineteenth century, ready-to-wear clothes did not exist. Women were expected to be able to sew, and most made their own clothes except for well-off women who could hire dressmakers to do it for them. Dry goods merchants and notion shops supplied the raw materials and implements for sewing.

This changed in the twentieth century as ready-made clothing became available. Expenditures per person for ready-made clothing grew from about $3 per year in 1869 to $21 in 1899 and $30.50 in 1929 (all in 1913 dollars).[1] That meant less demand for dry goods. This trend is reflected in the number of dry goods stores in Georgetown, which had consistently been between ten and fifteen into the 1930s and shrank to four by 1940. By 1948, there were none. Some dry goods stores went out of business, but other dry goods merchants (such as Louise Edlowitz and Joseph Gurewitz in Georgetown) broadened their inventory and started calling their shops department stores or clothing stores.

From the 1870s through the 1930s, there were around twenty-five stores on Georgetown's two main streets selling ready-made clothing. That seems like a large number for a small working-class community—in 1877 the population of Georgetown was about 11,500.[2] Clothing stores on the two main streets became even more numerous when Georgetown became a shopping destination, increasing to forty-three in 1975 and eighty in 1995.

CLOTHING STORES

DRY GOODS STORES

Dry goods is a foreign concept today. In his history of American department stores, Robert Hendrickson explains the term and its origin:

> *Dry goods stores take their name from shops run by New England merchants, many of whom were shipowners and direct importers in colonial times. Their two chief imports were rum and bolts of calico, which were traditionally carried on opposite sides of the store—a "wet goods" side containing the rum and a "dry goods" side holding the calico.*[3]

Long-ago advertisements give us a sense of what dry goods were. In 1880, Washington merchants Luttrell & Wine advertised "specialties in dry goods" including umbrellas, shirts, towels, white quilts, black silks, three-button kid gloves, and also "ribbons, cambric edgings, gloves, hosiery, furnishing goods, cloths, cassimeres and general variety of goods for spring use." In 1894, Pierce's dry goods store in downtown Washington announced a "Farewell Sale" of its entire inventory of "Dress Goods, White Goods, Black Goods, Silks, Linings, Muslin Underwear, Infants' Goods, Corsets, Embroideries, Ribbons, Gloves, Dress Trimmings, Handkerchiefs, Umbrellas, Jewelry, Toilet Articles, Notions, Laces, Neckwear, Hosiery and Underwear."[4]

One of Georgetown's first dry goods merchants was W. W. Corcoran, who, in 1815, started working in a dry goods store owned by his brothers. Later he opened his own store at the corner of today's Wisconsin Avenue and M Street. He lost the store in the depression that followed the Panic of 1819 but recovered from the setback and went into banking with George Washington Riggs. That partnership evolved into the Riggs National Bank of Washington, one of the city's largest financial institutions in the twentieth century.[5]

Between 1850 and 1852, Benjamin Mayfield and Stephen T. Brown opened a dry goods store on what today is M Street just west of 31st. Besides living next door to each other on P Street, they were brothers-in-law—Mayfield had married Brown's sister Charlotte.

In 1869, the partnership ended. Mayfield became a coal dealer, but Brown continued in the dry goods business on his own at the same location until 1880, and in partnership with William V. Lewis until 1896. Brown and Mayfield each also served as president of the Farmers and Mechanics' Bank in Georgetown.[6]

The "Mayfield and Brown" name would return in the 1880s when Brown's and Mayfield's sons ran an agricultural implements store (see chapter 2).

DRESSMAKERS AND TAILORS

If dry goods stores sold cloth, someone had to turn the cloth into finished clothing. Women with means could employ dressmakers to do that.

Throughout the years between 1900 and 1940, the number of dressmakers in Washington and Georgetown declined while the population of the District of Columbia more than doubled—further evidence of the increased availability of ready-made clothing. In Georgetown, dressmaking literally was a cottage industry—most dressmakers worked out of their homes. Of the twenty-two dressmakers in Georgetown in 1900, only two had addresses on M Street or Wisconsin Avenue, which likely were shops (but might have been their homes). All the rest worked from residential addresses.

In his history of American productivity, Robert J. Gordon attributes the increased availability of ready-made clothing in part to a wave of immigration from Russia after 1890. That wave included numerous tailors, many of whom worked making clothing in New York garment factories. The wave of Russian tailors is visible in Georgetown. Of the ten tailors who had shops on Georgetown's two main streets during the period of 1914 to 1920, eight emigrated from Russia or Poland, all arriving between 1892 and 1902. All but one of the eight were between twenty-six and thirty-six years of age when they emigrated, meaning they probably knew the tailoring trade when they arrived.[7]

CLOTHING STORES RUN BY IMMIGRANT FAMILIES

From the late nineteenth through mid-twentieth centuries, there were not just immigrant owners of Georgetown clothing stores, but in some cases multigenerational family networks of owners descended from immigrants. Successive generations of some families were part of the Georgetown business community for an extraordinarily long time.

The two largest family groups running clothing stores in Georgetown were the Brodofsky/Levy family and the Nordlinger/Baer family. Family trees in the following tables list members of each family who ran retail businesses and the locations and types of the businesses.

Brodofsky/Levy Family Tree

Hyman (Herman) Brodofsky
Shoes:
1901–1904 (2811 M St.)
Clothing:
1904–1910 (2811 M St.)
1911–1914 (**2815** M St.)
Bessie Brodofsky (wife)
Dry goods:
1914–1919 (**2815** M St.)

Katie Brodofsky Rosendorf
Dry goods:
1920–1929 (**2815** M St.)
Men's furnishings:
1930–1948 (**2815** M St.)
Married to Joseph Rosendorf, who ran a clothing store 1906–1926 (3048 M St., later 3072 M St.)

Meyer Levy
Married to Lillie Brodofsky, Hyman and Bessie's daughter
Dry goods:
1926–1929 (**3017–3019** M St.)
Men's furnishings:
1930–1943 (**3017–3019** M St.)

William Brodofsky
Men's furnishings:
1916–1919 (3322 M St.)
Men's clothing:
1920–1933 (**3128** M St.)
Men's furnishings:
1934–1942 (**3128** M St.)
Department store:
1943–1948 (**3128** M St.)
Men's clothing:
1954–1975 (The People's Store, **3128** M St.)

Sara Levy
Married to Harry Meyers
Women's clothing:
1930–1943 (3037 M St.)
Women's clothing:
1943–1968 (The Meyers Shop, **3061** M St.)

Samuel (Sam) Levy
Men's clothing:
1931–1944 (Sam's Men's Shop, 3057 M St.)
Men's clothing:
1944–1968 (David Richard, **3059** M St.)

Philip Levy
Books:
1980–2017 (Bridge Street Books, 2814 M St.; Pennsylvania Ave.); Philip died in 2017, but the store is still in business as of 2025

David Levy
Theater:
1973–1997 (Key Theater, 1222 Wisconsin Ave.)
1967–1973 (Partner in the Biograph Theater, 2819 M St.)

Note: Boldface street numbers indicate family-owned buildings.

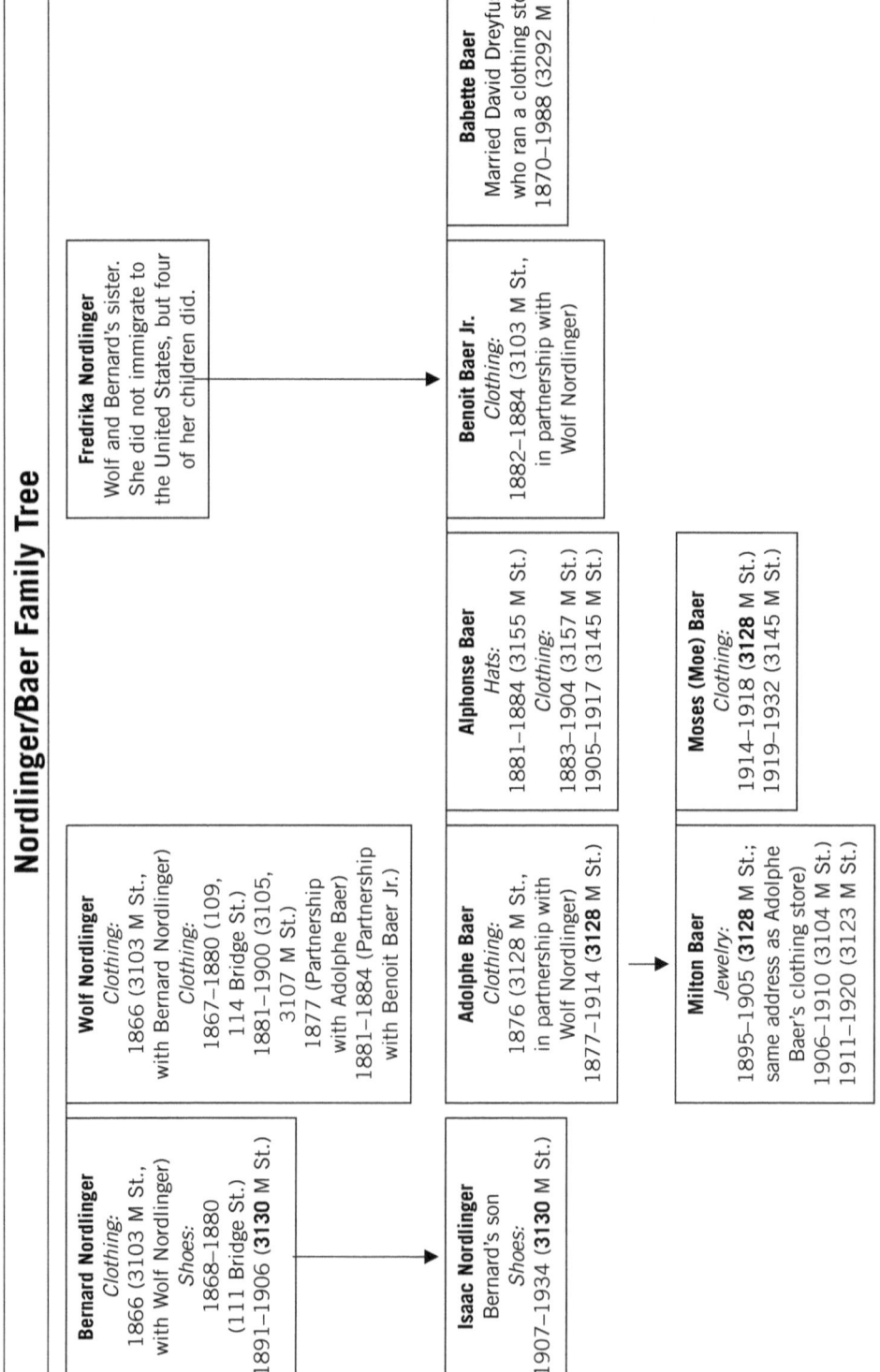

CLOTHING STORES

The Brodofskys and the Levys

The Brodofsky/Levy family in Georgetown began with Hyman Brodofsky, who was born in Poland in 1852 and came to the United States in 1892 at age forty. In 1901, he opened a shoe store that, by 1904, had become a general purpose clothing store. At some point, he began calling himself Herman instead of Hyman.

In 1910, Herman built a building at 2815 M Street to house his store and provide living quarters upstairs.[8] The building still stands. Herman's wife Bessie continued the clothing business after his death in 1914.

The building at 2815 M Street constructed by Herman Brodofsky in 1915. (*Photo by the author*)

Herman and Bessie had three children (Katie, William, and Lillie), all of whom were involved in the retail clothing business, two as proprietors and one by marriage.

Daughter Katie took over her mother's store in 1919 and sold dry goods until 1930 and men's furnishings after that. She lived upstairs at 2815 M Street with her husband Joseph Rosendorf, who ran his own clothing store

William Brodofsky's "The People's Store" at 3128 M Street is in the center in this 1966 photo. The building on the right earlier had housed Bernard and Isaac Nordlinger's shoe store. (*Library of Congress, Historic American Buildings Survey HABS DC,GEO,75—1*)

CLOTHING STORES

two blocks up M Street until 1926. She closed her store around 1950, after thirty years in business.[9]

Son William opened a men's furnishings store in 1915. In 1920, he bought a building at 3128 M Street and moved his business and his family there.

The Brodofsky/Levy and Nordlinger/Baer networks intersected in the building William bought. He purchased it from Benoit Baer, the nephew of Wolf and Bernard Nordlinger, who had constructed the building in 1893. Next door, at 3130 M Street, was Bernard Nordlinger's shoe store, now run by his son Isaac. There will be more about the Baers and Nordlingers shortly.[10]

In 1940, William started calling his business a department store, and later he named it "The People's Store."[11] He died in 1975 at age eighty-seven, after fifty-nine years in business.

According to a newspaper report of his death, William had found the recent gentrification and crowds of visitors in Georgetown so unsettling that for some years he had opened for business only sporadically. When the family sold the contents of the store after his death, some of those contents dated back to World War II and before, including

collarless shirts with separate collars, knickers, riding pants, riding boots, old hats, a baby's christening dress, an 1880 cash register, maids' uniforms, saddle oxfords, white buck shoes, suspenders, chemise-style ladies cotton slips, seersucker pajamas, boys' union suits, maids headbands, calendars from 1924 and 1925, [and] boxes of feathers for men's hats.[12]

Katie's and William's sister Lillie married Meyer Levy, an immigrant from Russia who had arrived in the United States in 1903 at age eighteen. Two of their five children, Sara and Samuel, would follow in their father's and grandfather's retail footsteps.

Meyer Levy ran a men's furnishings store on M Street for thirty years, opening in 1916. In 1931, he moved the business to a building he had purchased at 3017–19 M Street and continued to do business there until 1947, two years before his death.

Meyer and Lillie Levy's daughter Sara married Harry Meyers, who was born in Poland in 1903 and was brought to the United States as an infant. In 1930, when she was only twenty-four, Sara opened a women's furnishings store next door to her father's store.

Meyer Levy's clothing store was in the building on the left in this photo, 3017–19 M Street. His daughter Sara's store was in the building on the right. (*Photo by the author*)

Meyer and Lillie's son Samuel Levy, nicknamed Sam, was born in Washington in 1913. Sam opened "Sam's Men's Shop" at 3057 M Street in 1931, when he was only nineteen. According to his sons Richard and David, their grandfather Meyer Levy "put [Sam] into business."[13] (Sara's youth when she opened her store, and its location next door to her father's, suggest that he did the same for her.)

In 1940, Sam and Sara relocated their stores to neighboring sites. In 1938, Sam bought the property at 3059 M Street, next door to his store, for $12,000. In 1940, he tore that down and constructed a new store building, into which he moved Sam's Men's Shop. In late 1940, when Sam's construction project was under way or nearing completion, Sara and Harry Meyers bought the building next door to Sam's new one, at 3061 M Street, for $8,800. They moved Sara's store into that space in 1942.[14] Sara had started

CLOTHING STORES

out next door to her father, and now would be next door to her brother—a sign of family bonding, or perhaps just the potential for efficiencies and mutual help if they were neighbors.

At some point in the mid-1940s, Sara renamed her store "The Meyers Shop." It finally closed in 1968 after thirty-eight years in business.

Sam's son Richard recalled that Sam "over time upgraded [his] store from work clothes to middle class clothes to ultimately one of the finest men's stores in Washington." In 1945, he renamed the store after his two older sons, calling it "David Richard."

We know more about Sam's store than most Georgetown businesses because he advertised more. The ads confirm the change that Richard talked about.

In the first half of the 1940s, Sam's advertising was aimed at a cost-conscious clientele. For example, in January 1943, he advertised "selected irregulars" of men's nylon hose at three pairs for $1.25, touting them as

LEFT: In this detail from a 1935 photo, the building on the left with a vertical sign is 3057 M Street, the original location of Sam's Men's Shop. The building to the right of the shop no longer exists. (*Library of Congress, Historic American Buildings Survey HABS DC, GEO, 3—4.C26*)
RIGHT: In this detail from a 1957 photo, the building Sam Levy constructed at 3059 M Street is in the center, and his store's name has been changed to David Richard. The store's original home is on the right. Sam's sister Sara owned The Meyers Shop at 3061 M Street, on the left. (*DC History Center*)

Father's Day gifts. Many of Sam's ads during this period were for Hanes underwear. Hanes ran frequent, sometimes clever ads ("Now I'm unaware of underwear"), which listed local dealers including Sam's Men's Shop.[15]

After Sam renamed the store in 1945, the ads touted David Richard as a shop where sophisticated men bought their clothes. An ad in January 1946 features a drawing of an apparently suave, confident pipe smoker and says that "gentlemen prefer" Sakana shirts. Other ads in 1946 and 1947 touted a two-button zephyr-weight corduroy sport coat "tailored by Buckskin Joe" ($15), "fine woolen madras pajamas" ($4.95), and a "famous Botany Flannel Robe" ($15)—optional or luxury items, not basics.

In the ads were more images of refined-looking men, such as one in January 1950 featuring a drawing of a man wearing a hat, a Northcool tropical suit (available for $32.50), two-tone shoes, and what appears to be a Panama hat, strolling casually with one hand in his pocket and a long cigar in his mouth. "January in June is not impossible! Just try on one of our cool, comfortable Northcool tropicals." (The Hanes ads still appeared occasionally in the 1950s, though.)[16]

Perhaps the most interesting of Sam's ads featured the Airman Model Z, "the Greatest Shirt Idea in years . . . a business shirt that ZIPs closed." A great idea, perhaps, but it did not catch on.[17]

The shift to higher-end inventory and changes in the neighborhood brought occasional prominent customers. Richard Levy remembered working in the store in the 1950s and selling Hathaway shirts to Mrs. Dean Acheson, wife of the former secretary of state. Diplomats and generals were among other customers.

Sam, dubbed by some "the mayor of Georgetown," served on the boards of various business organizations and other associations including the Alexander Graham Bell Association of the Deaf. He played golf and tennis at Woodmont Country Club. In the late 1930s and early 1940s, Sam's Men's Shop had a bowling team, which played in the Georgetown Commercial League.[18]

After Sam built the new store in 1940, he and other members of the Levy family began investing in Georgetown real estate. At the time of a 1987 newspaper interview, Sam and a partner owned more than forty Georgetown commercial buildings.[19]

CLOTHING STORES

Sam's sons also became part of the Georgetown business community, Richard in property development and management, David as owner of the Key and Biograph theaters (see chapter 24), and Philip as founder and owner of Bridge Street Books, which he started in 1980 and operated until his death in 2017 (see chapter 27).[20]

The Nordlingers and the Baers

The Nordlinger/Baer family's history in Georgetown begins with Wolf and Bernard Nordlinger, who were born in the Alsace region, today part of France.[21] Wolf, born in 1836, sailed from Europe on a ship bound for Savannah, Georgia, in 1853, when he was seventeen years old. He lived in Savannah for eleven years, marrying and having two children. After serving in the Confederate army in the Civil War, he moved to Georgetown and went into business as a "clothing agent" in 1865.

Bernard, who was six years older, served in Louis Napoleon's army during the Crimean War. In 1858, he, too, arrived in Savannah, where he worked as a peddler. He followed his brother to Georgetown, and by 1866 the two were partners in a clothing store at what today is 3103 M Street. In 1867, Bernard left the partnership and opened a shoe store across the street and a few doors down, while Wolf continued the clothing business on his own.[22]

In 1893, Bernard tore down a building at 3130 M Street and built a new building into which he moved his store.[23] After his death in 1907, the store continued to be listed in directories as Bernard's, though his son Isaac was running it. Isaac changed the listing to his own name in 1918 and continued running the store until 1934. It was in business for a total of sixty-seven years.

Wolf helped two of his nephews get launched in the clothing business. In 1876, he and his nephew Adolphe (son of Wolf's sister Fredrika Nordlinger) went into partnership to run what was for Wolf a second clothing store at 3128 M Street, on the same block as his first, next door to Bernard's shoe store. After a year, Wolf moved on, and Adolphe continued to run the store at 3128 M Street until his death in 1914 when his son Moses (Moe) took over.[24]

The other supportive partnership was with Benoit Baer Jr. (another of Fredrika's sons). From 1882 to 1884, Wolf listed his original store in city directories as "W. Nordlinger & Co.," with Benoit as his partner. After 1884, Wolf listed the store solely in his own name again. In 1893, Benoit constructed a building at 3128 M Street, next door to his uncle Bernard's shoe store (see the photo earlier in this chapter). By 1897, he had opened a clothing store of his own in Alexandria, Virginia, and continued in the business there for twenty years. He sold the M Street building in 1920, to William Brodofsky, who moved his store into the space (see the previous section).

A third nephew, Alphonse Baer, started in business as a hatter in 1881, across the street from his brother Adolphe's shop. In 1883, he opened a clothing store next door at 3157 M Street on the corner with Wisconsin Avenue. He ran both stores for four or five years before closing the hat shop. In 1905, the Potomac Savings Bank took over the clothing store space, and Alphonse moved one door up the street. Alphonse was behind that, as he was one of the bank's organizers and would be a vice president and a member of the bank's board of directors. In 1919, Adolphe's son Moe took over Alphonse's store as he had done with his own father's business. Moe ran both stores until 1932, fifty-five years after Adolphe had started out in the business.[25]

Adolphe's other son Milton was a jeweler and watchmaker who had a store on M Street for twenty-five years (see chapter 8).

Alphonse's and Adolphe's sister Babette married David Dreyfuss, who in 1870 opened a clothing store at what is now 3292 M Street and ran it until his death in 1888.

Babette and David Dreyfuss had four children. Two of their sons, Joseph D. Dreyfuss and Benoit Dreyfuss, later ran a clothing store in downtown Washington under the name "Dreyfuss Brothers."

We can make several observations about the two families.

First, both families mostly did business in a short stretch of M Street. For example, these clothing and shoe stores were all open for business in 1916:

Meyer Levy at 2925 M Street

Joseph Rosendorf at 3073 M Street

William Brodofsky at 3322 M Street

Adolphe Baer & Sons at 3128 M Street

Alphonse Baer at 3145 M Street

Isaac Nordlinger at 3130 M Street

Joseph Dreyfuss at 3264 M Street

CLOTHING STORES

These stores cannot all have been selling the same things; they must have differentiated themselves by customer (men's, women's, children's), quality, style, and price. Unfortunately, in most cases there is little information about that because city directories provide little detail on the types of clothing sold (other than men's vs. women's, sometimes) and small Georgetown merchants did not advertise much if at all.

Both families had clusters of neighboring stores: Meyer Levy's clothing store was next door to his daughter Sara's Meyers Shop; Sara later relocated to space next to her brother Sam's store; and Adolphe Baer and his son Milton did business next door to Bernard Nordlinger's shoe store.

Second, both families helped their younger generations go into retail businesses. Meyer Levy provided capital for Sara and Sam to open their stores. Wolf Nordlinger was the partner of his nephews Adolphe and Benoit for brief periods. In both cases, the young entrepreneurs undoubtedly already had experience working in their father's or uncle's store.

Third, both families sought to own the buildings where their stores were located. Herman Brodofsky, Meyer Levy, Sam Levy, Sara Levy Meyers, and Bernard Nordlinger all constructed new buildings and moved their stores into them. We know that Herman, Meyer, and Sam's families all lived in their buildings, above the stores. Benoit Baer constructed a building that housed the businesses of his brother Adolphe and his nephew Milton. Sam Levy in particular owned other buildings besides the one where his shop was located. Members of the Levy family are prominent Georgetown real estate investors today.

Another Levy Family

A second Levy family (no apparent relationship to Meyer Levy and his descendants) ran clothing and shoe stores in Georgetown for more than fifty years. Barney Levy opened his store first, but his wife Rebecca (possibly nicknamed Betsy) built a retail business in her own right. The couple owned three clothing stores on M Street (at 2805, 2811, and 3047) but did not own them jointly. Their business styles seem different and their relationship was tumultuous, but Rebecca in particular exemplifies the entrepreneurial drive of many immigrant Georgetown retailers.

Rebecca Levy and her husband Bernard (nicknamed Barney) were both born in Russia in 1865 and came to the United States together in 1887, when they were twenty-two. They adopted the names "Barney" and "Rebecca" when they arrived; their native language was Yiddish (so they told a census taker), and their birth names no doubt were different.

Barney's name seemed to change from time to time. In 1893, "Bernard" Levy opened two clothing stores, at 2811 and 3047 M Street. Within a few years, the listings for these stores changed to identify the proprietor as "Barnett" Levy. It is likely that Bernard actually was Barney. Either there was confusion between two similar names (Barney and Bernie?), or Barney may have been trying to decide which Anglicized name to use. He settled on Barnett, but "Bernard" would come back later.

In August 1898, Rebecca began divorce proceedings, but the couple must have reconciled because the 1900 census shows them together as husband and wife, living with their two daughters at 2805 M Street. Three years later, Barney bought that building.[26]

Not long after that, Rebecca began an independent career. Was her desire for independence a cause of the earlier rift, or did the possibility of divorce convince her that she needed to be more independent? Or did she use her own name to buy real estate and open businesses as part of some business strategy the two of them had adopted? There is no way to know.

In 1906, Rebecca bought the building at 2811 M Street in her own name, not jointly with Barney.[27] That building formerly had housed one of Barney's businesses, and at the time she bought it was home to Herman Brodofsky's clothing store. That same year she opened her own men's furnishings store at 3003 M Street. Barney's store was the previous occupant of that space, so perhaps she just took over management of his existing business.

In 1909, Rebecca opened a second clothing store at 2805 M Street, where Barney was her landlord. At some point, she acquired the building from Barney (the second building in her portfolio). In 1910, Hyman Brodofsky left the space in Rebecca's building at 2811 M Street, and she moved her first store into that space, giving her two clothing stores three doors apart, at 2805 and 2811.

By this time, Rebecca and Barney appear to have divorced or at least separated. In 1910, she and her two daughters still lived above the store at 2805 M Street, and she told the census taker she was the head of the household; Barney was not there, but three boarders were. She also told the census taker

CLOTHING STORES

she was a widow, although Barney was very much alive. Divorced women at that time sometimes told people they were widows because of the stigma then associated with divorce. Barney's whereabouts are a mystery.

From 1911 to 1915, Rebecca bought three more buildings in Georgetown and two in Southwest Washington, all in her own name.[28] In 1916, she tore down the building at 2805 M Street and constructed a new one.[29]

Rebecca was nothing if not flexible. She changed the offerings in her two stores from time to time, sometimes selling new clothing, sometimes secondhand clothes, and sometimes dry goods. After 1918, Rebecca apparently found the business model that worked, selling shoes at 2805 and secondhand clothing at 2811 for the next decade. In 1930, she changed to men's furnishings at 2811 M Street and even ran a pawnshop there for a year or so in 1932 (probably reacting to the Great Depression).

One can see that Rebecca was entrepreneurial, even restless, taking advantage of whatever opportunity came along and unafraid to adjust and experiment to find her market niches. Barney seems different. He had multiple stores for a while but, by 1905, had settled on a single business, a shoe store, that he ran until 1919, when he went into the wholesale shoe business.[30]

At the time Barney closed his store he was embroiled in legal difficulties. In August 1918, Boston authorities accused him of selling clothing and shoes stolen in a series of Boston store burglaries. Rebecca posted his $3,000 bail, a significant sum. The matter would be dismissed in 1920 when the Boston prosecutors could not prove that Barney had been in Boston at the time of the burglaries. The publicity and official scrutiny, however, may have hampered Barney's business and led to its closure.[31]

There was further mystery about Rebecca and Barney's relationship. When Rebecca posted Barney's bail in 1918, she identified herself as his sister. When Barney died in 1925, his obituary also said Rebecca was his sister. We can only guess what was going on. It is possible that Rebecca and Barney reconciled again and resumed living together, but remained divorced. Unmarried cohabiting couples were frowned upon at the time, and so the two of them may have tried to keep their status secret, if not from everyone then at least from officialdom. If so, it is doubtful they fooled anyone in small-town Georgetown.[32]

When Rebecca died in 1931, her obituary said that she was active in charity work and "was affectionately known by her friends as 'Mother Levy.'" Her daughter Lillian and son-in-law Louis Yockelson took over both of her businesses, selling secondhand clothes at 2811 M Street until the late 1940s and shoes at 2805 M Street until the late 1950s. Lillian and her descendants continued to own those two buildings until 2003.[33]

CONSIGNMENT STORES

Stores selling secondhand clothing appeared in Georgetown in the early twentieth century. Their numbers never were large, frequently only one or two. The longest-running of those was the store run by Rebecca Levy and later her daughter and son-in-law, the Yockelsons (see the previous section). Consignment shops, now common in Georgetown but not numerous, came later on.

The late 1940s brought "The 1620 Shop," the first store that we know to have been a consignment shop from its start. Cecile de Rochefort owned the store. She was a native of Pennsylvania who had come to Washington in the 1930s and worked as a real estate agent and in public relations.

De Rochefort's newspaper advertising provides a feel for the inventory and gives the strong impression that this was not a thrift shop. An ad in 1950 explicitly referred to consignment and mentioned the availability of fur coats and jackets at "GREAT REDUCTIONS." A 1951 ad said the store sold "ALMOST NEW CLOTHES ON CONSIGNMENT" at "most reasonable" prices, including lightweight women's suits, linen suits for men, and women's sportswear. Another 1951 ad made clear the inventory was not limited to clothing and included "household articles in good condition—furniture, china, bric-a-brac, etc."[34]

The 1620 Shop closed in 1964.

Second Hand Rose, another consignment shop, opened in 1976 on the second floor of 1516 Wisconsin Avenue (near P Street), above a shoe store. A 1977 article referred to it as "A Real Find" and noted the presence on the rack of clothes designed by Geoffrey Beene, Pucci, Yves St. Laurent, Mollie Parnis, and Malcolm Starr. It also described the consignment terms, under which the shop received 50 percent of the sale price (40 percent on furs). Five friends started the shop: Cathie Kelly, Sue Gannon, Joan Bond, Sally Webster, and Carol Brumbaugh. They had a shared interest in starting a business and wanted to do something about high clothing prices. They ran the store for twenty-four years, selling it to Lynn Boynton in 2001. She continued to operate it at the same location until 2012, when she relocated the store away from Georgetown.[35]

UPSCALE BOUTIQUES

In the 1950s and 1960s, Georgetown became increasingly fashionable, and small clothing stores proliferated. In the 1960s and 1970s, the term *boutique* became popular as a label for such small shops. Boutiques in Georgetown had clever names, including Allen's Alley, Airport, Air Pollution, The Bum Steer, The Bootery, The Gentleman's Jodhpur, Jaipur West, Lady Madonna, Off the Cuff, Silhouette, Sporting Life, Trapeze, Up Against the Wall, and Yes.

Among the new shops were several that sold very expensive women's designer clothing and attracted a prominent clientele.

Saint-Aubin de Paris

Saint-Aubin de Paris opened in 1957 at 1661 Wisconsin Avenue, near the corner of Reservoir Road. The owner was Marguerite Paul, a Swiss immigrant who soon became known as Madame Paul. Her customers included Jacqueline and Ethel Kennedy and other women in the Kennedy family, wives of cabinet officers, the wife of a deputy attorney general, and the British ambassador's wife. Madame Paul would keep on hand a few pieces for some of her regular customers, which she designed using their individual measurements that she kept on file. Some of them would call, tell Madame Paul what type of outfit they needed, and trust her to make the selection for them. She emphasized elegance and simplicity in her designs and traveled to Europe yearly to purchase fabrics.

Madame Paul came to the United States with her American husband, whom she met when he was studying medicine in France. She told an interviewer that at the time she opened Saint-Aubin, "[m]y husband was busy with his career; Mimi [her daughter] was grown and a woman must do something or she becomes neurotic." This is very different from the stories of the immigrant shopkeepers a few decades earlier.

Saint-Aubin de Paris closed in 1988.[36]

GEORGETOWN'S RETAIL PAST

Dorcas Hardin

Dorcas Hardin was a Massachusetts native and boarding school graduate. Like Madame Paul, she was married to a physician. She started as a dressmaker and was hailed in a 1949 *Washington Post* article as "the best dressmaker designer" in Washington.

In 1954, she opened a small shop on Dumbarton Street, where she offered designer clothing that at that time was not available elsewhere in Washington. She, too, had Jacqueline Kennedy as a customer. Some of the clothes that Mrs. Kennedy bought from Dorcas Hardin were included in an exhibit at the Metropolitan Museum of Art in New York in 2001.

After Clark Clifford (the future secretary of defense) complained about the cramped space, Hardin moved to Wisconsin Avenue around 1960. Her new shop was just two blocks from Saint-Aubin de Paris, at 1513 Wisconsin Avenue.[37]

The prices were extraordinary even by today's standards. During a two-day visit to the store by designer Mary McFadden in the fall of 1976, Hardin sold $32,000 worth of McFadden's designs. A visit by Bill Blass brought more than $30,000 in sales. Many of the Bill Blass items were priced at $1,000.

By 1975, Hardin found that there were fewer customers looking for the top quality products she sold, and she did not like the newer designs of the day, which she described as "tents that make women look sloppy, quality that is poor, and prices that are outrageous." Given Hardin's own prices, one can only imagine the ones she found outrageous.

Hardin sold the store to Val Cook, one of her best customers, who would close it only two years later. Cook set out to run a less exclusive, more accessible shop that would appeal to younger women and carry a wider variety of styles at various prices. She also offered more gift items.[38]

The challenges Cook faced, related in a pair of newspaper interviews two years apart, are a catalog of the problems confronting a small Georgetown retailer:

- Buying the inventory: Cook selected the merchandise herself. In the higher-end clothing business, that meant trips to New York four times a year. To stock the store for one fall season, she spent twenty-two days in New York.

CLOTHING STORES

- Collecting from customers: one customer admitted to a reporter that

  I would say to myself, "Gee, if I don't pay those Saks bills right away I'll get awful hassle and dunning letters from their lawyers," but as for Val, I would reason, she's a pal and she'd understand. I'll pay her later.

- Paying for the inventory: manufacturers were reluctant to extend credit to a small business.
- Getting the inventory delivered: she found that manufacturers would deliver the latest styles to larger stores months before hers. She lamented that discounter Loehmann's sometimes received a product before she did.
- Shoplifting: Cook shied away from using electronic tags for fear they would offend her customers. She once caught a woman wearing three ultrasuede jackets under her coat.[39]

Cook closed the store in 1977. As with Saint-Aubin, one is struck by how much the shop's story differs from those of the earlier immigrant merchants. A hair salon now occupies the space.

Others

Other upscale dress shops during the 1950s and 1960s included a store run by Wilhemena Adams from 1942 through 1969. Adams started in the space that today is occupied by The Phoenix but, by 1948, had moved across the street to a space at the corner of Wisconsin Avenue and P Street that as of this writing in 2025 is a Thomas Sweet's Ice Cream shop.[40]

A few blocks away, the Mason Waters dress shop offered "carefully chosen feminine fashions" at 3003 P Street, next door to Morgan's Pharmacy. It closed in the early 1970s.

OTHER CLOTHING STORES
The Georgetown University Shop

The Georgetown University Shop (which we will abbreviate "GU Shop") did business in the neighborhood for fifty years, from 1930 to 1980. Rather than being on Wisconsin Avenue or M Street where other clothing stores were located, the shop did business at the corner of 36th and N Streets, next to the Georgetown University campus.

The shop was started by Stephen J. Barabas, a 1930 graduate of Georgetown University. Barabas was born in Jersey City, New Jersey, in 1905. His father was a custodian and later a saloon keeper. Census records variously say his parents were born in Czechoslovakia or Austria, depending on where the frequently changing European borders were in each census year. They had six sons, all born in New Jersey, of which Stephen was number three. He was a fullback on the football team during his years at Georgetown and was well known on campus.[41]

Not long after he graduated, Barabas opened a dry cleaning and shoe repair shop in a house just off campus at 1248 36th Street, on the corner with N Street. In the beginning, he also took in cleaning on campus. Students familiar with Barabas from his football days of course were early customers. He also began to sell some men's shirts and ties, on the second floor above the cleaning business; however, he continued to list the store in city directories only as a dry cleaner until the 1940s. The store was known as "The Georgetown Shop" until the late 1940s or early 1950s, when the word *university* was added to the name.[42]

In 1936, Barabas bought the building in which he was doing business, for $6,500. In 1940, he paid $5,000 to buy the property at 1246 36th Street abutting his on the south, which added another thirty-six feet to his street frontage.[43]

Later in 1940, Barabas married Helen O'Brien, a Maryland native. He served in the U.S. Navy in World War II, as a lieutenant junior grade. We do not know who ran the store during this period. Helen may have done so, or the store may have closed for a while.[44]

In 1946, Barabas leased the building at 1246 36th Street to a dry cleaning business, and expanded his clothing business to occupy the entire space at 1248. At some point, he installed handsome wood paneling in the clothing store.

Barabas sold the GU Shop in 1954 to Thomas Saltz. Stephen and Helen retired to a farm in Virginia but also had a residence in McLean, Virginia. She died in 1978 and he in 1980.

Thomas Saltz and his brother Samuel Lewis Saltz (who went by the name Lewis) were born in the Eastern Shore town of Crisfield, Maryland, Thomas in 1895 and Lewis in 1897. Their Russian-born father Max ran a general store, which is where as children they got their first retail experience. They

CLOTHING STORES

The Georgetown University Shop occupied this building at 1248 36th Street NW for fifty years. (*Photo by the author*)

moved to Washington in the 1920s, and for a while both worked for Raleigh Haberdashery, a men's clothing store that operated for decades. In 1936, after one false start, they founded their own men's clothing store, named "Lewis & Thos. Saltz" and located on G Street in downtown Washington.

They rented space that had formerly been a restaurant and spent $14,000 on renovations. They struggled to find the kind of store fixtures they wanted, until Thomas found some in the basement of a Cincinnati brewery and bought them for $4,000. Saltz's obituary in 1958 said that the Saltz store "was remarkable, within the trade, for its architectural simulation of 17th century English shop designs." The store also specialized in English merchandise. In 1955, Thomas told a reporter that "England is basically a man's country and center for men's fashions."[45]

In 1955, a reporter described the division of labor between the brothers:

> *Thomas is the aesthetic artist partner behind the club-like character and masculine good taste of the English décor of the G Street store. Lewis, the president, is the hard-driving businessman in charge of furnishings.*[46]

In 1955, Lewis Saltz became ill, and the brothers decided to sell the store (along with a just-opened branch on Connecticut Avenue) to a Chicago company. The brothers stayed with the company under its new ownership; however, three years later Lewis died at age sixty, and Thomas soon left as well. The stores (and other branches opened later) changed hands twice more before finally going out of business in 1986.[47]

After he left the company, Thomas Saltz spent nine years doing other things, among them working as a consultant and writing articles about "creative selling." He obviously missed the clothing business, though, because in 1964 he bought the GU Shop from Stephen Barabas. Barabas had just sold the two buildings at 1246–48 36th Street to Georgetown University for $16,000, so Saltz had to rent the store space from the university.[48]

The paneling that Barabas had installed must have appealed to Saltz's Anglophile tastes, and he embellished it until the GU Shop had what one reporter called "the mellow old wood and stained glass look that's as much a Saltz store tradition as the conservatively cut clothing."[49]

Despite its location, the GU Shop's customer base was not limited to students. Like other Georgetown stores, it had prominent figures among its clientele, including journalist Joseph Alsop and famed lawyer Edward Bennett Williams. Actors Lorne Greene, Henry Fonda, and Cary Grant all bought from the store during visits to Washington. Saltz played a hands-on role in the management of the store, including overseeing window designs and advertising. He added a women's department, run by his wife Julia. In 1974, Saltz opened a GU Shop branch in Chevy Chase, which had two floors and twice the selling space of the Georgetown location.[50]

In 1980, Saltz retired and sold the two GU Shop locations. By this time the $45,000 annual sales from the Barabas era had grown to $4.5 million. It had been forty-four years since Lewis and Thomas Saltz opened their store on G Street. The buyers of the GU Shop were a family group that included John Smoot Jr., a former manager of the menswear department at Woodward

& Lothrop, Washington's best-known department store. In 1990, the Smoot group decided not to renew the lease from the university, and the Georgetown location of the GU Shop closed. The Chevy Chase location continued in business for a time after that.[51]

The Phoenix

The Phoenix is the oldest clothing store operating in Georgetown today. Three generations of the same family have operated it for almost seventy years.

The founders were Betty and Bill Hayes, who in the 1950s ran the Launder-Rite Laundromat across the street from The Phoenix's future location. They had fallen in love with Mexican art and culture on a vacation, and when space became available at 1514 Wisconsin Avenue, they saw an opportunity to start a business selling Mexican art and jewelry. The space had previously been occupied by Fred Leighton's Latin American imports store, so it is possible they acquired some of their initial inventory from him. For the rest, they made a buying trip to Mexico. The store opened in 1955.

The Hayeses had no experience importing goods or running a shop; they were self-taught, on the job. They started off selling only Mexican imports, but as the years went by, they added merchandise from elsewhere, though retaining the Mexican flavor and the selection of Mexican folk art. Twice a year they went to Mexico on combination vacation/buying trips. They lived in the Palisades neighborhood just north and west of Georgetown.

In the 1980s when the Hayeses were ready to retire, their son John Hayes and his wife Sharon moved from Boston and took over the business. John and Sharon's daughter Samantha Gushner joined the business in 1998 and is the proprietor today (2025).

The family has changed the clothing inventory over the years, selling more regular clothing and less of the earlier folk art clothing. They focus on the ethics of the designers whose clothing they carry. The Mexican art and jewelry have remained a constant.

In 2000, the family bought the building that housed the business. The building contained two retail spaces, and eventually they were able to expand into the second space. In 2017, they completed a major renovation. The building had been built in 1896, so the renovation work encountered surprises, including a previously unknown fireplace that was hidden behind a rear wall and now is incorporated into the decor.[52]

Britches

Britches of Georgetowne, and its offshoots Britches Great Outdoors and Britches Western, began in Georgetown but ultimately grew to more than one hundred stores. Until the recent television success of Georgetown Cupcake with the series *DC Cupcakes*, Britches was the Georgetown store best known outside of Washington.

David Pensky and Richard Hindin, ages twenty-two and twenty-four, respectively, started Britches in 1967. In 1966, they had opened the Georgetown Slack Shoppe at 1269 Wisconsin Avenue (near N Street). They did it on a shoestring, building the store interior themselves. The inventory was sparse at first, so they folded slacks with tissue paper to make the piles of slacks look bigger.

In 1967, they opened the first Britches store at 1260 Wisconsin Avenue. The store's logo said, "founded 1967," a sign of their hopes for the future. Pensky did the buying, and Hindin handled the business side. The idea was to sell clothing off the rack that looked elegant or even custom made. In a newspaper interview, Hindin said that most retailers stock what they think people want, but "we stock what we think people should wear."[53]

Britches had its own brand of clothing, which hung in the stores alongside name brands. This enabled customers to compare prices and quality. Britches labels and advertising included the phrase "Clothing for Life." The store's advertising emphasized the Britches brand rather than price.[54]

In 1983, after sixteen years in business, Pensky and Hindin sold the business to CML Inc., a conglomerate that also owned very different chains like The Nature Company and NordicTrack. Years of aggressive expansion followed, and by 1995, there were 114 stores, 32 of them in the Washington area. Paul Davril, a California clothing manufacturer, bought the business in 1995 and tried a more youth-oriented marketing strategy. They changed the name to just "Britches." Britches filed for bankruptcy in 2002, and the remaining stores closed not long after.[55]

Rick Hindin then bought back the Britches name and, almost a decade later, resurrected it. His plan was for an online store and also a brick-and-mortar store called "Britches Bespoke" that would sell made-to-measure and custom-made suits. The online store does not seem to have materialized, but in 2020 Britches Bespoke opened a store in New York's Rockefeller Center. Hindin died in 2025, and the store closed.[56]

CHAPTER 6
Shoe Stores and Shoe Repair

The history of the shoe business in Georgetown parallels that of the clothing business in two respects: an increasing availability of ready-made shoes caused one type of shoe-related business (shoemakers) to fade away, and the number of shoe stores increased dramatically with Georgetown's emergence as a shopping destination.

There have been four kinds of shoe-related businesses in Georgetown: shoemakers, shoe stores, shoe repair shops, and shoe shine parlors. In the late nineteenth and early twentieth centuries, there were a dozen or more shoemakers on Wisconsin Avenue and M Street. Their numbers declined in the 1920s and they were gone by the mid-1930s, reflecting the advent of ready-made shoes. At the same time, a new kind of business appeared in Georgetown that had not existed before the second half of the 1920s: the "shoe repair" shop. The appearance and growth of shoe repair shops coincided with the demise of shoemakers—shoemakers responded to the growth of ready-made shoes by shifting their emphasis to repairing the new product.

The number of shoe stores dropped sharply between 1925 and 1935, from sixteen to eight, probably due to the Great Depression. Their number did not reach fifteen again until the 1980s, when the Georgetown Park mall opened.

SHOE REPAIR
Frank Bredice came to the United States from Italy in 1913, when he was twenty. In 1917, he opened his shoemaking business in a tiny building at 1434 Wisconsin Avenue (between O and P Streets).

The building shown here at 1434 Wisconsin Avenue housed the Bredice family's shoe repair shop from 1917 to 1978. (*Photo by the author*)

James Chamberlain had constructed the building in 1893 to house his grocery store. He died in 1910, and Frank purchased the building from Chamberlain's family between 1918 and 1920.[1] Frank and his American-born wife Maggie lived behind the store with their first child. The quarters must have been cramped; the building is only twenty feet wide and forty feet deep, and there is only one floor.

From 1926 through 1928, Frank's business was not listed at this address, and Sam Buttinelli ran a shoemaking shop there instead. Buttinelli was another Italian immigrant, who had worked as a shoemaker at various addresses around Washington.[2] In 1919, Buttinelli had lived in the building that housed the shop, probably before Frank and Maggie moved in (there was not enough room for two households).

It is unclear what Bredice was doing during this period. He briefly had a shoe repair shop in downtown Washington, which he advertised in the news-

SHOE STORES AND SHOE REPAIR

paper.[3] The family moved out of the Wisconsin Avenue building and into a house at 1320 Eye Street. Frank returned to Italy twice during this period, once on his own and once with his family.[4]

By 1929, though, Frank was back in business in the same Georgetown building as before, and the business would remain there for almost fifty years. This was when he made the switch from listing himself as a shoemaker to calling the store a shoe repair shop. The family also moved back to Georgetown, buying a house on Q Street.

Frank's sons Don and Anthony joined him in the business. Frank may have retired around 1960 (at age sixty-seven), because in that year the business was renamed "Bredice Brothers Shoe Repair." Frank died in 1981.

The Bredices' shop, like many longtime Georgetown businesses, acquired a prominent clientele in the 1950s and 1960s. Among the store's customers were President John Kennedy and his wife Jacqueline, each of whom paid by check during their years in the White House. The Bredice brothers chose not to cash the first check from each (written in 1961), instead framing the checks and displaying them in the shop. Other customers included Lyndon Johnson, senators Claiborne Pell and Charles Percy, Chief Justice Warren Burger, *Washington Post* editor Ben Bradlee, and film actress Myrna Loy, who

Ads like this ran in the *Evening Star* in March and April 1926 but disappeared after that. (Evening Star, *March 30, 1926, 44*)

lived in Georgetown in the 1950s while her husband was a State Department official. Don Bredice told a reporter, "We don't judge people by their shoes. There are some very fine ladies with pretty well-worn shoes."[5]

In 1978, the brothers moved the business away from Wisconsin Avenue to 35th Street near Georgetown University. They were still doing business there in 1990, when they were featured in a *Washington Post* article.[6]

Another longtime shoemaker in Georgetown was Libberante Sansone, who came to the United States from Italy in 1898 at the age of thirty-five. He set up shop in 1900 and continued in the business until 1930. At some point his son Frank joined the business, and it was Frank who made the change from "shoemaker" to "shoe repair." After only a year, though, the shop closed. Frank changed occupations entirely and became a stone mason. Joseph Speciale was another Italian immigrant, who with his wife ran a shoe-making (later shoe repair) shop on M Street from 1922 through 1940. His wife continued the business until at least 1943.[7]

SHOE STORES

Georgetown's longest-running shoe store was started by Bernard Nordlinger on what is now M Street in 1867. After his death, his son Isaac continued the business until 1934, a run of sixty-six years. See chapter 5 for the story of the Nordlingers and their relatives' clothing businesses. The family of Bernard and Rebecca Levy, including their daughter Lillian and granddaughter Louise Yockelson, ran shoe stores for seventy years, from 1895 through 1965. See chapter 5 for more about them as well.

Another longtime shoe business was Scott's Smart Shoes at 3139 M Street. Scott's was descended from a shoe store that Abraham Elliott (Abe) Felser opened in 1933 at 3111 M Street. Felser was already an established merchant when he opened the Georgetown store.

Abe Felser was born in Baltimore in 1884, the first American-born child of Joseph and Rachel Felser. Joseph and Rachel were born in Lithuania and came to the United States from Germany in 1881, along with Abe's older sister.

Joseph was a versatile entrepreneur. In the 1890s, he ran a furniture store in Baltimore. In the first decade of the twentieth century, he had a department store (later described as a dry goods store) and, a few doors

SHOE STORES AND SHOE REPAIR

away, a shoe store. His son Abe must have learned the shoe business working in his father's store.

In 1911, at the age of twenty-seven, Abe moved to Washington and opened a shoe store on H Street NE. He married Ida Kropp, whose parents had immigrated to Pennsylvania after her birth in Russia.

The Georgetown store was Abe's third, in addition to the H Street location and another on 8th Street SE. In 1940, six years after opening the Georgetown store, Abe moved it to 3139 Wisconsin Avenue, closer to the heavily trafficked intersection with M Street. He sold the business in 1944 to go into the real estate business, where he apparently was successful—land records show him owning thirty-five properties over the years. He died in 1961.[8]

We know nothing about the person who bought the business from Abe except that his name probably was Scott, because in 1945 he began advertising the stores as "Felser Scott's Shoes."[9] Scott took over during wartime, when shoes were rationed and subject to price controls. A 1946 newspaper ad assured consumers that, despite the end of the price controls, "Felser Scott's WILL NOT Increase Shoe Prices!"[10] The bottom of the ad listed three Felser Scott's locations besides the one in Georgetown: Abe Felser's original store on H Street NE and stores in Alexandria and Silver Spring.

At some point before 1950, Albert Kaplan bought the stores. Kaplan had been a branch manager for Abe Felser, probably in the Georgetown store—he lived on Wisconsin Avenue nearby. Like Felser, Kaplan was born in Baltimore to parents who had emigrated from Russia. He lived in York, Pennsylvania, in the mid-1930s before settling in Washington.

We know Kaplan owned the stores by 1950 because of a newspaper item about his generosity. In March 1950, the store on H Street was having a five-cent sale—anyone who bought one pair of shoes could buy another for five cents. A group of students from Mount Vernon College approached Kaplan, explained that they wanted to send clothing to war-displaced persons in Europe, and asked if he would just sell them two hundred pairs of shoes for five cents each. He not only gave them the shoes without asking for the five cents but also paid to ship the shoes to War Relief Services of the National Catholic Welfare Conference in New York, which would see to their distribution to displaced persons.[11]

Kaplan closed the Georgetown store in 1955. Brand names had long been an emphasis in the stores' advertising, and that continued right to the end. The ad for his store-closing sale offered 60 percent discounts and invited customers to choose from a long list of brand names: Buskens, Ederton, Fashion Bilt, Fortunet, French, Honeydebs, Johansen, Modern, Nunn-Bush, Official Scout Shoes, Poll Parrot, Polly Debs, Prima, Rand, Thrill Mates, Trim Tred, and W. L. Douglas.[12] The building was later replaced by an F. W. Woolworth store, and an Urban Outfitters store occupies that space as of this writing in 2025. The Silver Spring store closed later, perhaps because it was close to home—Abe lived in Silver Spring.

SHOE SHINE BUSINESSES

Shoe shine shops (or parlors, as they often were called) enjoyed popularity from World War I through World War II, fading out after that, at least on Georgetown's two main streets.

William H. Beall had a shoe shine business from 1919 to at least 1948, at various locations on Wisconsin Avenue between O and Q Streets. Beall was African American, born in Washington in 1875. He never attended school, but he did know how to read and write. He and his wife Mamie lived on 32nd Street.

In both the 1930 and 1940 censuses, Beall did not identify the shoe shine business as his occupation—in 1930 he said he was an "expressman" for his "own account," and in 1940 he said he was a truck driver for a furniture moving company. City directories, however, consistently list him as a shoe shiner in those and all other years between 1920 and 1948. Did he perhaps not want to tell the census taker his real occupation, or was he engaged in those other businesses as well? We do not know.

George Demetro had a shoe shine parlor from 1919 through the World War II years at 1214 and later 1225 Wisconsin Avenue. His and his parents' mother tongue was Greek, but he emigrated from Turkey and started the business when he was twenty-four years old. In 1941, he diversified and began taking in dry cleaning.[13]

CHAPTER 7
Barbershops and Hair Salons

BARBERSHOPS

In the nineteenth century, the barbershop was a social gathering spot for men as well as a place in which to be groomed. Many of the barbershops in Georgetown were owned by Italian immigrants or African Americans. The twentieth century brought two big challenges for barbershops: the advent of the safety razor early in the century, which enabled men to shave themselves rather than going to a barbershop; and the advent of longer men's hairstyles in the 1960s.

Because of the safety razor, the number of barbershops declined. In one group of surveyed barbershops, shaves fell from 50 percent of sales before World War I to 10 percent in 1930. There were 122,000 barbershops nationwide in 1939 but only 92,000 at the end of World War II.[1] King Camp Gillette, one of the inventors of the safety razor, preached that the socializing in barbershops was a waste of time anyway: "If all the time, money energy and brainpower which are wasted in the barbershops of America were applied in one direct effort, the Panama Canal could be dug in four hours."[2]

When longer hair later became fashionable for men, demand for haircuts of course fell. In self-defense, many barbers marketed "hair styling" at higher prices. Women hairdressers, who were more familiar with that kind of custom work, became competitors for barbers.[3]

Women's hair salons were rare in Georgetown before 1930. It was a largely working class neighborhood then, where probably few women could afford to visit a salon.

GEORGETOWN'S RETAIL PAST

The number of barbershops and hair salons on Georgetown's two main streets followed these trends. Barbershops shrank from nineteen in 1935 to nine in 1956, three in 1965, and none soon after that. There were only one or two hair salons until the 1940s, when the number grew to six or seven. In 1985 it rose to seventeen, many of which probably served both men and women. In 2023, there still were seventeen.

Writing in the 1980s, historian Mary Mitchell described the state of Georgetown barbering in 1868:

> *Barbershops did such a thriving business that the [town government] had to legislate against working on Sunday. The police found one barber at midnight Saturday dyeing his customer's beard black, with one-half of it still red. The officer kindly allowed him to finish the job, but dragged him afterwards into the justice of the peace to pay his $5 fine.*[4]

In 1987, Robert Sellers, who grew up in the 3400 block of M Street, shared reminiscences of his childhood in Georgetown decades before. Here is what he said about barbershops:

> *All barbers were black or Italian, all were artists, and all knew your dad and your grandfather and your uncles. No one in my family can remember the name of this barber shop, but the proprietor was a Tony, and he always had a fresh stick of Spearmint for you, and he always asked after the girl friend [sic] and calculated that it wouldn't be long before you'd be shaving. He was an expert on the Nats, and Georgetown's teams, and he listened respectfully as you analyzed Goose Goslin's swing. Fancy getting that kind of camaraderie in today's blaring blow-try unisex torture pits.*[5]

We do not know who Tony was. None of the long-standing barbershops on Wisconsin Avenue and M Street had owners named Anthony or Antony. The shop where Sellers got his hair cut may have been on a side street. Sellers's statement that all the barbers were black or Italian sounds flippant, but it is not far from the truth. City directories list a total of fifty-four barbershop proprietors in business on M Street and Wisconsin Avenue at one time or another during the years 1920 through 1940. Census, immigration, and draft records indicate that of those, 20 (37 percent) had African American or mixed-race owners and fourteen owners (26 percent) were Italian immigrants, for a total of 63 percent.

Albert Starke

One of the early barbershops was run by Albert Starke, an immigrant from Germany. He opened in 1865 on Market Space (next to the Georgetown Market), moving the next year to High Street (today's Wisconsin Avenue). He was born in Hanover and had come to the United States in 1856 at the age of twenty. He and his wife Mary (from New York) had five daughters and four sons.

In 1881, after fifteen years doing business at various locations on Wisconsin Avenue, Starke moved his business to the 2900 block of M Street, living above the shop or in the building next door. He closed the shop in 1904 at the age of sixty-eight, after thirty-nine years in business, and moved his residence to Valley Street (today's 32nd Street).[6]

Starke did not retire completely, however. In the early days of medicine, barbers doubled as surgeons. After the Civil War, at least one Georgetown barber included dentistry in the services he offered. Among other things, barbers were responsible for bleeding patients in the days when that was a common medical treatment. The modern barber pole originated then—the spiral ribbons around the pole represent linen bandages that were wrapped around the arm of the patient being bled.[7]

Starke went back to these roots and began holding himself out as a "cupper and bleeder." Even as late as the early 1900s, there was a "cuppers and bleeders" category in the classified section of Washington city directories, and in 1905 and 1906, Starke listed himself there. He had little company—there was only one other listing. Did Starke's listing disappear because he found demand for his services disappointing? There is no way to know. He lived on for sixteen more years, dying in 1922 at age eighty-six.[8]

The Coniglios

Frank Coniglio was born in 1886 and arrived in the United States in 1908, at age twenty-two. He came to Washington in 1911 and, after working as a barber in other parts of the city, he opened his own shop at 3251 M Street in 1912. It did business there for fifty-seven years. His wife Mary was a fellow

LEFT: Frank Coniglio's barbershop is in the center of this 1966 photo. (*Library of Congress, Historic American Buildings Survey HABS DC,GEO,80—1*)
RIGHT: In this photo of the interior, also taken in 1966, there are three chairs for the three Coniglio brothers. (*Library of Congress, Historic American Buildings Survey HABS DC,GEO,8—2*)

immigrant from Italy, and they had three sons and two daughters, all born in Washington. The family lived on Prospect Street, a block from the shop, until sometime in the 1930s.[9]

Frank's sons Stephen, Joseph, and Philip all became barbers and worked in the shop with their father. Philip started cutting hair when he was fifteen. The 1930 census, taken as the Great Depression began, asked how many hours each person had worked during the week of March 24 that year. Frank said sixty-six hours, and his sons each said forty-eight.

Frank died in 1949, and the three sons continued to run the business. Philip died in 1969, and the shop closed between 1970 and 1973.[10]

Joseph Fabrizio

Joseph Fabrizio (originally named Giuseppe) arrived in the United States in 1900 when he was sixteen. His cousin Pietro, who lived in New York, paid for his passage.[11] In 1905, when he was only twenty-two, he opened a barbershop at 1436 Wisconsin Avenue, just above O Street. Fabrizio's young age when he immigrated means that, unlike Frank Coniglio and others, he probably learned his trade in the United States rather than bringing it from Italy.

In June 1910, Fabrizio married Carmen Rubino, with his cousin Pietro as a witness.[12] Around the same time, he moved his shop next door to 1438 Wisconsin Avenue. He and Carmen lived upstairs and had two sons. Joseph owned the building together with someone named Sam Fabrizio, no doubt a relative.[13]

In 1925, Fabrizio's shop was heavily damaged in a freak accident. A streetcar southbound on Wisconsin Avenue jumped the tracks and plowed into the shop and the stores on either side of it. Two customers in Fabrizio's shop were showered with glass but escaped unharmed, fleeing the scene so quickly that they were not identified. The accident was front page news; forty people were injured, but apparently Fabrizio and his customers were spared.[14]

Fabrizio took an interest in current affairs. During World War II, the *Washington Post* published three letters that he wrote to the editors (one suspects he wrote more). He had left school after eighth grade, but he wrote with eloquence, as in this early 1939 letter:

> We should consider ourselves fortunate to be so far away from Europe, and all these different nationalities of people who found here a better place to live in and raise their families will stand by this democracy against any powers to try to put foot on this soil. So let us build those airplanes for ourselves and be ready for any emergency. Let us keep away from European trouble, and let us solve our own problems, as we have many still unsolved.

To the Ladies
JOSEPH FABRIZIO'S
TONSORIAL PARLOR
And
Beauty Department
WISHES TO ANNOUNCE SPECIAL
Summer Reduction Rates
MARCEL, 75c. RESET, 50c.
Expert Lady Operator
Appointment by Telephone West 419
3,8,,11

Joseph Fabrizio anticipated the future trend of hair-cutting shops that would serve both men and women. Services for women were only by appointment, since the ad does not include the shop's address. (Washington Post, *June 11, 1925, 12*)

In 1940, he wrote in praise of the high rate at which Italian Americans were enlisting in the military. As Italy was being freed from German occupation in 1944, he wrote in celebration of the restoration of mail service between the United States and liberated parts of Italy.[15]

Fabrizio lived just long enough to see the war end. He died in December 1945 at age sixty-one, and the shop space was taken over by a clothing store. Carmen owned the building, however, and she continued to live upstairs until her death more than thirty years later.

African American Barbers

Many of the African American–owned barbershops were clustered in two areas: the 3000 block of M Street (at the southern edge of the predominantly African American Herring Hill neighborhood) and the 1200 block of Wisconsin Avenue, just north of M Street. Three such shops competed on the latter block throughout the 1920s.

Among the African American barbers was Simon Burnett. Many of the African American barbers were born after the Civil War, but Burnett was born in 1858, probably into slavery. He came to Georgetown in 1877 and began working as a barber. He opened his own shop ten years later at 3003 M Street and did business at that address for more than fifty years, through 1943. He died in 1944.

The Merritt brothers also were African American, born in Georgia. Morgan was the older brother, born in 1872, and Matthew was ten years younger. Their father was a farmer. They opened their first shop in 1903 and were in business for twenty-nine years at various locations on M Street and Wisconsin Avenue.

Simon W. Sheffield, born in Texas in 1880, opened his first barbershop in 1910 at 1223 Wisconsin Avenue. One might not think of a barbershop as a target for burglary, but in 1914 thieves broke into the shop and stole ten razors, three pairs of clippers, and three pairs of scissors. One wonders if they were disappointed with that haul.[16]

In 1923, Sheffield bought a building on Wisconsin Avenue for $2,000. He did not move into his new quarters right away, instead leasing the building to an express company for two years. His shop finally opened in the space

BARBERSHOPS AND HAIR SALONS

In this detail from a photo taken around 1935, Simon Burnett's barbershop is the second from the right, with the barber pole visible on the left side of the store window. (*Library of Congress, Historic American Buildings Survey HABS DC,GEO,5—2*)

in 1926 and would operate there for thirty years. Sheffield also had a second shop downtown on H Street.

In 1931, Sheffield married Viola Williams, a West Virginia native. Simon died not long after that, probably in 1933. Viola took over the shop

The building at 1077 Wisconsin Avenue was home to Simon Sheffield's barbershop for thirty years. (*Photo by the author*)

on Wisconsin Avenue—she may have learned how to cut hair from Simon. (The H Street shop closed.)

At this point, Viola's path crossed that of another African American Georgetown barber, Robert H. Smith. There is not much information about Smith, who was born in Texas in 1870. In the early 1930s, he ran two barbershops in Georgetown.

In 1938, city directories began to list Smith at a third location: 1077 Wisconsin Avenue, the address of Viola Sheffield's shop. From 1938 through 1940, Smith was listed as proprietor of the shop, but after that Viola was again listed as the owner. Smith died in 1942. We do not know what the arrangement was between them. Viola owned the building, having inherited it from Simon.

There was one unfortunate incident in one of Smith's other shops, at 3280 M Street. Besides doing haircuts and shaves, barbers in years past made money selling hair tonic. The sales were profitable, because barbers either bought the tonic in bulk and rebottled it or made it themselves with their own formulas. In their shops, they often displayed an array of brightly colored bottles containing different tonics. The tonics contained alcohol, and that led to the mishap in Smith's shop. In January 1938, one of the tonic bottles fell on the floor and shattered, splashing hair tonic on a stove, where it caught fire. A customer was burned, and there was damage to the shop.[17]

African American barbers also did business in the Herring Hill commercial area of P Street, between 26th and 28th Streets. George Kent cut hair there from 1900 to 1923 and Hazzard Haywood from 1930 to 1938. For more about Herring Hill, see chapter 31.

HAIR SALONS

Learning about the owners of early Georgetown hair salons is challenging. Operators of salons were listed in directories under trade names more frequently than other Georgetown businesses, and those trade names often revealed only a first name, or no name: for example, Lillian's Beauty Shop, Ludie's Hair Styling, and Bonny Beauty Salon. We know little about Ludie Tillson, who ran Ludie's Hair Styling at 1524 Wisconsin Avenue from 1939 through 1969, and even less about Alice Lawson, whose Alice's Hair Salon was at 3263 M Street from 1937 through 1960.

A bit less mysterious is Lillian's Beauty Shop, which did business at 1336 Wisconsin Avenue (near N Street) from 1930 through 1960. The Lillian in the shop name was Lillian Randall, a Virginia native born in 1910. In 1930, shortly after they were married, she and her husband Harry Randall (a cleaner) were living on Connecticut Avenue. In 1940, when the shop had been open for ten years, they told the census taker that *Harry's* occupation was owner of a beauty shop, and the census listed no occupation at all for Lillian.

We know more about Rose Raynor Hitt, whose hair salon was on Wisconsin Avenue from 1963 to 1985. In 1952, she purchased a building at 1512

31st Street (just above P Street) for $20,000, and opened Rose Raynor's Beauty Salon. She sold that building in 1962 for $49,500 (it has continued to house various hair salons). Raynor moved to rented space at 1523 Wisconsin Avenue, near P Street, and did business there until 1986. She died in Alexandria, Virginia, in 2000.[18]

Activities in Rose's shop may have included more than just hairstyling. Emily Durso, who grew up nearby, began working in the shop in 1965 when she was fifteen, answering the phone and washing towels. She told her parents that Rose's husband, who always was nice to Emily, came to the shop once a week and spent an hour on the phone writing numbers in a notebook. Emily's parents realized that the salon perhaps was being used by a numbers betting operation, and urged Emily to find other employment. (Her next job was at the Francis Scott Key Book Shop [see chapter 27].)[19]

Some salons advertised their use of particular technologies or techniques. A 1937 newspaper ad for Lillian's Hair Salon said, "we specialize in Zotos Permanents for lasting and flattering waves." A Lillian's help wanted ad in 1937 sought a "beauty operator" who had to be "experienced in finger waving [and] marceling." When Rose Raynor moved her shop to Wisconsin Avenue in 1963, she took over space formerly occupied by "Larsen's Harper Method Beauty Salon."[20]

CHAPTER 8
Jewelers

In 1830, Charles Burnett and R. H. L. Villard had jewelry businesses on Bridge Street (today's M Street). In 1860, the town had three jewelers, one of whom was named Richard Nixon.

Until the 1970s, jewelry stores were not numerous in Georgetown—generally a half dozen or fewer on the two main streets. A handful more were added in the 1980s with the opening of the Georgetown Park mall. In the 1990s, the number sharply increased to thirty with the opening of many small jewelry businesses on Wisconsin Avenue; for more about that, see chapter 32.

3123 M STREET

For sixty-seven years, from 1910 to 1977, the building at 3123 M Street was home to three different jewelry stores. Benoit Baer Jr. built the building in 1909. His building permit application estimated the construction cost at $8,400.[1]

Milton Baer

The first occupant of the building was Benoit Baer's nephew Milton Baer, who had been a jeweler on M Street since 1894. He was born in Georgetown, where his father and uncle, Adolphe and Alphonse (Benoit's brothers), ran clothing stores along with a crowd of other relatives. For details on the family and their clothing businesses, see chapter 5.

In 1894, Milton opened his first store across M Street from Adolphe and Alphonse at number 3128, in a new building constructed by his cousin

This building at 3123 M Street was home to three jewelry stores during a sixty-seven-year period. (*Photo by the author*)

Benoit (see photo in chapter 5). In 1910, after a brief stay at 3104 M Street, Milton moved back across the street to 3123 M. For a while Baer's newspaper ads featured a mascot—a bear.[2]

In 1920, after twenty-five years in Georgetown, Baer moved his store to downtown Washington, where he remained in business until 1949. He also became a real estate investor. He was a member of the Association of Oldest

JEWELERS

MILTON BAER,
Jeweler and Optician.
A Special This Week—14-k. Hunting-Case Ladies' Watch, $16; Elgin or Waltham Movement.
PHONE WEST 693.   3123 M STREET N. W.

Milton Baer had a mascot, which appeared in a series of newspaper ads like this one. (Washington Post, *September 18, 1910, ES11*)

Inhabitants of the District of Columbia and was a Mason for fifty years. He died in 1957 at age seventy-seven.[3]

Charles Schwartz

In 1919, Milton Baer was succeeded in the 3123 M Street space by a branch of Charles Schwartz & Son, a long-established jeweler that already had a store in downtown Washington. At some point, Milton had acquired ownership of the building from Benoit, and he sold the building to Schwartz in 1924. Schwartz closed his Georgetown store in 1926, after only seven years in the neighborhood, but Charles Schwartz & Son is still in the retail jewelry business in Washington today (2025).[4]

The Tribby Brothers

The third occupant of 3123 M Street was J. Clinton Tribby. Clinton Tribby, his brother Charles, and his nephew Charles Jr. ran jewelry stores in Washington for sixty years, including two in Georgetown. Despite Clinton and Charles being brothers and both doing businesses under the Tribby name, the two jewelry businesses were separate.

The patriarch of the clan was silversmith Charles Elwood Tribby, born in Loudon County, Virginia. In 1857, he married Sidney Jane Gilbert, who would be among the family's entrepreneurs. In 1860 when the census taker called at his home in Winchester, Virginia, he was very specific about his occupation: "*master* silversmith."

Between 1859 and 1874, Charles and Sidney had six children, four of whom survived to adulthood. The oldest was Charles Ellsworth Tribby and the youngest was Joseph Clinton Tribby, who went by his middle name. Clinton Tribby never knew his father, who died three weeks after his birth.

In 1875 (the year after her husband's death), Sidney was the first Tribby to appear in business in Georgetown, opening a hat shop at 120 Bridge

Street, later redesignated 3115 M Street. Various members of the family would do business in that building for sixty-five years, and would reside in it for much of that time. As the years went by, Sidney's store changed from selling hats to selling notions to selling "fancy goods."

The building at 3115 M Street was the location of the first Tribby store. It is shown here when it was being demolished in 1940. (*Library of Congress, Historic American Buildings Survey HABS DC,GEO,46-*)

JEWELERS

Sidney's oldest son Charles Tribby began working as a watchmaker in 1881, when he was sixteen. One wonders how he learned such an intricate trade at such a young age. He was headquartered at the same address as his mother's hat shop, no doubt so she could keep an eye on him. Five years later Charles opened his own shop up the block, at 3143 M Street.

Not long after it opened, Charles's store was the site of a legendary burglary that was front-page news. Jewelry worth $3,000 (a sizeable sum then) was taken, including diamonds and gold watches. Less valuable goods were untouched.

The burglars were pros. This was not low-risk thievery—the Georgetown police station was less than a block away, and officers passed by frequently. There also was a fire station across the street. The thieves used drills and dynamite to open the safe, helped by a loud wind outside that covered up the noise. Several police officers walked by during the night and noted that the store's normally bright overnight gas lights were dimmer than usual, but they chose not to investigate. When Charles Tribby entered the store the next morning, he found a sledgehammer and a drill next to the open safe. What looked to be sawdust later was found to be dynamite. The drill and hammer turned out to have been stolen from Mason's carriage works nearby. The *Washington Post* declared the heist "one of the boldest safe robberies ever effected" and "the work of 'gophers.'"[5] It appears the robbers never were caught—there are no newspaper articles about their apprehension or trial. One hopes Charles had insurance.

In 1891, Charles moved his business back to 3115 M, apparently sharing the space with Sidney until she closed her business two years later. Also in 1891, young Clinton Tribby started working as a jeweler in Charles's shop.

After three years, the brothers apparently decided they would prefer to do business separately, and Charles moved back up the block to 3143 M, leaving Clinton alone in the 3115 space.

Robbery is a risk in the jewelry business, and in 1897 Charles was a victim again. This time the robber was less professional, breaking the store window and grabbing what he could. He was arrested within fifteen minutes.[6]

In 1898, Clinton Tribby went into partnership with George W. Offutt, his sister Gertrude's husband. The Offutts were established grocers in Georgetown. The partnership's jewelry store, under the name Offutt & Tribby, was located in Clinton's space at 3115 M Street.

Charles Tribby ran this ad in the *Evening Star* in November of that year:

> Mr. C. E. Tribby wishes to announce that he is not connected with the firm of Offutt & Tribby of 3115 M Street.[7]

This probably did not reflect hostility to his brother's venture; it more likely was intended to keep Offutt & Tribby's creditors from becoming confused and thinking that Charles was part of the venture and would back up its debts. The ad does make clear, however, that the two brothers were running distinct businesses.

The store sold eyeglasses as well as jewelry; a 1908 newspaper ad referred to "Offutt & Tribby Jewelry and Optical Goods." It is likely that Offutt provided capital but did not work in the jewelry business, as he had his grocery business to run.[8]

The Offutt & Tribby partnership lasted ten years. Its end was marked by newspaper ads for "J. CLINTON TRIBBY, successor to Offutt & Tribby."[9]

The situation was strange—from 1895 to 1903, brothers Charles and Clinton Tribby ran separate jewelry stores on the same block, both using the Tribby name—Clinton at 3115 M Street and Charles at 3143. The unanswerable question is whether the competition between them was friendly.

Whatever the nature of the competition, it ended in 1903, when Charles closed his shop and went into finance as a manager of the National Loan and Investment Company. He advertised an auction at which $30,000 of "diamonds, watches, etc." would be sold. "Owner retiring from business," it said. Another ad on the day of the auction offered more detail on what would be auctioned: "diamonds, gold and silver watches, silverware, clocks, bronzes, umbrellas, canes, cut glass and jewelry of every description."[10]

This was the beginning of years of family real estate activity, in which Clinton Tribby also would participate. Some of Clinton's tasks were perfunctory, such as being a trustee under deeds of trust securing loans the company made. Occasionally his role in the loan business led to difficulty, as in 1907 when Robert and Jane Smith accused him of usury and sought an injunction to prevent him from selling their household furniture.[11]

Twelve years after Charles Tribby had left the jewelry business, there again was a second Tribby jewelry store. Charles's son, Charles Ellsworth

JEWELERS

> **J. CLINTON TRIBBY,**
> Successor to
> **Offutt & Tribby,**
> Georgetown's Leading Jeweler,
> 3115 M Street N. W.
>
> Diamond sale for 30 days. 25% off on all diamonds. Very large assortment. ONE-KARAT Blue-white Diamond, $100.00. $30.00 Diamond Rings, $15.00. Take this chance to own a nice diamond ring.

This newspaper ad is evidence that Clinton Tribby's partnership with George Offutt had ended by August 1910. (Washington Post, *August 7, 1910, 6*)

Tribby Jr., opened one in 1915 in the Metropolitan Bank Building on 15th Street NW in downtown Washington. The strange intrafamily competition resumed, but at a greater distance, with one Tribby store in Georgetown and the other downtown.

Clinton Tribby inherited his father's pride in his work. In 1918, he ran a help wanted ad seeking not just a watchmaker but a "*first class* watchmaker," for $32 a week. He used the same terminology years later in 1936, when his ad said, "OPTOMETRIST wanted at once, first class."[12]

In 1927, Clinton Tribby moved his business to 3123 M Street, the building previously occupied by Milton Baer and Charles Schwartz. Jewelry shops using the Tribby name would be there for the next fifty years. In 1928, he bought the building from Schwartz. The building was only two doors away from the building at 3115 M Street where the family had started in business.[13]

In 1932, Clinton Tribby married Eleanor Cox Griffith, born in Tennessee in 1874. They had met when they were neighbors in the same apartment building on 19th Street NW. He and Eleanor were active in society. Newspapers in the 1930s and 1940s contained dozens of society column items about events that they hosted or attended.

In 1936, Tribby sold his jewelry business to Norman Siedenberg, who continued to run it for another forty years. Along with the business, Siedenberg leased the building and bought the right to use the well-established Tribby name. Siedenberg did not buy the building, which Tribby sold to someone else in 1940.[14]

With the business sold, Clinton Tribby retired at age sixty-two, but he remained in Washington. In 1939, he sold the family's other building at 3115 M Street. It was demolished in 1940, and a Woolworth's store replaced it.[15]

Clinton Tribby was a man of many interests. In 1911, he was granted membership in the Washington Chamber of Commerce, and over the ensuing years, he served on Chamber of Commerce committees regarding the development of Great Falls, Virginia; police and fire protection (a committee that had ninety-five members); the national guard; and parks, playgrounds, bridges, and retail trade. He was a director of the Potomac Savings Bank. In 1931, the 7th Police Precinct pistol team won first place in the annual tournament of the Washington Pistol League, winning a trophy donated by "Maj. J. Clinton Tribby, Georgetown Jeweler, who is an aficionado of the sport." In 1935, Clinton applied for membership in the Sons of the American Revolution, based on his descent from a Barnabas Gilbert (Sidney's ancestor), who had fought in the Revolution. In 1948, when Mrs. B. J. Erkenbeck won a golf tournament at the Army-Navy Country Club, she was awarded the J. Clinton Tribby Cup.[16]

Clinton Tribby had served in the U.S. Army in World War I and continued to serve in the reserves after the war. When he died in 1953, he was buried in Arlington National Cemetery. His headstone says he was a lieutenant colonel.[17]

Norman Siedenberg, who bought Clinton Tribby's jewelry business, was a Washington native whose father owned a retail ice business. Siedenberg was only thirty-two when he bought the Tribby store. He had learned the trade working as a jewelry salesman.

Siedenberg did little newspaper advertising for many years. In 1950 and 1951, however, he started running display ads in the *Evening Star*, concentrated around May and June (when the ads mentioned weddings and graduations) and in the fall and early winter (anticipating Christmas). The ads touted an "exciting collection" of engagement rings, Girard Perregaux watches for $46 and $71.50, Gorham silver flatware, a Reed and Barton silver tea and coffee service for $450, and a Krements gold and crystal brooch and earrings for $39. The results of this ad campaign must have been disappointing, because the ads disappeared after 1951.[18]

In 1977, a reporter interviewed Siedenberg for an article about the store's closing, not quite one hundred years after Charles Tribby had begun working as a watchmaker and forty-one years after Siedenberg had bought the store. The reporter described Siedenberg as "a courtly gentleman with silver hair and an erect military bearing." Siedenberg's lament about change was common among Georgetown merchants in the 1970s:

JEWELERS

It's a different class of people now. The hippies and people in mod clothes took over. More people walk around eating and drinking. They drop their paper cups on my doorstep and their soda cans on the sidewalk. Fifteen years ago, ladies in parties of three and four, all dressed up, would go to lunch and browse in the antique shops and jewelry stores. But with the advent of the street vendors, you can't walk around in leisure anymore.[19]

Siedenberg said the high-end jewelry market had peaked in the late 1940s. He listed some of his customers from back then: General George Patton, Admiral William Leahy, Mrs. Felix Frankfurter, Mrs. Dean Acheson, and actress Myrna Loy (who lived in the neighborhood for a few years). Siedenberg also lamented the recent scarcity of good craftsmen and watchmakers.

Harris Krick

Another long-lived Georgetown jewelry store belonged to Harris Krick, who opened on M Street in 1894. Five years later, Krick moved his store to

Harris Krick's jewelry store can be seen on the left in this detail from an 1896 photo. (*Peabody Room, D.C. Public Library*)

3053 M Street, next door to the Old Stone House, where it remained for forty-nine years.

Harris Krick was born in Russia, with the birth name Krigsonof. He arrived in the United States in 1882, at the age of twelve. He, his wife Olga, and his two children lived on Dumbarton Street. Krick did not advertise in the *Washington Post* or the *Evening Star*, leaving us little information about his business. He was active in his community. He was the president of the Congregation Ohev Sholem and spearheaded the construction of the congregation's new synagogue dedicated in 1906. He also was an officer of the Odd Fellows Lodge.

Krick died in 1946. The store continued on for at least two years, possibly run by his daughter Rose, who had worked in the store. By 1954, the building housed a delicatessen. It was torn down in 1958.[20]

CHAPTER 9

Laundries

The Evolution of Cleaning Clothes

The history of laundries and dry cleaners in Georgetown mirrors changes over the decades in the technology for washing and cleaning clothes and in the structure of the industry.

Doing laundry was a laborious task in the nineteenth century. It involved scrubbing tubs of wash against a washboard, hefting wet laundry in and out of tubs for rinsing, drying it outside, starching it, and ironing it with heavy flat irons. Because of the time required to dry, it was a two-day process.[1]

Middle-class women seeking relief from this drudgery hired "laundresses" or "washerwomen," who either came to their homes to do the wash or did it in their own homes. In 1877 and 1881 city directories, Mary Donegan, Harriet Hamblin, Ann Meeks, Edmonia Ray, Harriet Williams, Clara Canter, Martha Donnelly, and Lucy Harris all were listed as "washer" or doing "washing" or "laundress" at addresses on today's M Street and Wisconsin Avenue. These probably were the women's homes rather than separate places of business.

Later in the nineteenth century, "laundries" developed that received people's dirty laundry, did it by hand, and returned it. Chinese immigrants ran many such laundries (in Georgetown virtually all of them).

On Georgetown's two main streets, there were only seven laundries and dry cleaners in 1914. That number grew to fifteen in 1935 and remained at about that level for twenty years. After that it declined to seven in 1965 and to only one in 1975 and later.

The decline in the 1960s no doubt was due to Georgetown's newfound popularity as a shopping destination. With that development, laundries and cleaners no longer were the best use for retail space on major streets, and retail shops could and would pay higher rents there than laundries and cleaners could. There still are laundries and dry cleaners in Georgetown today, but they are largely on the side streets.

CHINESE LAUNDRIES

There long has been an association between laundries and the Chinese in the United States. For decades, legislation and local regulation shut Chinese immigrants out of many occupations, and laundering was one of the few open to them. Between 1914 and 1938, individuals with Asian surnames opened ten laundries on Wisconsin Avenue and M Street. The names tell the story: Charlie Wing, Han Lee, Quong Lee, Ling Lee, Charlie Lee, Horn Lee, Sing Lee, Hem Lee, Frank Lee, and Sam Moy. Many of those businesses were later run by others with Asian surnames, many probably relatives: Charlie Chinn, Ling Lee (a different one), Loy Lee, Ying Lee, Arkee Lee, Roy Lee, Charlie Gong, Sou Wong, and Sing Wong.

This was a citywide phenomenon. The classified section of the 1912 city directory had separate categories for businesses that washed clothes: "laundries" and "Chinese laundries." There were 29 "laundries" and 116 "Chinese laundries." Nineteen of the latter group had proprietors with the last name Lee.

It is difficult to find out much about the people who ran the Chinese laundries in Georgetown because many had similar names and they were born in other countries. In many cases, they also seem to have eluded census takers.

The group about whom we know the most is the family of Hem Lee who opened their laundry business in 1929 at 1440 Wisconsin Avenue.

Born in China in 1895, Hem Lee was thirty-five when he opened the business. In 1940, he lived above the shop with his father Fee Lee, then seventy-two; his younger brother Fow Lee, twenty-eight; and his cousin Sing Lee, forty. Fee Lee was born in California, but his children were born in China—he must have returned from the United States to China for some years.

In 1948, Ying Dong Lee bought the building for $23,000, but Hem Lee remained the proprietor of the laundry. By 1954, Ying Dong Lee had taken

This photo shows 1440 Wisconsin Avenue, home of the Lee family's laundry business. (*Photo by the author*)

over as proprietor. In 1966, he benefited from Georgetown's rising cachet when he sold the building for $300,000, and the laundry business closed.[2]

Two other Asian groups ran laundries on M Street across from each other. Sing Lee opened a store in 1924 that operated until 1934, under various proprietors who may or may not have been relatives. Sam Moy's laundry lasted much longer, opening in 1936 and closing in the early 1960s. Over those twenty-three years, the business was run in succession by Sam Moy, Charlie Gong, Sou Wong, and Sing Wong. Here, again, family relationships are unknown.[3]

INDUSTRIAL LAUNDRIES

In some cities in the late nineteenth century, businesses arose that did laundry on an industrial scale, in factory-like facilities. Several factors drove this development: the advent of machinery that could do wash on a large scale; the increasing difficulty of drying clothes outside in polluted, often sooty urban air; and the development of urban water systems providing ample clean water. Some of these firms picked up and delivered laundry, while others collected it at a network of branch storefronts.

The industrial laundries started out washing hotel linens and men's shirts and separate collars. Later, however, some marketed themselves as able to do all of a family's wash. Three such laundries had storefronts on Wisconsin Avenue or M Street: Frazee-Potomac Laundry, the Palace Laundry, and, briefly, the smaller Elite Laundry.

In 1898, John D. Frazee opened "Frazee's Laundry," operating from a single location at 12th and D Streets NW in downtown Washington. There is little information about Frazee, except that he was a bicycling enthusiast.

In 1901, Frazee started another business alongside Frazee's Laundry, under the name "Palace Laundry." The Palace Laundry made a major play to do all the family's washing. It ran large newspaper ads saying, "you pay by the pound at this new laundry" (five cents per pound), and referring to this as "our twentieth century way of doing your family wash."

> *The slavery of "Wash Day" is to be relegated to the past. Washing by the pound is a great success in other cities and we shall make it a success here. All work is called for promptly and returned. A neat canvas bag is furnished. Wear and tear are saved. All flat work is ironed. All starched goods are starched and the balance*

is returned "rough dry," ready to be ironed at home. Shirt Collars and Cuffs are laundered in the best manner and charged for at the usual rates by the piece.[4]

This arrangement sounds appealing today.

Frazee was serious about this effort—he had made a significant investment in new machinery and had remodeled a laundry plant he already owned at 21st and E Streets NW, pictured in some of his ads. The plant did laundry for both his existing business and the new venture. The Palace Laundry provided laundry bags, and an image of one of their bags appeared in their advertisements from the start. One series of ads was headlined "Have You Met Her? Who? Miss Monday Bag." (Monday was laundry day in many households.)[5]

This illustration appeared in many of the Palace Laundry's ads. (Evening Star, *February 9, 1901, 17*)

The Palace Laundry relied on pickup and delivery and did not have stores in Georgetown or any other neighborhood. Despite the big investment and aggressive marketing, it did not last long, disappearing in 1905.

Frazee now concentrated on Frazee's Laundry, which he had continued running alongside the Palace Laundry, and applied lessons from the Palace experience to Frazee's. Rather than relying solely on pickup and delivery, this time there was a network of storefronts for receiving laundry, which grew to twenty-four branches in 1939. The first store in Georgetown opened in 1913 at 3421 M Street, later relocating to 3423. There was a second branch at 1456 Wisconsin Avenue from 1930 to 1932. In 1933, the M Street location closed.

Ads extolled "the Frazee Finish" for shirts, cuffs, and collars.[6] In 1905, a merger with a competitor, Potomac Laundry, provided additional capital for Frazee to remodel a plant at 18th and D Streets NW and install new machinery. In 1907, Frazee sold his controlling interest in the merged company to Charles Jacobsen, the president of a bottling company, and Louis Levy.[7]

In 1914, the name "Palace Laundry" reappeared, this time used by an industrial laundry concern run by Thomas Hill Marshall. Marshall was from West Virginia, where he had been a laundry manager before he came to Washington. He died in 1918, and his son George Preston Marshall inherited the business. George Marshall later was known for his ownership of the Washington Redskins professional football team. Another of his sports ventures was Washington's first professional basketball team, which he named "The Palace Laundry Five."[8]

Marshall's Palace Laundry was the biggest of Washington's industrial laundries, growing to thirty-six branches citywide in 1932 and fifty-two in 1939. From its 1913 beginning, it had a Georgetown branch on Wisconsin Avenue, and another opened on M Street in 1919. The locations of the two Georgetown branches changed from time to time, but there always was a Palace branch on each of the two streets. As the 1940s began, Palace scaled back to a single location at 1410 Wisconsin Avenue, finally closing that in the late 1950s.

The approach of these large laundries truly was "industrial." As in a mass production factory, the task of laundering clothes was broken down into specialized jobs. Classified ads sought "collar girls," experienced "bundle wrappers," and experienced individuals to "iron coats on press machine" and to run "mangles." A mangle was a large-scale ironing machine, into which entire sheets could be fed. One of John Frazee's mangle operators was injured when her hand got tangled in a sheet and was pulled into the machine. She sued Frazee, who finally prevailed in 1908, but only after the case went all the way to the United States Supreme Court.[9]

One would think the industrial laundries would have driven their Chinese competitors out of business, but that did not happen—Chinese laundries continued to operate on Wisconsin Avenue and M Street into the 1960s. They offered lower prices than the big laundries because they were family businesses with low labor costs.

Increasing labor costs, the advent in the 1920s of feasible home washing machines, and the invention of coin-operated washing machines in the 1950s led to the decline of industrial-scale processing of household laundry. Some of the large laundries evolved into linen services and did laundry for hotels.[10]

DRY CLEANERS

Before dry cleaning was invented, re-dyeing was the common treatment for garments like men's suits. Dyes eliminated spots and restored color, and businesses called "dyers" provided that service. At various times between 1881 and 1920, John Knorr, Maurice Michael, and Randall Morris were listed in directories as dyers with locations on Wisconsin Avenue or M Street.

By the 1890s, techniques developed for cleaning nonwashable garments with solvents like gasoline and benzene. The problem was that these substances were toxic, volatile, and expensive. Dyers did such cleaning rather than laundries because dyers were accustomed to working with chemicals and with nonwashable fabrics. In the absence of machinery, however, the dry cleaning process was labor intensive and involved rubbing and scouring. Hence, the classified section of Washington city directories in the late nineteenth and early twentieth centuries had no category for "cleaners" but did have a category for "dyers and scourers."[11]

The first three stores in Georgetown to call themselves "cleaners" were run by men with two things in common. All were immigrants from Russia, and all were tailors before they went into dry cleaning. Edward Gantz and Arthur Bardt were the first to open, in 1920.

Gantz was born in Russia in 1886 and came to the United States in 1909 at the age of twenty-three. By 1917, he was living on Fuller Street NW and working as a tailor. His dry cleaning shop at 1436 Wisconsin Avenue opened in 1919 and lasted for eleven years, until 1930. Edward, his wife Sarah, and their two sons lived above the shop. Later in the 1920s, Sarah ran the shop, and Edward went back to work as a tailor, soon winding up as an employee of Jos. A Wilner Co., a Washington clothier.

It is not clear that Bardt actually was a tailor, though he said he was. He unquestionably was an entrepreneur, trying first one business and then another. He was born in Russia in 1865 and came to the United States in 1888. Before opening his dry cleaning shop at 3310 M Street in 1919, he ran a corner grocery on Third Street NW and later on Massachusetts Avenue. In 1920, he told the census taker he owned a tailor shop; perhaps he was still doing tailoring work in the new shop. After only two years, he moved the dry cleaning store to L Street NE. Another year later, he switched from dry cleaning to running a candy store at that address.

Burnett Niemetz opened his dry cleaning shop in 1920. Niemetz was born in Russia in 1883 and arrived in the United States in 1904. He really was a tailor, with a shop at 14th and P Streets NW from 1913 to 1919. In 1919, he made a short-lived detour, joining forces with Milton Abel to run a fish market on the Southwest Washington waterfront. That venture lasted only a year. Abel continued to sell fish for another three years, but Niemetz went into the dry cleaning business.

Niemetz called the business "Reliable Cleaners and Dyers" and located it at what then was 1302 Wisconsin Avenue.

In 1922, Niemetz bought the building next door at 1304 Wisconsin Avenue and moved the business there. The building just to the north was the factory of the Fussell-Young Ice Cream Company (see chapter 12). Unlike many Georgetown merchants, Niemetz had a home elsewhere in Washington (near the Soldiers' Home on Quincy Street NW) and never lived above the store.

Reliable Cleaners did business for thirty years, the longest-running dry cleaner on Wisconsin Avenue or M Street. It closed in the late 1950s.

LAUNDRIES

The building at 1302 Wisconsin Avenue (on the left) was the first home of Reliable Cleaners, which later moved to 1304, on the right. (*Photo by the author*)

A problem with early dry cleaning was that the chemicals used left odors in the clothing. Solvents with less odor were invented later on. This odor problem clearly inspired the name of Howard's Odorless Cleaners, which followed an industrial model. Its shop at 1500 Wisconsin Avenue did business from 1931 through 1940 and was part of a group of twenty-two storefront locations that took in cleaning to be done at Howard's central plant on South Capitol Street.

CHAPTER 10

Grocery Stores

Corner Store to Supermarket

THE EVOLUTION OF FOOD STORES

The way people bought food changed dramatically over the first half of the twentieth century, in three phases. That evolution can be seen in the history of Georgetown food stores.

In phase 1, food stores were local, small, and specialized. One bought fish at a fish market, vegetables at a produce market, meats from a butcher, and other supplies from a grocer. There was no refrigeration, so one had to shop daily. Many storekeepers extended credit and provided delivery, because their customers were neighbors. There was no self-service; clerks retrieved items for customers. The number of small grocery stores was enormous.[1]

Alongside the small stores, many cities, including Washington, had large markets where shoppers could buy from stalls selling a variety of food. The sellers rented their stalls from the city or other market owner. They were small businesses like the grocery stores but were clustered together in a single building.

In phase 2, national chains operated networks of local grocery stores. A&P began this evolution in the 1870s and had sixty-seven stores by 1876, but it started to expand more rapidly after 1912, as did other chains. The chains focused on creating efficiencies in the supply chain, but the retail end did not change much. These stores were not supermarkets—they still were small, local stores where there still was no self-service. By 1920, national chains operated seventy-five hundred such stores, and by 1930, there were thirty thousand.[2] Between 1919 and 1932, the combined market share of the five biggest chains grew from 4.2 percent to 28.8 percent.[3] Changes made by the chains included the debut of store brand goods and the elimination of credit and deliveries. The new stores' sometimes poor selection of local produce and meats left some opportunities for local butchers and produce markets to survive, but small grocers faced a challenge competing with the better inventory and lower prices of the chains.

In phase 3, beginning in the 1930s, supermarkets came on the scene. They were made possible by refrigeration (people could go to the store less often and stock up on each trip); by the development of nationally advertised, branded goods independent of the chains' store brands; and by the automobile, which enabled customers to travel longer distances to the stores. They took advantage of scale and other efficiencies not only in the supply chain but also at the retail level. The stores were large and self-service, often located in outlying areas to take advantage of low rents. They featured lower prices and advertised extensively. The first shopping cart appeared in 1937. The competition from supermarkets led to A&P closing more than half of its small stores between 1936 and 1941. Supermarkets' share of grocery sales went from 3.2 percent in 1932 to 22.8 percent in 1948 to 53.8 percent in 1958 to 74.5 percent in 1972.[4]

SMALL GROCERS IN GEORGETOWN

In 1877, the number of food stores in Washington and Georgetown was staggering—1,302 of them, not including stalls in the city markets. The D.C. population at the time was 175,000, so there was a food store for every 134 people. In Georgetown, which had a population of 11,571 (measured in 1878), there were 49 grocers and five produce markets on Wisconsin Avenue and M Street, 20 more grocers on the side streets, and 27 food stalls in the market—a food store for every 114 residents.[5]

Walking west on what is now M Street in 1877, one would have encountered multiple grocery stores on every block. In the block between 30th and 31st Streets, there were five grocers on the south side of M Street and three on the north. In the next block, between 31st Street and Wisconsin Avenue, there were two on each side. On the south side of M Street between 33rd and 34th, there were eight grocers, no doubt clustered there because of the Georgetown Market just east of 33rd.

Eugene Lyddane

Among the small grocers was Eugene T. Lyddane, who opened a grocery store between 1871 and 1874 at today's 1408 Wisconsin Avenue, just north of O Street. Born in Maryland in 1847, Lyddane was in his late twenties when he started the business. He died fifty-six years later, in 1932, and census records show his son Eugene Jr. running the store for a while after that. The store closed between 1935 and 1938, after more than sixty years in business.

The store occupied only the left half of a two-store building until 1914 when Lyddane expanded into the rest. The two spaces remain combined today.

Shown in this photo, 1408 Wisconsin Avenue was home to the Lyddane family's grocery store for sixty years. (*Photo by the author*)

GROCERY STORES

Eugene Lyddane III, in an oral history interview, was asked whether members of Georgetown's prominent Peter family (owners of the Tudor Place estate) ever came into the store. His reply again tells us how different the grocery business was then.

> No. They never came in. They would call on the telephone. But they wouldn't come in. Not many people came in grocery stores those days. There was no Safeways and things. No chain stores. People would order by telephone, and it would be delivered by truck. Those were the days.[6]

When the chains arrived, the Lyddanes faced intensifying competition. Another small grocer, Benjamin Baker, had been located just three doors down the street. As we have seen earlier, it was not unusual for small grocers to operate in close proximity. By 1920, however, Baker's store had been replaced by a Sanitary Grocery outlet, which A&P took over in 1926. There is no way to know whether the nearby chains were a factor in the Lyddane family's decision to close in the 1930s, but they must have faced an increasing competitive challenge as the years went by.

The Cropley Family

The Cropley family, an entrepreneurial clan, ran several retail businesses in Georgetown during the nineteenth century.

The patriarch was Samuel Cropley, born in England in 1803. His wife Eleanor came to the United States with him, and the two of them had eight children, all of them sons. One son died at age nineteen and another became a flour merchant and later a brick dealer, but the remaining seven all were retailers. George and Thomas were druggists (see chapter 11); Robert, Arthur, and Edward (who went by his middle name Maurice) were in the grocery business; and youngest son Charles was a dealer in agricultural implements (see chapter 2).

Samuel Cropley was already in the grocery business in Georgetown by 1830. For a few years in the 1860s, he was in two partnerships: one with Artaxerxes Offutt selling dry goods (rather than groceries), and another with his nephew George B. Barnard running a drugstore. By 1867, the partners were gone and Samuel was back in the grocery business together with his sons Arthur and Robert, under the name "Samuel S. Cropley & Sons" in a space next to the Georgetown Market. Son George took over the drugstore that Samuel had formerly run with Offutt.

Samuel was prosperous—in the 1860 census he said he owned real estate worth $10,000. Besides running his own businesses, he was a director of the Firemen's Insurance Company of Washington & Georgetown and the Farmers and Mechanics' National Bank.

In 1860, his prosperity also included ownership of three enslaved individuals, ages fifteen, thirty-one, and thirty-five. We do not know if all of these worked in his business or were household servants. Earlier censuses did not show him owning enslaved people, and he did not own them much longer. When Congress emancipated slaves in the District of Columbia in April 1862, Cropley did not apply for the compensation that the legislation provided for. Searching for an explanation, we can speculate about two extremes: he might have decided to free his slaves without compensation, or he had already sold them. There is no way to know.

Samuel Cropley died in 1869. Arthur and Robert continued to run the grocery store near the market, and the name "S. Cropley & Sons" remained on the door, until they closed it in the mid-1880s. Their brother Thomas then took over the space for a drugstore.

In 1874, Albert and Robert had opened a second grocery store under their own names at what is now 3101 M Street. They bought the one-story building, added two additional floors to it in 1877, and created a cellar in 1880. Around the same time that Robert and Arthur closed the original store in the mid-1880s, their younger brother Maurice took over this new one, running it alone in some years and in others with a partner named Ewing. He went out of business in 1892 or 1893.[7]

GROCERS ON THE SIDE STREETS

Though there are only a few corner groceries on Georgetown's side streets today, architectural evidence of many others remains. Corner houses with doors set at a diagonal were once stores, mostly grocers. Occasionally one sees two such houses at a single intersection.[8]

This photo shows 3101 M Street as it appeared in 2019, much as the Cropleys had left it. For an older photo of the building, see chapter 11. (*Photo by the author*)

This building at 28th and Olive Streets was occupied by Daniel Harris's grocery store in 1908, and between 1914 and 1920, it housed Nathan Broidie's grocery store. (*Photo by the author*)

This building on the corner of 34th Street and Dent Place was home to Arthur Donaldson's grocery store in 1908 and, later, was the site of grocery stores run by Donaldson's widow, by Albert M. Hilleary, and by the Kogod Brothers. (*Photo by the author*)

GROCERY STORES

Albert Hilleary

Albert Hilleary was born in Georgetown in 1876. His father was a bricklayer who also sold produce from a wagon. In 1917 Albert opened a grocery store at 34th and Dent Place, but around 1921 he moved the store a block north, to 34th and Reservoir Road.

Albert and Flora Hilleary lived above the store. Albert worked in the store until just a few months before his death in 1962, and his son Cecil continued to operate the store after his father's death. Students from nearby Western High School knew Albert as "Pops." A historical marker in front of the house says that the intersection was known as "Hilleary's Smiling Corner":

> *Like many other corner stores in Georgetown, this was a gathering place for the neighborhood. Children played marbles on the sidewalk, barbershop quartets sang*

The building at 34th Street and Reservoir Road was the location of Albert Hilleary's grocery store for more than forty years. (*Photo by the author*)

GEORGETOWN'S RETAIL PAST

in the store, and hunters met there almost every Friday night to discuss their triumphs and smoke cigars.

The marker says that Hilleary gave away groceries to neighbors in need, helping many to get through the Great Depression. The building is a private home now, but the shop windows still are there.[9]

Scheele's Market

The recollections of Tyler Abell about Scheele's Market during his childhood in the 1930s and 1940s tell us much about how small grocers operated:

> *Everybody bought their groceries at Scheele's and they were delivered. And Scheele's had a fantastic meat department....*
>
> *The old man always wore a paper sack on his head—a great big, tall paper sack, they all wore white coats and white aprons and they'd get back there in the meat department and if you wanted a steak two inches thick, they'd make it two*

Scheele's Market at 29th and Dumbarton Streets. (*Photo by the author*)

inches thick. If you wanted it three, they'd make it whatever you wanted, that's the way they did it. . . .

They made deliveries to our house which was right across the street, two or three times a day. . . .

Self-service was unthinkable, because if you'd let people pick their own stuff off the shelves, they'd run off with it. . . .

Scheele's, they'd put the groceries for everybody, all their customers, would go in old cardboard boxes that they saved up from all the deliveries that were made. . . . I don't know how far away they delivered. I'm sure it was a pretty long ways. Certainly to the other side of Wisconsin.[10]

David F. Scheele, a Washington native born in 1855, opened a butcher shop at 28th and Dumbarton Streets in 1892. After a few years, he listed the business in directories as a grocery store, but given its roots it probably emphasized meats. Between 1898 and 1900, he relocated to the store's present location at 29th and Dumbarton. After David's death in 1922, his brother George A. Scheele ran the business. George's son George Jr. worked in the store as well.

Scheele's market, though no longer owned by the Scheele family, still does business in 2025 under the Scheele name at the Dumbarton Street location.

PUBLIC MARKETS

The largest of Washington's public markets was Center Market, opened in 1801 on Pennsylvania Avenue where the National Archives building now is located. Four others had opened by 1813. Public markets were regulated, with laws prohibiting resale of food purchased in the market and fraud in weights and measures. The intent of the resale prohibition was to keep wholesalers out and have consumers deal directly with food producers.[11] The Eastern Market is the only one of the city's original markets that still operates as such.

Georgetown's market has always been located at what is now the corner of M and Potomac Streets. A market house built in 1803 remained in use until 1864. It was replaced in 1865 by a new structure that still stands today. The market was operated by the Town of Georgetown until the town was consolidated with the City of Washington, when the Georgetown Market was merged into the city's market operation.[12]

This photograph (ca. 1920) of Stephen Frank in front of the Center Market bacon stand of the Auth Provision Company shows what a stall in the Georgetown Market may have looked like. (*Library of Congress National Photo Co. Collection LC-DIG-npcc-29263*)

A symbol of the automobile's prominence in Georgetown was the Southern Auto Parts store that occupied the historic Georgetown Market from 1956 to 1980. (*Library of Congress, Historic American Buildings Survey HABS DC,GEO,82—1*)

GROCERY STORES

While the new town market was being built, its tenants occupied temporary quarters in some old tobacco warehouses between the C&O Canal and what is now M Street. When the new market was completed in 1865, a group of butchers decided they wished to remain independent. They first purchased temporary quarters at Wisconsin Avenue and N Street. In the mid-1870s, they built a new market house on that same site.[13] Known first as the Farmers & Butchers Marketing Company and later as the West Washington Market, the facility operated into the early twentieth century.

CHAIN FOOD STORES IN GEORGETOWN

The chains of small grocery stores made their first appearance in Washington around 1908. That was the first year the city directory listed A&P, with one store. It also was the first time the directory listed the Sanitary Grocery Co. Inc., a Washington/Richmond chain that would become the biggest player in the market until it was merged into Safeway in 1928. Safeway continued to run stores under the Sanitary name for some time after the merger.[14]

By 1914, A&P had expanded to twelve locations in Washington, including one at 3139 M Street in Georgetown. Sanitary had grown to twenty-seven stores, including one on the same block as A&P, at 3103 M Street.

Unlike the independent small grocers, the chains did not extend credit or deliver orders. Judy Davis, who grew up on P Street, remembered her neighbors' solution to the lack of delivery by the Sanitary Grocery Store at 3003 P Street:

> Little boys would come after school with their wagons. My mother would walk across the street, get her groceries, and then she'd give the little boy 10 cents, which was quite generous, to bring the groceries home in the wagon.[15]

Many of the chain stores indeed were small. Survey atlases[16] show the dimensions of the Georgetown buildings in which some stores were located. Assuming only the lower floor was used for the store, space was very limited.

GEORGETOWN'S RETAIL PAST

Miscellaneous Grocery Stores by Floor Space

Store	Location	Footprint
A&P	1400 Wisconsin Ave.	3,150 sq. ft.
A&P	3139 M St.	1,440 sq. ft.
Safeway	1305 Wisconsin Ave.	3,700 sq. ft.
Safeway	3075 M St.	2,300 sq. ft.
Sanitary	1524 Wisconsin Ave.	4,000 sq. ft.

Safeway sometimes constructed its own buildings for these small stores and even developed its own architectural template for them. An example is 3255 M Street, where Safeway did business during the 1940s. The small-store strategy is apparent: a one-story building only 19 feet wide with a floor area of only 3,190 square feet. Similar former Safeway buildings can be found around Washington, all one story with an arched or peaked roof, decorative elements in the facade, and a double door entrance.[17]

This building at 3255 M Street, former home of a Safeway store, is an example of the small spaces in which early chain stores did business. (*Photo by the author*)

THE IMPACT OF SUPERMARKETS IN GEORGETOWN

The first appearance of the word *supermarket* in the Washington *Evening Star* was on March 19, 1933, in an article about industries' hopes for recovery from the Great Depression:

> All over the country these big markets are arising. A large supermarket was opened in New Jersey in early December and within six weeks it had totaled more than $500,000 sales, equaling the operations of 100 average chain stores.[18]

The article went on to say that independent grocers had learned they could compete with the supermarkets by sprucing up their stores, freshening their merchandise, and advertising.[19]

By 1954, A&P, which in 1930 had 125 stores in the District of Columbia, operated only 9 stores in the Washington area, presumably all supermarkets. Giant Food, whose name almost shouts "supermarket," had only 26 stores throughout the metropolitan area.

SURVIVORS

Since 1960, the shops selling food on Georgetown's two main streets, with two exceptions, have been purveyors of high-end ("gourmet") meats and foods. The two exceptions are convenience stores and Food Mart, a small self-service market that operated from 1956 to 1980 at 3075–77 M Street, a space that had been a grocery store since Sanitary opened there in 1938. In 2023 Streets Market, another small self-service market, opened at 27th and P Streets NW.[20]

Fisher's Market

Fisher's Market was in business longer than any other Georgetown food store. Henry W. Fisher, a Maryland native, opened the store in 1863, when he was thirty-four years old. After short-term stays at a couple of locations, the business settled in 1882 at 1267 Wisconsin Avenue, on the southeast corner with Dumbarton Street, where it remained for eighty years.

Henry and his family lived a stone's throw from the business, on O Street just across Wisconsin Avenue. Henry died in 1901 at age sixty-nine. His son Henry Wellen Fisher, then thirty-eight and known as Wellen, took over the

GEORGETOWN'S RETAIL PAST

This building was the home of Fisher's Market for eighty years. (*Photo by the author*)

business. Wellen's son Henry Wellen Fisher Jr., known as Henry, would take over in turn shortly before Wellen died in 1934.

Fisher's Market finally closed its doors in 1963, a century after it opened. The *Evening Star*, in an article about the impending closing, recounted the long-term loyalty of the market's customers:

> Householders' routine has been to telephone Mr. Fisher, or one of his assistants, each morning to order the day's groceries and meat. Apparently, few persons have ever been disappointed. One customer has been ordering by telephone the last 57 years and has never seen the inside of the store. She has promised to do so before the closing, May 31. Another customer has been dealing with Fisher's for 70 years.[21]

Purchases listed on a 1911 receipt from Fisher's included several chickens for sixty-two cents, a pound of peaches for thirty-five cents, a cantaloupe for fifteen cents, and a ham for $1.54. As was common for neighborhood grocers, Fisher's extended credit—the receipt is for a month's purchases during July 1911.[22]

GROCERY STORES

In the early twentieth century, Fisher's bills and receipts featured elaborate graphics, like this from a receipt in 1911. (*Tudor Place Archive*)

Offering deliveries was a long tradition at the market. One of the younger Henry's duties as a child was to deliver groceries to customers who had summer homes along the streetcar line that led to Rockville. The *Georgetowner*, in its May 16, 1963, report on Fisher's closing, told of Fisher salesmen in the nineteenth century personally visiting customers to get their daily grocery orders:

> *If you had lived in Georgetown in 1861 and were considered "quality," a salesman from H. W. Fisher, Provision Dealer, would have called on you [in person] each morning for your order. . . . Fisher's store had the first telephone in Georgetown, which helped them expand and it was then that they called off their traveling salesmen.*

The *Evening Star* reporter described the store's interior, with a high ceiling, worn wooden chopping blocks, and an "ancient" ceiling fan over the meat counter. Henry said that it was his father, Wellen, who had added the meat department. Wellen also added bay windows to the building's Wisconsin Avenue frontage when his father (who did not like the idea) was away.[23]

Henry Wellen Fisher Jr. said that one of the store's early customers had been Robert Todd Lincoln, who lived on N Street in Georgetown. Emphasizing the freshness of what the Fishers sold, Henry also said "we have never cut a piece of meat until someone has ordered it."

Neam's Market

Neam's Market did business for forty years at 3217 P Street, on the corner with Wisconsin Avenue. Najeeb Neam was Lebanese and immigrated to the

United States from Syria in 1908. He opened a food store at the P Street location in 1909, calling it a delicatessen for his first few years in business but later calling it a grocery store.

For a three-year interval starting in 1936, George Atohl ran the store, and Najeeb and his wife Amelia worked for him as clerks. In 1939, Najeeb again became the proprietor. We do not know what this was all about. Did the Neams temporarily lease the store to Atohl, or did they sell it to him and buy it back? Amelia ran the store during World War II, presumably in Najeeb's absence.

Najeeb's sons Jack, Edmond, and George took over the business in the mid-1950s. As Georgetown became more upscale in the 1950s and 1960s, so did the market and its clientele. According to Jack's 1988 obituary:

> *Blessed with an exquisite taste for precious perishables and exotic delicacies, the family filled the market with more than 60 varieties of imported cheese and 24 kinds of mustard. They carried Mennonite wheat flour, litchi nuts and papadum, a wafer-thin Indian bread.*

Humorist Art Buchwald (a Georgetown resident) said that "Mr. Neam… is to fresh fruit what Bulgari's is to jewelry." Neam's still took telephone orders as late as 1981, with a $100 per month minimum. With a gift for understatement, Jack Neam told the *Washington Post* in 1981, "We do a classy trade here."

The market's customers included Nancy Kissinger, Elizabeth Taylor, Jacqueline Kennedy, and Nancy Reagan, as well as households with the family names Mellon, Harriman, and Vanderbilt. In 1985, Neam's was used as the location for a short scene in Mike Nichols's film *Heartburn*, in which Jack Neam briefly appeared as a butcher serving Meryl Streep. Jack liked to say that Meryl Streep costarred in his movie.[24]

The Neams sold the business in 1989 but stayed on as consultants to the new owners. Neam's Market was still doing business at the same location in 2000 but closed shortly after that.

The French Market

The French Market was a nearby competitor of the Neams and another example of how the increasing presence of affluent families in Georgetown spawned premium food stores. George Jacob, who came to the United States

GROCERY STORES

in the late 1940s with his father and brothers, learned the meat business in his father's butcher shop on K Street. The premium meats that his father sold attracted customers from the diplomatic community.

George and his brothers opened The French Market around 1957, in space at 1632 Wisconsin Avenue (between Q Street and Reservoir Road) that had since 1920 housed Mrs. Rose Collins's grocery store. By 1965, they had combined that space with two neighboring buildings, one a former antique store.

The French Market was a family enterprise. George's wife Elizabeth said that she never worked in the store, but her sister and all of her children did. A nephew worked there for twenty years.[25] Like Fisher's Market and Neam's Market, The French Market claimed prominent customers, including Henry Kissinger and Jacqueline Kennedy.

The French Market closed between 1995 and 2000. Asked why he closed, Jacob cited change in Georgetown: rising crime, parking issues, and competition from the Dean and Deluca gourmet food store in the Georgetown Market and from Sutton Place Gourmet on New Mexico Avenue. He also noted that the Georgetown Safeway had improved its meat department so that customers could get some of the same cuts there that they had been buying at The French Market.

This 2014 photo shows three merged spaces that were occupied by The French Market and still house a single store. (*Photo by the author*)

CHAPTER 11

Drugstores

LIKE THE GROCERY BUSINESS, DRUGSTORES EVOLVED OVER THE DECADES, due to the growth of medical knowledge and the advent of drug regulation, among other things.

In the late nineteenth century, pharmaceuticals were not regulated. Drugstores sold (a) a few truly effective drugs that are still in use today, such as aspirin; (b) heavily advertised patent medicines of dubious usefulness; and (c) narcotics like opium and cocaine. Many of the patent medicines, unbeknownst to customers, contained alcohol or opium. Though doctors wrote prescriptions to instruct patients what to buy and take, any drug could be purchased without a prescription. Because prescriptions were not necessary, pharmacists had a higher status relative to physicians than they do today, and customers often asked them to diagnose ailments and suggest treatments. There was no large-scale drug manufacturing, so pharmacists formulated (compounded) drugs by hand.

Legislation brought change. The Pure Food and Drug Act in 1906 required alcohol, cocaine, opium, and other such ingredients to be disclosed on the medicine's label, though they still were permitted as ingredients. Between 1914 and the 1930s, opium, cocaine, and the like were banned. Legislation in 1938 established the foundations of today's drug regulatory system, requiring both FDA approval of new drugs and doctors' prescriptions in order to buy most of them. After 1940, medical knowledge accelerated, the number of available drugs grew rapidly, and more of them were manufactured.[1]

In 1830, there were two "apothecaries" on Georgetown's two main streets. William Berryman ran one near the corner of 30th and M Streets, and Otho

DRUGSTORES

Linthicum ran the other near Wisconsin Avenue and M Street. (Otho Linthicum's brother Edward ran a hardware store in the same space.)

In 1860, there were five drugstores. Writing in the 1980s about Georgetown in 1868, Mary Mitchell said that "[f]or ladies, a greater joy sprang from the new drugstores mushrooming on convenient corners. Here they found patent medicines, fine French perfumes, braids, curls and invisible wigs."[2]

In the twentieth century, drugstores were consistently plentiful in Georgetown. In most years from 1914 to 1940, there were seven to nine of them on the two main streets, plus a few others on the residential streets. The number of drugstores did not shrink during the Great Depression but did drop after World War II. Still, there were four or five on Wisconsin and M Street until the 1960s.

Surprisingly, the arrival of the Peoples drugstore chain did not drive out the independent pharmacies at first. In Georgetown, Peoples did not

LEFT: The exterior of Peoples Drugstore at 3101 M Street in 1909. The building previously housed the Cropley family grocery store (see chapter 10). (*Library of Congress, National Photo Co. Collection LC-USZ62-129873*)
RIGHT: The interior of the same store, also in 1909. (*Library of Congress, National Photo Co. Collection LC-USZ62-129887*)

expand by buying existing drugstores, or perhaps the owners of those stores were unwilling to sell to them. It opened its first Georgetown store in 1921, in space at 31st and M Streets formerly occupied by Cropley's grocery store and later by a meat market. In 1930, it opened a second store at Wisconsin Avenue and M Street, replacing a restaurant. No decline in the number of neighborhood pharmacies followed either of these openings. Peoples did not expand in Georgetown again until 1970, when it opened a store at 1403 Wisconsin Avenue, on the former site of a bakery. CVS now (2025) operates a drugstore at that location.

THE CROPLEYS

The previous chapter described the grocery business of Samuel Cropley and his family. In the 1860s, Cropley was a partner in three Georgetown businesses, including the George Barnard & Co. drugstore at the corner of today's Wisconsin Avenue and M Street.

Samuel's sons George and Thomas Cropley both followed him into the drugstore business, each with his own store. George opened his in 1866 at 31st and M Streets, across 31st Street from his brother's grocery store. Thomas opened his store ten years later at M and Potomac Streets, on the other side of Wisconsin Avenue. George briefly had a second location on High Street in the 1870s. His store closed around 1890 and Thomas's five years later.

> **T. L. CROPLEY,**
> **DRUGGIST,**
> 186 Bridge and 110 High street,
> GEORGETOWN, D. C.,
> Offers to Physicians and to the Public a fine assortment of Drugs, Medicines, Essential Oils and Pure Powders. All the new remedies procured as soon as noticed in the medical journals. Glass, Paints, Oils and Dyes.

This ad for Thomas Cropley's drugstore appeared in an 1877 city directory. Note that the store also sold glass, dyes, and paints. (Boyd's Directory of the District of Columbia, *1877, 220*)

DRUGSTORES

Thomas's profile (paid advertising) in an 1884 guidebook and directory said:

Among the leading pharmacists of the District is Mr. Thomas L. Cropley at 3269 M Street. . . . He carries a full and judiciously selected stock of medicines, chemicals, drugs, patent medicines, &c., also toilet articles, perfumery, sponges, brushes, &c., in fact everything pertaining to a first class establishment. Employment is given to two assistants, and prescriptions are compounded with skill, promptness and accuracy. Mr. Cropley was born and educated in the District, and is a young man who is very popular, and is a member of the Potomac Boat Club. He has had a long experience in the drug business, and his practical knowledge of all its branches and facilities for properly conducting it are unsurpassed.[3]

The phrase "medicines, chemicals, drugs, patent medicines" suggests the expansive and unregulated nature of the business at the time.

BRACE'S PHARMACY

Russell Brace, a physician, opened his pharmacy between 1864 and 1866 at today's corner of 30th and M Streets. Brace was from Rochester, New York. He went to medical school in Baltimore and for a while practiced medicine in Montgomery County, Maryland, before moving to Washington to open his store. The 1867 city directory listed him as "Brace R., Dr. and druggist." His son William later took over the store.

Receipts from Brace's Pharmacy tell us that medicines the store sold included citrate magnesium (a laxative), dioxogen (an antiseptic), Platt's Chlorides ("The Odorless Disinfectant"), Ellerman's Embrocation (a muscle rub); tincture of benzoid (to treat canker sores), and alophen pills (another laxative). Some items would not be available over the counter today: morphine tablets and strychnine tablets. The store also sold turpentine, boric acid (a bug killer), glue, almond oil, rose water and glycerine, and alkanet root (a red dye).

Receipts from Brace's Pharmacy identify many items in the above list by chemical formula rather than a brand name. The receipts also record numerous sales of numbered "recipes," such as "Recipe 5653" and "Recipe 3555," sometimes referring to a renewal, as in "renewal recipe 3107." Were

A 1912 receipt from Brace's pharmacy. (*Peabody Room, D.C. Public Library*)

these standard or pre-prepared formulations that Brace offered, or were they a shorthand for custom formulations that Brace had previously provided the same customer, or were they references to doctors' prescriptions? We do not know.[4]

Brace's Pharmacy would operate at the same location for fifty-five years, though the Brace family sold the business in later years to George Latterner. Russell and William Brace both lived on 30th Street less than two blocks from the store. The store closed in 1931, and its building has since been replaced by a bank branch.

THE O'DONNELL FAMILY

Thomas O'Donnell was born in Ireland in 1825 and came to the United States in 1850. In 1858, he married Catherine Kinnerk, another immigrant from Ireland. Thomas worked as a truck driver, but he spawned a clan of pharmacists—three of his children and a grandchild.

DRUGSTORES

Brothers James and William J. O'Donnell were the first to enter the drugstore business, and they did so aggressively. After opening two stores elsewhere in Washington in 1897, they branched into Georgetown in 1899, when "James O'Donnell & Bro" began running two pharmacies, at the intersections of Wisconsin Avenue with M Street and P Street. William had studied pharmacy at night at the Washington College of Pharmacy. Members of the O'Donnell family would operate those two stores for many years to come.

James and William's sister Ellen "Nellie" O'Donnell earned a pharmacy degree from what is now George Washington University at age forty. From 1914 through 1922, she ran the Wisconsin Avenue and P Street store.

Another brother, named Thomas after his father, became a tinner (a welder or metal worker). In the next generation, however, his son Thomas E. O'Donnell, born in 1886, did go into the family business. He started as Nellie's employee in the Wisconsin Avenue and P Street store, and later he was the proprietor of the Wisconsin Avenue and P Street store from 1925 to 1943.[5]

The Wisconsin Avenue and P Street branch of O'Donnell's Pharmacy was located in this building at 1442 Wisconsin Avenue. (*Photo by the author*)

In 1922, the family moved the Wisconsin Avenue and M Street drugstore to 3204 M Street and opened a paint store next door at 3206–8 M Street, which Thomas ran. The drug and paint businesses both involved working with chemicals, and so it is not surprising for the family to have branched out in that direction. (Thomas Cropley's drugstore also sold paint.)

While these stores were listed in directories under individual siblings' names, the movement of family members between stores suggests that this may all have been one enterprise. Because of pharmacists' sometimes close relationships with customers, the identity of the pharmacist at each location was important information, and the stores may have been listed under the names of different siblings for that reason.

The family's drugstore empire extended throughout the city. The 1927 directory listed O'Donnell pharmacies at six other locations besides the two Georgetown stores. William O'Donnell also was a real estate investor—tax records in 1931 show him owning ten buildings on Wisconsin Avenue and M Street.

The M Street store closed in the mid-1930s, but the store at Wisconsin Avenue and P Street continued in business until the early 1960s.

MORGAN'S PHARMACY

Morgan's Pharmacy at 30th and P Streets is one of Georgetown's oldest surviving businesses, having operated for 110 years. Malcolm and Joseph Morgan, D.C. natives who were only twenty-two and twenty-four at the time, opened the "Morgan Brothers Pharmacy" in 1912. Their father, Daniel Morgan, was a lawyer. Malcolm graduated in 1912 from the George Washington University pharmacy school, and Joseph received his pharmacy degree two years later from Georgetown University.

The pharmacy occupied space that had been the home of Henry Beattle's grocery store since 1893. In 1911 Beattle retired, and the mortgage on the building was foreclosed. The *Washington Post* reported that the buyer, whose name was not announced, intended to remodel the first floor for a drugstore and the upper floors into apartments. The buyer probably was druggist William J. O'Donnell (see the previous section), because it was from him that the Morgan brothers eventually bought the building in 1923. There is no evidence that O'Donnell ever ran his own drugstore in the space. Perhaps he began with the intention to open a store in the building and then changed his mind and leased it to the Morgans instead. The Morgans may have bought some of their store's fixtures at a 1911 auction of items from Beattle's store, where items for sale included counters, shelving, showcases, and an icebox.[6]

By 1920, the brothers and their families were living across the street at 2928 P Street. Malcolm owned the building and lived in one apartment, Joseph lived in another apartment, and the third apartment was leased to a tenant. Living across the street enabled them to keep an eye on their business. That came in handy in May 1941, when Malcolm saw a burglar exiting the store and shot and wounded him when he did not halt on demand.[7]

The Morgans built an addition on the rear of the building sometime between 1924 and 1931.[8] In 1928, they opened a second store on Wisconsin Avenue near Tenley Circle,[9] which did business until about 1940. The Morgans changed the name of the Georgetown store from "Morgan Brothers Pharmacy" to "Morgan's Pharmacy" around 1936.

Around 1942, after twenty-nine years in business, the Morgans sold the Georgetown store to Joseph Schenick, who continued to use the Morgan name.[10] In 1944, Schenick bought the building from the Morgans for $35,000.[11]

Schenick was born in 1908 in Pennsylvania. His parents were Lithuanian immigrants who ran a grocery store. He and his wife Leah ran Morgan's Pharmacy until the 1960s. Joseph Schenick died in 1984, but Leah continued to own the store building until 2003.[12]

When he bought the business, Schenick decided to staff up. In the months after he took over the store, he advertised for "WOMEN, part time, to work at neighborhood soda fountain" and a "PORTER, over 18, to work in drugstore, must ride bicycle." The soda fountain required a split shift, working 9 a.m. to 2 p.m. and 5 p.m. to 8 p.m. daily, for sixty cents per hour. The porter would receive a salary of $22 per week.[13]

The Morgans had not advertised, at least in the daily newspapers, but Schenick began doing so in 1946.[14]

Morgan's was an old-fashioned drugstore and, indeed, still looks like an old-fashioned drugstore now, with many of the interior fixtures dating to the 1920s. Joseph Morgan's 1963 obituary said that the brothers "kept the old apothecary tradition in their establishments, with glass jars and scales in the windows and ice cream chairs and tables." The glass jars and scales still are in the window today.[15]

A 2005 obituary for Catherine Misner described how the soda fountain in Morgan's had been a hangout for Misner and her friend Millie Boland.

> *In high school, they hung out at the soda fountain inside the venerable Morgan's Pharmacy at 30th and P streets NW. Sipping their 5-cent Cokes, the girls would cast furtive glances at the adolescent "drugstore cowboys" slouching insouciantly on the sidewalk.*[16]

Janet Bohlen, a Washington writer who also grew up in Georgetown, remembered that

> *[w]e ordered chocolate sodas with malt sprinkled on top at Morgan's Pharmacy at the corner of 30th and T [sic], spinning on the high round stools while we waited. Here we bought our first illicit cigarettes from "Doc" [Schenick], claiming that they were for our mothers, and thumbed through equally verboten racy magazines, tame by today's* Playboy *and* Playgirl *standards. Doc kept an eye on us, but never moralized.*[17]

This tile work continues to greet visitors to Morgan's today (2025). (*Photo by the author*)

DRUGSTORES

Barry Deutschman, a Washington native, bought Morgan's Pharmacy in 1992 and ran it until his retirement in 2018. The exterior of the store had long been painted black, which he described as "a very Dickensian look." He repainted it green, having observed "everything going green these days."

In an oral history interview, Deutschman mentioned his grandmother, who had been married to Malcolm Morgan. Known to have a sweet tooth, she told Deutschman that people had joked she married Malcolm to get unlimited access to ice cream from the soda fountain. Deutschman also told of gourmet chef and Georgetown resident Julia Child running into the store and asking for a pack of Tums.[18]

GEORGETOWN PHARMACY

The building on the southwest corner of Wisconsin Avenue and O Street was a drugstore for 107 years. Harry "Doc" Dalinsky, one of the more colorful people in the history of retail Georgetown, ran the Georgetown Pharmacy in the building for the second half of that long period.

This building at Wisconsin Avenue and O Street once housed Doc Dalinsky's Georgetown Pharmacy. (*Photo by the author*)

A. H. Herr built the building in 1879.[19] His first tenant was J. D. Bowman, who in 1879 moved his drugstore from the corner of Wisconsin and P Streets into the new building. Only a year later, George B. Lockhart took over the business. Lockhart, twenty-five years old, was from Virginia and had come to Washington in 1872. In an 1884 business directory, Lockhart's entry (really paid advertising) said:

> *A large stock containing everything usually found in a first-class drug store is constantly kept on hand, among which are drugs, medicines, toilet soaps, perfumery, shoulder braces, trusses, sponges, and all kinds of druggists' sundries.*[20]

In 1897, Lockhart sold the store to Morris Waters, a Georgetown native and the fourth of six sons of a plumber. He was young when he bought Lockhart's business, age nineteen or twenty. About five years later, he also became a partner with Robert Wrenn in the Wrenn & Waters drugstore at 35th and O Streets, but it lasted only about a year. After that Waters concentrated on the Wisconsin Avenue Store. He, his wife Katherine, and two daughters lived above the store. He died in 1918 at age fifty.[21]

Thomas F. Donahue probably bought the business from Katherine Waters, and by 1920 it was doing business under the name "Donahue's Pharmacy."[22] Donahue was a D.C. native, born in 1892. His father Matthew, a D.C. government supply manager, and his wife Mary were both born in Ireland. The family was fond of the name Mary; Thomas and Mary named their daughters Mary Ellen and Mary Francis. At the time he bought the

MORRIS W. WATERS,
PHARMACIST,
S. W. COR. 32D AND O STREETS, N. W.,
WASHINGTON, D. C.

Pharmacist Morris Waters's will consisted of a single page, handwritten on the stationery of his store, with this logo at the top of the page. The stationery used an old address from before 32nd Street was renamed Wisconsin Avenue in the early 1900s. (*D.C. Probate records*)

store, Thomas and Mary were living with Thomas's parents on P Street in Georgetown. During the 1920s, they moved to Bethesda.

In 1928, Donahue bought the building that housed the store.[23] That same year, he made some improvements, removing partitions and building showroom windows. He and his descendants would own the building for sixty years.[24]

In 1938, Harry Dalinsky, who became known in the neighborhood as "Doc," bought the store together with his brother and renamed it the Georgetown Pharmacy.[25] Donahue still owned the building, so the Dalinskys rented the space from him. We do not know when Doc's brother withdrew from the business.

Doc Dalinsky was born in Russia in 1910 and was brought to the United States as a child. By 1920, his family was living in Baltimore, where his father made caps in a factory. By the time of the 1930 census, the father was in business for himself as a cabinetmaker. In later interviews, Dalinsky described a poor household but a loving family.

Doc graduated from the University of Maryland's pharmacy school in 1930; he began working at Sugar's Drugstore at 35th and O Streets for $40 a week. He married Marion Tenn, a D.C. native, in 1938. By 1940, he and Marion and their children were living in Chevy Chase.

Dalinsky was a character and a local institution, referred to sometimes as the "Mayor of Georgetown."[26] His 1992 obituary said that "what he did best was dispense a mixture of schmaltz, patience and good humor that made his store a nice place to visit." He was a confidant to some, and an observer of what went on around him. A 1970 profile in the *Washington Post*'s *Potomac Magazine* said:

> He knows which of the teen-age sons is stealing the magazines (and which of the boys ought to be straightened out by his parents). He knows who has the cancer that the wife knows nothing about yet. He knows which daughter is unhappier than she ought to be at her expensive boarding school. He knows who is between positions and who is drinking too much and who is seeing a psychiatrist. And who ought to be seeing a psychiatrist.[27]

Dalinsky said he always knew when President Franklin Roosevelt was visiting his son (who lived in Georgetown) because the family would order a pint each of vanilla and chocolate ice cream and a carton of Chesterfields.[28]

For eleven years, Dalinsky hosted a closed-door Sunday brunch for his friends in the store's back room, with coffee, pastry, and grits provided by Collins Bird, the manager of the nearby Georgetown Inn. The friends, all Georgetown residents, included journalist David Brinkley, novelist Herman Wouk, humorist Art Buchwald, and presidential advisor and cabinet secretary Joseph Califano. Word got around and attendance increased, so Dalinsky moved the food from the back room to the front and added bagels, lox, sausage, and sometimes caviar to the menu. Finally the crowd became too big (at one point fifty people), and in 1979 the brunches came to an end.[29]

From 1973 into the early 1980s, Marion Dalinsky ran a cosmetics and gift shop called "Powder and Smoke" a block up the street.[30]

Doc Dalinsky had a sense of humor. Shortly after the release of the hit movie *The Exorcist*, which was set and partially filmed in Georgetown, a product called "The Beginner's Exorcism Kit" was on display in the store window. A warning on the box said, "for serious problems see a priest or a shrink."[31]

Dalinsky retired in 1983 and sold the business to Jacky Boroukhim. Boroukhim closed the business in 1988, saying he was forced out of business by his $5,000 monthly rent (ironically being charged by the building's owner Matthew Donahue, a descendant of the earlier owners of the same store). Many of the customers who had patronized the store when Dalinsky owned it had died, and Boroukhim said others "are afraid to come out because of the rowdiness on the street." He also acknowledged, however, that he might have alienated some of his clientele by selling gold jewelry that in those years was attracting young customers who, some neighbors suspected, got their money from the drug trade.[32]

By 1965, the competition from chains had had an impact. There were only two drugstores on Wisconsin Avenue and M Street, Peoples and the Georgetown Pharmacy, plus Morgan's and the Dumbarton Pharmacy on side streets. Harold Sugar, proprietor of the Dumbarton Pharmacy, later lamented the chains' arrival:

> *Chains were getting much more important. When I started [1968] there were about five drugstores in Georgetown. Three or four on Wisconsin Avenue. There was Potomac Pharmacy, there was O'Donald's [sic], there was the Georgetown Pharmacy, Harry Zelinski [sic], who was a good friend, [laughingly] a block*

away. All gone. The only one remaining is Morgan's, where I started. The pressure from the chains changed. When I started, pharmacists have always cooperated with one another. If I needed an item that I did not have, I could call Peoples, which became CVS, I could call them, and the pharmacist would say, if he had it, "It's yours," and they sell it to me at their cost. That changed when Gray Drug bought Peoples.[33]

The remaining independents did stick together, it seems. In 1981, several of them refused to sell an issue of *Life* magazine that included an interview with Bernard Welch, the alleged murderer of Michael Halberstam. The stores joining in the boycott included Doc Dalinsky's Georgetown Pharmacy, Morgan's, Dumbarton Pharmacy, and Sugar's Campus Store at 35th and O Streets. Doc Dalinsky said, "We just felt this is a terrible thing to pay some guy and make him look like some kind of hero . . . I just had to do it [remove the magazine from his store's shelves]. If I didn't, I'd feel lousy about it."[34]

CHAPTER 12

Candy Stores, Ice Cream Shops, and a Factory

Georgetown always has been a place to go for a treat. Before today's prewrapped candy on shelves at the grocery checkout counter, there were specialized candy stores, often selling candy made by the proprietors. Because the grocery business was specialized, bread and pastries were sold in bakery shops. Some stores sold all three.

In the late nineteenth century, there were eleven "confectioners" and four or five bakeries on Georgetown's two main streets. "Confectioners" sold candy but might sell ice cream as well. The number of confectioners fell to six or so in the 1920s and 1930s and down to two in 1943. After that, there were only one or two. A big factor in the disappearance of candy stores in the mid-twentieth century must have been the growing availability of mass-produced candy, which could be sold in drugstores and grocery stores and did not have to be handmade on store premises.

Joseph Arney, an immigrant from Austria, ran one of the early confectionaries with his wife on M Street near Thomas Jefferson Street. Brittania Peter Kennon, who was born in 1826 and grew up at Georgetown's Tudor Place estate, visited the store as a child. The experience was so memorable that at age ninety-two she described it in detail for an oral history compiled by her grandson:

> When I was a girl there were but three kinds of candy—horehound, lemon and peppermint sticks. The latter striped with red. They were kept in tall glass jars and as the variety was limited one had little trouble to select what one wanted. It cost

CANDY STORES, ICE CREAM SHOPS, AND A FACTORY

six cents (or a fif and a bit) [sic] *an ounce! Mrs. Arney was the confectioner of the place—not only of Georgetown but of the north side of Washington as well. . . . They had no boxes in those days neither* [sic] *the nice wrapping paper of today. How well I remember when I would stop* [at the Arneys' shop] *for some candy— after selecting the kind I wanted old Mrs. Arney would rummage about under the counter until she found old newspaper in which to wrap it up!*[1]

Some of the early confectionaries had very long runs. Christian Beck, an immigrant from Germany, opened his bakery on Dumbarton Street in Georgetown in 1863. He moved twice but then settled in the 2900 block of M Street, where his store did business for seventy years. After Christian's death in 1884, his son Henry took over the business. Benjamin Gissel, another German immigrant, started his bakery between 1864 and 1866, and it did business at 1419 Wisconsin Avenue for more than seventy years, run first by Benjamin and then by his sons Henry and Frederick, finally closing in the early 1940s.

STOHLMAN'S

The purveyor of sweets that produced the most memories was Stohlman's, at 1254 Wisconsin Avenue. It began as Arnold's Bakery and later evolved into an ice cream parlor and candy store. Mr. and Mrs. Phillip May bought the business in 1845 and twenty years later sold it to Frederick Stohlman, whose wife was Mrs. May's niece. Frederick Stohlman's son J. William Stohlman later took over the business, and his son J. William, Jr. in turn ran the business until it finally closed in 1957.[2]

Recollections by longtime Georgetown residents are filled with references to Stohlman's. Judy Davis said:

I remember every time I got an A in school, my reward was a chocolate eclair at Stohlman's. That seemed such an enormous gift to receive. That was worth working for.[3]

Grace Dunlop Ecker recalled that "[b]ack in my girlhood it was 'quite the thing' to go down to Stohlman's and have a saucer of ice cream in the back parlor at one of the little marble-topped tables." J. Bernard Wyckoff remembered that, when he moved to Georgetown in 1922, locals instructed

129

A 2025 photo of 1254 Wisconsin Avenue, which once was the home of Stohlman's Confectionary. (*Photo by the author*)

him to "[b]uy your meats at Scheele's, ice creams at Stohlman's and shoes at Nordlinger's." Other residents reminiscing about the neighborhood would include Stohlman's in any list of stores they fondly remembered.[4]

The store closed in 1957 when J. William Stohlman was ready to retire and his sons had chosen other careers.

The family donated the interior of Stohlman's to the Smithsonian, where it was displayed in the new Museum of History and Technology (now the Museum of American History). Besides marble-top tables, cabinets, cash registers, and display cases, the donation included tools of the trade, such as molds and plaster casts for chocolate candies and ice cream, which Stohlman's would create in the shapes of Washington, Lincoln, Santa Claus, and a cherub. Also included were wooden tokens that waiters would leave at a

The donated interior of Stohlman's was a "star attraction" when the Smithsonian Museum of History and Technology opened in January 1964. (*Smithsonian Institution Archives Image SIA2010-3405*)

customer's table instead of a check. The customer would hand the token to the cashier, who would know the amount of the customer's bill.[5]

After Stohlman's closed, its building housed a series of hair salons, but in 1980 it became the home of a Swensen's Ice Cream parlor that for ten years recalled its earlier life.

THE CANDY KITCHEN

Another longtime confectionary institution was the Georgetown Candy Kitchen. Mary Colbert Mose, who grew up working on a canal boat with her parents, recalled what she and her family did while in port in Georgetown:

> One place we used to visit very much was the Candy Kitchen. Oh, I thought they had the best candy up there that ever was. They had all kinds and oh, there's none today that could touch it. They made candy and sold ice cream. There's where my first banana split came from. It was delicious. It couldn't have been any better.
>
> Then another thing. My father bought boxes, whole boxes of candy there. There was a taffy—one was chocolate, one was vanilla, one strawberry.... He would buy a box each. It wasn't pulled taffy; it wasn't that type. We used to get it in blocks. They wasn't even. More like chunks. Then there was another kind. He would buy cough drops—the little long ones, only they was bigger [than now]. They'd be licorice, strawberry, lemon and orange. He'd buy maybe a couple of boxes of them.
>
> And peanuts by the can. He'd buy them there too. They were in the hull. Every time we went in port, he'd have to get that gallon of peanuts.[6]

Evelyn Pryor Lison, another canal boat child, said:

> After our dads came back with the pay, they'd always give us kids so-much money; so we'd just go up to M Street to the Candy Kitchen. We was all crazy about those banana splits.[7]

Peter J. Chaconas and his son Theodore came to the United States in 1893 and opened "The Candy Kitchen" in 1900, at 3065 M Street. Eliza Palmer previously ran a candy store in the space, and the Chaconases probably bought her business. Peter gradually withdrew from the business—in 1912 the name changed from "Chaconas & Chaconas" to "TH Chaconas & Co.," and after 1913 Theodore was the only proprietor listed in directories.[8]

CANDY STORES, ICE CREAM SHOPS, AND A FACTORY

In 1921, after twenty years in business, Theodore and his wife Mary paid $17,500 to buy the building, which contained a second retail space (3063 M Street) besides the one occupied by the Chaconas store. The Chaconas family (including five children) lived in the building, above the store, for more than thirty years. Theodore never went to school but was able to read and write. Mary could not.[9]

This photo shows 3063–65 M Street, former home of The Candy Kitchen. (*Photo by the author*)

From 1918 through 1923, the store next door at 3067 M Street was Adolphe Nielson's confectionary business—the competition. We have to presume that Chaconas and Nielson were selling different product lines within the broad category of "confectioner."

The Candy Kitchen also sold ice cream, and bread—a 1924 newspaper ad for "Dad's Bread" included "T. H. Chaconas 3065 M St." in a list of "Dad's dealers."[10] Sports pages told of the ups and downs of the store's bowling team.

Also in the 1920s, Theodore expanded the retail candy business into the wholesale realm, as shown by a 1924 advertisement for "Apex Chocolates" (the distributor of which was the Columbia Wholesale Confectionary Co., located on 9th Street NW) in the *Sligonian*, a monthly student publication of Washington Missionary College in Takoma Park, Maryland.[11]

The 9th Street address was in or adjacent to the downtown Center Market, an efficient location for wholesale distribution. When the Center Market

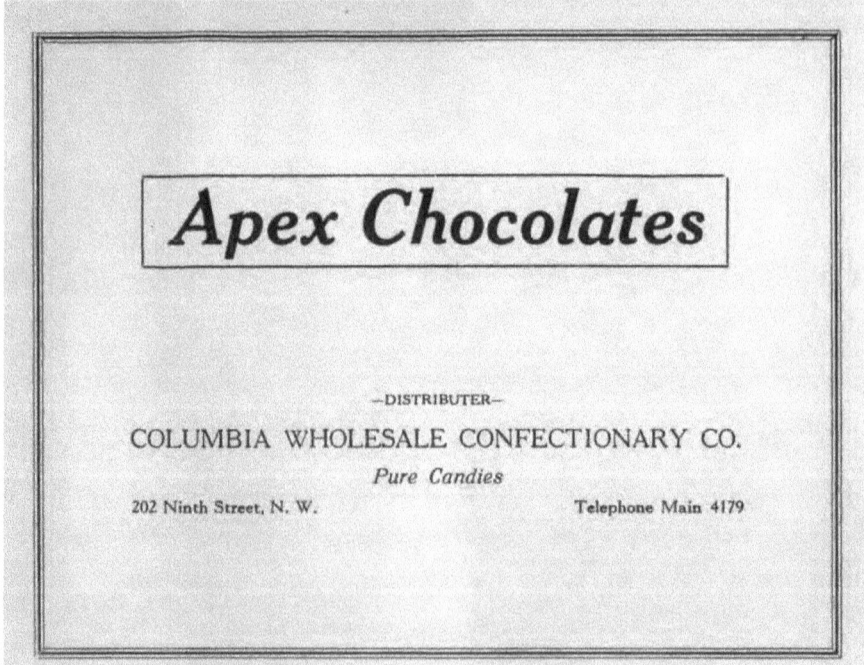

A 1924 advertisement mentioned the Chaconas family's wholesale candy venture. (Sligonian *9, no. 3 [December 1924]: 25)*

closed in 1931, Theodore, identified in a press announcement as president of Columbia Wholesale Confectionary Co., moved the wholesale business to space in the Union Terminal Market on Morse Street NE.

The repeal of Prohibition became effective in December 1933, and the family's next business decision recalls the Ogden Nash couplet "candy is dandy but liquor is quicker": they promptly opened a liquor store. A March 1934 list of applicants for newly available D.C. liquor licenses included "Peter Theodore Chaconas and Georgetown Candy Kitchen and Liquor Store, 3065 M Street."[12] Peter T. Chaconas was one of Theodore's twin sons, then twenty-eight years of age. In April, Theodore and Mary bought the neighboring property at 3067 M Street, and the liquor store opened in that space a few months later. This was in the depths of the Great Depression, and they were able to buy the building for only $4,000.[13]

In 1934, the family opened a restaurant at 3063 M Street, in the other half of the building where the candy store was located. Eugene Daly and Harry Dodge had previously run restaurants in that space. The candy store at 3065 closed in 1937 and the restaurant expanded into its space. Mary died in 1942 and Theodore in 1946, but their sons continued to run the restaurant until 1947 or 1948 and the liquor store until at least 1967. The family sold the two buildings on M Street in 1995 and 1996, after son Paul's death. Son Peter lived on for another twenty-five years and died at age 101 in 2005.

THE FUSSELL-YOUNG ICE CREAM COMPANY

Georgetown always has had shops that sell ice cream, but for thirty years ice cream actually was manufactured there. The Fussell-Young Ice Cream Company's factory was located on Wisconsin Avenue just north of N Street, on the site now (2025) occupied by the Georgetown Inn.

Until the mid-nineteenth century, there was no mass-produced ice cream; it was available only in small quantities from caterers and other custom sources. Jacob Fussell was a Baltimore milk dealer faced with an erratic demand for cream that periodically left him with an excess supply. Using the excess, he was the first in the country to make ice cream in commercial quantities and sell it wholesale.

The new venture proved so profitable that Fussell gave up the milk business to concentrate on ice cream. In 1856, he moved to Washington and opened his second ice cream factory, at 12th and F Streets NW downtown. A retail ice cream shop was on the ground floor. Among Fussell's customers was the Union army during the Civil War.

In 1863, he moved to New York and opened a third plant and retail store there. By 1884, the Washington plant, relocated to 14th Street and New York Avenue, was making three hundred to six hundred gallons of ice cream a day and supplying most of the city's restaurants.

Jacob Fussell was a Quaker, was active in the abolitionist movement, and was a friend of Abraham Lincoln. He retired from the business around 1875, and other members of the family took over, including his grandson Norris Fussell. Jacob Fussell died, back in Washington, in 1912.

Around 1917, the Fussell Ice Cream Company merged with a competitor that had been started in 1915 by former Fussell employee Ford E. Young, and the merged company was called the Fussell-Young Ice Cream

The Fussell-Young Ice Cream Company had a fleet of delivery trucks, as seen in this 1923 photo of its Georgetown factory. Note the Christmas tree in the window of the retail store. (*Library of Congress National Photo Co. Collection LC-DIG-npcc-30453*)

Company. Shortly after that, in 1919, the company began construction of a new ice cream plant in Georgetown, on Wisconsin Avenue. As with other Fussell-Young plants, there would be a retail store on the ground floor.

In 1931, the company acquired and tore down brick buildings just to the north and expanded the plant onto those lots.

Twenty years later, only a year after Fussell-Young had occupied a newly built factory in Alexandria, Arden Farms Co. of Los Angeles bought the company. The new management apparently decided the Georgetown plant no longer was necessary. It was demolished in 1953, and the Georgetown Inn occupies the site today.[14]

CHAPTER 13

Tobacco Shops

Georgetown was founded on tobacco. It began as a small settlement around a warehouse for the official inspection and grading of tobacco for export. For more on that history, see chapter 1. While the tobacco economy declined in the second quarter of the nineteenth century and the inspection, storage, and export of tobacco figured less in the town's economy after that, tobacco was a sizeable neighborhood *retail* sector until the 1930s.

In 1830, Albert Waugh ran Georgetown's one tobacco store near the intersection of today's 31st and M Streets. In 1860, there were a half dozen tobacco stores in the neighborhood. After the Civil War, there was a boom in the retail tobacco industry. Citywide, there were only 6 tobacco stores in 1874, but fourteen years later there were 160 of them. Only a little of that boom happened in Georgetown, but there were a dozen or so tobacco stores on Wisconsin Avenue and M Street until the 1930s, after which the number shrank. As of this writing in 2025, there are two tobacco stores, along with several shops selling vaping and CBD products.

Cigars long were the hot item; until the late 1930s, many of the tobacco stores listed themselves in directories as selling cigars specifically (in one case "segars") rather than using the more general word *tobacco*.

PETER AND JOHN MAY

Peter May was born in Washington in 1855 and grew up in Georgetown. His father worked as a laborer but apparently was frugal, and by the time of the 1870 census, he owned $2,000 worth of real estate (probably the family home) and personal property worth $600. Peter had two younger sisters and a younger brother.

TOBACCO SHOPS

By the time Peter turned fifteen, he was working as a cigar maker's apprentice. For at least some time, his employer and teacher was tobacconist John Albrecht (more on him later in the chapter).[1]

In 1880, Peter went out on his own, opening a store at 1318 Wisconsin Avenue. In 1894, he moved the business up the street to 1340 Wisconsin Avenue, where it would remain for more than twenty years.

Peter never married. For the last few years of his life, he lived with his younger sister Annie and her family. Peter's fierce loyalty to his family was revealed in 1901, when he pursued a libel charge against Durand Shackelford. May's complaint said Shackelford had "reflected on the character of" May's sister-in-law. That would have been John's wife Bertha. We do not know how the dispute was resolved, or why it was Peter rather than John who took legal action.[2]

Peter died in 1912, and his younger brother John took over the store. John told the census taker in 1900 that he was a cigar maker, so he had already been working in the store for years when he became the proprietor. He left the business in 1921, and for the next four years, Daniel Dobbins ran a cigar store in the same space, no doubt having bought the business from John.

A photo taken between 1895 and 1912 shows the store when Peter was still the proprietor. Lettering in the store windows says, "Peter J. May, Cigar Manufacturer" and "Tobacco, Cigars, Snuff." Three gentlemen stand in the doorway, all wearing suits and bowler hats. A classic cigar store Indian, perhaps four feet high, fills one window.

JOHN SCHULTZE

John Henry Schultze emigrated from Germany and opened a tobacco store in 1864. The store originally was located on the ground floor of the Union Hotel at 30th and M Streets but, after fifteen years, moved east to what today is 2913 M Street. It did business there until 1897.

A sketch of Schultze's store appeared in an 1884 business directory. The sketches probably were paid advertising—this one certainly reads like Schultze wrote it, and reveals how he viewed his business and himself:

> *A large and well assorted stock is carried, embracing everything to be found in a first-class tobacco store, including the most popular brands of cigars, tobaccos, cigarettes, smoking tobacco, pipes, &c. The cigars are principally of his [Schultze's]*

> JOHN H. SCHULTZE,
> MANUFACTURER AND
> **DEALER IN HAVANA & DOMESTIC SEGARS,**
> SUPERIOR CHEWING AND SMOKING TOBACCO,
> SNUFF, PIPES, FANCY ARTICLES, &c.
> **No. 62 Bridge Street, under Union Hotel,**
> GEORGETOWN, D. C.

This ad for John Schultze's tobacco store appeared in the 1867 city directory. (Boyd's Directory of Washington & Georgetown, *1867, 496*)

> own manufacture, of which he makes a specialty, and in which only the best stock is used.... For nearly twenty years he has successfully followed this business, and has established a reputation for keeping on hand a good supply of the very best goods to be obtained in the District, and has a large trade throughout the city. He has a host of friends who appreciate him personally and his efforts to please all.[3]

Schultze closed his store in 1896; he died in 1907.

THE ALBRECHT FAMILY

The Albrecht family ran a tobacco store on M Street for forty-seven years, from 1869 until 1915.

Born in Germany in 1846, John C. Albrecht came to the United States at age four and may have grown up in Maryland. The first sign of his tobacco store in Georgetown was a newspaper ad that ran for much of December 1869, the Christmas season, inviting readers to "come and see the handsome presents," including "a choice selection of MERSCHAUM and FANCY PIPES."[4]

John may have chosen to open his store in Georgetown because he had become fond of Agnes Emrich, also born in Germany. She lived in Georgetown, and her mother Marie ran a "fancy store" on M Street, near John's store. John and Agnes were married in 1870.

Albrecht relocated the store for a few years in the 1870s and then did so again in 1881, settling at 3119 M Street, where the store would remain for thirty-five years. The building no longer exists.

At times John and Agnes used an Anglicized version of their name, calling themselves "Albright" or "Allbright." They may have used that name for the store. In 1882, "*Allbright's* Cigar Store" ran a classified ad offering to sell a retail liquor license at a reduced price.[5]

After John's death, Agnes and her son Harry carried on the business, listing it in directories under Agnes's name. In 1910, they went in an intriguing direction—they began to sell sporting goods in the store along with tobacco, a combination that today would be laughable. Perhaps the logic was that the customer base for both products was predominantly male. They advertised "Albrecht's Sporting Goods, Cigars and Tobacco." Note the Albrecht name. Harry ran the sporting goods side of the business and Agnes the tobacco. One wonders if there was a generational difference of opinion, with Harry wanting to branch out into new things.[6]

Both businesses closed in 1915, and a Sanitary Grocery Store moved into the space. Agnes died in 1928 and Harry in 1935.

GEORGETOWN TOBACCO—TWO INCARNATIONS

Philip Helig was the son of Russian immigrants, born in 1888. He was a farmer in New Jersey until his mid-thirties, when he moved to Georgetown and opened a tobacco store in 1927 in space at 3207 M Street that since 1906 had housed Theophilis Wrenn's tobacco store.[7] Helig may have bought his initial inventory and his store fixtures from Wrenn. In the late 1930s, he branched out from retail trade into wholesale tobacco sales, calling the business "Georgetown Tobacco Co." In 1956, Helig and his wife Mamie changed the retail space into a liquor store, though the wholesale tobacco business continued to operate elsewhere. They sold both the tobacco business and the liquor store in 1959.

The second store to use the "Georgetown Tobacco" name still exists. David Berkobile, then twenty-four, opened the store in 1964 at 1261 Wisconsin Avenue, under the name "Georgetown Tobacco and Pipe." In the late 1970s, he shortened the name to "Georgetown Tobacco." Around 1972, Berkobile moved the business to new quarters at 3144 M Street, three doors from Wisconsin Avenue, where it remains today. He installed antique paneling and shelves from a Pennsylvania apothecary dating to 1880. A sign displayed in the store said, "Thank you for smoking."[8]

Before long, there were other branches, three by 1969: Alexandria, Montgomery Mall in Bethesda, and Tysons Corner in Virginia. Two more branches opened in the following year, at the Iverson Mall in Maryland and a mail order department in Vienna, Virginia. By 1976, though, the business was back to three branches (Georgetown, Tysons Corner, and Montgomery Mall) with the mail order operation located in the Georgetown space. As of this writing, only the Georgetown store remains.

In the store's advertising, Berkobile and his staff sought to project an image of an elegance and refinement perhaps lost in modern times. A 1969 ad read:

> *Men will have a fine time here: We feature a variety of pipes and tobacco under our own label and famous brands. We also carry a large selection of choice hand rolled cigars.*

In 1978, Georgetown Tobacco advertised a four-hour fourteenth anniversary celebration to be held on a Friday night:

> *A leisure opportunity to shop, meet old friends, swap tales and enjoy a particular comaradery [sic] not attainable during a busy day. Expert counseling and guidance prevail. The man still practicing the ancient art of smoking will find an eager audience within our walls. The proprietor will often be present to greet you and exchange esoteric knowledge about the pursuit of smoking pleasures.*

The ad also promised bartering, pipe trading, and tobacco sampling. Note the reference to smoking as an "ancient art." J. William Grady, who was a vice president of Georgetown Tobacco and Pipe for ten years, may have put this philosophy in a nutshell as he left the company to open his own cigar store downtown. When interviewed by a reporter, he observed that "[t]here is too much ye olde tobacco shop. There is a lot of romance to the products here."[9]

Like many tobacco stores, Georgetown Tobacco sells other items as well. Its website describes "an in-depth selection of accessories and gifts from the familiar to the fantastic including Venetian masks, canes, hats, cufflinks, original lithographs and beautiful cigar humidors."[10]

CHAPTER 14

Florists

IN 1878, THERE WERE TWENTY-SIX FLORISTS CITYWIDE, BUT THERE WERE none in Georgetown. In 1900, the citywide total was seventy-seven, but still there were none in Georgetown. After that, there were consistently two to three florists on Georgetown's two main streets until the 1950s when the number grew to five and remained there until it dropped in 1980. As of this writing in 2025, there are no florists on the two main streets, though there are at least two on side streets.

George Comley's flower shop (described in the following section) and Blackistone Florists had the sector to themselves until the 1930s.

THE COMLEY FAMILY
The florist business started by George A. Comley in 1902 was a true family enterprise that lasted until 1969.

Comley was born Abraham George Comley in 1869, in Wiltshire, England. When he was four, his family immigrated to Canada, where several of his siblings were born in the ensuing years. In 1890, he moved to the United States. He settled in Arlington, Virginia, and married Phoebe Sherier in 1894. Arlington was largely agricultural at the time, and he worked in a dairy. By the time of the 1900 census, he had reversed his first and middle names, calling himself George A. Comley.

Comley started his florist business in 1901 or 1902, opening a stall in Washington's Center Market. The market, opened in 1801 on the site of today's National Archives, was the largest of several public markets that were part of Washington's food distribution system.

In 1908, George opened a second location, this time a shop in Georgetown at 1204 Wisconsin Avenue. Within two years, he abandoned the Center Market stall, and Georgetown became his sole retail location. He may have chosen the Georgetown location in part for the convenient commute from his home in Arlington's Clarendon neighborhood. In about 1920, the business moved around the corner to 3209 M Street.

George and Phoebe had four children: sons Francis G. and Milton, and daughters Lillian and Louise. Both sons became florists, as did a son-in-law and a daughter-in-law. Francis reversed his first and middle names as his father had, and became known as George F. Comley. (To avoid confusion, we will refer to them as George A. and George F.)

George A. sought to move beyond selling plants bought from wholesalers and start growing some of his own supply. He and Phoebe started buying property in Arlington in 1907 and, by 1928, had acquired twelve properties.[1] Among them was a parcel of several acres on Lee Highway (now Langston Boulevard) near George Mason Drive, where they established a nursery.[2]

The extended family lived in three houses on that land. George A. died in 1930. After that, Milton ran the nursery and George F. ran the Georgetown store. Misfortune struck again a year later, when George F. also died. George F. and Phoebe's son-in-law Linden Shenk, who had married their daughter Lillian in 1930, stepped in to manage the store, and did so for thirty years. The store, however, continued to bear George A.'s name until it closed in 1969.

A 1934 newspaper ad around Easter began with the headline "*Remember—* COMLEY'S" and touted a

> [l]arge assortment of specimen potted plants, including Easter Lilies, Tulips, Hydrangea, Azalea, Spirea, Jonquils, Begonias, Etc. Beautiful Baskets of Assorted Flowers. Reasonable Prices—Prompt Deliveries.[3]

A December 1932 ad offered "living evergreen Christmas trees in tub," ranging in height from three to seven feet (and priced from $1 to $4), as well as "cut spruce trees." It too offered delivery, in this case out of necessity: the Georgetown store—only twenty-two feet wide by fifty or so feet deep—had little room for an inventory of trees.[4]

FLORISTS

It stood to reason that as Arlington grew there would be an opportunity to sell flowers directly from the nursery. In 1937, Milton opened a florist shop of his own on the Lee Highway property. The Georgetown and Arlington stores had distinct names and advertised separately, suggesting they were separate businesses, not a common enterprise. For example, the 1937 ad about Christmas trees mentioned only the Georgetown store.[5]

Also in 1937, Phoebe bought the building that housed the Georgetown store for $30,000.[6]

Lillian's marriage to Linden Shenk did not last. It is not clear when they parted company, but when Linden registered for the draft in 1942 and was asked for the name of someone who always would know his whereabouts he listed not Lillian, but Reita Comley, his brother-in-law George F.'s widow. At the time, he was living on Conduit Road (today's Macarthur Boulevard) as a boarder in someone's home, without Lillian. Despite the apparent breakup, though, Linden continued to manage the Georgetown store until at least 1960. In the census in both 1940 and 1950, Reita said she was a designer for a florist. She might have been working with her brother-in-law Milton out in Arlington, but her being listed in Linden's draft registration suggests she was working with him in the Georgetown store. He had remarried by the time he died in 1965, but not to Reita. We do not know who ran the Georgetown store after Linden Shenk, but it probably was Reita.

After the Georgetown store closed in 1969, Lillian and her sister Louise, as Phoebe's executors, sold the M Street building. Like many other longtime Georgetown business owners, they benefited from the neighborhood's newfound cachet: the building that Phoebe had bought for $30,000 in 1937 sold for just over $1 million.

CLAIRE FLORIST

Sally W. Peters (not related to the author) was the proprietor of Claire Florist, which did business in Georgetown for more than thirty years, from 1935 through 1969.

She was born Sarah Canada in 1907. Her parents ran a grocery store, and her mother was the postmaster of Glen Echo, Maryland. As a teenager, Sally was part of a small scandal in 1926, when a Prohibition enforcement agent was forced to resign over his conduct in an investigation involving Sally. The agent, hoping to "get something" on eighteen-year-old Sally, dated her for two months, taking her to dinner and on trips to Washington and Baltimore. He later charged her with selling liquor and alleged she had bought it with money he gave her "as his messenger." The case was dismissed.[7]

Sally married Clifford F. Peters, a fellow Maryland native whose father also was a merchant. Clifford worked variously in the construction and coal businesses and as a chauffeur. They settled in Glen Echo.

In 1935, when she was twenty-eight, Sally opened a florist shop at 1265 Wisconsin Avenue (near N Street), in space that had been occupied for the previous two years by Simon B. Wiseman, another florist. She probably bought his business from his estate. It is unclear whether she used the name "Claire Florist" from the beginning, but she definitely had adopted the name by 1949, when she temporarily relocated the shop to 1205 Wisconsin.[8] In 1947, Sally sponsored a team in the D.C. Recreation Department's West End basketball league.[9]

Around 1950, Sally decided to move up the street a few doors to 1243 Wisconsin Avenue. When she applied for a permit to remodel the space, Sally encountered the newly established architectural requirements of the Old Georgetown Act, passed in 1950, which forced her to accept a multipane store window with an eighteenth-century flavor in lieu of the plate glass window that would have been ideal for displaying flowers. For more about Sally's application, see chapter 1.

From 1951 through 1960, Sally had two locations, continuing to operate in the old 1265 Wisconsin space as well as in the new shop at 1243—the two were only a half block apart. She had a staff; over the years, she ran frequent classified ads seeking salespeople and delivery drivers. She did not advertise much beyond the classifieds, but in 1954 Claire Florist did advertise "a beautiful display of Mamie Eisenhower Carnations" and "artistic flower arrangements by Sally W. Peters."[10]

In the late 1940s, Sally and Clifford had moved from Glen Echo to a home on T Street in Glover Park, no doubt to be closer to her business. He died in 1953. They had no children. She continued to operate the florist shop until 1970. She died in 1973.[11]

Claire Florist called 1243 Wisconsin Avenue home from 1950 to 1970. (*Photo by the author*)

CHAPTER 15

Furniture and Home Furnishings Stores

Selling furniture in Georgetown's small retail spaces is a challenge, but there have been furniture stores in the neighborhood throughout its history. Several stores have compensated for the cramped quarters by opening branch locations in the neighborhood, often within a couple of blocks. Businesses selling furniture in the neighborhood have included cabinetmakers, furniture stores, sellers of home furnishings, antique dealers, and dealers in secondhand furniture.

In 1830, the five furniture stores all called themselves "cabinetmakers," perhaps because ready-made furniture was rare at the time.

In the prosperity of the 1920s, the furniture business in Georgetown boomed, with the number of such stores on the two main streets growing from three to ten. The impact of the Great Depression was apparent by 1932, when the number of stores selling new furniture had dropped to six, but three additional stores were selling used furniture. In the 1960s and 1970s, there was another boom, with around ten stores selling new furniture and a similar number selling home furnishings. That boom ebbed only slightly, and in 2023, there still were twelve stores selling furniture and two selling home furnishings.

THE MAYS

One of the three cabinetmakers working in Georgetown in 1860 was John M. May, whose business was located at the southwest corner of today's Wis-

FURNITURE AND HOME FURNISHINGS STORES

consin Avenue and Prospect Street. May and later his son did business at that location for at least forty years.

May was born in 1822 in Hesse, Germany. He married Barbara Yost, also born in Hesse, and the two of them came to the United States in time for the birth of their third child and only son, John George May, in 1847. By the time of the 1850 census, they were living in Georgetown, and the elder John was working as a confectioner. By 1853, he had changed careers and had become a cabinetmaker. In 1864 he began calling his business a furniture dealer, not just a cabinetmaking shop.

We know little about May's business. He did not advertise, and he is seldom mentioned in the press. We do know a few things about his other activities, however.

May seemed to have an affinity for wandering animals. In 1856, he ran an ad seeking help locating a stray cow. In 1864, he found a stray horse and advertised in search of its owner. A Major Kerrigan claimed the horse, and a Sergeant Frankie swore before a judge that Kerrigan did indeed own the horse. Sixteen days later, the real owner appeared. May, obviously scrupulous about returning animals to their rightful owners, called the police. The major was arrested, and the horse was returned to its owner. In April 1865, May advertised seeking the return of another stray horse.[1]

People who buy furniture generally cannot carry it home, so furniture stores have delivery trucks or, in May's time, wagons. Furniture dealers sometimes used their wagons for other hauling on the side. May did that, using his wagon to transport mail between the Georgetown and Washington post offices. In 1865, in his ad seeking the return of a horse that had "strayed away from the Post Office in Washington," he said, "the horse is used in conveying the U.S. mails" and that anyone providing information leading to recovery of the horse "will be suitably rewarded by the mail contractor."

May displayed a few pieces of furniture on the street in front of the store. In November 1873, he encountered a shoplifter who was not afraid of heavy lifting and stole one of those display pieces, carrying it off on his back.

May did at least some business with the Town of Georgetown. An 1860 newspaper item noted that the town had agreed to pay May $2 for "a writing table furnished to [the City] Council chamber."[2]

> $5 REWARD—Stolen from in front of my store, No. 69 High street, Georgetown, a green and yellow striped REP. LOUNGE. A colored man was seen several times on Bridge street, between 5 and 6 o'clock p. m., with it on his back. I will give the above reward for the apprehension of the thief and the return of the Lounge.
> It*
> JOHN M. MAY.

In 1873, John May encountered a shoplifter who was not afraid of heavy lifting. (Evening Star, *November 11, 1873, 2*)

May's business was successful, and he and Barbara were well off. In the 1870 census, he said he owned real property worth $8,000 and personal property worth $2,000, significant amounts then. In addition to son John G., they had three daughters. John M. May died in 1878, from injuries he suffered in a fall from a ladder.[3]

After some experimentation in other lines of business, son John G. May had taken over the business by 1880; he continued it for another twenty years, until 1900. He and his wife Emma lived above the store at first, but later bought a house across the street.

Like his father, John G. May had a sideline: moving people's furniture. In 1894, there was a misunderstanding when May, having moved a Mrs. Blundon's things from Dumbarton Avenue to Northeast Washington, was unable to find her to collect his fee. He took her sewing machine as security, and she called the police. He was arrested and released on bond. We do not know how the matter was resolved.[4]

The last years of John G. May's life were troubled. The furniture store closed in 1900, and over the next few years, he was in and out of St. Elizabeth's Hospital (the District of Columbia's public mental hospital). He died in 1914, but Emma lived on until 1943, when she died at age ninety-two.

In 1927, the building that had housed the Mays' furniture store was replaced by a bowling alley.

THE SCHUTTS—HOME FURNISHINGS

The term *home furnishings* refers to goods for the home other than large furniture: linens, draperies, and other window coverings; small furniture; knick-knacks; and the like. William H. Schutt and his son Charles R. Schutt ran

FURNITURE AND HOME FURNISHINGS STORES

a home furnishings store on M Street for almost seventy years, from 1870 through 1938.

William Schutt was born in New York state in 1819. He began his career in Ithaca, New York, where he worked as a clerk. There he met and married Hannah Welsh. They had one child, Charles, born in 1855.

In 1866, William and Hannah moved to Washington. After a brief stint as partner in a Center Market produce stand, he started learning the furniture business by working for a year as a salesman in Moses Solomon's furniture store in downtown Washington.[5]

In 1870, William opened his own store at what is now either 3064 or 3066 M Street in Georgetown. He listed it in city directories as selling "house furnishings," china, and glassware. By 1881, he and his son Charles were running the store as partners.

The Schutts' home furnishings store was located in one or both of these two buildings at what is now 3064–66 M Street. (*Photo by the author*)

William Schutt died in 1891. In his will, he left his half interest in the business to Hannah and expressed the wish that, as long as she lived, the business should be "directed and carried on in the same manner and under the same name." As it turned out that did not happen, and Charles was sole owner of the business two years later, probably after some negotiation with Hannah.[6]

As often happens when sons take over businesses from fathers, Charles had plans of his own and made changes. In 1894, he added stoves to the inventory. He also sought a better location, moving the store four times between 1895 and 1914 but finally settling at 3120 M Street. He opened a second store downtown on 7th Street NW.

Ironically, it is the closing of the store after Charles's death in 1939 that tells us the most about just what the store sold. An auction company advertised a list of inventory that would be liquidated in a sale on May 9 of that year, including the following:

> *High Grade Aluminum, Enamel and Iron Cooking Utensils; Wheeling and Buckeye Galvanized Iron Tubs, Buckets, Pails, Watering and Refuse Cans; Mop Buckets, Mops, Brooms; Gas, Coal and Oil Stoves and Heaters; Ovens, Kitchen Requisites, China, Glass, Cutlery, and Lanterns, Chair Rentals, Metal Flower Boxes, Bird Cages, Etc.*[7]

Note that the store still carried the stoves Charles had added to the inventory back in 1894.

Under Charles, the store was a dealer for the Wear-Ever Company. Wear-Ever ran periodic ads for its products in the *Evening Star*, listing numerous Washington stores that carried the products, including Schutt's. Products touted in the ads included a four-quart "handy kettle" for ninety-eight cents, a five-and-a-half-quart cooker for $3.65, a percolator for $1.98, and an aluminum "cooky pan" [sic] for $1.98.[8]

Charles, his wife Virginia, and their three daughters lived above the store on M Street, later above the 7th Street store, then back above the M Street store. In the 1930s, they moved to the Cherrydale area of Arlington, Virginia. Charles was active in the Grace Episcopal Church in Georgetown and, on at least seven occasions, was elected to a one-year term as a warden or vestryman.[9]

FURNITURE AND HOME FURNISHINGS STORES

Charles may have had an eccentric side, though. In 1907, as a juror in a criminal proceeding, he earned a rebuke from a judge when he explained his late return from the lunch break by saying he was accustomed to taking a nap at noon.[10]

3140 M STREET

The building at 3140 M Street is the only Georgetown building constructed specifically to house a furniture store, and it has been home to four of them.

The building at 3140 M Street has been home to four furniture stores. This photo was taken in the 1960s. (*Library of Congress, Historic American Buildings Survey, HABS DC,GEO,76-*)

Store Number 1: John F. Darcey

George Wise constructed the building to house the furniture store in which he and John Darcey were partners.

Darcey was born in Montgomery County, Maryland, in 1857, one of ten children of a farmer. His twin brother Charles would grow up to be a carpenter and contractor.

In his early twenties, Darcey moved to Washington and worked as a farm laborer and later a clerk. In 1887, he married Sarah Jennie Cunningham, a D.C. native. They lived on Potomac Street for many years and had five children.

George W. Wise was a few years older, born in Pennsylvania in 1845. Since 1879, he had been doing business as an undertaker and had built a building for that business at 29th and M Street.

In 1899, Darcey and Wise entered into a partnership known as J. F. Darcey & Co., which opened a furniture store at 3120 M Street. Wise would have been busy with his successful funeral home business, so he must have provided the capital for the venture and Darcey the expertise. We do not know what brought the two men together; there was no family relationship. Whatever each brought to the table, though, the business succeeded and lasted for twenty-six years.

In 1911, Wise constructed a new building for the furniture business. He had purchased a building at 3140 M Street in 1909, and in 1911, he tore it down to build something bigger. An *Evening Star* item announced the plans for the building, said it was intended for J. F. Darcey & Co., and offered this description:

> *The entire front will be of iron and glass, from the ground floor to the top, so as to give not only an abundance of light and air to the interior, but also affording a chance to display goods. The building will have a depth of nearly one hundred feet.*[11]

The building's retail space was (and still is) large for Georgetown: 25 feet wide and 105 feet deep. Its four floors contain a total of 10,000 square feet of space. The floors are unobstructed except for a row of thin support columns running down the middle of each floor from front to back. This was a modern building for Georgetown in 1911. To this day, no building on M Street is quite like it.[12] When J. F. Darcey & Co. moved into the new building, the

Schutts' home furnishings store (discussed earlier in the chapter) moved into their old space at 3120.

In November 1912, the store was one of fifty polling places for a mock D.C. election—D.C. residents did not have the right to vote in presidential elections until 1960. Besides voting for their preferred presidential candidate, residents were asked to vote on questions about the structure of the D.C. government: should the people of the District manage their own affairs? Should the D.C. commissioners be elected rather than appointed? Should the District have a delegate to the Congress, and should that person be elected or appointed by the president? The movement seeking full voting rights and congressional representation for District of Columbia residents continues today in 2025, more than one hundred years later.[13]

In 1922, the store moved down the block and across the street to 3106 M Street. This seems odd; if Wise was a partner in the store and owned its custom-built quarters, why move? A falling-out perhaps? A desire to downsize into less space?

In 1926, George Wise died at the age of eighty-one. Wise's will gave Darcey the right to buy Wise's interest in the partnership for $15,000. It appears that Darcey, who by then was sixty-nine years of age, turned down the offer. The store closed that same year.[14] Darcey and his wife Jennie continued to live in Georgetown with their daughter. He died in 1930 at age seventy-three.

Store Number 2: Kendrick-Harrison Furniture Co.

When John Darcey & Co. moved out of 3140 M Street in 1922, the Kendrick-Harrison Furniture Co. moved in. It did business there for only four years.

William H. Kendrick (who probably called himself Herbert) was born in Iowa and grew up in Centerville, Virginia. In 1899, he married Virginia-born Debora Davis, they moved to Washington, and he began a career as a carpenter.[15]

In the early 1920s, when he was in his mid-forties, Kendrick went into business with fellow carpenter William W. Harrison, who was married to Kendrick's younger sister Corinne. Harrison was born in Mississippi and lived in Pennsylvania before coming to Washington.

GEORGETOWN'S RETAIL PAST

In 1922, the Kendrick-Harrison furniture store featured baby carriages. (*Library of Congress National Photo Co. Collection LC-F82-9210*)

The pair's first store was at 3255 M Street. A photo feature in the *Washington Herald Rotogravure Magazine* in early 1922 included a picture of the store, the sign on which read "second hand goods." The caption under the photo said, "anything from chandeliers to saucepans at Kendrick and Harrison's."[16]

In 1923, Kendrick and Harrison joined with Kendrick's younger brother Luther Garland Kendrick and opened another Kendrick-Harrison furniture store in Wise's building at 3140 M Street. They continued doing

> **Kendrick-Harrison Furniture Co.**
> **3140 M STREET N. W.**
> *Furniture, Bedding, Carpets and Stoves*
> *Headquarters for Toys in Georgetown*
> *A Small Deposit Will Lay Aside Any Article*

Kendrick-Harrison ran small newspaper ads like this 1924 example, which appeared in a full page of similar-sized ads. Note the layaway offer and their claim to be Georgetown's "headquarters for toys." (*Washington Post, January 28, 1924, 10*) business at 3255 M Street as well, until replacing it in 1925 with a store at 1230 Wisconsin Avenue. From then on, their two stores were within two blocks of each other.

Perhaps Kendrick-Harrison expanded too rapidly. In 1927, as suddenly as it had appeared, the entire operation closed. For a year, William Kendrick was in the transfer business at the 1230 Wisconsin Avenue location—another example of the delivery wagon coming in handy. After that he went back to carpentry, as an employee at the Woodward & Lothrop department store. He died in Northern Virginia in 1966 at the age of eighty-nine. William Harrison became an accountant for the federal government and, during World War II, worked as a foreman at the Baldwin Locomotive Works in Chester, Pennsylvania. Harrison died in 1944 and is buried in Arlington National Cemetery.

Store Number 3: William E. Miller
The William E. Miller furniture store had been doing business on 7th Street NW in downtown Washington since 1905. In 1927, it opened a branch in the building at 3140 M Street, which operated until the late 1930s. After that, the space became a Sears, Roebuck store and later a Western Auto store.

Store Number 4: The Door Store
When The Door Store opened in July 1954 at 3144 M Street, it was unique: it sold not complete items of furniture, but parts for furniture, which the customer could either assemble himself or (later) have the store assemble for him. *Washington Post* reporter Eileen Summers put it perfectly:

> Sooner or later it was inevitable that the do-it-yourself craze would simmer down to "do some of it yourself." That's the hypothesis behind the Door Store."[17]

Norman and Connie Tolkan started The Door Store along with Norman's cousin Warren Rubin. (Rubin left the store after a year.) Norman Tolkan was a recent graduate of Georgetown University's School of Foreign Service and spoke Italian and Arabic, among other languages. He had previously worked for the State Department and for the Marshall Plan, and both he and Connie had worked as editors for publishers. They actually started the business while Norman was waiting for a new State Department job to come through. He never made it back to State.

People had long been making tables from unfinished doors, and the Tolkans set out to make such projects easier and more elegant. They invested $4,500 and began with an inventory of nineteen flush doors, which quickly expanded. Besides the doors, the store had a supply of legs (wrought iron, aluminum, brass, or wood); cushions; and paint and varnish.[18]

A newspaper ad eight months after the store opened listed the store's offerings:

> custom furniture by the part . . .
>
> Table tops: birch, mahoganies, walnut, Formica—to size . . .
>
> Legs: brass, wood, aluminum, iron—from $2.95 for 4. Foam rubber couches, etc.[19]

A later ad reveals how diverse the inventory of legs was:

> *Only the Door Store has such an exciting variety of legs—high quality high-fashion legs for furniture in any style, from Danish tapered teak to Queen Anne brass . . . Italian provincial walnut to three-prong iron . . . chrome center-stalk pedestals to carved Venetian frames.*[20]

The doors were not ordinary, either—the Tolkans imported them from Sweden, Finland, and the Netherlands, in search of the best finishes. A few months after opening, the Tolkans expanded the raw material they offered for table tops to include marble slabs. Then they added mosaic tiles, including nineteen colors of Venetian glass.[21]

Not long after they opened, the Tolkans discovered that many of their customers did not wish to be do-it-yourselfers. They began giving buyers a choice: assemble the item yourself or let the store do it. They created a workshop above the store and hired part-time workshop assistants to help with assembly.[22] The top floor was warehouse space. Connie kept the books and ran the store itself, while Norman ordered the inventory and went on periodic buying trips.

The store's name sometimes caused confusion. Once the author, while in the store, heard employees explain to a disappointed customer that the store did not actually sell doors for use as doors.

FURNITURE AND HOME FURNISHINGS STORES

The Tolkans also carried some more traditional items. They imported reproductions of eighteenth-century Italian furniture from a workshop in Florence, with floral patterns that they updated with more contemporary colors. Here as elsewhere, they did not take themselves too seriously: a 1967 advertisement said, "Louis XIV potty chairs are to be had at The Door Store."[23]

This business model required a lot of space, which must have made 3140 M Street, the building George Wise had built, attractive. The Door Store moved there in the summer of 1956.[24]

Some furniture stores coped with the limitations of Georgetown retail spaces by opening branches elsewhere in the neighborhood, and The Door Store, despite its spacious quarters at 3140 M Street, did the same. In 1968, Door Store Inc. bought the building at 3146 M Street, just up the street and, in March 1969, started operating in both locations. Fabrics became a big part of the business, and from 1974 to 1982, the location at 3146 M Street was called "Door Store Fabrics."

Also in 1969, the store adopted a new slogan: "The Eclectic One." It used that phrase in its advertising for two years.[25]

In the early 1970s, The Door Store rented space on the waterfront at Wisconsin Avenue and K Street and opened a warehouse and retail outlet there. The warehouse seemed plagued by disasters. A flood in June 1972 did $137,000 in damage. Five months later, fire in a defective gas heater spread to wicker and wood stored in the warehouse, leaving another $100,000 in damage. Six engine companies and three hook and ladder trucks responded to the fire. The Tolkans repaired the damage both times, and the warehouse continued to operate until 1974.[26]

The Door Store was succeeding wildly, and more expansion followed. During the 1970s, branches opened in Rockville, Maryland, as well as Springfield, Bailey's Crossroads, and Winchester, all in Virginia. Ultimately, the shop that the Tolkans had started in Georgetown grew to sixty stores in nine states with sales of $50 million a year.

The Georgetown store displayed whimsical art alongside furniture. During the 1980s, the displays of beds included sculptures of a man and a woman made by Philadelphia artist Leo Sewell from odds and ends like Tinker Toys, Lincoln Logs, piano hammers, rulers, and baseball bats. The two sculptures were reclined and intertwined on the beds; Tolkan called them the "copulating couple" and thought they increased bed sales.[27]

In 1973, Stephen B. Newman, identified as "an owner of the Door Store," was quoted in a newspaper article about Georgetown street vendors, saying that street vending should be prohibited because street vendors offer "merchandise of the lowest quality and type . . . and appeal to low quality customers." It is possible the Tolkans had taken Newman in as a partner, but more likely he only was an employee and the reporter was mistaken about his role. There are no other references to him in the press in connection with The Door Store.[28]

Norman Tolkan did seem to take a dim view of changes in the neighborhood in the 1970s. He complained about crowds of tourists who came to Washington for the national bicentennial in 1976:

> *The streets [of Georgetown] are thronged from about 11 a.m. to 4 p.m. It's quite absurd. It's been a disaster, with troops of people coming through—all eating ice cream cones and dragging their feet. They look so hot.*

Tolkan dissented from other merchants' expressions of concern about general neighborhood decline. In a 1976 newspaper article about that issue, he said,

> *Georgetown is alive and well and living in Washington. I find it very difficult to accept the theory that Georgetown is on the skids. We find the competition in our area is acute. [Competitors] force us to run faster and find a product which is fresh and which is competitively priced.*[29]

The Tolkans owned the company throughout its forty-year life—it never went public. By the 1990s, large competitors like IKEA and Crate & Barrel were taking a toll on the business, and The Door Store started consolidating and closing branches to try to survive. In May 1996, the last two stores (in Georgetown and Bailey's Crossroads) closed. Norman and Connie's only child, Victor, had been president of the company for a year and had overseen the consolidation effort. Connie had died in 1992.[30]

Norman Tolkan later opened a store in Northeast Washington called Homeward. It started out selling furniture parts, but later, like The Door Store, the business began selling complete pieces as well. He died in 2014.

KELLY FURNITURE COMPANY

Kelly Furniture Company did business in Georgetown from 1924 to 1943, except for a hiatus from 1940 through 1942. Unlike some of the other Georgetown furniture stores of the 1920s and 1930s, there is little mystery about what it sold and what its business model was.

Edmund M. Cohn founded Kelly Furniture Company in 1924. He was born in Cincinnati, Ohio, around 1887. His father, an immigrant from Germany, was a clothing merchant. Edmund was born Edwin, but at some point in his late twenties or his thirties, he began calling himself Edmund. (This was the first of two name changes.) In 1921, Cohn moved to Washington and found work as a salesman for Philip Levy & Co., a downtown furniture store.

In 1924, Cohn formed a corporation called Kelly Furniture Co. Inc. to operate a furniture store. The store opened that same year on Wisconsin Avenue near N Street. The reason for the choice of the Kelly name is a mystery.

The store's first advertisement, appearing in the classified section in 1924, was very brief: "Handsome, new, full vanity, etc., very cheap; other furniture."[31]

In 1928, Kelly Furniture Co. Inc. bought and moved to a building at 1245–47 Wisconsin Avenue (between M and N Streets).[32]

In the midst of getting the business started, Cohn married Winifred Borck, a native of Colorado, in 1926. Winifred had three children from a previous marriage, and the family lived on 37th Street NW, just north of Georgetown.

Newspaper advertising suggests that, for its first ten years or so, the store carried brand-name furniture and appliances. Manufacturers published product ads that listed dealers where the products could be purchased. Kelly was listed in such ads for Lawson Odorless Radiant Heaters, Congoleum flooring, Stewart-Warner radios, Leonard Electric Refrigerators, and Grunow Teledial Radios, among others.[33] Furniture and appliances are expensive, and sellers of these products had to accept credit. That Kelly did so is confirmed by a 1936 ad in which the store offered the Naxon electric washer for $21.95, $1.95 down and $2.00 a month.[34]

In 1931, Kelly Furniture Company did what other Georgetown furniture stores had done when short of space—it opened an auxiliary showroom just down the block, at 1229 Wisconsin Avenue. In 1932, Cohn bought that building. The showroom lasted only two years, perhaps because

This photo shows 1245–47 Wisconsin Avenue, the one-time home of Kelly Furniture Co. (*Photo by the author*)

of challenges from the Great Depression. In 1935, Cohn opened a liquor store in the showroom space; however, that venture apparently did not pan out either, and he closed it after a year. Despite the Depression, though, the company was doing well enough give all employees a 10 percent raise at Christmas 1936.[35]

Changes came in 1938, when Kelly Furniture announced that the store was going to move to new quarters in downtown Washington at 829 7th Street NW. The announcement said "we are not going to move any of our present merchandise. Therefore we have cut our prices to cost and below." The following month, the company announced an auction of its remaining inventory. "Plenty of everything for everybody," the ad said.[36] The corporation continued to own the building at 1245 Wisconsin Avenue after the closing, and it still used it from time to time after the move. A 1940 advertisement said, "Kelly Furniture Co. celebrates its 16th birthday" and touted fourteen hundred items available at discounts of 25–60 percent. The ad listed both the 7th Street location and 1245 Wisconsin Avenue.[37]

All was not well between Cohn and Winifred, and they divorced in 1935. The split apparently was not amicable, as he was sentenced to jail in 1940 for failing to make alimony payments.[38]

In 1942, Kelly Furniture closed the 7th Street location. An advertisement for the going-out-of-business sale there said the company had lost its lease.[39]

And then, in 1943, Kelly Furniture reopened at the Wisconsin Avenue location. Cohn bought the building from the corporation. There was another wrinkle: around this time, Edmund Cohn changed his name to Edmund M. Cole. Why he did so is again a mystery, but this was the second time during his life that he changed his name.

This time Cole tried an entirely different business model. He no longer offered credit terms—all sales were for cash. He announced the new strategy in a series of ads, saying, "we have a new policy where you can buy furniture AT PRICES EQUAL TO WHOLESALE FOR CASH!!" They ran from February 27 (just a week after he bought the building) through March. Other ads said that Georgetown was "out of the high-rent district," a statement that seems strange today but was true at the time.[40]

Furniture is a challenging commodity to sell only for cash. All prices of course were lower in the 1940s, but even with that Kelly's prices seem extraordinarily low. For example, it offered a three-piece bedroom suite for $49.50 and a "three-piece solid maple living room suite" for $79.50.[41]

The new venture did not last long. The store's last display ad appeared in the *Evening Star* in October 1943. By January 1944, Edmund and his second wife, Elinor, had moved to Miami, and in December Edmund sold the former store building at 1245 Wisconsin Avenue for $32,000.[42]

LITTLE CALEDONIA

The phrase "Georgetown institution" often is tossed around, but it truly does apply to Little Caledonia, which did business for sixty-five years on Wisconsin Avenue just south of P Street.

Little Caledonia's vast and varied inventory makes it hard to classify. We include the store in this chapter because it sold home furnishings, but there was much more. A description by a *Georgetowner* writer is worth quoting in full:

> It isn't an antique shop, although some of the items in the store could qualify. It isn't a furniture store, although there is furniture and just about everything you need to start up a stylish, unique home. It isn't a fabrics shop, although there are reams and reams of fabric. It isn't a card shop, although a whole section is devoted to unique and classy cards. It isn't a toy store although any child would be enthralled in the children's section.... It isn't a silver-glass-ceramic ware store, although the room fronting the street contains a boundless array of such treasures. It isn't a kitchenware shop, though you feel as if you are walking into a time-bound, warm and tight-quarters kitchen in the kitchen department.[43]

All of this was arrayed in the thirteen rooms of two adjacent townhouses, where getting lost was a common experience. A map of the store even appeared in the *Georgetowner* in 1987, locating each of the rooms and listing the types of items to be found there.[44]

Two sisters started the business and ran it through all but its last five years. Eleanor and Marian Wells were born into a prosperous Washington family in 1908 and 1914, respectively. Their father was a physician and their grandfather was a former judge and Tennessee congressman. The family lived in a series of apartments in Dupont Circle and Kalorama, often with a live-in servant.

FURNITURE AND HOME FURNISHINGS STORES

In the 1930s, the sisters, then in their twenties, learned that a storefront at 1324 Wisconsin Avenue was available at a rent of $35 a month. They liked antiques and enjoyed frequenting auctions, so they decided to open an antique shop even though, they admitted years later, they knew nothing about running such a business. Named after London's Caledonian market, it opened in May 1938. The early inventory included odds and ends from the family's apartment.

The opening was briefly reported by Betty Beale in her "Top Hats and Tiaras" column in the *Evening Star*, where she referred to the new store as "Vilma Schmidt's, Eleanor Wells' and Marian Prichard's 'junk shop.'" Little Caledonia shared the building with Georgetown Galleries, an art dealer. Beale described it as a "small white house with its brilliant blue doors and red room, with its antiques in every nook and cranny and lovely modern paintings on the second floor." (Marian Wells was married three times; Prichard was her married name at this point. We do not know who Vilma Schmidt was, and the sisters did not mention her name when interviewed years later about the shop's origins.)[45]

The business got off to a slow start. The opening party attended by Beale attracted lots of friends who bought little. Business continued to be disappointing for a while. As the sisters later told the story, a turning point came when a friend wanted to buy three or four dozen each of several types of glasses. The sisters said they would get them and, the next day, traveled to New York, not quite knowing what they were going to do. When they got there, a hotel clerk asked if they were going to the gift show. They had not known about any such show, but they went and explored it in depth, learning much about the business and finding the friend's glassware as well as other inventory.

Early customers who bought antiques also wanted paper to wrap them as wedding gifts, and adding wrapping paper to the inventory led the sisters to expand into other goods. A late 1938 newspaper ad suggested the inventory expansion already was well under way. It described "Chinese wrapping papers" for eight to eighteen cents, some in an antique gold and green design, others featuring deep red and purple with lotus flowers. Also available were Currier and Ives Christmas cards from five cents, woodblocks of Washington and Williamsburg for ten to fifteen cents, and "cards designed by contemporary American artists" including Norman Rockwell.[46]

After the slow start, the business was successful. Late in 1941, the sisters paid $4,500 to buy a building at 1417 Wisconsin Avenue that had previously housed a fruit market. By 1943, they had moved the store to the new quarters. Two years later they paid $14,000 to buy the building next door at 1419 and created a connecting door between the two.[47]

Little Caledonia became known for its selections of lampshades and wastebaskets. The sisters advertised frequently, giving us a picture of the breadth and charm of the inventory. Among the advertised items in 1948 through 1951 were these:

Short little apron in assorted prints with clever pocket arrangement for cigarettes and matches

Willow suitcase in five sizes

Copper heart mold for mousses, aspics, jellies and oven baking

Colonial porridge bowls in a modern non-tarnishing alloy

A transparent egg for gift wrapping

Chinese straw table mats

The Spice Island Pepper Mill in a gift box with a sack of peppercorns

Whole Louisiana Strawberry preserves in a wooden basket

Wooden Swedish Christmas tree with candle ring

Tea Cozy with removable slipcover in Old Fashioned Chintz.[48]

For a while, Little Caledonia shared space in its new quarters with Anne Payson's yarn and woolens shop. A Little Caledonia ad in 1948 said that Payson's shop was "making Georgetown famous," perhaps an exaggeration. By 1954, Payson's shop had moved up the street, probably because Little Caledonia needed the space.

Little Caledonia's neighbor was the Christ Child Opportunity Shop. Although the Opportunity Shop concentrated more on antiques and sold many items on consignment, there was considerable overlap between the two stores' offerings, an outstanding opportunity for customers with time to make their way through both. For more on the Opportunity Shop, see chapter 16.

Several newspaper profiles of the shop and the sisters appeared in the 1980s and 1990s. By that time, the shop had five thousand square feet of space in thirteen rooms, an inventory of sixty thousand items, and a staff of thirty-five employees, many with long tenure. Among them was Leon Carpenter, who had been there forty-five years by 1988 and had started by delivering lampshades on a bicycle. Like other Georgetown shops, Little Caledonia had famous customers, including Jacqueline Kennedy, Lady Bird Johnson, Tricia and Julie Nixon (daughters of the president), actor Lorne Greene, and Madeleine Albright.

One of the newspaper profiles described Eleanor as having a husky voice, a frequent smile, and a love for cooking and Victor Herbert. The profiles also described Eleanor as more of a business person while Marian was more artistic. Eleanor devoted more time to the business in its early years than Marian, who spent time in Europe, occasionally buying and sending back items for the shop.

The sisters did experiment with expansion. They opened branches in Spring Valley and in Rhode Island, but those did not last. They also briefly had a catalog. Both sisters also dabbled in real estate, including properties in Georgetown and near Massachusetts Avenue and Van Ness Street.

The sisters did not experiment with technology, however. The shop did not have a computer until 1997. The twelve hundred customer charge accounts were tracked on index cards. It took a month to complete the annual inventory.

In several of the profiles, the sisters admitted the shop had not made a profit since 1979. Eleanor said, "I'd rather subsidize it the rest of my life. I love the way people enjoy it. And it's worth having it just so people don't have to go to malls. I hate malls." She identified one of the drags on profits when she said "we just buy things we like. I'm afraid we are buyaholics. Salesmen love us."[49]

Eleanor died in March 1997. Later that year, Marian sold the business to Erika Emery, the longtime store manager. Emery altered the name to "The Little Caledonia Shop," consolidated into one of the two buildings, installed a computer, and repainted but, otherwise, left the business model unchanged. Five years later, she was forced to close the business when the building was sold and she lost her lease.[50]

CHAPTER 16

Antique Dealers

What makes something an "antique" is in the eye of the beholder. The word *antique* can refer to a rare, collectible item of historic art or furniture, or it can refer to any piece of old furniture, or it can refer to what some might call junk.

Antiques were not a big business in Washington until the 1920s. In 1881, the classified section of the city directory did not even have an "antiques" category. The number of antique stores citywide grew to nine in 1914, nineteen in 1925, and thirty-five in 1935.

Georgetown has had two antique boomlets. The first was in the 1930s. On the neighborhood's two main streets, the number of antique shops grew from one in 1925 to ten in 1935, and the number of stores selling used furniture grew from one to four. Although hard to confirm, it seems likely that the Great Depression created a market for both buyers and sellers of used furniture, and that at least some owners of the multiplying used furniture stores may have called their businesses "antique stores" to provide broader appeal and less stigma for their customers. In the 1950s and after, renovation gave Georgetown historic charm that began to attract affluent shoppers, while retail space was plentiful—an attractive combination for antique dealers. The number of antique stores grew from one in 1948 to twenty-one in 1956. There were only five antique stores on the two main streets in 2023, plus a handful on side streets.

In the 1930s and 1940s, there was a concentration of antique stores in the 1500 block of Wisconsin Avenue, between P and Q Streets. During that decade, many houses on the block were converted from residential to retail

ANTIQUE DEALERS

use—in 1925, there were nine retail stores on the block, and ten years later there were eighteen. So at a time when the antique business was growing, space for those new stores was available in the 1500 block. In the 1960s, the number of antique dealers in the 1500 block shrank but the number in the 1600 block grew, and there still are three on that block today. In past years, there also was a concentration of antique shops on O Street just west of Wisconsin, though as of this writing in 2025 none of those shops remains.

ANTIQUE STORES NORTH OF P STREET
George H. Kernodle

George Howard Kernodle was a serious student of antiques. In 1933, he was part of the first antiques boom when he opened a shop in two buildings at 1525–27 Wisconsin Avenue (numbered 1525 and 1529 today). He lived upstairs at 1527.

George Kernodle's antique shop was in the building at right center in this 1966 photo. (*Library of Congress, Historic American Buildings Survey HABS DC,GEO,68-*)

Kernodle was born in North Carolina in 1896, the second of five children of George Washington Kernodle, a physician, and Katherine Kernodle, who owned a hat shop. The younger George was known to his parents as Howard, no doubt to distinguish him from his father, and he may have gone by that name as an adult. The family moved to Washington in 1910, and Howard graduated from Western High School (today's Duke Ellington School for the Arts, in Georgetown). He went to the University of Virginia (though he did not graduate) and was a corporal in the army in World War I. He never married.

Kernodle particularly focused on glass, and was an expert on glass paper weights. At the time he died, he was working on a study of early glass bottles. After his death, Sloan's Art Galleries conducted an auction of his shop's inventory, which included

> 7 clocks until recently on loan to the Smithsonian Institution; a superb collection of 17th and 18th Century Candlesticks; Early American Glass; Andirons, Fire Hooks and Screens, Fire Tools; Oriental Rugs; very early Antique Furniture . . . [and] an unusually Valuable Working Library on Antiques, Glassware, China, etc.

The auction notice described Kernodle himself as "a recognized authority in many fields of early Americana, a collector and consultant to museums and historic shrines in the east." A later newspaper account of a controversy about the location of the country's first iron works described him as "a scholarly gentleman with a passion for the truth."[1]

Besides antiques, Kernodle was a flower aficionado. In 1944, he found a rare orchid in a field in Fairfax County, Virginia. He said that there were hundreds of them growing there, but he refused to say where the field was because the flowers "only would by trampled by tourists."[2]

Although he took his work seriously, Kernodle had a sense of humor. He once described a visitor to his shop as "the dear lady, be-minked and bemused, who remarked that she 'wouldn't know the difference between Chippendale and mahogany.'" He also opined that "the badly overworked term 'Early American' is entitled to a long rest."[3]

Kernodle's store did business on Wisconsin Avenue for twenty-three years, until his death in 1957. He is buried in Arlington National Cemetery.[4]

ANTIQUE DEALERS

Isabella Jones

Isabella McCoy was born in Annapolis, Maryland, in 1876. Among her ancestors were families who had arrived in Maryland and Virginia in the 1600s. Her father died when she was a teenager.

In 1896, Isabella married Lewis Benson Jones, a civil engineer from Albany, New York. They soon had two children: Harry, named after her father, and Harvey, named after Lewis's father. The marriage lasted only a few years, however. By 1900, the couple had separated, Isabella living with her mother in Annapolis and Lewis back in Albany.[5]

Isabella, her children, and her mother moved to Washington in 1908. Isabella told the 1910 census taker she was a widow, no doubt to avoid the stigma attached to divorce at the time. She worked as a teacher from 1918 to 1920. When her mother died in 1926, Isabella inherited the family home at 1908 Belmont Road NW in the upscale Kalorama neighborhood.[6]

Two years later, at the age of fifty-two, Isabella went into business for the first time. She opened an antique store on 19th Street, NW, close to her home and to Dupont Circle. She also tweaked her name a bit, calling herself Isabelle rather than Isabella. We do not know what experience she had with antiques, if any. Later she moved the store to DeSales Street, just off Connecticut Avenue and across the street from the Mayflower Hotel. Her sons worked in the store. The DeSales street store closed in 1931.

In 1934, Isabelle (the name she used at the time) returned to the antiques business, this time in Georgetown. She opened in space at 1574 Wisconsin Avenue, probably buying the business and the inventory of Nellie Wick, who had run an antique store there since 1931, under the name "Old Georgetown Shop." Isabelle continued using that name.

Around 1935, she began calling herself Isabella again. In 1937, she sold the Belmont Road house and moved into an apartment above the store.

In 1938, Isabella moved the store a few blocks down the street to rented space at 1560 Wisconsin, and she moved her residence there as well. The new location was a detached building on a large lot, set back from the street—not what one typically would think of for a retail store. In 1946, Harry and Harvey bought the building that housed her shop and her apartment for $18,000.[7]

Isabella was not alone in using the name "Old Georgetown Shop." Ads reveal that, at least in 1943, Sidney Solomon was using the same name for his antique shop two blocks away.[8]

Isabella's only advertising took the form of a few classified ads under "Miscellaneous For Sale." They provide only a tiny glimpse into her inventory. At various times she offered a "pine hunt board," a "large assortment of early pressed glass," an inlaid bureau for $85, a marble slant-top desk in "perfect condition," a pine water bench, and a "full dinner set, blue Minton."[9]

Isabella closed her store sometime between 1948 and 1954—in 1954, the city directory listed the building as vacant. In 1956, however, a new shop opened in the same space under the name—what else?—"Old Georgetown Shop." It operated there through 1965. We do not know whose store it was—by this time directories had reversed their prior practice and often listed a store's trade name without identifying its proprietor. Isabella's sons did still own the property, so conceivably she could have reopened.

Isabella died in Chevy Chase, Maryland, in 1975, at the age of ninety-eight. Her obituary identified her as "Isabel." The building where she had lived and done business was replaced in the 1960s by a nine-unit townhouse complex.[10]

Caroline D. Meggs

Across the street from Kernodle and just a few doors down from Isabella Jones was Caroline "Callie" Meggs's antique shop, opened in 1930 at 1530 Wisconsin Avenue.[11]

Mystery and tragedy surround Caroline Meggs. She was born in North Carolina in 1884. Nothing is known of her childhood or family. At the time of the 1920 census, she and her husband John Meggs were living in Marion County, South Carolina, where he was a money order clerk in the post office. With them was a son from John Meggs's first marriage to Monica Hayes, who had died in 1917.

John and Caroline Meggs came to Washington at some point in the 1920s, where he had a government job, probably with the post office department. The marriage apparently fell apart before long, and in 1929 John Meggs married Thelma Gandy in Florida. He and Thelma lived back in Marion County, where he was the postmaster. Caroline listed herself in the

This photo shows 1530 Wisconsin Avenue in 1966. Thirty years earlier, it had been the home of Caroline Meggs's antique shop. (*Library of Congress Historic American Buildings Survey HABS DC,GEO,69-*)

city directory as the widow of John S. Meggs, avoiding the stigma of divorce as Isabella Jones did.

Caroline ran her shop for seven years, until 1938. She appears in the 1940 census as a patient at St. Elizabeth's Hospital, the public mental hospital in Washington. Her illness probably is what led the shop to close. She remained at St. Elizabeth's for another twenty-seven years, until she died there in 1967.

Later in his life, John Meggs became a Baptist minister. He died in 1964. His obituary mentioned his earlier marriage to Monica and the later one to Thelma, but makes no mention of Caroline.

Jacob Kasab

Jacob Kasab ran a multifaceted business at 1508 Wisconsin Avenue from 1936 to 1945. His characterization of the business in city directories changed from year to year, sometimes saying he sold antiques, sometimes secondhand furniture, sometimes art goods. On his World War II draft registration form, Jacob gave his occupation as "antique shop." The evidence suggests he had an eclectic inventory that included all of these things.

Kasab was of Armenian descent, born Jacob Kasab Kelejian in Turkey in 1898. He came to the United States in 1922 and initially settled in New York, finding work as a shipping clerk. He became a citizen in 1928 and, at the same time, changed his name to become just Jacob Kasab.[12]

Shortly after that, he came to Washington. In 1931, he married Lydia Nazarian, a fellow immigrant from Turkey who was eight years younger. Jacob and Lydia lived with Lydia's family near Dupont Circle. Lydia's brothers George and Jake had started a rug business in 1920, with a store on Connecticut Avenue and a cleaning plant at 3316 P Street in Georgetown (the plant building is now a private home). In the early and mid-1930s, Jacob worked in the Nazarian family business as a rug repairman and later as a "rug dealer." We do not know which came first—his employment by the Nazarians or his relationship with Lydia, who also worked in the business as a bookkeeper.[13]

As the mid-1930s passed, Kasab decided to go out on his own, opening a shop in 1937 at 1508 Wisconsin Avenue. He and Lydia and their daughter Eleanor lived upstairs. At some point, Kasab started using the name "Georgetown Art and Craft Shop." That name, for example, appears in a 1941 classified ad in the *Evening Star*, offering "Rugs. Orientals, all sizes; antique drop leaf tables; chest of drawers."[14]

The merchandise listed in the ad does not jibe with the "art and craft" name. One can imagine the store full of rugs, used furniture/antiques (the line between them being blurry), and artist supplies.

In 1942, like many successful Georgetown merchants, Jacob and Lydia moved to the suburbs, buying a house in Chevy Chase. In 1943, they bought the building at 1508 Wisconsin Avenue that housed the store.[15]

Only two years later, in June 1945, Jacob closed the store, held a closing-out sale, and sold the building. But Jacob did not really go out of business. Instead, he opened another store under the name Georgetown Art and Craft in rented quarters two blocks away, at 3204 O Street. He continued to do business there at least through 1960. The new store may have focused more on the art side of the business than on antiques—that would explain the close-out sale of antiques at the old location. In 1949, the *Evening Star* reported that a fire had caused damage to the roof of the new store's building. "Jacob Kasab, proprietor, said he did not believe the water which seeped down from the attic did any damage to his valuable art objects."[16]

Jacob lived on for more than thirty years, dying in 1994 at age 96.

Joseph Esunas

Joseph Esunas's antique shop was in the next block north, at 1661 Wisconsin Avenue, between Q Street and Reservoir Road. That block was still mostly residential when Esunas opened his store in 1931—at the time there were only four stores on that long block.

Esunas was born in Lithuania in 1978 and came to the United States in 1911. He and his wife Teresa, an immigrant from Russia, were married two years later. Esunas initially found work as a carpenter for a construction company, and the family lived in Southwest Washington.

Esunas found himself briefly on the wrong side of the law in 1921, during Prohibition. Police raided a hardware store on Pennsylvania Avenue that was selling stills disguised as gasoline cans for $16.50. Something led the police to search the Esunas home, where they found a twenty-gallon still and two hundred gallons of mash. Esunas was charged, but we do not know the final outcome.

Joseph and Teresa separated in the early 1920s. In 1928, after a few more years living in Southwest Washington, he bought a building in Georgetown at 1661 Wisconsin Avenue for $7,500 and moved there with his two sons. He was not yet operating a business there, however; he worked for someone else as a cabinetmaker.

That changed in 1932, when Esunas left his job and went into the upholstering business, operating out of his home. The business soon became successful. He needed help and, in 1935, advertised for an experienced upholsterer and cabinetmaker. He also needed more space, so in 1934 he built an addition on the front of the building, as shown in the photo. The

Addition on the front of 1661 Wisconsin Avenue, constructed by Joseph Esunas in 1934. (*Photo by the author*)

addition provided 140 square feet of new space as well as a store window right on the sidewalk. Several buildings in the 1600 block of Wisconsin Avenue have such additions.

By 1936, Esunas was calling his store an antique shop. He continued to provide upholstery and other services, though. Esunas closed the business and sold the building in 1945, when he was sixty-seven years old. With the proceeds from selling the building, he bought a house on Foxall Road where he lived until his death in 1962 at age eighty-four.[17]

SOUTH OF P STREET: TWO INSTITUTIONS

The term *institution* often gets applied to Georgetown stores, but the 1400 block of Wisconsin Avenue, just south of P Street, has been home to two neighboring businesses that do deserve the title.

Little Caledonia

Little Caledonia was in business for sixty-five years, under the management of its founders for all but the last five. It was not strictly speaking an antique shop, but it did have antiques for sale, along with many other home furnishings items. For more on Little Caledonia, see chapter 15.

The Christ Child Opportunity Shop

The Christ Child Opportunity Shop has been at 1427 Wisconsin Avenue (next door to Little Caledonia) since 1938. Over that time, it has evolved from a Depression-era thrift shop into an upscale antique and consignment store. In 2015, a reporter said the shop "comes off like a cross between your upmarket grandmother's townhouse and the estate sale of an elegant hoarder." Visiting the shop today, one finds a vast inventory of often elegant used items, and affluent-looking fellow shoppers. This combination at first blush sounds "uncharitable," but what counts is that it works and helps fund the Christ Child Society's charitable activities.[18]

The Christ Child Society, which owns the shop, was founded in 1885 by Mary Virginia Merrick, a young woman born into a prosperous Washington family who from childhood had ambitions to spend her life caring for children less fortunate than herself. A fall when she was fourteen left her severely disabled, but that did not stop her. From an initial effort to deliver layettes at Christmas to new and expectant mothers, the society grew to operate a settlement house, summer camps, and boys clubs. Society branches sprang up in other cities, and the National Christ Child Society was established in 1916. Mary Merrick served as president of both the original Washington chapter and the national organization. She died in 1955.[19]

The Opportunity Shop grew out of periodic rummage sales. In 1935, it appeared in the city directory for the first time, in space at 1508 Wisconsin Avenue that had previously been a meat market and in another year or two later would be occupied by Jacob Kasab's Georgetown Art and Craft Shop.

After a four-year stay at 1415 Wisconsin Avenue, the store moved to 1427 Wisconsin in 1940, and it remains there today. The society bought the building in 1945 for $13,800.

Some of the shop's early newspaper ads in 1935 suggest an emphasis on people's practical needs (except perhaps for fur coats). In addition to a ten cent sale, it advertised new shoes and rubbers for ten cents and fifteen cents, as well as a washing machine. A Thanksgiving clearance sale included "furniture, fur coats, etc.," greatly reduced because the store "must clear space for new stock."[20]

In the 1940s, the shop held annual Christmas doll sales. The *Evening Star* reported on the 1943 sale:

> DOLLS TO DELIGHT THE HEARTS OF MANY. *It will be a case of "come and choose" at the doll sale to open Thursday at the Christ Child Opportunity Shop, 1427 Wisconsin avenue N.W. Dozens of dolls to suit every taste have been dressed by 80-year-old Mrs. Catherine Collins, a member of the Christ Child Society, who has outfitted approximately 100 dolls since September.*[21]

Mrs. Collins's efforts highlight what has perhaps been the shop's biggest asset: a workforce of dedicated volunteers. In the early 1950s, the store was operated by twenty-five to thirty such volunteers. (By 2015, that workforce would grow to seventy.) Prices were set by a seven-member "store committee." The committee also had to decide whether some offered donations were saleable enough to be accepted. Some donations were passed onto the Salvation Army instead of being offered for sale in the shop. One newspaper item said all proceeds go to the society's convalescent home for children and "no items are handled on a commission [consignment?] basis." On a typical day, seventy-five to one hundred customers visited the shop, many of them needy.[22]

Occasionally there were bonanza donations. In 1952, the shop received a trunk from a society member that contained carefully preserved forty-year-old gowns, several never-worn kimonos, figurines, and powder boxes. The next year the shop received a collection of 1890s gowns from an estate, which were modeled by a volunteer store worker. Included were high-necked embroidered shirt waists, evening wraps, feather boas, and parasols.[23]

From its opening until the late 1950s, the shop listed itself in the city directory as selling secondhand furniture, though the inventory was far broader than that. Later listings for a while said the shop sold "general merchandise," and after that, the listings did not say what the business was—by that time its reputation made such detail unnecessary.

In 1956, the society in effect divided the shop in two—the traditional thrift shop on the ground floor and an antique and consignment shop on the second floor. In the early 1960s, ads reflected a changed inventory, touting "antique crystal stoppers to fit any 19th cent. decanters, paintings, furn., silver, china, crystal, curios" as well as brand-new bridal gowns for $25.[24]

A burglary of the shop in 1976 underscored that the donated and consigned inventory included valuable items—the thieves made off with $37,500 worth of jewelry.[25]

During the 1960s, occasional September newspaper items announced that the shop would be reopening for the fall. Perhaps it closed during summers because of slow business and vacationing volunteers.

In 1970, the shop was taking a 25 percent commission on consignments and a committee determined the prices. By 2009, the system had changed, with the store receiving 40 percent of the sale proceeds for items selling over $100 and the consignor receiving the other 60 percent. For items selling for $100 or less, the split was fifty-fifty. In 2015, the shop was using a scheduled markdown scheme, under which the price of an item was reduced 10 percent after thirty days, and 50 percent after ninety. Such a system keeps the interest of bargain hunters, who might come back in hopes that an item they could not afford earlier will still be there, with a lower price.[26]

In 1970, the *Washington Post* ran an article about looking for bargains in the city's more upscale thrift shops. It said that according to the shop's manager "[w]ives of Republican cabinet members rub elbows with the wives of Democratic senators on the second floor . . . where French and Canadian embassy wives are frequent customers." Twelve years later, another shop manager told a reporter that "often a diplomat will come dashing in for extra forks or glasses when they're expecting to entertain a bigwig from home." The shop also has had prominent donors, among them the Kennedy family.[27]

Notwithstanding the prominent clientele, the shop still beat the bushes for donations. A 1970 newspaper ad said:

HELP US HELP OTHERS
Now—while you're spring cleaning—keep an eye open for salable items you can no longer use . . . and bring them to Christ Child Opportunity Shop.[28]

In 2002, the society abandoned the thrift store on the building's ground floor, renovated the space, and made the entire store an antiques and consignment shop.

Hundreds of people have volunteered to work in the Opportunity Shop over its eighty-five-year history. One gets a sense of this from the archives of the *Evening Star* and the *Washington Post*, where multiple obituaries from the 1960s and later mention the deceased's service in the shop.

CHAPTER 17

Hardware Stores

Hardware stores have been less numerous than other kinds of Georgetown businesses, but several have been long-lived.

In most years from 1877 to the mid-1960s, there were four to six hardware stores on the two main streets. The number of hardware stores gradually declined after that, as local industry and farmers became less of a market and retail rents rose to levels that did not work for retail hardware businesses. As of this writing in 2025, there is only one hardware store in Georgetown.

EDWARD LINTHICUM

Edward M. Linthicum owned one of the two hardware stores operating in 1830, at the corner of High and Bridge Streets (Wisconsin Avenue and M Street today). Born in Maryland in 1797, Linthicum had an uncle, Dr. Ninian Magruder, who was prominent in Georgetown and may have helped him get started in business.

To say Linthicum prospered is an understatement. In 1846, he bought the estate on R Street that today is known as Dumbarton Oaks. In 1860, he told the census taker he owned real estate worth $50,000 and personal property worth $6,000.

Linthicum's prosperity also included ownership of enslaved individuals, five of them in 1850 and four in 1862. We do not know if these people worked in his business or his household.[1]

Linthicum was in the hardware business for at least fifty years. He retired five years before his death in 1869. The 1864 directory described the store as "Linthicum, E. M. & Co. (C. A. Buckley and J. Marbury, Jr.)," suggesting new owners using the old name.

In his will, Linthicum left $50,000 in trust for the establishment of a school for "indigent white boys and youth of Georgetown," which became known as the Linthicum Institute. It operated as a tuition-free night school, teaching (according to a 1930 advertisement) "Mechanical and Architectural Drawing, Typewriting, Penmanship, Industrial Art, Mathematics, bookkeeping, etc." "Everything Free," the ad said.[2]

In 1887, the institute erected a building near 31st and O Streets that housed both the school and a second floor hall that was the site of frequent dances and social events. When the institute's former president G. Morris Steinbraker died in 1975, his obituary described the institute as "a foundation that provides scholarships for needy boys." We do not know when the transition from school to scholarship foundation took place, but it must have been complete by early 1957, when the institute sold its building to Christ Church Georgetown. The building now is the church's parish hall.[3]

HENRY P. GILBERT

Newspaper portrait of H. P. Gilbert. (Evening Star, *June 29, 1889, 11*)

Henry P. Gilbert ran a hardware store from 1877 to 1891. Gilbert was born in 1830 in Columbia County, New York, on the Hudson River south of Albany. He and his wife Mary moved to Washington in 1862, where they lived on D Street NW, and he found work as a clerk. In 1867, he went into business for himself on the waterfront, a few doors west of Wisconsin Avenue (then High Street) on Water Street. At first he held himself out as a dealer in iron, then in 1869 as a hardware dealer. From 1870 through 1876, he called it a junk business. He was located in an industrial area, and so he dealt not in the nails, hand tools, and smaller products that one finds in today's typical retail hardware store but, instead, in bigger, heavier hardware for the industrial firms found on the waterfront.[4]

HARDWARE STORES

```
H. P. GILBERT,
    91 and 93 Water street, Georgetown, D. C.
STONE WAGONS, CARTS,
    HARNESS, SINGLE AND DOUBLE,
        WAGON COVERS, DERRICKS,
            STEEL BARS, AXES, SHOVELS,
                WHEELBARROWS, SCALES,
BLANKETS, CANVAS HORSE COVERS,
    SACKS, SASH. B. S. WORKING IRON,
        NUTTS, ANVILS, BELLOWS,
            SLEDGES,
                STEEL STRIKING HAMMERS,
                    STONE BREAKERS,
            At fair prices for Cash.
    Iron, Rope, Brass, Lead, and Copper bought for
cash.
    Come and see for yourself.          no25-1m
```

A December 1872 newspaper ad describes the heavy-duty hardware that was H. P. Gilbert's stock-in-trade. (Evening Star, *December 9, 1872, 11*)

In 1870, Gilbert bought the machinery of a marble works just north of the Capitol building. The machinery had been used to saw marble for the recently completed enlargement of the Capitol. It is unclear whether Gilbert bought the machinery as part of his junk business or actually intended to use it.[5]

In 1880, Gilbert opened a second location at what today is 1208 Wisconsin Avenue, just north of M Street. The old location ceased to be a hardware store soon after that. Besides running the hardware store, Gilbert developed a stone and gravel business at the waterfront location. In 1883, for example, he provided four thousand cubic yards of stone used for rip-rapping in the land filling operation that created Haines Point. In 1893, he was part of an investor group that planned to build a water-powered factory in Cabin John to produce brick (sixty thousand pieces a day), tile, and sewer pipe.[6]

In 1882, Gilbert was one of the founders of the First Cooperative Building Association of Georgetown. He served as president for at least ten years, and as a director for years after that.[7]

Gilbert's other activities included bicycling and founding a temperance organization.[8]

In 1889, storm damage led to the abandonment of the Alexandria-Georgetown canal, which had run from Georgetown across the Aqueduct Bridge and south to Alexandria. Gilbert purchased timbers from a canal causeway. One of his employees, Walter T. Weaver, told author Arthur G. Peterson that he had helped saw the timbers into planks.[9]

In 1891, Gilbert sold the hardware store business to Walter Weaver and his brother, F. (for Francis) Baker Weaver. After the sale, Gilbert concentrated on his stone and gravel business and became a contractor.

W. T. WEAVER & SONS

W. T. Weaver & Sons hardware is one of Georgetown's oldest businesses, founded in 1889 by Walter T. Weaver and his brother F. Baker Weaver, and still operating today although with more of a niche business model.

The Weaver family had already been in Georgetown for generations by the time Walter Weaver started his business. Michael Weaver, Walter's grandfather, was born in 1786. The Weavers were one of several families of butchers who owned most of the land that today is Glover Park and a good deal of land to the west of that. They bought live cattle at a market on what is now MacArthur Boulevard and supplied meat to Georgetown and the City of Washington. The Kengla and Homiller families also were part of this group.

Several of Michael Weaver's sons also became butchers. An exception was Charles Weaver, the father of Walter and F. Baker, who gave up the butcher's trade to be a farmer, probably working family land west of Glover Park.

Around the same time Walter and F. Baker Weaver started the hardware business, their brother John L. Weaver and cousin William H. Barnes started a real estate and mortgage banking business. Brothers Charles and David soon joined the business, and it became Weaver Brothers, a mainstay of the Washington business community for a hundred years. Another cousin, Robert D. Weaver, was a cofounder of the Washington Metropolitan Railway (a major streetcar line) and served as president of the Farmers & Mechanics Bank and the Washington Gas Light Company.

The family Walter Weaver grew up in was prosperous. Charles Weaver told the census taker in 1870 that his personal estate was worth $5,000, a large sum at that time. It was another nineteen years before his sons started their businesses. According to Walter's grandson Jim Weaver, Charles's wife

HARDWARE STORES

Artwork on a 1908 Weaver's receipt acknowledges the connection to H. P. Gilbert, seven years after the Weavers bought his business. (*Tudor Place Archive*)

Augusta gave each of her children $5,000. That no doubt provided the capital to start the real estate and hardware businesses.

Walter and Baker Weaver started by buying H. P. Gilbert's hardware business at 1208 Wisconsin Avenue. Even years later, Weaver Hardware receipts said the Weavers were "successors to H. P. Gilbert." Gilbert was still prominent in Georgetown business circles, and his name must have provided some credibility.

Except for one brief interval, the hardware store has been in the same location since it opened. The store was located on the ground floor of the Masonic Hall, built in 1858, which was the meeting place of four different Masonic lodges. Walter Weaver was active in the Masons, and that probably helped him obtain the lease, or at least made him aware of the space's availability.

The clientele of Georgetown hardware stores changed over time. When Weaver's opened, the customers were farmers from the surrounding area. Jim Weaver, Walter's grandson, said that in those early days they were selling "farm implements and belts."[10]

Weaver's store also supplied harnesses, made by Lewis N. Shearer (who Jim Weaver called "Mr. Louie"). Shearer joined the store at or shortly after its opening, when there were dozens of harness makers in Washington and Georgetown. According to Jim Weaver, the store supplied all the harnesses for mules that towed canal boats on the C&O Canal. Shearer remembered that the canal used to order eighty to one hundred sets of harness at a time. Shearer at one point had three assistants working with him.[11]

Weaver Hardware's original building, in 1911. The wagon says "Weaver's" on the side and must have been used for deliveries. Note the Masonic symbol at the top of the facade. (*D.C. Public Library, Willard R. Ross Postcard Collection*)

HARDWARE STORES

Shearer lived on Dent Place in Georgetown, and worked at Weaver's for fifty-two years until retiring in 1940. He had two sons, one of whom was named Walter—named after Walter Weaver, one wonders?

F. Baker Weaver died in 1925 and Walter Weaver in 1933. Walter's obituary listed several Masonic leadership posts that he held. His son James Bryce Weaver, who went by his middle name, continued running the store.[12]

The Weavers did not advertise a great deal, but they could be creative. A 1962 ad featured a drawing of a stylishly dressed woman like one would see in a department store ad. The text said, "HARDWARE ... FASHIONABLE??!! Certainly—hardware is fashionable from W. T. Weaver & Sons, Inc."[13]

On July 8, 1963, the store was destroyed by a mammoth five-alarm fire, the biggest fire in Washington in five years. Jim Weaver, who lived in Northern Virginia, received a phone call from a manager at the bank across the street, telling him about the fire. He drove to the store and knew the situation was bad when he could see the smoke as he drove past the Pentagon. There was water damage to two neighboring buildings and smoke damage to most buildings on the block. Besides the building, the Weavers lost $150,000 in inventory.[14]

The family relocated the store temporarily to 1271 Wisconsin Avenue, space that until recently had been occupied by Fisher's Market (see chapter 10). They managed to open at that location just two weeks after the fire. Jim Weaver recalled that the Weavers' competitors called Bryce and offered to sell him inventory and building materials at cost. The Weavers had to have the basement of the new location dug out to create storage space for inventory.

The local business community celebrated the opening of the temporary location with a party at Billy Martin's Carriage House. Competitor John Meenehan (see the following section) joked that he had tried to burn Bryce Weaver out but had not succeeded.

That December, the Weavers bought the site of the burned-out building from the Georgetown Masonic Lodge Association for $52,000, with the understanding that the association would be given a lease for space in any new building at a dollar a year.

In November 1964, there was a Masonic cornerstone-laying ceremony to begin construction of a new building. Officials of forty-eight Masonic lodges in the District were there. Masons in white gloves symbolically checked the

GEORGETOWN'S RETAIL PAST

LEFT: The new Weaver Hardware building. Weaver's occupied the ground floor space until 2000 and since then has been located upstairs. (*Photo by the author*)

RIGHT: A Masonic symbol also appears at the top of the new building's facade. (*Photo by the author*)

cornerstone with a square, a level, and a plumb, and anointed it with oil, wine, and corn. Grand Master Harry B. Savage tapped the stone into place using the gavel that George Washington had used to do the same for the cornerstone of the U.S. Capitol.[15]

The building was complete and the hardware store was in its new quarters by 1967. Like the old building, the new one has a Masonic symbol on its facade.

Like some other Georgetown businesses, Weaver's Hardware has had celebrities among its clientele, including Vincent Price and Goldie Hawn. NBC journalist David Brinkley lived in the neighborhood and was a regular customer. According to Jim Weaver, Brinkley was good at woodworking. He bought a table saw at Weaver's and asked that it be delivered. When Weaver arrived at Brinkley's house with the saw, Brinkley told him he had just won a similar saw in a charity raffle. Weaver offered to take the saw back, but Brinkley said he had only paid five dollars for the raffle ticket and would give the extra saw away to someone.

In 1975, Jim Weaver was one of the organizers of Georgetown's first "Good Old Days Parade," which featured as many as one hundred antique cars along with marching bands, to benefit Children's Hospital. As thanks after the

HARDWARE STORES

Georgetown Visitation school and convent made its gymnasium available as overnight housing for visiting parade personnel, Weaver staged a small repeat of the parade in the Visitation parking lot so that the cloistered nuns could enjoy it. The parade was repeated for several years, but it finally became so time consuming to organize that Weaver had to turn it over to someone else.[16]

Bryce Weaver died in 1981, and Jim Weaver continued the business, with his own two sons. Around 2000, they changed the focus of the business to specialize in decorative hardware, moved it to the second floor of the building, and leased out the ground floor. The new business involves more interaction with architects and decorators and less with homeowners. Jim Weaver died in 2013, and his sons run the business today, the fourth generation to do so.[17]

MOLLOY AND MEENEHAN

The building at 3241–3243 M Street (just west of Wisconsin Avenue) housed a hardware store for sixty years, owned in succession by Thomas J. Molloy and

This building at 3241–3243 M Street was home to Meenehan's Hardware. (*Photo by the author*)

John F. Meenehan. They had much in common: both emigrated from Ireland and both were saloon keepers before they went into the hardware business.

Molloy was born in Ireland in 1875 and came to the United States in 1900. Within a year, he opened a saloon in Northeast Washington. In 1906, he closed that and opened a saloon in Georgetown at 3243 M Street. In 1908, the saloon became a wholesale and retail liquor dealer.

Prohibition came to the District of Columbia on November 1, 1917, more than a year before the Nineteenth Amendment to the U.S. Constitution made Prohibition national (see chapter 22). Like all other bar owners and liquor dealers, Molloy had to change his line of business. By 1919, he had opened Kentucky Hardware at 3241 M Street. He may have expanded into his former saloon space next door at 3243. We do not know why he chose the name "Kentucky Hardware."

The Molloy family lived on North Capitol Street. Thomas's wife Mary also was from Ireland, having come to the United States in 1904. They had six children.

Prohibition ended in 1933, and Molloy was able to return to the liquor business. His oldest son, Leo, was among the first 107 applicants for D.C. liquor licenses in February 1934. Later that year Leo had his license and was selling beer at 3245 M Street, next door to his father's hardware store. A year later he was selling liquor as well as beer.

In 1938, Thomas Molloy sold the hardware store to John F. Meenehan. Meenehan's grandson Patrick recalled his father John F. Meenehan Jr.'s story about buying the store. Molloy invited the senior Meenehan into a back room at the store and poured two glasses of whiskey with which they drank to their agreement. Meenehan said, "Don't I need to fill out some papers or something like that?" Molloy said, "Ain't me, we're good." The papers did materialize later. (The Molloys' liquor store continued to operate next door.)[18]

Meenehan had come to the United States from Ireland in 1885, when he was seven. Around 1900, the same year he became a U.S. citizen, he started working as a bartender. A year later, he was working as a bartender for Michael Morris, known as "Uncle Mike," who had a saloon at 3004 M Street in Georgetown. Meenehan soon married Morris's daughter, Mary.[19]

Morris helped his new son-in-law open his own saloon on 14th Street NW in 1902, along with brother Martin Meenehan and another partner. It

HARDWARE STORES

was successful but had to close in 1917 when Prohibition came to Washington. Meenehan took his family to Ireland for a few years but brought them back to Washington in 1921.[20]

In 1924, Meenehan started a hardware store on 14th Street. Thus, the Georgetown store acquired in 1938 was not Meenehan's first, nor was it his last—the family eventually owned four other hardware stores, two in Maryland and two in Virginia.

Meenehan's Georgetown location differed from modern hardware stores. It was not self-service—a customer had to tell one of the many clerks what he was looking for. At the same time, it was very much full service. John Meenehan himself would deliver bulky items to a customer's home. If a customer needed help with a task like installing a toilet valve, someone from Meenehan's would come to his home and do it—at no extra charge.

In the early years, Meenehan's had exclusive franchises from some manufacturers. Meenehan's stores were the only places in Washington where one could buy GE light bulbs, Kem-Tone paint, and Johnson outboard motors. The store sold some of these franchised products on consignment, so it did not have to pay for the merchandise until it sold—a winning business model for sure.

In 1947, John Meenehan Sr. retired, and his sons John Jr., Frank, and Vincent took over the business. (John Sr. died ten years later.) In 1948, the three sons bought the M Street building from Leo Molloy and other members of the Molloy family for $67,500.

Multiple Meenehans worked in the stores. John Jr.'s son Patrick served as an all-around troubleshooter, assigned to stores where problems needed attention. At one point, John Jr. fired all the employees of one of the Maryland stores and sent Patrick there to take over and rebuild the staff. Two of Patrick's siblings ran the office. Patrick's cousin recalled inventorying small hardware:

> *I remember counting all those nails and bolts and screws and all these little items. They were all in these bins. For the inventory, we had to hand-count each one and report it on this grid.*[21]

There was no alley access to the store, so all deliveries had to be made through the front door, on crowded M Street. Meenehan finally constructed a trap door, so deliveries could go directly to the basement storage area. (The trap door no longer exists.)

Meenehan's did advertise. They ran spots on the popular Harden and Weaver morning radio show, with the jingle "Meenehan the hardware man, the hardware man is Meenehan." An ad in the *Evening Star* on April 12, 1951, promoted the celebration of Georgetown's bicentennial and urged readers to "Come Down and See Commercial Liza." One wonders who or what Commercial Liza was.[22]

Like Weaver's, Meenehan's had celebrities as customers, including Benjamin Bradlee (editor of the *Washington Post*), Wilbur Mills (powerful chairman of the House Ways and Means Committee), novelist Herman Wouk, and Senator Eugene McCarthy. When the movie *The Exorcist* was being filmed nearby on Prospect Street, people from the film crew would come to Meenehan's to buy hardware they needed for the day's filming: fishing line and wire for a scene where star Linda Blair levitated, and Sapolin paint in a brick red shade for blood.

The advent of big box lumber/hardware stores like Hechinger's and later Home Depot led to tough competition for smaller hardware stores. The Meenehan full-service concept made it hard to compete because the store needed more clerks than a self-service store. Some family members wanted to consolidate the stores and become part of the True Value or Ace Hardware groups, but John Sr. refused, not wanting to cut off business with his existing suppliers.

In 1955, the family sold the M Street building to finance the opening of additional stores and became a tenant of the buyer. As Patrick later said, that proved to be a strategic mistake. Twenty-five years later, the landlord to whom they had sold the building raised the rent by 400 percent. The store could not be profitable at that rent, and so it closed. Two stores in Virginia continued to operate.[23]

CHAPTER 18

Paint and Glass Stores

The retail paint business in Georgetown has been notable for its concentration through the twentieth century, when it consisted largely of just five long-lived businesses.

Paint and Glass Stores

Becker Paint & Glass	1885–1968
DeMaine & Co.	1900–1941
Columbia Glass & Mirror Co.	1954–1982
Jones Paint Store	1935–1970
Gilbert Paint & Glass	1939–1959

The ownership of the five changed, but their names were a constant. In this chapter, we will take a closer look at three of the five.

There were only a handful of other paint stores, which came and went after only a few years. Druggists sometimes either sold paint in their stores (Cropley's Pharmacy) or opened paint stores of their own (O'Donnell's). Perhaps this was because they were used to working with chemicals (see chapter 11).

BECKER PAINT & GLASS

The Becker family opened a paint store in 1885 that did business on Wisconsin Avenue for eighty-four years. The founders sold the business in 1913, but under other owners it continued to operate, using the Becker name until 1971. The store illustrates the value of a strong brand name—for decades after the Beckers themselves were gone, none of the several successor owners dared to drop the Becker name, even one owner who already had an established paint business under his own name.

The business started with Charles Becker, who was born in Hanover, Germany, in 1832. By 1860, he and his wife Mary, born in Bavaria, were in New York, where their oldest son Charles A. Becker was born. (To minimize confusion we will refer to the son as Charles Jr.)

At some point in the 1880s, the family relocated to Washington, and Charles opened a drugstore at what now is 1367 Wisconsin Avenue. The 1880 census lists "apothecary" as the occupation for both Charles and Charles Jr.

In 1884, Charles opened a paint store next door to the drugstore at 1365 Wisconsin Avenue. Charles apparently decided to concentrate on the paint business and allowed Charles Jr. to take over the drug business, which he did in 1889 with a partner, George M. Sothoron. That venture was short-lived, and the drugstore was gone by 1890. Charles Jr. continued to work as a druggist, though, running a store in Tenallytown and later one downtown. He disappeared after 1906, and we do not know where he went or what happened to him. Charles does not mention Charles Jr. in the will he signed in 1914, suggesting either that Charles Jr. already had died or that there was some estrangement.

In 1893, Charles moved the paint store to 1239 Wisconsin Avenue, where it would remain for seventy-three years.

Starting in 1900, the store advertised that it sold glass as well as paint and oils. In 1904, Charles brought his son Harry (brother of Charles Jr.) into the business.

In 1913, Charles and Harry sold the store to Elkanah M. Hook, and Hook replaced Charles as president of the corporation that ran the store. In May 1913, the store ran a classified ad offering for sale "one young mule." We do not know if the sale of the mule came before or after the sale of the business, or what role the mule might have played in the business. Pulling a delivery wagon, perhaps? After selling the business, Harry worked in sales for the Pittsburgh Plate Glass Company, no doubt applying knowledge he had acquired during his years in the store in Georgetown. Charles became a corn merchant.

Hook, the new owner, was born in Massachusetts in 1871 and arrived in Washington around the time he bought the store. In the 1914 directory, he

PAINT AND GLASS STORES

THE CHARLES BECKER PAINT CO., Inc.
DEALERS IN
Paints, Glass and Painters' Supplies

Washington, D.C., Oct. 31 1912

Mr. W. B. Orme

Telephone West 67
1239 WISCONSIN AVENUE, N.W.

1912			
July 26	2 lbs.	Butcher's Polish	.90
Sept. 23	2 lts.	Glass 12 X 28 & putty	.55
Oct. 10	1 qt.	546 Devoe Paint	.60
	¼ lb.	Blue	.15
14	1 qt.	546 Devoe Paint	.60
	1	Brush	.15
16	1 can	Green Paint	.15
24	1 lb.	Butcher's Polish	.45
28	1 gal.	546 Devoe Paint	2.10
	¼ lb.	Blue	.15
	1 qt.	Turpentine	.20
	2 4"	Brushes	1.00
31	1 gal.	546 Devoe Paint	2.10
	½ "	Enamel	1.35
	1	Brush	.60
	1 pt.	Turpentine	.10
			11.15

This 1912 receipt details three months of purchases at Becker Paint by William B. Orme. Orme was the secretary/treasurer of the Washington Gas Light Co. He lived in Georgetown and must have been doing some redecorating at home. (*Peabody Room, D.C. Public Library*)

listed himself as affiliated with both the Charles Becker Paint Co. and the Huntsfield Paint Co. Huntsfield Paint was a paint manufacturing concern owned in partnership by Hook, William M. Mansfield, and John W. Hunt, and located on the Georgetown waterfront. Selling paint to the Becker store may have been how Hook learned there was an opportunity to buy the store.

Under Hook's ownership, the store was a distributor of DeVoe paints. Ads in 1916 recommended DeVoe Gloss carriage paint for porch and lawn furniture "and yes, for baby carriages, too." They also touted the benefits of DeVoe Vernosite Long Life Spar Varnish, which displayed "the exact formula on every can." An ad in 1921 urged boaters to "Get your Craft 'Ship-Shape' with yacht paint at $4.25 a gallon and yacht enamel at $7.50 a gallon."[1]

In 1921, the store changed hands again. The owner was Harry W. Taylor, who had started out as a painter in 1912. He had joined forces with George A. Pennington in 1914, and they had built a business doing painting, wallpapering, and window treatments. As with Hook, Taylor may have found out that the Becker store was for sale because he and Pennington bought paint and other materials there.

Hook, ever the entrepreneur, joined with two partners to start the Metal Repair and Supply Company, with quarters on Wisconsin Avenue a few blocks north of Georgetown. Later he went into sales work for the Frigidaire Corporation.

Then the unexpected happened. In 1926, only five years after he bought the Becker paint store, Harry Taylor died suddenly at age forty-one. Hook realized this was a chance to reacquire the store. He must have looked for a partner, and found William A. Craig. Craig had sold real estate and, in 1920, was the proprietor of a garage. He had no apparent background in paint, so it seems likely that he provided capital and Hook provided the know-how. They bought the business and the building in March 1927. Again, though, the Becker name was a big asset, and they did not want to change it—a 1927 ad referred to "Craig & Hook, Inc, trading as Becker Paint & Glass Co."[2]

This second Hook paint venture did not last, either, and William R. Winslow took over the business in December 1928. Winslow had resources—

This 1927 ad shows us that Craig & Hook retained the Becker Paint name. (Evening Star, *June 20, 1927*)

immediately after buying the business, he paid off the $12,000 mortgage on the building, in cash.³

Winslow was born in Elizabeth City, North Carolina, and came to Washington in 1919, working as a salesman for the Hugh Reilly Co., which sold paint. In 1921, he started his own wholesale paint business at 921 New York Avenue NW, under the name W. R. Winslow Company. Soon he branched into retail sales as well, buying existing paint and hardware stores and operating them under their original names rather than putting his own name on them. Consistent with this strategy, Winslow kept the Becker name for his newly acquired Georgetown store.⁴

Although Winslow kept the original names on the stores he bought, they advertised together under the Winslow name. A 1943 ad listed six Winslow stores, all with different beginnings to their names but all ending

Becker Paint & Glass was located in the building on the right in this 2025 photo, at 1239 Wisconsin Avenue. (*Photo by the author*)

with "Paint & Glass Co." or "Paint & Hardware Co." Ads like this were frequent through the 1950s.[5]

Many years later, in 1969, Winslow moved the store to 3255 Prospect Street. He continued to use the Becker name at his new location for a while.[6] After 1971, the Becker name disappeared from Winslow's advertising. The former Becker's store continued to operate under the Winslow name at the Prospect Street location for fifteen more years, long after Winslow's death in 1973. The last display ad referring to it promoted Benjamin Moore Paint's Labor Day Sale in 1986.[7]

Winslow was a philanthropist. He was on the board of directors of the Boys Club of Washington, and he donated 110 acres of land in Point No Point, Maryland, for a Boys Club Camp. In 1950, the camp was named Camp Winslow in his honor. He established a foundation that awarded four college scholarships each year. He also was a member of the Rotary Club of Washington and served on the board of Western Maryland College.[8]

DEMAINE & CO.

The DeMaine family ran a paint store on M Street for forty-one years, starting in 1900. Alice K. DeMaine, the matriarch of the family, was a driving force behind the business.

The DeMaines were an established family in Alexandria, Virginia. William H. DeMaine, born in 1818, was a cabinetmaker in Alexandria. His son Charles, born in 1843, lived in Alexandria and was a railroad engineer. His three children included William H. and Charles W. DeMaine, born in 1865 and 1867, respectively. William and his son Windsor became undertakers, running a funeral home in Alexandria for decades.

Charles W., who was probably nicknamed "Charlie" but will be referred to here as "Charles II," married Alice Kyle, the daughter of a farmer in Boutetort County, Virginia, near Roanoke. The year 1895 brought the birth of Charles II and Alice's only child, also named Charles W. DeMaine, who we will refer to here as "Charles III." By 1900, they had settled on N Street in Georgetown.

Charles II and Alice opened a paint store that year at 3202 M Street, under the name "DeMaine & Co." We do not know who the "& Co." was.

PAINT AND GLASS STORES

The business soon moved to 3213 M Street, where it would remain for almost forty years.

Charles II was not in robust health, and in October 1910 he died at the age of forty. His funeral was held in the chapel at his brother William's funeral home in Alexandria.[9] Alice continued running the business, and Charles III soon was part of it as well—the name remained "DeMaine & Co.," but now it is clear who the "& Co." was. Within a few years after Charles II's death, Alice and Charles III bought the building that housed the store.[10]

Charles III served in World War I with the 110th Field Artillery. He returned from France in June 1919.[11]

The DeMaine store was an "exclusive agent" for Lowe Bros. Paint, identified in one newspaper ad as a "high standard" paint. The store also sold Monarch Paint, which ads referred to as "Monarch Paint 100% pure."[12]

The DeMaines' business was not limited to paint, however. A 1917 ad said Monarch Paint was available from "DeMaine & Co." at the M Street address, but below that appeared "Goodyear Service Station, The only one in Georgetown." In 1917 through 1919, ads for tires and inner tubes ("a bear for wear," "Chilled Rubber Process greater strength, service, savings") included DeMaine & Co. in lists of Goodyear dealers.[13]

Alice's involvement in the business continued at least through 1920, when she told the census taker her occupation was "paint store, own business." She was fifty at the time. Like his father, Charles III died young, in 1936 when he was only forty-one. The store continued to operate through 1941, probably under Alice's leadership. She died in 1942 and the store closed then.

COLUMBIA GLASS & MIRROR CO.

Columbia Glass & Mirror was established around 1948, probably by Donald F. Lenehan and a partner whose identity is unknown. The store started out at 2904 M Street, in quarters that had long been home to William Lee's feed store (see chapter 2). More recently Frank F. Davis had bridged two eras by running a combination feed store and gas station in the space.[14]

Donald Lenehan was born in Washington in 1922. His father was a film salesman who had moved the family from New York to Arlington, Virginia, a couple of years before Donald's birth. The 1950 census lists

Donald as a "glazier" working in a "glass and mirror retail store," probably the Columbia store in Georgetown. He and his wife Betty lived in Arlington and had two daughters.

In 1952, the store ran what may have been its first display ad, in the *Evening Star*. "Rooms too square? Ceiling too low? Correct that defect with MIRRORS!," the ad began. It boasted of "Washington's finest collection of mirrors and mirrored furniture." Most unusual for M Street even then, the ad said, "Always Plenty of Free Parking Space!" The parking was behind the building, reached by an alley from M Street.[15]

We know Lenehan had a partner because in 1953 he ran a newspaper ad announcing that he had "acquired complete ownership of Columbia Glass & Mirror Co.," implying the departure of a co-owner. The ad said that Lenehan would "continue to give his personal attention, and the benefit of his sixteen years of experience as glass and mirror specialist, to Washington area home owners."[16] The sixteen year reference tells us that Lenehan first started working in the glass business when he was in his mid-teens, since he was only thirty-one years old when the ad ran.

In 1959, Lenehan paid $25,000 for a building at 3232 M Street and moved the business there. The building, which is architecturally quite distinct from its neighbors, was built in the nineteenth century, probably before the Civil War, and since the early twentieth century had been the home of Charles Reckert's grocery store.[17]

Columbia Glass did business at the new location for twenty-six years, finally closing its doors in 1982. Donald Lenehan lived on until 2011, when he died in Washington State.

The Columbia Glass & Mirror Co. in 1966. (*Library of Congress, Historic American Buildings Survey HABS DC,GEO,79—1*)

CHAPTER 19

Appliance Stores

Keeping Up with Innovations

Today home appliances and electronics are found in "big box" stores, but for much of the twentieth century, there were between one and four neighborhood appliance stores on Wisconsin Avenue and M Street in Georgetown. The relatively constant number of stores belies a dramatic evolution in what the stores were selling, from stoves early on to electric home appliances later and to electronics after that. To last in the appliance business in the twentieth century, a business had to hold its own in a race with developing technology. That race is apparent from the history of Georgetown's longest-lived appliance store, Georgetown Electric.

Before 1920, the main home appliance was the stove. In 1860, Robert Boyd had a store selling stoves at 88 High Street (today, Wisconsin Avenue between Prospect and N Streets). In 1877, five stores were selling stoves. Decades later, from 1965 to 1990, B. A. Coe & Co. would be a specialized dealer in gas ranges at 3330 M Street.

Another early non-electric appliance was the pedal-powered sewing machine. J. B. Wells's store at 74 High Street sold them for several years starting as early as 1877, and George Smith had a sewing machine store on Wisconsin Avenue from 1915 through 1931. William Lear had a sewing machine store from 1937 to 1948, but by that time, the machines probably were electric.

Stores selling electric appliances did not appear until the 1920s. That was when electricity had become commonly available in urban areas and home electric appliances first became widely available. In 1910, there were only fourteen thousand electric meters in Washington, a city of 331,000. Essentially no American homes had refrigerators in 1920. By 1930, 8 percent of homes had them, and by 1940, the number rose to 44 percent (56 percent in urban areas). The first electric washing machines appeared in the 1910s but were expensive. By 1925, though, a moderately priced washing machine could be had for $125 to $150, and sales increased.[1]

Earlier in the twentieth century, newspaper articles had hailed as technological marvels devices that are commonplace today. In 1905, the *Washington Post* reported that the electric refrigerator was "about ready for general introduction." Two years later, the *Post* reported on a convention of the Electric Light Association and talked of displays of "hundreds of different contraptions electrically powered."

> *The reporter tried to find out something about an electric refrigerator, but everybody who should have known were extremely reticent and looked hurt when the question was put.*[2]

In the early 1920s, a range of appliances came onto the market. In 1922, W. H. Tuberville ran an advertisement inviting newspaper readers to come to "The House Electric" on Connecticut Avenue for demonstrations of electric dishwashers, washers, ironing machines, sewing machines, refrigerators, and "fireless electric cookers." A *Washington Post* article a year later, headlined "Home Electrical Appliances Make Women's Life Easy," declared "[d]rudgery removed from household now" and talked of electric refrigerators, kitchen exhaust fans, vacuum cleaners, ranges, and percolators.[3]

Citywide, there was no general "appliances" category in the classified section of the city directory in 1930. There was a category for electric refrigerators, which listed only two dealers.[4] In 1938, the number of listings under "electric refrigerators" had grown to fifteen. There now was an "electrical appliances" category, listing three stores.

GEORGETOWN ELECTRIC

Harry Reuwer and his son Henry "Duke" Reuwer ran Georgetown Electric for sixty years.

Harry was born in Harrisburg, Pennsylvania, in 1886. He came to the Washington area in 1926, settled in Arlington, Virginia, and worked as a mechanic for Sterrett & Fleming Inc., a Hubmobile auto dealer on Connecticut Avenue.

Harry started the business in 1926 at 1242 Wisconsin Avenue. His son Duke started working in the family store early. Duke's World War II draft registration, when he was eighteen, said that Georgetown Electric was his employer. (He enlisted shortly after registering.) In 1950, the Reuwers told the census taker that Harry was the proprietor of the store and Duke was a "radio technician, electrical appliances."

For their business to survive for sixty years, the Reuwers had to keep up with technological improvements in products they already sold, but they also frequently had to add newly invented products to their inventory. Because they also repaired appliances, they had to be able to service the new products as well as sell them. Comparing the store's advertising early and then later in its life illustrates this. Ads run by appliance manufacturers during the store's first year (1927) said Georgetown Electric sold Johnson's Wax Electric Floor Polishers and Iroquois Refrigerators—straightforward, largely mechanical appliances. Sixty years later, one of the store's last ads was for Sony Camcorders, a technology that would have been science fiction in 1927 (as, indeed, was television itself in 1927).[5]

Georgetown Electric only occasionally ran newspaper ads of its own. Westinghouse and General Electric (GE), however, for whom the store was a dealer, ran frequent ads for their products that listed local stores selling those products, including Georgetown Electric. In these ads, one can see the progression of appliance technology and the changes in Georgetown Electric's inventory:

1920s: Georgetown Electric sold Savory Airator fans and RCA Radiola radios—"there's an RCA Radiola to fit [every room]." There also was the Iroquois refrigerator, producing "the crisp, dry cold of a frosty night." A Westinghouse ad said that the dealer who displays the sign of a Westinghouse Electrification Dealer "offers you a complete service in things electrical, made or supplied by Westinghouse—from wiring devices to motors and appliances of every kind." This tells us that Georgetown Electric maintained an inventory of parts, or at least could order them.[6]

APPLIANCE STORES

1930s: In 1931, the Reuwers moved the business closer to M Street, to 1205 Wisconsin Avenue, where it would operate for twenty-five years. There were more ads for refrigerators, confirming that they really had begun to sell. Radio technology was advancing, as shown by a 1938 ad for a General Electric radio with "the Amazing New Beam-A-Scope," which "overcomes the necessity of 'anchoring' a radio in a fixed location in a room" and "eliminates the need for unsightly aerial and ground wires." It also featured "keyboard touch tuning—another General Electric first."[7]

1940s: General Electric contributed to the war effort with an ad in which Uncle Sam said, "Your idle electric appliances are needed. Bring them in today. Sell them for cash or war stamps." Georgetown Electric was one of the dealers ready to receive those appliances. Later in the 1940s, another new technology appeared in the form of FM radio: "You've never heard anything like Westinghouse Rainbow Tone FM."[8]

1950s and 1960s: These decades brought television. A General Electric console TV (black and white) could be purchased at Georgetown Electric for $199. (Ten years later a color console would cost $449.) The store also carried General Electric ranges and air conditioners. A 1954 General Electric ad invited readers to pick up an entry from any dealer (including Georgetown Electric) for a contest in which they could seek to win a GE Swivel-Top vacuum cleaner by "just complet[ing] the G-E Swivel-Top cleaner jingle."[9]

Harry Reuwer died in 1959. Also in the late 1950s, the store lost its lease on Wisconsin Avenue when its landlord and neighbor, the Riggs National Bank, wanted to demolish the building to create the parking lot that occupies the site today. Georgetown Electric moved to its third and last location, at 3135 M Street, just around the corner. The Reuwers never bought any of the three buildings in which their store was located over the years. They always were in leased space, but that space always was in a prime location, close to Georgetown's nerve center at Wisconsin Avenue and M Street. Some of their ads in the 1960s touted their location "in the heart of Georgetown."[10]

1970s: Georgetown Electric became a dealer for Sony, whose products were the epitome of Japanese-made, high-tech TVs and other electronics.[11]

1980s: In 1981, an *Evening Star* directory of dealers in television and stereo equipment said that Georgetown Electric repaired TVs for flat rates: black & white TVs $27.50, color TVs $45, "minor repairs cost $12.50 or less."[12]

Duke Reuwer died in June 1986, and the store soon closed. The last newspaper ad mentioning the store was a Sony ad for its camcorder line in December of that year.[13]

OTHER STORES

The same march of technology that we see in Georgetown Electric's history is also visible in Georgetown store names. The first store with "radio" in its name was the Georgetown Radio Shop at 3320 M Street, which opened in 1924. Georgetown Electric was the first store with the word *electric* in its name. Colonial Electronics was the first with a name including the word *electronic*, opening in the early 1950s.

Radios needed to be repaired, and three shops specializing in radio repair opened in 1933 and 1934, run by Thurman Centers (3354 M Street), Charles Eaton (3534 M Street), and someone named Tutts (3005 M Street).

The first store specializing in air conditioners belonged to Roy Klomparens, who opened the business in 1937. The first vacuum cleaner specialist was Guarantee Vacuum & Radio Co., which was open by 1939 at 2810 Pennsylvania Avenue.

In the early 1950s, Shrader Sound at 2803 M Street was the first business whose name emphasized high fidelity sound. It remained in business through the 1960s. Later there were others, such as Sound of Georgetown and the Sound Warehouse in the 1970s. And, of course, there was national chain Radio Shack, which sold electronic parts and equipment from a location in the Georgetown Park mall from 1983 until the early 2000s.

CHAPTER 20
Staying Overnight
Early Taverns to Hotels

TAVERNS
BEFORE THERE WERE HOTELS IN GEORGETOWN, THERE WERE TAVERNS. Historian Oliver Wendell Holmes (named for but not related to the U.S. Supreme Court justice of that name) thought there were as many as fifteen at the close of the eighteenth century. Some were located on or near the waterfront. Others were located on the northern side of town, to serve farmers and others coming to sell crops and buy supplies. And some were located in the center of town, to serve the local population.[1]

Taverns provided lodging for travelers (usually in shared rooms), stables for their horses, and food for both them and the local public. Meals generally were served at appointed times rather than as diners came and went.

Taverns also served as community centers. Georgetown in the late eighteenth and early nineteenth centuries had no courthouse, no city hall, no library, no auditorium. Meetings and social events took place in the taverns.

Belt's Tavern
While there were one or two taverns in the area before the Maryland Legislature authorized the creation of the Town of Georgetown in 1751, the first tavern in the newly established town was Belt's Tavern. In August of that year, Frederick County, Maryland (of which Georgetown was then part), granted Joseph Belt a license to open a tavern. The tavern was initially located on what today is Wisconsin Avenue just south of Grace Street and the future

> *Frederick* County, *September* 8, 1771.
>
> THE Subscriber continues to keep a House of Entertainment in *George-Town*, at the King's Arms, and as he is provided with good Entertainment, Stabling, and Provender for Horses, would be obliged to all Gentlemen travelling and others for their Custom, and they may depend on kind Usage, by their most Humble Servant,
> (w3)   JOSEPH BELT.

A 1771 newspaper ad announcing the opening of Belt's Tavern. (Maryland Gazette, *September 19, 1771, 3*)

right-of-way of the C&O Canal. Some years later, Belt moved to a site across Wisconsin Avenue and close to M Street.

By 1752, the new town had been laid out and subdivided, and Belt's Tavern was the site of the first sale of lots. Town records tell us that the commissioners who governed the unincorporated town until 1789 held meetings at Belt's starting in 1757 and possibly earlier.

Belt did business for more than twenty years. He called his establishment the "King's Arms," a common name for taverns—there were others under that name in Alexandria, Baltimore, and Annapolis. People in Georgetown, however, continued to refer to Belt's establishment as "Belt's Tavern." Belt closed in late 1774 or early 1775.

White Horse Inn

One of the outlying taverns was the White Horse Inn, at the corner of today's Wisconsin Avenue and Q Street. There was a market nearby where enslaved people were bought and sold. Buyers and sellers would stay at the inn, and the enslaved individuals awaiting sale would be confined in the large cellar, which extended under Wisconsin Avenue. Tradition has it that the proprietor was German, and that the Rhine wine she served was popular. Another legend says that George Washington, who was a frequent customer of the competing Suter's Tavern (more on Suter's later), stayed at the White Horse Inn only once. He was offended in some way by the owner, and he never returned.[2]

STAYING OVERNIGHT

A historical marker on a house at 1528 33rd Street NW says incorrectly that the tavern was located in that building. While the marker gets the location wrong, the rest of it is worth reading:

> *When George Town was a leading port, the tavern was a favorite stopping place for travelers and tobacco merchants from Frederick Town, also a popular meeting place of Thomas Jefferson and other notables. Here Mayor John Cox entertained General Lafayette; dinner of reed birds followed by dancing to music from the balcony.*

Suter's Tavern

Suter's Tavern, opened in 1783, was Georgetown's most historically important. The location of Suter's has long been debated, but Oliver Wendell Holmes convincingly makes the case that Suter's was at the former site of Belt's Tavern, on the east side of today's Wisconsin Avenue, just south of M Street. Others have suggested it was at 31st and K Streets or at the site of today's Georgetown Club, 1530 Wisconsin Avenue.[3] Suter named his business the "Fountain Inn," but it was known to Georgetowners as Suter's Tavern.

Suter's was a prime meeting space. Until Georgetown's incorporation in 1789, the town commissioners met at Suter's Tavern as well as at Belt's. Suter's also was the meeting place for the District of Columbia's first Masonic Lodge, and it was from Suter's that a procession set out to lay the cornerstone for the White House, which had been designed by James Hoban, a Mason. Sales and auctions of real estate were frequent events at Suter's, and there was at least one auction of enslaved people. A lending library operated at Suter's, though the books may well have been stored elsewhere. When the Bank of Columbia, D.C.'s first bank, was chartered, the subscribers to its stock met at Suter's to elect the first board of directors.

Suter's biggest distinction, though, was its role in the creation of Washington, D.C. George Washington had been a Suter's customer from time to time since 1785. In March 1791, Washington spent three days and two nights at Suter's, where he met with the major landowners of the future District of Columbia to negotiate an agreement for them to contribute property for the creation of the new city. It seems likely the final agreement was signed at Suter's, because John Suter signed it as a witness.

The three commissioners who governed the new District met often at Suter's. In September 1791, they were there with Thomas Jefferson and James Madison to discuss details about the project. Among other things, this was the meeting where the names "District of Columbia" and "City of Washington" were adopted. The first sale of lots happened a few weeks later on October 17, also at Suter's.

John Suter died in 1794. His wife Sarah continued the business for another year or so, but she left the business in 1795 when her son John Suter Jr. became a partner in a competing tavern.

The Suter's Tavern site housed a number of other taverns after Sarah's withdrawal. They had various names, but locals still called it Suter's Tavern. George Pitt finally took over in 1803, under the name "Anchor Inn":

Anchor Tavern and Oyster House

George Pitt having taken and entered upon the above Inn and fitted up at a considerable expense respectfully solicits the patronage and support of his late friends, when a resident at the Eagle Tavern, those who frequented the Fountain Inn, and the public in general.[4]

The Anchor Inn operated until 1816. By 1824, when the Marquis de Lafayette visited Georgetown, the deserted tavern building was the only Georgetown structure that he recognized from his previous visit decades before.[5]

The City Tavern, Lang's Hotel, and the Morgan House

The City Tavern, at 3206 M Street (just west of Wisconsin Avenue), is the only one of the early taverns still standing. In the 1790s, three new taverns appeared on the scene, all of which were in substantial, newly constructed brick buildings. The Union Tavern (later renamed the Union Hotel—see the following section) opened in 1796 at today's corner of 30th and M Streets. The Columbian Inn opened in 1799, at the corner of Wisconsin Avenue and Cherry Street. The third was the City Tavern, which opened in 1796. It was initially run by Clement Seawall, who had run Suter's Tavern for a while after John Suter's wife left it.

STAYING OVERNIGHT

Besides the brick main building, the City Tavern had a separate kitchen building and a third building used for storage or as a stable.

As Suter's had been before it, the City Tavern was the site of countless meetings of local government, associations, and other groups. The Georgetown Corporation (which governed Georgetown after the town's incorporation) met there for the first time in December 1796 and did so frequently after that. Around that same time, the tavern hosted an organizational meeting of the Georgetown Bridge Company, formed to build the first bridge across the Potomac at Little Falls (the site of today's Chain Bridge). These meetings would have taken place in the tavern's "Long Room," later called the "Assembly Room."

Charles McLaughlin took over the tavern in 1799. The next year, President John Adams stayed and dined at the City Tavern when he visited Washington to learn about the progress of construction of new government buildings. The press reported that at a banquet in his honor at the City Tavern, there were no less than seventeen toasts, among them toasts to the United States, Congress, the State of Maryland, the State of Massachusetts, and the City of Washington, the spirit that achieved independence, and the new nation's treaties with foreign powers. (Abigail Adams was not impressed with Georgetown, which she described to a correspondent as "the very dirtiest hole I ever saw for a place of any trade or respectability of inhabitants."[6])

Joseph Semmes became the tavern keeper in 1801, opening under "the sign of the Indian King." The sign was to guide out-of-town visitors; locals of course ignored the new name and referred to "Mr. Semmes' Tavern." Under Semmes, the City Tavern became a regular stop for stagecoaches on a route between Port Tobacco and Leonardtown, Maryland. Semmes also became a partner in a line running stagecoaches to Annapolis. Stagecoaches passed through a high archway where the building's entrance is today, to load and unload passengers in a courtyard behind the tavern.[7]

The Bank of Columbia was in the building next door (which also still stands), and the bank's directors often met at the City Tavern. In 1801, the new town tax collector announced that he would be at Semmes' Tavern every Tuesday, Thursday, and Saturday, presumably to receive tax payments that he could then immediately deposit in the bank. When the City Tavern building was rehabilitated in the early 1960s, a bricked-up connecting doorway was discovered between the tavern and the bank.[8]

Semmes later renamed the establishment the "Columbian Inn." Perhaps the most intriguing gathering at the City Tavern was a "chemical lecture" in 1820, tickets for which were purchased at a nearby apothecary shop. The advertisement for the lecture promised that "the exhilarating gas will be administered to the first thirty gentlemen registered."[9]

Semmes advertised new prices in 1825. A meal for a passing traveler was 37.5 cents. Overnight accommodations were a dollar a day. A year's room and board could be had for $250. "Best Madeira Wine" was 12.5 cents a glass or $1.50 a bottle. If a lodger wanted a fire in his room, it cost extra.

In 1834, Eleanor Lang took over the City Tavern. She called it the "Georgetown Hotel," but as with previous attempts to name the business, Georgetowners ignored the name and referred to it as "Mrs. Lang's Tavern." Eleanor and her descendants ran a hotel in the building for most of the next sixty years.

Eleanor Lang was a widow, born in Maryland in 1790. In the 1860 census, Eleanor's household consisted of herself, her son John, and five apparently unrelated people. The census does not reveal her residence address, but we can assume she lived in the hotel and that the five other people were guests: a harness maker, a merchant, a clerk, and a woman who gave no occupation, probably a widow. There also was someone who gave his occupation as "servant." He probably was a guest rather than Eleanor's employee, because Eleanor relied on enslaved labor.

In April 1862, Congress passed legislation that freed all enslaved individuals in the District of Columbia, months before President Lincoln would free them in Confederate states by signing the Emancipation Proclamation. Owners of freed individuals were entitled to compensation for their lost property, to be determined by appraisers. Eleanor requested compensation for ten enslaved individuals, four adults and six children. Among them were these six people, whose occupations, taken together, look like a hotel staff:

Mary Dyer, forty-eight, "an excellent cook, washer and ironer."

Lizzie Clark, thirty-three, who "does chamber work and the like."

STAYING OVERNIGHT

Henry Clark, twenty-eight, "a house servant."

George Dyer, twenty-three, "a house servant."

Mary Jane Clark, sixteen, "a good cook."

Eliza Ann Clark, fourteen and a half, "a house servant."

The petition for compensation also listed three other children, ages three months to ten years, and described each individual by color and height. Eleanor was awarded $3,504 for the group.[10]

After Eleanor's death in 1865, her son John took over and continued to operate the hotel, probably until his own death in 1870. The business clearly was successful; in the 1870 census, John estimated the value of his real estate at $28,000 (which of course included the City Tavern Building) and his personal property at $2,000.

There was no hotel in the building for a number of years, but in 1877, Richard W. Morgan opened a new hotel in the building, called the Morgan House. He advertised rates of $2 per day or $9 per week. Morgan was a native Washingtonian born in 1843, who may have worked previously in the printing business. While he was listed in city directories as the hotel's proprietor, John R. Lang, Eleanor's grandson, had some role in the business, probably because he owned the building or had a lease on it.

Extensive regrading of Georgetown streets in 1871 lowered the level of M Street by ten feet, and the basement of the building became its ground floor (see chapter 1).[11]

In 1893, the hotel moved to 1218 Wisconsin Avenue, on the other (north) side of M Street. The relocation apparently did not work out, as the hotel disappeared shortly after that.

During the first half of the twentieth century, the City Tavern's former quarters on M Street housed a fruit market, a paint store, a printer, a grocery store, an auto supply store, and a series of liquor stores.

In 1959, a group of Georgetown residents formed the Georgetown Redevelopment Corporation for the purpose of preserving historic buildings in the neighborhood. The corporation's first purchase was the City Tavern, which otherwise would have been turned into a mirror factory. When John

The City Tavern building in 1959, when it housed a printing business. (*Library of Congress, Historic American Buildings Survey HABS DC,-GEO,57-*)

Colle heard about the building, he recruited a group of twenty people to buy and restore the building. They formed the City Tavern Association, which bought the building from the Redevelopment Corporation in 1960. The building long was the home of the City Tavern Club, a private club. In 2024, the building was sold to investors who announced their intention to operate it as a for-rent event space.[12]

The City Tavern Club in 2014. (*Photo by the author*)

A sign of the Indian King still hangs over the City Tavern entrance, harkening back to the days of Joseph Semmes. (*Photo by the author*)

HOTELS
The Union Hotel

The Union Hotel, on the northeast corner of today's 30th and M Streets, opened in 1796 and would remain in business for decades, under a succession of owners. It seemed to have everything going for it, including a prime location, but it would fail repeatedly.

The hotel was initially prestigious. In June 1800, the federal government relocated from Philadelphia to Washington. On June 3, a local delegation met President John Adams on the outskirts of town and escorted him to the Union Tavern (as it was then known). Marines fired a salute in his honor, and a reception was held at the tavern in Adams's honor.[13]

By August 1824, the building was known as Crawford's Hotel. In 1825 came the first of many announcements about changes in management. In January, under the heading "Union Tavern Revived," Curtis Grubb Late from Philadelphia announced that he had taken over. Another change came later the same year, when Henry W. Tilley announced that he had assumed management, calling it the "Union Hotel."[14]

In 1832, the building burned down. As part of the rebuilding it was doubled in size.

In 1854, a notice in the *Evening Star* announced the first of what would be a series of auctions of the hotel's contents. It listed in detail "superior and well-kept furniture of the Union Hotel, all of which has been laid in new within the past 18 months." The auction began on Monday, November 20, and continued for several days. Each time over the years that an auction of the hotel's contents took place, the newspaper notice exhaustively listed the items to be sold. In this case, the list included seventy-five mattresses, French china dinner and tea ware, wardrobes, window blinds, mahogany wash stands, and "chamber sets."[15]

The hotel remained empty for five years, though the stables continued to operate through at least 1856, run by Hiram Wright.[16] In 1859, newspaper announcements of meetings held there tell us the hotel was back in business. It failed again, however, and in March 1860, the second auction of furniture, bar fixtures, and such was announced.[17] This may be when John Waters took over.

By 1861, Waters was running the building as more of a boardinghouse, occupied by a number of families, some young lawyers, and a music teacher.

STAYING OVERNIGHT

Behind the building were a stable and quarters for enslaved people. Although the public areas were still in good shape, boarders may have had to provide some of their own furniture.

Early in the Civil War, the government compelled Waters to lease the building to the government as a hospital.[18] Louisa May Alcott arrived in Georgetown in December 1862 to work as a nurse in the hospital. In *Hospital Sketches*, her book about the experience, she described the scene:

> *Long trains of army wagons kept up a perpetual rumble from morning until night. Ambulances rattled to and fro with busy surgeons, nurses taking an airing or convalescents going in parties to be fitted for artificial limbs. Strings of sorry looking horses passed, saying as plainly as dumb creatures could, "why in a city full of them is there no horsepital [sic] for us?" Often a cart came by, with several rough coffins in it and no mourners following; barouches, with invalid officers, rolled round the corner and carriage loads of pretty children, with black coachmen, footmen and maids.*
>
> *Round the great stove was gathered the dreariest group I ever saw—ragged, gaunt and pale, mud to the knees with bloody bandages untouched since put on days before; many bundled up in blankets, coats being lost or useless; and all wearing that disheartened look which proclaimed defeat.*[19]

Alcott nursed the soldiers until January 1863, when she fell ill and her father had to come and take her back to Massachusetts.[20]

By 1863, notices reappeared of events held at the hotel, including Professor Goodall's Floral Festival—the building no longer was a hospital. In 1864, an ad announced that the hotel was open "and has been refurnished with extreme care and taste." Board was $2 a day. The ad did not identify the new proprietor.[21]

The year 1866 brought the third auction of the hotel's contents, this time including the opportunity to take over the lease, which had three years to run. The buyer of the lease and probably the contents was Riley A. Shinn.[22]

Shinn, aged forty-one, was from Burlington, New Jersey (near Philadelphia). During the war, he split his time between his New Jersey farm and Georgetown, where he had a beer and ale bottling plant just up the street from the hotel, at Thirtieth and Olive Streets. He also was among the initial officers of the newly formed National Capital Insurance Company.[23]

He prospered wildly during the war. In the 1860 census, he said he owned real estate worth $10,000 and personal property worth $8,000, not insubstantial. In the 1870 census, he cited real estate worth $200,000 and personal property worth $30,000. Those figures would have included the hotel as well as the bottling business.

Shinn embarked on an extensive and time-consuming renovation of the hotel. The remodeled hotel featured a facade in the popular second-empire style, and Shinn referred to the hotel as a "Pocket Tuileries," a reference to the Tuileries Palace in Paris. Additions included fifty more rooms, a bar serving fresh New Jersey oysters, and an ale vault.[24]

In 1867, Shinn leased the hotel restaurant to "the celebrated restaurateur John O'Leary" but informed the public in November that the rest of the building was being run as an apartment hotel, not open to transients. He did rent overnight rooms in two houses next to the hotel. That model apparently did not pan out, and in September 1868, Shinn announced that the hotel again was open to travelers, at $3 per day. The restaurant must have done a good business, though, as Shinn ran a help wanted ad in April 1868 seeking five meat cooks and five vegetable cooks.[25]

Shinn sold his bottling business in early 1871, perhaps to concentrate on the hotel.[26]

In 1871, the District of Columbia government began an extensive public works program that included paving streets throughout the city. Ever enterprising, Shinn became a paving contractor. Ironically, the government assigned Shinn a paving project on M Street near his hotel. The workers had to blast their way through rock at one point, and they accidentally breached a sewer line. The gas fumes filled the hotel and devastated its business for a while.[27]

In 1876, Shinn renamed the business the "West End Hotel." In 1871, Congress had consolidated Georgetown with the City of Washington and with the still rural parts of the District of Columbia, to create a single municipality. Over the next several years, there was an informal effort to rename the neighborhood "West Washington." Shinn's choice of name may have been in response to that.[28] (The effort to rename Georgetown failed—see chapter 1.) Shinn's younger brother Vinecomb Shinn was the hotel manager.

The hotel failed again in 1880. Again there was a newspaper notice, this time for the fourth auction of the hotel's contents, including a piano, feather beds, mattresses, "black walnut chamber suites," walnut parlor furniture, and marble top tables. The ad said the furniture was "made to order by Adolphe & Bro, Philadelphia, for Mr. Shinn." It also said the hotel had about fifty rooms. Riley Shinn returned to farming in New Jersey.[29]

The buyer of the hotel was William C. Davis, who was listed as proprietor in the 1881 directory. He advertised lower room rates, $1.50 a day.

The hotel closed around 1884. It was converted to five apartments in 1908, and the building was torn down in 1935 to make way for a service station.

West Washington Hotel

Joseph Schladt ran a saloon and later a hotel at 1238 Wisconsin Avenue from 1881 to 1937. From 1887 on, the hotel was known as the West Washington Hotel, again reflecting the 1870s movement to call the neighborhood West Washington rather than Georgetown. The restaurant and the bar were notorious, and Schladt had numerous brushes with the law.

Schladt was born in Germany in 1850 and came to the United States in 1866. He traveled on the SS *America*, whose passenger list shows no other Schladts—he either traveled alone or came with relatives who had different last names. He was sixteen years old.[30]

Sometime after that, Schladt became a crewmember on a German ship, probably a merchant vessel. His name and birth year appear on an official list of deserting German sailors, which indicates that he was a "scullery man" and deserted in New York in October 1873, at the end of a return voyage from Bremen. The record identifies his residence as Baltimore.[31]

Schladt first appeared in Washington four years later and worked as a bar manager from 1877 through 1880. In 1881, at the age of thirty-one, Schladt opened his own saloon in rented space at 1238 Wisconsin Avenue, which had been built some time before 1850.[32] In 1883, he bought the building, enabling him to expand and diversify. In 1884, he started calling the saloon a restaurant, and then in 1885 he began calling the business a hotel and restaurant. The earliest mention of the "West Washington Hotel" in the press was an 1891 newspaper item saying that "Mr. Joseph Schladt will put a new front in [sic] the West Washington Hotel."[33] The Schladt family lived in the hotel.

This 2025 photo shows 1238 Wisconsin Avenue, former home of the West Washington Hotel. (*Photo by the author*)

In 1892, the hotel advertised the opening of its "summer garden":

OPENING OF THE ONLY SUMMER GARDEN in Washington, giving concerts every day and night. Special arrangements have been made to entertain my many patrons and friends who may attend WEDNESDAY, JUNE 15, the day of opening.[34]

An undated photograph depicts a space that probably was the summer garden, decorated with hanging paper lanterns and hanging plants. A few men are seated at tables with mugs of beer, but there also is a family with two small children. Small ads emphasizing the summer garden ran in the summers of 1901 and 1902, noting that in the garden there was an orchestrion and (in

STAYING OVERNIGHT

1902) phonograph music. The phonograph was a novel technology then. An orchestrion was an automated device that used piano rolls or a pinned cylinder to produce music through pipes with accompanying percussion.[35]

Census records tell us that besides Schladt's wife and four children, the hotel's residents consisted of hotel employees and middle-class working people: carpenters, painters, restaurant workers, and government clerks. Most of the residents were Schladt's relatives or employees. The number who were neither ranged from a high of six in 1910 to a low of one in 1930. More than half of the people shown in the census were born in D.C., Maryland, or Virginia, which suggests that those individuals were residents rather than transients. Either the hotel was small and more of a boardinghouse than a hotel, or the census taker did not list guests who were transient. Perhaps the bar and restaurant were the real business, and the hotel was a sideline.

Two individuals were there for more than ten years, appearing in the census in both 1900 and 1910: George Hesselberger (more about him shortly) and John Divine, a carpenter. An even longer-term resident was John Kemp, Schladt's German-born nephew, who lost a hand at age sixteen in an accident while cleaning a "cotton seed machine" in the rear of the hotel. (It is unclear what such a machine was doing in a hotel.) Kemp lived in the hotel for at least ten years and, possibly, more than twenty.[36] Among the 1920 residents was Thomas Fullalove, whose brother Richard had sold the building to Schladt back in the 1880s.

Schladt was a homing pigeon enthusiast. The *Evening Star* carried this announcement in 1893:

> *Three days later, Schladt released six pigeons from the front of the hotel. They headed at once for their home coop at 1238 8th Street NW, arriving there in just two minutes.*[37]

> Mr. Schladt of the West Washington Hotel has introduced a cote of carrier pigeons into his establishment. He will send a few down next week to Wert's Wharf, Va., per steamer Harry Randall. There they will be liberated. Several will be turned loose from Baltimore.

Announcement about carrier pigeons at the West Washington Hotel. (Evening Star, *May 3, 1893,* 10)

In 1891, police raided the hotel based on suspicions that "a gaming table was being run . . . by Joseph Schlatt [*sic*]." They arrested several players and confiscated packs of cards, chips, and other paraphernalia.[38]

In 1894, police in disguise arrested Schladt for illegally selling liquor on Sunday to people who were not registered guests of the hotel. Schladt claimed that the man from whom the patrons bought their drinks was not a hotel employee. Schladt's lawyer made much of the fact that the officers had used disguises to sneak in, but the jury was told to ignore that, and Schladt was convicted.[39]

In 1895, the D.C. government refused to renew Schladt's liquor license, which had been opposed (and would be in the future) by the Anti-Saloon League. Schladt responded by placing the hotel in a corporation, of which he was the treasurer. The purported hotel manager was G. A. Hesselberger, who lived in the hotel and was another corporate officer. A hearing in March 1896 was devoted to exploring whether the corporation was a sham and Schladt was actually still in control.

The unsavoriness of the bar was a big issue at the hearing. The league's lawyer said that

> *the character of the place is bad. It is common talk about town that the place is frequented by women from the city.*[40]

Georgetown had been consolidated with the City of Washington for more than twenty years, but this tells us that some Georgetowners still considered Georgetown distinct from "the city" of Washington. After someone mentioned they had seen two drunk couples emerge from the hotel on a Sunday, Schladt replied:

> *But they didn't get drunk in the hotel. Because they were coming out drunk and you saw them is no sign they got anything to drink there.*[41]

Owners of college-oriented Georgetown bars would make exactly the same argument in the 1960s (see chapter 23).[42]

The hotel was ordered closed on March 31, 1896, and more litigation about Schladt's role followed as he sought to get his liquor license back. At the end of a hearing in April, a reporter said, "it is understood that Schladt will retire and application will be made for a new license." A license was granted to Hesselberger on June 30. The summer garden had been closed while the hotel lacked a liquor license, but it promptly reopened on July 18.[43]

There was more excitement in store before the year ended. On October 12, John Collins entered the bar, accused a Mr. Gwynne Tompkins of having come there to meet Collins's wife, and shot Tompkins twice. Schladt hit Collins over the head with a billiard cue, preventing him from firing a third shot, and probably saving Tompkins's life. Mrs. Collins was nowhere in the hotel.[44]

In early 1901, Schladt had different legal problems. In January, he was arrested on charges of illegally tapping into a gas line in order to avoid paying for service. In February, he was found guilty of tapping into a water main. In 1905, Schladt was again convicted of selling liquor on Sunday, and in 1908, a jury convicted him of selling liquor with no license at all.[45]

In 1908, an acetylene tank in the rear of the hotel exploded. The technician who Schladt had brought in to fix the malfunctioning tank was killed. Schladt was severely burned while attempting to rescue the technician and was hospitalized in critical condition.[46]

Congress legislated Prohibition in the District of Columbia effective November 1917, months before the Constitution was amended to enable Prohibition nationwide. Given Schladt's previous difficulties complying with alcoholic beverage rules, it is no surprise that he ran afoul of the Prohibition laws. On April 4, 1918, police raided the hotel and found $1,500 worth of liquor, including a barrel each of gin and whiskey, two barrels of beer, and several cartons of liquor. Schladt posted $2,000 bail (a sizeable sum then), but one of his employees spent the night in jail.

In 1925, federal authorities attempted to sell the hotel for payment of $2,139.38 in taxes, possibly levied on unlawful liquor stored there.[47]

In 1932, there was another raid, which yielded a quantity of liquor that was smaller (nine gallons) but still was sufficient to charge Schladt. Three months later he spent a night in jail when he was unable to pay the $500 fine that the court had given him ninety days to raise. He was released only after his attorney got the fine reduced to $200.[48]

Schladt died in 1937 at age eighty-seven, and the hotel closed. Schladt's daughter and son-in-law continued to live in part of the building, but most of it was vacant. In 1941, Schladt's estate sold the building to William G. "Billy" Martin, who ran a well-known restaurant there (see chapter 21).

The Georgetown Inn

For thirty-five years after the West Washington Hotel closed, there was no hotel in the M Street / Wisconsin Avenue retail core. By 1962, when the Georgetown Inn opened, Georgetown was becoming a tourist, entertainment, and shopping destination. The contrast to the West Washington Hotel could not have been greater.

The 105-room inn was built on the former site of the Fussell-Young Ice Cream Company on Wisconsin Avenue at N Street, only a block up the street from where the West Washington Hotel had been. (For more on Fussell-Young, see chapter 12.) American Metropolitan Investment Company owned the site and leased it to a group including Julius Epstein of Chicago and Collins Bird, who became the inn's first general manager and stayed in that job for thirty years. The lessees built, furnished, and operated the hotel. Seeking to create Washington's most elegant hotel, they hired Chicago decorator Richard Himmel. Of the $3 million spent to build the inn, $450,000 was for interior decor.[49]

Considerable hype preceded the hotel's May 1962 opening, including a multipage advertising spread in the *Evening Star*.[50] Promotional speeches and materials described the prospective guests as "the happy few to whom elegant living is a way of life," and said, "[t]he Georgetown Inn provides the essence of life in the grand style for those chosen few who know how to live it." The spread in the *Star* concluded by saying that

> the Georgetown Inn is conceived in the tradition of the Union Hotel and Suter's Tavern—and it is dedicated to the kind of old Georgetown hospitality that characterized the era when its erstwhile predecessors were in their prime.

The logic of this is a bit hard to follow. Suter's was not remotely luxurious. The Union Hotel aspired to luxury but, as we have seen, failed repeatedly. It is unclear just what the traditional connection was.

The guest rooms in the inn were in several distinct styles. Among them, the "Toile Rooms" had sleigh beds, wing chairs, empire desks, and reproductions of eighteenth-century French oil lamps. The "La Librairie Rooms" had shutters, canvas wallpaper depicting shelves of books, and art nouveaux rocking chairs. Rooms all had bidets, with instruction manuals for guests unfamiliar with such devices. Not only was room service breakfast available, but on request it would be served to guests in bed, at no additional charge. On each floor, a different color predominated: blue, gold, green, red, and black/white.

A butler and maid were assigned to each floor twenty-four hours a day. Guests were escorted to their rooms not by a bellman but by an assistant manager, who introduced them to the two servants. The inn had a Rolls Royce available to transport guests. Guests registered using quill pens, and message slips, instead of being headed "while you were out," said "whilst thou were out."

There were four restaurants, called "The Four Georges." The George I Room had English decor from the early eighteenth century when George I was the king of England. The George II Room served seafood, and it featured an azure skylight and a waterfall that sprayed down one wall. The George III Room was the most formal, and the George IV Room's decor revolved around an eighteenth-century Waterford Chandelier, under which the food was salads and other cold dishes. Each room served a different kind of cuisine, but all four menus were available in any of the four rooms. Despite the formality, there also were playful touches—waiters wore brown tailcoats with pink linings, for example.

The hotel was a big hit when it opened. The first affair held at the inn was a benefit dinner for the Washington Ballet Guild, at which the Duke and Duchess of Windsor were guests. The local fashion industry was a source of loyal customers who held frequent fashion shows there. The inn served as the Washington base for the seven original Project Mercury astronauts. Other frequent guests included Vice President Hubert Humphrey, Dallas Cowboys owner Clint Murchison, members of the Kennedy family, the cast of the film *The Exorcist*, and Marlon Brando. In 1976, the Four Georges closed for the first time for a private party, which celebrated *Playboy* magazine's "Girls of Washington" spread.[51]

The prices were high for the time, though they seem laughable today for such luxury. When the hotel opened the rates were $20 for singles, $25 for doubles, and no more than $60 for suites.

Luxury and service like this require well-trained and motivated employees, fastidious property maintenance, intensive management, and customers willing to pay very high prices. All of these things are difficult to economically sustain. Ultimately the inn had to lower its prices and reduce some of the luxurious perks. Eighteen months after it opened, the inn advertised rooms from $13 a night.[52]

In 1968, Collins Bird and some other investors bought the hotel lease from American Metropolitan, eliminating the rent they had been paying. Bird and his colleagues continued to run the hotel for another twenty-two years.[53]

The inn's piano bar was popular in the 1970s, featuring pianist Mel Clement, a forty-five-year veteran of the music business. A piece in the *Washington Post* described Clement as "a large, grandfatherly, tuxedo-clad gentleman, with crinkly eyes and thinning, slicked-back hair . . . super-genial."[54]

Donald Dresden, the *Washington Post*'s restaurant critic, gave the Four Georges scathing reviews in 1970 and 1973, complaining of cold food and even saying that "no one seems to be running the place."[55] In 1981, a relocated Rive Gauche replaced the Four Georges (see chapter 21). In 1983, another change of restaurants was announced in this curious fashion:

**WE'D LIKE TO ANNOUNCE A CHANGE THAT
MAKES ABSOLUTELY NO DIFFERENCE**
WASHINGTON'S PREMIERE RESTAURANT IS
NOW CALLED LES AMBASSADEURS
Everything else at our Georgetown Inn location remains the same.
Our fine continental cuisine.
Our legendary service.[56]

Bird and his partners sold the inn in 1980 to a Washington-based investment group. By 1991, the hotel had become part of the troubled real estate portfolio of Washington investor and philanthropist Conrad Cafritz. The hotel closed in September of that year but reopened the following spring. It still is in business in 2025, though it has changed hands at least once more.[57]

CHAPTER 21

Restaurants

GEORGETOWN WAS NOT ALWAYS A DINING DESTINATION. ON WISCONSIN Avenue and M Street, there were about fifteen restaurants from 1914 to 1930. That number grew to twenty in the early 1930s and twenty-eight in 1935, which is curious in light of the Great Depression. The number remained in the high twenties or low thirties until the 1960s, when Georgetown became more of an attraction, and the number of restaurants on Wisconsin Avenue and M Street grew to forty. That was followed by a spurt of spectacular growth in the late 1970s and 1980s. While the 1981 opening of the Georgetown Park mall increased the number of stores in the neighborhood, it did not contribute many new restaurants; in 1985, only seven of the neighborhood's eighty-seven restaurants were in the mall. The number of Georgetown restaurants began to decline in the late 1990s, as other neighborhoods became competitors for dining customers, but there still were sixty in 2023.

A history of Georgetown restaurants would be a book in itself. In this chapter, even more than others, we are limited to examining snapshots of just a few.

EATING AT TAVERNS

In the eighteenth and into the nineteenth century, someone seeking a meal in Georgetown would have gone to a tavern. Some taverns were located on or near the waterfront. Others were located on the northern side of town, to serve farmers and others coming to sell crops and buy supplies. And some were located in the center of town, to serve the local population.

Taverns provided lodging and stables as well as food. There is no reason to think the food was memorable, though occasionally festive dinners were held in taverns. Food generally was served at an appointed time rather than as diners came and went.

For more about taverns, see chapter 20.

Restaurants began to appear in Washington in the early nineteenth century. They were more convenient for diners, who could eat at times of their own choosing and at private rather than communal tables. Restaurants had menus from which diners could order what they wanted instead of accepting a fixed bill of fare.[1]

THE RODIER FAMILY

A. P. Rodier ran an oyster house and hotel on what is today Thirtieth Street just north of M Street. In 1822, he advertised that he had just opened a tavern on Bridge (M) Street. The ad said that the tavern had "a most excellent billiard table" and that the tavern was "for those who whilst they seek the freedom of a public house wish to avoid its bustle and often licentiousness." Later that year, Rodier advertised an oyster house and billiard room at a different location, on High Street (Wisconsin Avenue).[2] Both businesses were gone by 1830.

Thirty years later, sometime between 1853 and 1858, an Anthony Rodier opened the White House Hotel and Billiard Parlor on Wisconsin Avenue near the C&O Canal. This was Charles Anthony Rodier, born in Georgetown in 1827. He sometimes went by Charles but, more often, by Anthony; we will refer to him as Charles to avoid confusion. He was not A. P. Rodier's son—Charles's father was Jean François Philibert Rodier, an immigrant from France. Given that the two men had the same last name and ran the same kind of business, however, there may well have been some relationship. By 1867, the business had expanded to include bowling facilities.

Charles's older brother James worked in the business with him. The exact nature of James's role is unclear. In 1864, the city directory suggested they were partners. In 1867, it listed Anthony as proprietor of the restaurant and James as running the bowling alley.

In the 1870 census, Charles Rodier's household also included Richard Hall, who was a bartender but was only fifteen years of age. He probably worked in Rodier's restaurant.

White House Restaurant
AND BOWLING SALOON,
33 High Street.

The Bar is Stocked with Choice Wines Liquors and Cigars.

☞ Meals at all hours. Oysters and Game in season.

Anthony Rodier, Prop.

A 1974 ad for the White House Restaurant. (Boyd's Directory of the District of Columbia, *1974, 557*)

After the White House closed in 1875, Charles may have worked as a bartender in the 1880s. He also was a caterer and known for his recipe for terrapin stew. He was active in the Fraternal Order of Elks, and with the announcement of his death in 1901, there appeared an announcement of a special meeting of the local lodge to honor their deceased brother.[3]

LUNCH COUNTERS

The days of fine dining in Georgetown came in the 1960s. Before that, most of the restaurants were casual. Between 1910 and 1960, casual restaurants with the word *lunch* in their names were common in the neighborhood. Among them were Coney Island Lunch, Connecticut Lunch, Earl's Quick Lunch, Gem Lunch, Everybody's Lunch, Georgetown Lunch (of course), Kymingham Lunch, Prospect Lunch, Ramey's Lunch, Expert Lunch, and University Lunch.

The Augers

The owner of Expert Lunch was George Auger, who came to the United States from Turkey in 1906 at age fifteen. Auger moved to Washington around 1920, working as a chef. Two years later, he opened his own restaurant on 14th Street NW, which he ran for five years.

It is not clear what he did for the next year or two, but Auger opened a new restaurant in 1928 at 2919 M Street NW, in rented space that had been

Expert Lunch (2919 M Street) in 1935. (*Library of Congress, Historic American Buildings Survey HABS DC,GEO,50-*)

RESTAURANTS

a tailor shop. A 1935 photograph tells us he called it "Expert Lunch," though he did not list it in city directories under that name. The photo was taken not long before he closed the business. The building still stands and remains in use as a restaurant.

Auger's son Ulysses grew up to have a big impact on the restaurant business in Washington. After dropping out of high school and working as a busboy to help support the family, Ulysses, whose nickname was "Blackie," opened Blackie's House of Beef on 22nd Street NW in 1952. Capitalizing on the increased availability of and demand for beef after wartime rationing, Blackie's became one of Washington's best-known restaurants. He later opened other restaurants, all with names that included the word *black*. He briefly owned Britt's Cafeteria in Georgetown (discussed later in the chapter). He also was an investor in two Washington hotels (the Madison and the Marriott on 22nd Street) and in the Madison National Bank.[4]

Newton Malone and Gem Lunch

Newton A. Malone ran a restaurant in the 3400 block of M Street for thirty-four years. He is notable for having lived and worked on that one block for his entire adult life.

Malone was born in Sharpsburg, Maryland, in 1885. By 1900, his parents had moved to Georgetown, and the family lived at 3500 M Street. His two older brothers and their father Charles were day laborers. The C&O Canal was behind the house, with about 150 feet of vacant land in between. Charles and the brothers probably worked many days in the port or on the canal. Malone completed school only through the sixth grade.

In 1911, when he was twenty-six years old, he opened a restaurant at 3414 M Street. It probably was the construction of the Key Bridge that in 1920 caused him to move it across M Street from its original location to number 3401. He and his family moved with it and lived upstairs. The restaurant became known as Gem Lunch. We do not know just when he adopted that name, but it was in use by the 1930s.

Restaurants demand hard work. Malone told the 1940 census taker that he worked seventy-hour weeks.

In 1987, Robert Sellers, who had lived in the 3400 block of M Street in the 1930s, reminisced about those days and about some of the shops on the block. Malone's eatery was not a genteel place, and Sellers described it in colorful terms:

> Newt Malone's was a horse of an entirely different hue. My Uncle John, of the rhinoplastic nose and the never-empty glass, sat quietly in the corner and kept an eye out for the lads from #7. Uncle John "took numbers." His compatriots comprised a company that came as close as any to a redneck saloon. Brawls were commonplace, ladies of the night spiced the air space, raids were frequent and payoffs predictable. The Gem Lunch was wonderful.[5]

"Took numbers" refers to Uncle John's role in an illegal numbers game, taking numbers from individuals placing bets. The "lads from #7" refers to police officers from the 7th Precinct, of which Georgetown was part.

Malone died in 1949. After his death, the space continued to house a restaurant called Gem Lunch through the mid-1950s, but we do not know who ran it. The space later became Mac's Pipe and Drum, a bar and restaurant that attracted a youthful crowd and was at times viewed with suspicion by neighborhood residents. (For a photo of the building, see chapter 23.)

Columbia Lunch and Britt's Cafeteria

William Britt was in the restaurant business in Georgetown for twenty-nine years. After he left the business, others bought and continued to run his restaurant, Britt's Cafeteria, for another twenty-eight years.

Born in Washington in 1877, Britt moved to Georgetown in 1900 and, for some years, worked as a clerk. In 1912, he opened a restaurant at 3200 M Street, on the southwest corner with Wisconsin Avenue. He named it "Columbia Lunch." Britt may have been in partnership with Walter T. Weaver, the founder of Weaver's hardware store, though that arrangement, if there was one, ended in 1918.[6]

In 1900, a crowd gathered outside to see election returns that were projected from a stereopticon projector in Columbia Lunch onto a screen on the south wall of O'Donnell's drugstore across M Street.[7]

In 1924, Britt moved diagonally across the intersection to 1205 Wisconsin Avenue, where he was the northerly neighbor of the Farmers and Mechanics' Bank (now PNC Bank). The bank was his landlord.

RESTAURANTS

In 1930, Britt closed Columbia Lunch and opened a new restaurant called Britt's Cafeteria, just up the street at 1211 Wisconsin Avenue. Britt's Cafeteria would remain in that space for thirty-seven years. See chapter 25 for a photo of the building.

In 1941, Britt sold the business to John Heatwold. (Britt died four years later.) The restaurant became a family operation. Heatwold and his son and daughter, James and Janet, ran the business during the day, and another son, John, ran it at night.

Britt's under the Heatwolds was known for Southern comfort food. An *Evening Star* article in 1966 described the menu:

> [H]ot homemade biscuits, red-eye gravy, Southern-fried steak, grits, baked Virginia ham, old-fashioned chicken and dumplings, Southern-fried butter fish, fresh collard greens, fried apples and cornbread.[8]

Prices were low—the reporter said it was hard to spend more than $1.50 for dinner; that was cheap even in the 1960s.[9]

Britt's was open at all hours, and it was the place to go for people who were hungry in the middle of the night. Britt's would close at 8 p.m. and reopen at midnight, using the time in between to get ready for the late-night rush. It was a hangout for other restaurant owners who had closed for the night, cab drivers and other night workers, and entertainers who had finished their evening acts. Late-night patrons also included Georgetown University students who would drink Britt's coffee while they pulled all-nighters.[10]

Customers also included politicians and celebrities, among them Secretary of State Dean Rusk. The Alger Hiss case in the late 1940s and early 1950s provided another kind of celebrity customer. The controversial espionage case against Hiss, a State Department official, became an issue in the 1948 election and after. The case hinged in part on a conversation that journalist Whittaker Chambers claimed to have had with Hiss—in Britt's Cafeteria. The role of then-congressman Richard Nixon in the case provided an initial boost to Nixon's political career.[11]

In 1966, Heatwold sold Britt's to Ulysses (Blackie) Auger, who had grown up upstairs from Gem Lunch (discussed earlier in the chapter). Auger's plan was to keep Britt's more or less as it was, except for expanding its hours from twenty per day to twenty-four and expanding the kitchen. That did not last long; he closed Britt's in 1969.[12]

HEON'S RESTAURANT

In the 1920s and 1930s, George and Peter Heon and their partner Henry Mantzuranis ran a series of food-related businesses in Georgetown, frequently changing the type of store in apparent search for the best result. At various times and places they ran a fruit market, two candy stores, and a delicatessen. By 1938, they had slimmed the empire down to one business, Heon's Restaurant, located in a building at 3150 M Street that they had purchased between 1918 and 1923.

This 2025 photo shows the building at 3150 M Street that from 1920 to 1967 was the home of Heon's Restaurant and the Heon family confectionary that preceded it. Later this was the location of Nathan's restaurant. (*Photo by the author*)

RESTAURANTS

The brothers were immigrants from Greece. George was the first to arrive, in 1897, when he was seventeen years old. Peter, nicknamed Pete, arrived in 1911 at age eighteen. George started out with a short-lived florist business, and then a fruit stand in Alexandria, Virginia.

George and Pete Heon expanded into other businesses. In 1927, they opened a swimming pool at Chevy Chase Lake, which operated until 1972. In the 1940s, each of the brothers began investing in real estate. Between 1922 and 1956, George bought thirty-one lots and buildings in Georgetown, in Southeast Washington just south of the Capitol, and in other locations. Pete bought several buildings along the south side of M Street just east of the restaurant.[13] In 1949, they took over the Dumbarton Theater at 1349 Wisconsin Avenue (see chapter 24).

George Heon died in 1959, and his sons ran the restaurant after that. Pete apparently was not active in the restaurant business by then, perhaps

This sign of the Heons' past presence remains today at the front door of 3150 M Street. (*Photo by the author*)

focusing on the family's other businesses. Heon's Restaurant closed in 1968. Pete died in 1979.

We know little about the menu at Heon's. The Heons did not advertise in the newspapers, and restaurant critics never got there. We do have one hint about the decor, however. In 1964, George's sons remodeled the restaurant and renamed it the Heritage House. Son Louis told a reporter "for many years Heon's was a working man's restaurant. The redecoration gave the restaurant a more traditional Georgetown flavor." Among other things, carpeting replaced sawdust floors.[14]

THE MARTIN FAMILY

Martin's Tavern is the oldest restaurant in Georgetown today and is thought to be the oldest family-owned restaurant in Washington. Four generations of the founding Martin family have run the business. They all have the first name William, and so to avoid confusion we will call them Williams 1–4. Williams 1 and 2, William S. Martin and his son William G. Martin, opened the tavern at 1264 Wisconsin Avenue in 1933, just after the repeal of Prohibition. Because William 2 lived in Virginia, the license was issued to William 1, who lived in the District. It is possible that rumors of William 2 having a relationship with bootleggers during Prohibition may have been an additional impediment to him being the licensee.[15]

Athletic talent ran in the family. William 2 was a baseball standout at Georgetown University and went on to play professional baseball for the Boston Braves and the New York Giants. William 3 went to Georgetown Preparatory School and Georgetown University, and he too was an athlete, a Golden Glove boxing champion.[16]

Martin's Tavern became popular soon after opening. Being the first tavern in Georgetown after Prohibition had to have helped. Martin's strived for respectability, enforcing a dress code and frowning on table-hopping. Some of the waiters in the early days were brusque, however. *Evening Star* reviewer Richard Slusser, comparing his experience dining at Martin's in 1971 with his earlier visits back in the 1940s, said "the waiters no longer live up to their reputation of being the rudest in town."[17]

Gangster Emmitt Warring was such a fan of Martin's crabcakes that, in 1939 and 1940, while serving a prison term for tax evasion, he somehow managed to have them delivered to him at Lorton Reformatory.[18]

RESTAURANTS

Martin's Tavern in 2025. (*Photo by the author*)

Martin's attracted some famous customers. Every president from Harry Truman through George W. Bush ate there at some point. Senate Majority Leader Lyndon Johnson and House Speaker Sam Rayburn (a longtime friend of William 2) were regular patrons, sitting in the back room called "The Dugout" (note the baseball metaphor). John F. Kennedy had breakfast at Martin's most Sundays after Mass, and proposed marriage to Jacqueline Bouvier in a booth (now known as the "Proposal Booth"). Office of Strategic Service (OSS) head William Donovan met with other OSS agents at Martin's. The tavern later was a meeting place for KGB chief of foreign counterintelligence Oleg Kalugin and FBI agent David Major. Accused spy Alger Hiss also was seen at Martin's. The tavern was one of the settings for the novel *Murder in Georgetown*, written by Harry Truman's daughter Margaret, a customer of Martin's.[19]

In his 1971 review, Slusser complimented Martin's on its fried soft shell crabs, broiled red snapper, and breaded veal cutlet. The prices back then of course seem low today: forty cents for a small tossed salad and $1.50 for a shrimp cocktail. Slusser recommended Martin's as a good place to take a foreign visitor looking for American food.[20]

When William 2 died in 1949, Billy Martin (William 3) took over the business.

In 1941, William 2 had paid $5,000 to buy the nearby building at 1236–38 Wisconsin Avenue that, from the 1880s until 1937, had housed the West Washington Hotel.[21] (See chapter 20 for more on the hotel and a photo of the building.) The building, which still stands, is located a block south of Martin's Tavern, at the corner with Prospect Street. William 2 began remodeling the building in 1941, but wartime restrictions forced him to stop work. In 1943, the public housing authority, trying to address the wartime housing shortage in Washington, leased the building and created fourteen apartments on the upper floors. The ground floor remained vacant.

In 1953, William 3 opened an upscale restaurant in the ground floor space. He called it "Billy Martin's Carriage House." In an oral history interview years later, William 4 recalled an article referring to the Carriage House as "the White House of restaurants in Washington, D.C."[22] An ad in 1956 said:

> *Complete dinners for the entire family are offered by* **Billy Martin's Carriage House**, *where famous people meet famous food. . . . When tourists express a desire to visit a restaurant then it must have a national reputation. Such is the standing of* **Billy Martin's Carriage House**, *famous for its wonderful food and economical prices.*[23]

The space was divided into several rooms. The Georgetown Room and the red-decorated Sam Rayburn Room were the most formal. The Horse Parlor had dark walls and an equestrian theme. A private event space with a large wine vault was called the Cognac Room. The Snuggery was a piano bar. An ad in 1976 said "Retreat to the SNUGGERY. Relax with a drink at the intimate piano bar as John Eaton plays your favorites." (Pianist John Eaton was still performing in Washington as of 2022.)[24]

One of the bars, thirty-five feet long and built of mahogany, had been in the West Washington Hotel since 1870. William 3 told a reporter that the lamps hanging on either side of the entrance had hung on a carriage used by President William McKinley.[25]

Like Martin's Tavern, Billy Martin's Carriage House attracted well-known diners. William 4 recalled his father telling him that Jacqueline Kennedy and Marlon Brando had waited in a long line for a table.[26]

In 2011, Georgetown resident Al Wheeler reminisced about the food:

> *The flounder, they get a small flounder, about that big, and they cook it in bacon grease. . . . It was delicious. [O]f course, the eggs Benedict was tremendous. And they had good roast beef. It was a very good restaurant.*[27]

In 1976, Michael O'Harro, a promoter from California, leased the Sam Rayburn Room and opened the Tramps disco there. William 3 invested $100,000. William 4 later recalled that Tramps "was a huge success, was well-known all up and down the East Coast [and was] well-known all the way to the West Coast as being one of the first discotheques on the East Coast, way before New York had discotheques."[28]

Disco was a fad, but while it was in vogue Tramps made money. O'Harro said in 1978 that William 3's $100,000 investment would yield $400,000 profit on a gross of $900,000. A disc jockey cost less than live entertainment would, and drinks at Tramps averaged $2.50, which was steep then. In 1978, Tramps expanded, and the other rooms in the Carriage House were remodeled into a more informal restaurant called "Tramps at the Carriage House."[29]

Tramps attracted celebrities. Among those seen there were Sylvester Stallone, Telly Savalas (who bought wine for everyone in the place), Olivia Newton-John, Cher, Pelé, Margaret Trudeau, Peter O'Toole, Peggy Fleming, Fleetwood Mac band members, Cliff Robertson, and Lloyd Bridges.[30]

O'Harro was colorful and then some. He was *Cosmopolitan* magazine's Bachelor of the Month and made the *National Enquirer*'s list of Ten Most Eligible Bachelors. When interviewed by a reporter in 1978, he wore a white jumpsuit and patent leather platform shoes.[31]

Tramps closed in 1982 and the Carriage House not long after. William 4 remembered that the hundred-year-old building was deteriorating and his father chose to close rather than pay for the extensive repairs that were needed.[32]

William 4 started working for his father at Martin's Tavern in 1982, initially as a bartender. William 4's parents had divorced in the late 1960s, and the relationship between father and son was fraught. Rather than inheriting the tavern, William 4 had to buy it from his father. William 3's initial asking price was $2 million, but negotiation brought it down to $1.1 million, enabling William 4 to complete the deal in 2001 using several layers of financing.[33]

William 4 tells the story of a customer who was refused when he requested that the chef further cook a steak that was not well done as ordered. William 4 intervened and ordered the cook to make it more well done. When approached years later by William 4 about financing for his purchase of the tavern, the former customer recalled the experience with the steak and agreed to help.[34]

RIVE GAUCHE

At the top end of the Georgetown gastronomic scale was Rive Gauche, once widely deemed the best French restaurant in Washington and a spawning ground for dozens of chefs who started other French eateries in the city.

The postwar years through the 1950s were not good years for fine dining in Washington. During the Great Depression and the war, people had gotten out of the habit of eating out, and some wartime price controls and rationing continued into the early 1950s. People who ate out generally did so at places in their neighborhoods.[35] Rive Gauche was a big factor in changing this, not only by virtue of the food it served but also because the people who learned the business at Rive Gauche went on to create other high-end restaurants.

Blaise Gherardi, who was born in Corsica and came to the United States from France in 1949, opened his first restaurant, Place Vendome, on 17th Street NW, in 1952. In 1957, he moved the restaurant to 3200 M Street (at the southwest corner with Wisconsin Avenue) and renamed it "Rive Gauche–Place Vendome." (*Rive gauche* means "left bank"). The space had been a Peoples Drug Store for twenty years, and before that it was the home of Columbia Lunch (discussed earlier in the chapter).

In April 1957, Gherardi ran classified ads for three days seeking waiters and busboys "for new restaurant," but saying nothing else about job qualifications. Apparently he did not get the kind of applicants he wanted, and so he ran this more specific ad a month later:

RESTAURANTS

Restaurant requires waiters with French service experience and knowledge of French language. Also experienced busboy. Apply in person, 3200 M st. n.w. (White only.)[36]

Most of these were unusual qualifications in Washington in the 1950s. The "white only" requirement was not.

Gherardi's objective was to run the best restaurant in town. He hired his chefs from France, making scouting trips there as necessary to seek talent, and arranging special visas for them.[37] Although he assumed the persona of a temperamental chef, Gherardi told a reporter that he himself never cooked anything except that he would "open a can of Campbell's soup on Sundays. I am so sick of this damn French food."[38]

Customers arriving at Rive Gauche were met and seated by Jannine Cusson, who had previously been a hat check clerk at Place Vendome. She was known for her strong personality, and the *Washington Post*'s Sally Quinn described her as a "blonde Gallic terror" who had distinct likes and dislikes and was feared by many. On the other hand, Donald Dresden, the *Post*'s restaurant critic, said that she "charms a variety of diners . . . and runs the place with the efficiency of an airline hostess that she once was." Her title was manager, but she was quick to say that she had nothing to do with the kitchen or the cooking.[39]

To say Gherardi was temperamental is an understatement. One chef whose departure led to a lawsuit told the court that his reason for leaving was not money but dissension in the kitchen. As Gherardi himself put it, "I am not a masochist. If anyone who works for me does something wrong, I fire him. I have quite a temper." In 1971, Gherardi fired Jannine Cusson after she had worked for him for almost twenty years. He also was free with public criticism of his alumni, holding forth at length about their faults and mistakes in a lengthy *Washington Post* article in 1973.[40]

The alumni succeeded elsewhere, however, founding a series of French eateries that dominated the Washington restaurant scene for years, including Sans Souci, Chez Camille, La Nicoise, Jean-Pierre, and Le Bagatelle.[41]

The reviews of Rive Gauche were favorable, but reviewers did note the prices. In 1969, *Evening Star* critic John Rosson described his four-course meal: a cocktail to start, then vichyssoise, sliced tomato and cucumber salad, quenelles de mantua (poached dumplings topped with tiny shrimp in a shrimp sauce), and for dessert diced fruit au Kirsch, all washed down with a $4 half bottle of Chablis Premier Cru. The check was $15.87. His comment was that Rive Gauche "is worth every dime of it. If you've got it, the Rive Gauche is one of the places to spend it. . . . Start saving your pennies." He did note that a condescending attitude on the part of the staff seemed to have been corrected since his previous visit. The *Washington Post*'s review that same year was similar.[42]

In 1973, Gherardi sold the restaurant, citing arthritis that made moving around difficult. The buyers were an Alexandria investor group, together with existing Rive Gauche maître d' Pierre Sosnitsky and chef Michel Laudier. Sosnitsky and Laudier, both in their twenties, had a 50 percent interest. The investors told a reporter that because of that employee ownership they intended to be hands off and let the staff run the business. Gherardi died five years after the sale.[43]

The decor in Rive Gauche was part of the experience: banquettes covered in burgundy leather, a high ceiling, an impressive crystal chandelier, and framed oil paintings.[44] The new owner group took that to a higher level in 1974, when they arranged for a long-term loan of Cezanne's "House of Picasso at Ste. Victoire" to hang in the dining room. Extra security was necessary because the painting was worth $250,000—they would take it off the wall and put it in the safe every night.[45]

Rive Gauche, like other upscale Georgetown restaurants, attracted a celebrity clientele. John and Jacqueline Kennedy dined there from time to time during his presidency, and Jacqueline continued to do so after John's death when she lived in the neighborhood. Other well-known patrons, according to Gherardi, included Robert McNamara, Frank Sinatra, and David Frost. As one of his reasons for firing Cusson, Gherardi said she made Marjorie Merriweather Post stand and wait for hours and then refused her a table.[46]

In 1981, Rive Gauche moved up Wisconsin Avenue to space in the Georgetown Inn. It closed three years later. In the old space at Wisconsin and M Street it left behind Place Vendome, which was converted to a French brasserie under the name Place Vendome–Rive Droite (meaning "right bank"). Reviewers said good things about the food and noted that the prices were lower, the decor was less stuffy, and the atmosphere was more stylish. It only lasted a couple of years.[47]

BISTRO FRANÇAIS

Among Rive Gauche alumni who went on to success on their own was Gerard Cabrol, who opened Bistro Français in 1975, in partnership with Jean-Paul Amsellem and Alain Gooss, who were investors in other French restaurants in Washington. Bistro Français occupied two adjoining buildings with the dividing wall removed: 3124 M Street, which had been the home of the Silver Dollar Café (discussed later in the chapter), was turned into a little French café, and 3128 M Street, which had been William Brodofsky's People's Store (see chapter 5) became a somewhat more formal dining room. A partial photo of Bistro Français appears on the cover of this book.

Cabrol was from Castres, France (near Toulouse), and worked for a time as a chef at the Hotel Plaza Athenee in Paris. As Cabrol told the story, one day a hotel guest who had noticed his skill came up to him and offered him a job in Washington at four times the salary. The guest was Blaise Gherardi, proprietor of Rive Gauche in Georgetown. Cabrol accepted the offer and headed for Washington.[48]

Cabrol's vision for his own future was a restaurant specializing in rotisserie chicken. In 1975, after two years at Rive Gauche, he leased the two buildings on M Street and launched Bistro Français. There were two thousand customers in the first three days.

On opening day the rotisserie was not yet installed, but soon it arrived from France. While the restaurant offered a broad menu, a signature dish was the "poulet Bistro Français," chicken sprinkled on the inside with thyme, brushed on the outside with butter, and roasted on a spit for forty-five minutes.[49]

Two weeks after the opening, John Rosson of the *Evening Star* raved about the food, which included traditional French fare like trout amandine, sole meunière, and sauteed frog legs. He called the pastries "outstanding." Donald Dresden of the *Washington Post* was similarly positive about both the food and the service when he reviewed Bistro Français four months later.[50]

The decor of Bistro Français was a relaxed and modern yet still elegant version of French. The walls were light, the floors were wood, the chairs were country style, and plants and art exhibit posters were scattered about. The round windows from the Silver Dollar Café days were replaced by plate glass windows to allow in more light.

Perhaps the most unusual characteristic of Bistro Français was its late-night hours. At the time of Rosson's early review, the restaurant remained open until 5 a.m., seven days a week. Cabrol later dialed that back a bit, but in 2001 it still was open until 3 a.m. on weekdays and 4 a.m. on weekends. The late night crowd included entertainers after their shows ended and chefs from other restaurants who were looking for a bite after their own places closed.[51]

In 2015, the restaurant lost its lease on 3128 M Street but continued on in the 3124 M Street space, which Cabrol and Amsellem had bought in 1985. It finally closed in 2016.[52]

ECONOMICAL FRENCH RESTAURANTS

French restaurants in Washington in the 1960s and 1970s ran the gamut from high end to more economical. Two of the more popular economical ones had roots in Georgetown.

Maison des Crepes

Jacques Vivien, born in France, came to Washington after working as a chef at the Ritz and Crillon hotels in Paris. He worked briefly at Rive Gauche and, in 1960, opened the high-end Jockey Club Restaurant, known for its good food and popularity with the Kennedys and other glamorous people.

In 1968, Vivien and Hugo Fregnan opened the first Maison des Crepes at 1305 Wisconsin Avenue, in space that had been occupied for ten years by the Tasty Bake Shop and, for forty years before that, by a series of grocery stores. At one time it had been a movie theater (see chapter 24).

As the name suggests, the menu consisted almost entirely of crepes, both main courses and desserts. The concept was so novel that restaurant critics had to explain to readers what crepes were: "those paper-thin French 'pancakes' filled with a wide choice of delicacies."[53]

Maison des Crepes became wildly popular. In June 1968, the *Evening Star*'s restaurant critic John Rosson gave it a review that most restaurateurs would die for, confessing to be a "glutton" for Vivien's crepes, describing the house salad as "plain but remarkable," calling the interior decor "a

Maison des Crepes initially occupied the tall building in this photo, at 1305 Wisconsin Avenue. Earlier the building had housed the Scenic Theater. (*Photo by the author*)

delight," and observing that "Maison des Crepes" was "superbly" managed. He described the decor in detail:

> *The setting is right out of the French countryside. The walls are done in old sides of barns. Here and there one sees old farm implements—from hayrakes to plowheads. The tables are small and candlelit. And the pretty young waitresses (most of them are French) are in provincial costumes.*

"Don't miss it. It's a spot for everybody," he concluded.[54]

Two years later, Donald Dresden, the *Washington Post*'s restaurant critic, was less enthused. His review was titled "Maison des Crepes probably won't remind you of your last trip to Paris," and he complained that his crepe was served cold.[55]

Nevertheless, Vivien and Fregnan were on to something. In 1968, they opened a second Maison des Crepes in Bethesda, and in 1973, they opened a third in Alexandria. The decor and menu were the same in all three. Entrée crepes included asparagus béchamel; caviar with sour cream; piperade and ham; and crabmeat in a white wine sauce. In 1973, prices for crepes ran from $1.35 to $3.50. In 1976, they expanded the Georgetown branch into the space next door.[56]

In the mid-1970s, Vivien and Fregnan, and their newly added partner Serge Barbe, became unhappy with the produce they were buying; they saw quality declining while prices rose, and they missed the quality that was available in markets in France. Vivien flew to France and recruited Louis Calza, a French farmer he knew slightly who previously had worked in the United States as a gardener. The partners helped Calza return to the United States and start a farm along the Rappahannock River in Sperryville, Virginia. Calza used French agricultural techniques to produce the kind of greens and vegetables they were looking for, along with crayfish and escargots. Fregnan drove two round trips a week from Washington to Sperryville (eighty miles each way) to pick up the produce. This was an extraordinary effort to supply a low-priced restaurant. We do not know how long the arrangement continued.[57]

Things changed in 1979. According to the *Evening Star*'s restaurant columnist, the popularity of small, inexpensive French cafés declined, and French restaurants with more substantial menus (akin to brasseries in France) became the thing, offering a middle ground between the cafés and the top tier. Vivien sold his share of the business to Fregnan, who turned the Georgetown Maison des Crepes into Brasserie-Bretonne. The brasserie continued for seven years, closing around 1986.

Chez Odette

The other "bargain" French restaurant of the period was Chez Odette. In the mid-1950s, Mrs. Odette Pantelich, from St. Vrain, France, opened Chez Odette with her husband Voya, at 3027 M Street. The space soon proved too small. "We wanted a bigger place and one where we could serve drinks," Mrs.

RESTAURANTS

Odette said. So in 1959, the Odettes opened a second, larger location just down and across the street at 3063 M Street, in space that since the 1930s had been home to the Chaconas family's restaurant (see chapter 12).[58]

Rather than closing the original Chez Odette right away, the Odettes ran both locations for several years, under the same name. One can imagine the confusion of out-of-town visitors looking to dine at Chez Odette. In 1962 or 1963, the Odettes finally closed the 3027 M Street branch.

John Rosson, the *Evening Star*'s restaurant critic, was fond of Chez Odette. In a 1961 review headlined "Truly, Truly French," he noted the presence in Washington of top-notch French restaurants like Rive Gauche, and then went on to say the following:

> *But the District also has a French restaurant like the ones you'd find on the Left Bank—small, intimate and informal, the type most often patronized by Paris' man-on-the-street. This, Parisians will tell you, is how the Frenchman, who isn't actually a millionaire, actually eats when he dines out.*
>
> *Aside from a few paintings, the Chez Odette décor is practically nil, yet you know in an instant that it's French. . . . It makes no attempt to be elegant, yet among its habitués are members of the diplomatic corps, Capitol Hill legislators and a number of well-known gourmets.*[59]

Reviews ten years later were just as good, and prices were still low by the standards of that time (and laughably low by today's standards). The only entrée over $3 was a $4 filet mignon with béarnaise sauce. A meal consisting of soup, the filet mignon, a side order of vegetables, a salad, and coffee came to $5.60.[60]

One Georgetown resident who entertained a guest from New York at Chez Odette described it as "just the kind of fun comfortable place you would take a slightly, not necessarily wacky but certainly highly inventive artist from New York."[61]

Chez Odette closed in the late 1980s.

CHAPTER 22
Prohibition in Georgetown

PROHIBITION WAS A UNIQUE ECONOMIC EVENT—IT DECLARED AN ENTIRE commercial sector illegal. The people who owned bars and liquor stores had to find other things to do, as did their employees.

Congress enacted Prohibition for the District of Columbia two years before the Eighteenth Amendment to the U.S. Constitution enabled nationwide Prohibition. The amendment did not take effect until January 15, 1920, but Congress had authority to ban alcohol in the District without the amendment, and did so effective November 1, 1917. (This did not make the District unique. Some states had already been declared dry by their legislatures.)[1]

City directories before Prohibition identified bars separately from restaurants. (After Prohibition, directories stopped making that distinction, perhaps because all bars were legally required to serve food as well as alcohol.) We know that in 1916 there were sixteen saloons located on Wisconsin Avenue and M Street. The table on the next page shows what happened to them when D.C. Prohibition took effect.

Six of the sixteen saloonkeepers closed, and three went into other businesses. The other seven changed their business model to sell "soft drinks." This was a new phenomenon; before 1916, there were no businesses on the two main streets that listed themselves as soft drink stores, though of course soft drinks were available in grocery stores and drugstores.

There was not as big a market for soda pop as the presence of seven soft drink stores suggests—the seven probably were selling "near beer." Under Prohibition, beer with an alcohol content of under 0.5 percent was permitted,

Former Bar Businesses on Wisconsin Avenue and M Street during Prohibition

Proprietor	Address	1918 Listing for Same Address
Patrick F. Carr	3605 M St.	Fred Jawish restaurant
Patrick J. Cook	3214 M St.	Peter J. Cook soft drinks
Richard Cook	3401 M St.	Vacant
William T. Doyle	1218 Wisconsin Ave.	John Williams soft drinks
George F. Harper	3285 M St.	George F. Harper soft drinks
Robert R. Hogan	3033 M St.	Vacant
Mary E. Holohan	3400 M St.	Mary E. Holohan soft drinks
John J. Keady	3314 M St.	Vacant
John F. Killeen	1314 Wisconsin Ave.	John F. Killeen soft drinks
Edw. E. Mannix	3059 M St.	Edward E. Mannix soft drinks
Michael V. Moran	3011 M St.	Michael V. Moran soft drinks
Michael Morris	3004 M St.	Vacant
Conrad Schroeter	3258 M St.	Abr. L. Mitchell pool
Francis J. Stanton	1205 Wisconsin Ave.	Vacant
Joseph F. Tennant	3219 M St.	Vacant
Jas. W. Wardell	3603 M St.	George Jawish fruits

and was popularly called "near beer."[2] Many "nonalcoholic" beers sold today have similar alcohol content. Many breweries and bar owners tried to survive by making and selling near beer.

We can confirm that one of the seven soft drink stores did indeed sell near beer. A newspaper item in 1924 described a series of raids that resulted in the arrests of several bookmakers, one of whom conducted his business in a small room in the rear of "John Killeen's near-beer saloon at 1314 Wisconsin Avenue." Killeen must have convinced the authorities that he was unaware of the bookmaking, because he was not charged.[3]

Occasional newspaper articles described charges against owners of near beer bars elsewhere in Washington for selling whiskey. It is possible that someone among the six was doing so as well; there is no way to know.[4]

The near beer model apparently worked better for some than for others. Mary Holohan's soft drink business was gone by 1920, but that may have been because her side of the block was demolished for Key Bridge construction. Patrick Cook and his family gave up on soft drinks after two years and converted their space into a meat market. Others lasted longer. John Killeen stuck it out until 1926, when he opened a truck dealership and a gas station. Michael Moran made it all the way to 1933.

People still managed to buy alcohol in Washington, including in Georgetown. A 1931 map based on police department records used dots to indicate the locations of speakeasy raids in that year. There were at least five dots on M Street and Wisconsin Avenue, and twenty or more elsewhere in Georgetown. Few of the Georgetown raids made the press.[5] One of those dots was the West Washington Hotel on Wisconsin Avenue, which was raided several times (see chapter 20).

When Prohibition ended, some of the saloon and liquor store owners who had changed business lines went back to selling alcohol. Thomas Molloy, who had opened Kentucky Hardware when Prohibition forced him to close his liquor store, joined with his son Leo to open one of Georgetown's first post-Prohibition liquor stores two doors away from the hardware store, at 3245 M Street (see chapter 17). John Killeen closed his filling station and opened another of the first post-Prohibition liquor stores at 1333 Wisconsin. In 1935, Patrick Cook converted his grocery store and meat market at 3214 M Street back into a liquor store.

The end of Prohibition actually came in two stages. Quickly fulfilling a campaign promise by Franklin Roosevelt, Congress legalized the sale of 3.2 percent beer, effective in April 1933. In 1934, the city directory listings of two former saloon owners (Leo Molloy, son of Thomas Molloy, and John Killeen) identified their business as "beer."

The rest of Prohibition did not end in the District until the Twenty-First Amendment was ratified in December 1933. The next month,

PROHIBITION IN GEORGETOWN

Congress passed legislation concerning the licensing and taxation of alcohol in the District, and the first bars and liquor stores in the District opened on March 1, 1934.[6]

Michael V. Moran's story is poignant. He was the third generation in his family to own a business in Georgetown. All of the businesses involved alcohol sales. His grandmother Alice, born in Ireland, ran a grocery store near today's intersection of 28th and M Streets, starting at some point before 1860. The grocery store also sold liquor. In 1893, she converted the grocery to a saloon but closed it two years later, after thirty-three years in business.

Alice's son and Michael V.'s father, Michael F. Moran, opened a liquor store near 29th and M Streets in 1862. In 1867, he opened a second liquor store in a building he had bought at what is today 3011 M Street. He and his family lived upstairs. The family would run businesses at that location for seventy years.

After Michael F.'s death around 1870, his wife Margaret closed the store near 29th Street but continued to run the store at 3011 M Street until she retired in 1895. The liquor store became a saloon either just before or just after her retirement. Her son Michael V. Moran became proprietor of the saloon, and his twin brother Patrick was bartender.

When Prohibition came, Michael V. turned to serving near beer along with hot dogs and other simple food. For ten years he operated on that basis, passing up offers to sell the business because he was sure Prohibition had to end soon and he could go back to running a saloon. Not knowing he had almost made it, he decided to quit in 1933. Just a few days after he agreed to close and move out of the building, the legislation authorizing 3.2 percent beer was passed. Michael was committed by then and could not back out. He closed the business in September 1933, and the space became part of John Lavezzo's grocery store.[7]

Because directories after Prohibition did not identify bars as distinct from restaurants, we cannot tell how many bars opened in Georgetown after Prohibition; they all were lumped into the restaurant category. We do know how many liquor stores there were before and just after Prohibition, however, and that comparison is dramatic, as seen in the table that follows. If anyone hoped that fourteen years of Prohibition would reduce alcohol consumption, these numbers suggest otherwise.

Liquor Stores by Year

Year	Stores
1860	3
1877	2
1916	4
1918–1932	0
1935	12
1938	11
1943	12
1956	9
1965	7
1975	9
1985	6
1995	4
2014	4
2023	4

CHAPTER 23

Bars and Bar Wars

THE LINE BETWEEN A "RESTAURANT" AND A "BAR" IS IN THE EYE OF THE beholder. Most restaurants serve alcohol. Some would say a business should be called a "bar" when alcohol is a major part of the business and is the predominant reason for patrons coming. Others might place the line elsewhere. This definitional challenge is magnified by the fact that in the District of Columbia, with a handful of exceptions, all businesses serving alcohol must also serve food; except for that handful, there are no "pure" bars. Because of that requirement, city directories after repeal of Prohibition did not distinguish between bars and restaurants. Directory listings of "restaurants" include all types: college bars, nightclubs, carry-outs, fine dining restaurants, and others.

In this chapter, we will consider three categories of "bars": upscale saloons, nightclubs, and the less upscale, youth-oriented Georgetown bars that in the 1960s and 1970s were concentrated on a stretch of Wisconsin Avenue sometimes called "The Strip."

UPSCALE SALOONS

A 1962 change in the District of Columbia liquor laws led to the advent of a new type of Georgetown business that sits squarely astride the restaurant/bar dividing line: the upscale saloon. Before 1962, the liquor laws allowed cocktails and wine to be served only to customers seated at tables or lunch counters. At the bar itself, only beer could be served and only to patrons actually seated at the bar. In May 1962, Congress made two changes: liquor and wine could be served to customers at the bar, and drinks could be served to stand-up customers who were waiting for tables, if they were in a separate room or screened-off area.¹

The upscale saloons resemble restaurants in that they serve food, generally good but not of the gourmet quality one would have found in a Rive Gauche. They resemble bars in that many of their customers are there for the drinks more than for the food, and the bar is an important part of the space. Two of the upscale saloons described here are still in business in 2025, and the genre is definitely alive and well.

Clyde's

Clyde's was the first. Stuart Davidson saw an opportunity in the new law. He was a fan of P. J. Clark's, a popular New York saloon, and set out to create something similar. B.J.'s, a biker bar at 3236 M Street, was for sale, and Davidson bought it.²

Clyde's opened in 1963, and it still is in business sixty years later. The idea, as Davidson later put it, was that "it's more fun to eat in a saloon than to drink in a restaurant." Clyde was the name of a mythical friend of Frank Sinatra and Sammy Davis Jr. Years later, addressing a business club audience, Davidson described the business during its first year as "hopeless, not serious."³

An *Evening Star* writer described the decor:

> Clyde's is an elegant looking saloon and Dad and Grand-dad might look in silent wonder at it.... The decorations are all reminders of the turn of the century or not later than World War I. The walls are covered with prints of posters advertising cigarettes that are no longer made; World War I banners; pictures of anonymous men with celluloid collars and handlebar mustaches and women wearing the bulky clothing of that era.⁴

There was a juke box (now long gone), filled with carefully chosen pop and jazz tunes. "Their taste is matchless," said the *Star* reporter. The menu was small, including a London Broil for $2.

Clyde's did not appeal to the college crowd. There was a dress code—men had to wear jackets after 6 p.m. Drink prices were higher than in other nearby bars. At least at the time of an *Evening Star* report in 1965, Clyde's did not serve customers under twenty-one, even though the minimum age to drink beer and wine was eighteen.⁵

A year after the opening, nineteen-year-old John Laytham, a Georgetown undergraduate, began work at Clyde's as a dishwasher. He later said he took the job to earn date money. His educational goal was a career in the Foreign Service, but he took to the restaurant business and never looked back. By 1968, he had become general manager of Clyde's, and two years after that Davidson made him a partner with a 20 percent stake.

Laytham was a font of ideas. It was his suggestion that they open on Sundays, which was a little aggressive—Georgetown was not yet a Sunday brunch destination. Sunday became the highest-volume day of the week for Clyde's.[6]

Davidson and Laytham expanded the original restaurant in stages. Initially, it consisted only of the bar in front and the room directly behind that. In 1968, they added a rear bar. After that, they constructed an atrium behind the rear bar. Then they added the Omelet Room in front.

In 1970, Davidson and Laytham bought the Old Ebbit Grill on 15th Street for only $11,250, when the IRS auctioned it for back taxes. Davidson had gone to the auction with the idea of just buying the iconic wooden bar that had originally been in the Ebbit House Hotel. When he saw the low prices that people were bidding for the entire package, he joined the bidding and bought everything.[7]

In 1974, Davidson and Laytham bought the building in which Clyde's had been leasing space since it opened. They paid a surprisingly low price: $275,000. Within a year or two, they also bought the buildings on either side.[8]

In his "1975 Guide to Dining Out," *Washington Post* restaurant critic Donald Dresden said this about Clyde's:

> You can get a sandwich here till 1 a.m., an omelet till 1:30 and a drink until 3. You can also have lunch at $2.50 for an average main course and $6 at dinner. A recent Irish stew and a cup of chicken soup were good dishes, and some others have been about the same. Omelets? Not bad, but not peerless.[9]

Clyde's restaurants opened in other locations: Tysons Corner in 1978, then Chevy Chase, Reston, Columbia, and downtown Washington.[10] While the suburban locations were bigger, they had similar decor. Part of the menu was standard across all locations, and part was left up to the chef in each restaurant.

Clyde's in 2014. (*Photo by the author*)

The dress code became the subject of controversy in 1976. Two signs in the restaurant laid out the detailed rules:

> *Jackets and Ties are requested after 8 p.m.—Sundays Excepted. Sport coats (leisure coats worn over collared dress shirts are acceptable) or ties are required on Friday and Saturday nights after 8 p.m. No short sleeve jackets or short jackets can be substituted for the sport coat. T-shirts are not acceptable on any night after 6 p.m. Tank tops are not acceptable at any time day or night.*

Three people filed suit under a D.C. law prohibiting discrimination on the basis of sex or personal appearance, pointing out that a woman wearing a T-shirt was admitted to the restaurant and a man without a tie was not. We do now know how that particular case was resolved, but the strict dress code has long since been dropped.[11]

In 1985, Davidson and Laytham bought three more restaurants from Richard McCooey: 1789, the Tombs, and F. Scott's, all located on 36th Street near the Georgetown University campus. As a freshman at Georgetown in 1948, McCooey had the idea of creating a rathskeller near the campus to cater to a student clientele. In the early 1960s, Rev. Edward B. Bunn, president of the university, had the same idea. He and McCooey joined forces at Bunn's suggestion. The university bought the building, and McCooey bought the existing café that was operating there. When the lease on a laundry occupying the rest of the building expired, McCooey took over that space and built two restaurants. The basement rathskeller of his dreams he named "The Tombs"; the more upscale restaurant upstairs became 1789. Both became Georgetown institutions.

McCooey opened F. Scott's in 1975. It featured dramatic art deco decor, chrome furniture with rich blue upholstery, edge-lit glass partitions between booths, vintage posters, on all the walls, and 1930s swing music played through a state of the art sound system. It had the overall feel of a set from a 1930s movie musical, and it was a sensation when it opened. In 2018, it became a private club and event space, and in 2021, it reopened as Fitzgerald's, with the art deco theme gone.[12]

This 2025 photo shows the former location of F. Scott's. (*Photo by the author*)

Clyde's made a contribution to popular music. Bill Danoff and other members of the Starland Vocal Band lived in the Washington area, were Clyde's customers, and used the title of the Clyde's happy hour menu as the name of a song: "Afternoon Delight." Their recording of the song became a hit in 1976.

One expansion plan did not work out. In 2001, Clyde's proposed to construct a 350-seat restaurant on a barge that would float in the river next to the proposed Georgetown Waterfront Park. The proposal met opposition from people who feared it would reduce the water area available for recreational uses, consume parking needed by boaters, and pose safety and environmental hazards. On June 8, 2001, a floating protest took place, with 50 canoes, kayaks, and other vessels "marching" in the river. Among the signs they carried: "we want oars, not hors d'oeuvres." The floating restaurant never was built.[13]

Nathan's

In 1969, Howard Joynt and two partners leased the former Heon's Restaurant space at Wisconsin Avenue and M Street—the most prime of Georgetown locations—and opened Nathan's, originally called Nathan's Mustache. Descendants of the Heon family were the restaurant's landlords throughout its life. Joynt and his partners leased not just the restaurant space but the entire building, and the group took on responsibility for the entire building's maintenance and taxes. This was a tough economic deal that would come back to haunt Howard Joynt and his wife Carol.[14]

According to Howard Joynt's wife Carol, the restaurant was named after Nathan Detroit, a well-known bartender and bookie who was one of Joynt's original partners. Joynt later bought out both partners and continued running Nathan's until his death.

Like Stuart Davidson, Joynt was inspired by P. J. Clark's and similar bars in New York. Also like Davidson, Joynt initially required male customers to wear a jacket and tie. He deliberately set drink prices high to discourage undergraduate customers.

There were two rooms. A long, narrow front room was the bar. The other room was a more elegant dining room, which in the 1980s served an Italian menu. On a Saturday night, one had to walk through the crowded and noisy bar to reach a second door into the quiet serenity of the dining room. After Howard's death, Carol hired a new chef, and together they changed to a more American menu, though retaining a few of the Italian favorites.[15]

As one St. Patrick's Day approached, Howard Joynt and the bartenders told customers they were having sod shipped in from Ireland. The sod actually came from a sod farm in Maryland, but they did cover the entire barroom floor with sod. It damaged the carpet underneath, but everyone had fun.[16]

Howard Joynt died suddenly in 1997. Carol knew little about the business and had in mind selling it, until she discovered that she was liable for millions of dollars in back taxes that her husband had failed to pay. She had to continue running the restaurant in order to pay off the debt. She went through a trial by fire to learn the restaurant business and eventually free herself from the debt. Initially she ran the business while continuing her career as a journalist, but the career gradually was eclipsed by the demands of the restaurant.

In 2011, Carol Joynt wrote a memoir about the experience, titled *Innocent Spouse*. The book lays out some of the challenges of running a Georgetown saloon:

- Theft by employees was a big problem. At one point Howard Joynt hired detectives to investigate, who reported that the staff was stealing cash and selling cocaine in the bar. In one episode, a waiter was caught headed out the back door with a live lobster under his shirt.[17]
- Rats were a perennial problem. Once some of the younger kitchen employees, annoyed at a reduction in overtime, cut the screens that kept rats out of the building.[18]
- There were "episodes." A customer ripped a plumbing fixture off the men's room wall because he had had a bad day. A cook and a coat check girl got into a fight that included a knife.[19]

Carol's memoir also summarizes the economics of Nathan's:

> *All the money was made in the bar. In a good year we grossed about $4.7 million. Approximately $300,000 of that went to rent, another $50,000 to insurance, and about the same amount to property tax. . . . The payroll, repairs, utilities, goods, equipment rental and so on.*[20]

Carol had to be a landlord as well as a restaurateur. The upstairs tenants included a tailor, a tuxedo rental shop, and a family of fortune tellers.[21]

Among Carol's innovations was the Q&A Café, where she conducted interviews with famous people at Nathan's. Since long before marrying Joynt, she had been a journalist and in recent years had been a producer of *Larry King Live*, responsible for recruiting prominent people to be interviewed on King's show. She put that experience to good use. She started the Q&A Café in the aftermath of the September 11 attacks, when people were thirsty for more information. Many of the early interviewees were experts on the Middle East and terrorism. Among later interviewees were former CIA agent Valerie Plame, NBC anchor Tom Brokaw, and Scott Simon, the host of NPR's *Weekend Edition*. Carol continued the Q&A Café after Nathan's closed and still continues it as of this writing in 2025, conducting interviews in various D.C. venues.[22]

Eventually Carol negotiated an early termination of her lease and closed Nathan's in 2009, after running it for twelve years.

Mr. Smith's

Mr. Smith's, at 3104 M Street, opened in 1964 in space formerly occupied briefly by a restaurant called the Velvet Inn. The owners of the Velvet Inn had made the garden behind the building into an inviting space, which Mr. Smith's continued. There was live entertainment both inside and outside. A piano player held forth inside, while in the garden jazz guitarist Al Harvey was a fixture from Mr. Smith's opening until at least 1975. One reporter observed that "while the young frolic in the garden patio, older patrons get melancholy around the piano bar" singing old standards. Later Mr. Smith's closed the garden, but the piano bar continued, becoming the restaurant's defining feature for decades. "The Friendliest Saloon in Town" was the restaurant's tagline.[23]

In 1990, a branch of Mr. Smith's opened in Tysons Corner, Virginia. The live music in the branch was discontinued when the piano bar concept proved unsuccessful there.

In 2014, Mr. Smith's announced that it would be closing because its landlord had raised the rent to an impracticable level. Several employees, including the two piano players, saw that there still was a market for a piano bar and made plans to open the Georgetown Piano Bar on M Street. Around the same time, Chadwick's at 3205 K Street announced it would be closing, and Mr. Smith's was able to purchase the entire business, including the lease and all licenses. Since the K Street space was already improved and supplied, the contents of Mr. Smith's M Street space were auctioned off, including kitchen equipment, glassware, and beer signs. The employees planning the Georgetown Piano Bar were already committed to that before they found out about the Chadwick's deal, so they went ahead with the new business.[24]

Mr. Smith's was at this M Street location from 1965 to 2014. (*Photo by the author*)

Mr. Henry's

Mr. Henry's opened in 1967 at 1225 Wisconsin Avenue, in space it took over from the Tivoli restaurant. It was part of a small chain run by Henry Yaffe, a former Baltimore hairdresser who came to Washington in 1965 and opened a restaurant on Capitol Hill. The Capitol Hill location was a launching pad for popular singer Roberta Flack. Other locations were in Tenley Circle, Alexandria, and College Park.

This building at 1225 Wisconsin Avenue was the home of Mr. Henry's. (*Photo by the author*)

Mr. Henry's was popular with the LGBTQ community. A 1982 newspaper profile about Georgetown nightlife reported that gays and straights both frequented Mr. Henry's, but that families who occasionally wandered in tended to depart quickly.[25]

At one point, Yaffe toyed with the unusual idea of creating condominium tables in a back room in the Georgetown restaurant, to be called "Roberta Flack's Music Room." Customers would pay for ownership of tables ($2,000 for a table for four for nine and a half years), and then lease them back to Yaffe. An owner would be able to reserve their own table any time, though customers without reservations could use the table when the owner was not doing so. Owners would pay regular prices for food and drink. The economic benefit to the table owners is hard to see, which may be why Yaffe never carried out his plan.[26]

Yaffe gradually sold the restaurants in preparation for his eventual retirement. The sale of the Georgetown location came in 1986.[27]

The Third Edition

The Third Edition opened in 1971 at 1248 Wisconsin Avenue. It was so named because it was the third restaurant owned by Michael Kirby, who also owned Chadwick's (discussed in the next section). At first, the same chef supervised the kitchens at both the Third Edition and Chadwick's.

A few months after the opening, Donald Dresden of the *Washington Post* wrote a generally favorable review. He described the decor:

> *This is a plain and quiet and modest place. . . . Tables and booths seat 66; a comfortable bar takes the overflow. The modest décor is agreeable. The noise level is low.*

Dresden praised the soups and stews, as well as the London Broil. Often one for understatement, he said, "the executive sandwich pleased me." It consisted of toast topped by Russian dressing, sliced tomato, cold roast beef, and Swiss cheese.[28]

With the 1970s came the advent of the "fern bar," a type of bar/restaurant that was intended to part ways with dimly lit bars of the past by featuring wood furniture (often lighter colored), pleasant lighting, plants (hence the reference to ferns), and camp art work such as advertising posters of the

GEORGETOWN'S RETAIL PAST

past. The decor, together with a menu of salads, sandwiches, a few entrées, and light and unusual cocktails, was intended to appeal to women and create a gathering place for singles. The second floor of the Third Edition in the 1970s and 1980s was the quintessential fern bar. In 1983, *Washington Post* restaurant critic Tom Sietsema confirmed this when he said that "the standing menu differs little from that of any generic fern bar." He also said, "this restaurant wears middle age pretty well." Later on, the fern bar craze faded, and the fern bar ambience upstairs was displaced by a party atmosphere and a crowded dance floor.[29]

This 2025 photo shows 1248 Wisconsin Avenue, former home of the Third Edition. (*Photo by the author*)

At some point, Kirby sold the Third Edition to Greg Smith. In 1983, Smith in turn sold it to Greg Talcott, who had started as a Third Edition bartender in 1977. The restaurant was an occasional backdrop in the 1985 film *St. Elmo's Fire*. In 1990, the Third Edition opened an outpost in Rehoboth Beach, Delaware. Early in 2013, Talcott sold a part interest to Richard Sandoval Restaurants, though he remained in management and said the intent was that the Third Edition continued. By April that plan had changed, and Sandoval and Talcott replaced the Third Edition with El Centro, a Mexican restaurant.[30]

Chadwick's

Michael Kirby opened Chadwick's in 1967 in space on the Georgetown waterfront at 3205 K Street. The location was unusual—this was long before

The former Chadwick's space on K Street, now occupied by Mr. Smith's. (*Photo by the author*)

the waterfront was redeveloped with office complexes and a blocks-long national park. Instead, the restaurant's neighbors were a power plant for federal buildings, storage lots for federal and District government vehicles, coal yards (for power plant fuel), and a variety of industrial uses. Among those uses was a rendering plant producing foul odors. The elevated Whitehurst Freeway loomed over K Street. The only neighbor open in the evening was the Bayou nightclub, in the block just to the east (see more on the Bayou later in the chapter).

Kirby later opened the Third Edition, and the same chef oversaw both kitchens, at least at first.[31]

Despite its dark and foreboding surroundings at night, Chadwick's proved popular. In his "1975 Guide to Dining Out," *Washington Post* critic Donald Dresden noted Chadwick's prices (including dinners for $4.95) and pronounced the food "a good buy." He also praised the "warm, saloon ambience [and] excellent service." Branch locations opened in Alexandria and Landover. To mark its twenty-fifth anniversary in September 1992, Chadwick's offered a "two for $25" special—for $25, a couple could share one appetizer and have two entrées and two desserts. Anyone turning twenty-five in 1992 was given a 25 percent entrée discount for the rest of the year.[32]

Yet another hazard of the K Street location was flooding, with the Potomac River across the street. In 1972, floodwaters brought by Hurricane Agnes touched the Chadwick's building but never got in. When another flood threatened in 1985, manager Joe McGuinness said Chadwick's would remain open and would take no particular measures to protect against flooding. McGuinness and the managers of a nearby parking garage and floor covering concern had a friendly competition to see who would receive the most media requests for comments on the flood. McGuinness claimed victory, and again there was no damage to the restaurant.[33]

At some point Kirby sold Chadwick's to Michael Russo. Russo was a 1975 graduate of Georgetown University. Besides his interest in Chadwick's, Russo was active in charity work, including the Bartender's Ball Foundation. When Russo died in early 2014, Kirby returned to help Russo's family keep the business going. Nine months later the family announced that Chadwick's would close. Mr. Smith's took over the space (see more on Mr. Smith's earlier in the chapter).[34]

J. Paul's

J. Paul's was the creation of Paul Cohn, a native of Baltimore who for a time was the manager of the popular music duo Peaches & Herb. In 1983, he bought a failing restaurant called Wall's Grill at 3218 M Street for $150,000 and invested another $500,000 in renovations.[35] Cohn obviously was the Paul in the J. Paul's name.

A centerpiece was a thirty-eight-foot bar shipped in pieces from a bar near the Chicago stockyards. In a later seminar on how to start a restaurant, Cohn advised attendees "[i]f you're going to have a restaurant where people have to wait, have a big bar where they can spend money." The decor also included elevator doors from New York's Waldorf-Astoria and a pair of $5,000 sterling silver lamps from a Pittsburgh bank. Besides the eighty-nine seats, there was more open space than usual for a saloon—a place where people could mingle. The raw bar was located in the window, looking out on the street where it might lure people in.[36]

During the renovations, Cohn met Barry Silverman, who had paid his way through college working in restaurants. After a month try-out period, Silverman became a part of the organization. It was a classic combination of the creative, conceptual thinker and enthusiast (Cohn) and the methodical manager and "numbers guy" Silverman.

Reviews of J. Paul's commented on a preppy atmosphere. One review in the year J. Paul's opened, headlined "J. Paul's Preppy Pub," said that in order to enter one needed "a rich tan . . .; blond, dirty blond or light brown hair; a polo shirt with some sort of animal or mammal applique; a pair of madras pants or Bermuda shorts." Another review three years later said: "the fern bar is alive and well on M Street, flourishing as J. Pauls' saloon." It noted the dark wood, molded ceiling, brick walls, and numerous plants. The second review described the food as good though not consistent, saying "you don't expect serious food here, although the menu reflects the higher standard to which pub food is put nowadays." One customer said, "I'll tell you, I've never seen so many people wearing eyeglasses in one place before." It's a fascinating observation, but the significance is unclear.[37]

A threat of sorts appeared in 1983 in the form of a proposal for the opening of a Burger King fast food restaurant next door to J. Paul's. Cohn was a vehement opponent of the proposal, even though the owner of the neigh-

GEORGETOWN'S RETAIL PAST

J. Paul's in 2014. (*Photo by the author*)

boring building was repairing and renovating what had been a deteriorated historic building (the former Bank of Columbia—[see chapter 30]). "We are trying to upgrade the clientele here in Georgetown. We don't need young kids hanging around eating Burger King burgers until the early morning hours," Cohn told a reporter.[38]

Cohn joined forces with Bechara Nammour in a new company called Capital Restaurant Concepts, which ran J. Paul's and started three other new restaurants in the next couple of years (Paolo's, the Georgetown Seafood Grille, and the River Club), and more after that. In 2014, after thirty years, Cohn left the organization to do other things but remained in the restaurant business. J. Paul's closed in 2018. Capital Restaurant Concepts still is in business and still owns restaurants in Georgetown.[39]

NIGHTCLUBS

Georgetown has been home to a variety of nightclubs, but two of them stand out.

The Cellar Door

The Cellar Door was a major nightclub that developed a national reputation. It was located squarely in the middle of what became known to some as "The Strip," at the corner of 34th Street and Wisconsin Avenue.

Sometime before 1963, a club began operating in the building on that corner, called The Shadows. It is not clear whether this was an earlier iteration of The Shadows that later did business at 3125 M Street (see more later in the chapter) or the name was a coincidence. In 1963, when he was twenty-seven years old, Jack Boyle bought the club with (according to him) poker winnings and renamed it the Cellar Door.

Boyle was an important figure in the Georgetown bar and entertainment industry. He was born in 1936 in Youngstown, Ohio, and began working in neighborhood bars when he was a student at Georgetown University after

The former home of the Cellar Door at 34th and M Streets. (*Photo by the author*)

service in the U.S. Air Force. He went back to Youngstown briefly after graduation but returned to Washington in 1961. Over the ensuing decades, he would at one time or another own several bars besides the Cellar Door.

Boyle owned the Cellar Door twice. The first time, he hung onto it for only two years and then sold it to Tom Lyons. Charlie Fichman started as a Cellar Door waiter in 1964, became a part owner in 1966, and finally became sole owner.

The next few years under Fichman were what one commentator called the first golden age of the Cellar Door. Folk music was becoming increasingly popular, and folk artists like Judy Collins, Joni Mitchell, Odetta, Gordon Lightfoot, and Phil Ochs appeared at the Cellar Door early in their careers. The cover charge was fifty cents, and the draft beer was cheap. Each Sunday night there was a hootenanny where anyone could take the stage and sing, sometimes with people like Mitchell and Ochs in the audience.

In 1970, Boyle bought the Cellar Door from Fichman. Boyle at that time already owned the Crazy Horse and Mac's Pipe & Drum, and he had previously owned the Apple Pie. Over the next decade, the Cellar Door became a club of national reputation booking major performers. In 1978, the fire marshal reduced the allowed seating capacity from 199 to 125, which reduced the club's revenue-generating capacity and made it harder for it to compete for those major acts.

Boyle and Dave Williams, a nightclub manager, formed Cellar Door Productions, which became one of the country's biggest concert booking and promotion companies. Besides booking nightclubs, they booked performances at other major venues like the Kennedy Center, Constitution Hall, and the Capital Center. From 1980 to 1987, they also owned the Bayou (more on the Bayou later in the chapter). As famed as the Cellar Door nightclub would become over the coming years, the production company would grow into a far bigger enterprise.

John Denver performed from time to time at the Cellar Door. In 1970, Bill and Taffy Danoff, his backup singers, showed him the skeleton of a song that Bill had written. Denver liked it, and the three polished it in Denver's Cellar Door dressing room. It became "Take Me Home, Country Roads," Denver's biggest hit and now the official state song of West Virginia. (None of the three composers had ever set foot in the state.)

Boyle withdrew from active management of the Cellar Door club in 1973, when he was thirty-seven. Cellar Door Productions continued to operate it until selling it in 1981 to Paul Kurtz and Howard Bomstein. Kurtz and Bomstein operated it for a year under the name "The Door" but encountered financial difficulty and closed the club in January 1982.

Boyle remained engaged in Cellar Door Productions, however. He and Williams finally sold the company in 1998 to SFX Entertainment, a booking conglomerate. By that time, it had been the highest-grossing U.S. concert promoter for five years running, with $75 million in annual revenue, seven regional offices, and three hundred employees, booking concerts and events all over the country. Williams died before the sale closed. Cellar Door Productions remains in business today.[40]

The Bayou

Vincent Tramonte opened the Bayou in 1953 in a former warehouse at 3135 K Street, under the Whitehurst Freeway, in space that back in the 1930s had housed a bar called the Pirates Den. Tramonte was a lawyer, born in New York in 1915. His father was a barber, born in Italy. Tramonte went to the University of Virginia and married Helen Mowbray, a Virginia native.

From its opening until the mid-1960s, the Bayou featured Dixieland jazz; the Bayou name may have been a reference to Louisiana. In the 1960s, after a short time trying out an exotic dance club format, it switched to rock music and became very popular, with lines around the block. The drinking age for beer and wine was still eighteen, so the Bayou and other clubs attracted eighteen- to twenty-one-year-olds as well as young servicemen.

When the D.C. drinking age rose to twenty-one, the Bayou lost that younger customer group. It previously had not booked major acts on the weekends because it could rely on hundreds of young drinkers showing up every weekend. When that steady income source disappeared, the Bayou began booking bigger names on weekends. It helped that the space was large—two levels accommodating 475 people. Joe Hackson and U2 both played the Bayou, as did Bruce Springsteen, Billy Joel, and the Dave Matthews Band.

In 1980, Cellar Door Productions bought the Bayou and owned it until 1997, when Jack Boyle's son bought it. It was forced to close in 1998 when a major redevelopment of the site was to begin.[41]

"THE STRIP"

People whose home renovations changed Georgetown in the 1940s and 1950s had a vision of a quiet, dignified, historic neighborhood. In the mid-1960s, that vision collided with a boom in the bar business, particularly bars catering to college students and other young customers. The boom was initially fueled by features of the District of Columbia's liquor laws and Georgetown's proximity to two universities (Georgetown and George Washington). In 1968, riots triggered by the assassination of Martin Luther King made suburban visitors to downtown Washington fearful, crime rates in D.C. rose, and Georgetown became the city's main center for entertainment and dining, because its streets were filled with people and felt safe. The opening of more bars collided with the residents' vision and led to virtual warfare between bar owners and neighborhood groups including the Georgetown Citizens Association.

There was a particular concentration of youth-oriented bars on M Street west of Wisconsin Avenue, which came to be known as "The Strip." The number of restaurants on the three blocks of M Street west of Wisconsin Avenue grew from eight in 1960 to fifteen in 1965. The composition of the group changed, too. In the 1950s, it had included several diners and lunch counters like the Little Tavern hamburger shop, Gem Lunch, Julie's Café, and Everybody's Lunch. By 1965, all of those except the Little Tavern were gone. Many of the new bars offered entertainment, ranging from DJs to local bands to one or two places that featured big-name acts.

The Silver Dollar

The Silver Dollar, at 3124 M Street (just east of Wisconsin Avenue), had perhaps the most interesting of Georgetown storefront facades. The business had several incarnations.

Monroe Michael and Hilda Ansell opened the Silver Dollar Grill in 1937, in space at 3124 M Street that had been the home of Max Rosenthal's dry goods store. In 1934 and 1935, before they opened the business, Hilda Ansell had worked as a saleswoman and a clerk. She might have been Canadian. We know nothing about Monroe Michael.

The Silver Dollar Café in 1966. Note the poster for the featured musical act, the "Party Makers." (*Library of Congress, Historic American Buildings Survey HABS DC,GEO,75—*)

In September 1937, not long after the Silver Dollar opened, a *Washington Post* item about goings-on in Washington after dark included this:

> *Lights flare in the "Silver Dollar" around the corner on M street. A young man raises a violin to his shoulder, ripples through a popular song and bows into an aria from "Samson and Delilah." There is nothing unusual about the young man, in his well-tailored gray suit, which would lead the audience to suspect that he is a police officer by day.*[42]

We do not know who built the unusual art deco facade, but it seems logical that Michael and Ansell would have done it—the round windows were consistent with the Silver Dollar motif but would not have been suited to displaying Rosenthal's dry goods merchandise.

In early 1943, Joseph Pasqual and Danny Frese applied for an alcoholic beverage license for the Silver Dollar, a sign that they recently had bought it. Frese previously owned a restaurant on Pennsylvania Avenue SE. He was born in Naples, Italy, in 1895, and came to Washington after living in New Haven, Connecticut. He told the 1940 census taker that he worked as a "host" in the "retail liquor" industry. We know nothing about Pasqual.[43]

Frese and Pasqual had occasional regulatory problems. In 1944, a municipal court judge fined them $25 for "allowing decomposing garbage to accumulate." Theirs was one of nine establishments fined at the same time for sanitary violations in a continuing crackdown. Price controls during World War II introduced a new complexity to retail businesses. Danny Frese was cited by the Office of Price Administration for violating the controls—he had served less than an ounce of alcohol to someone but charged them the set price for a full ounce. He admitted the violation and paid a $25 penalty.[44]

A newspaper ad in 1950 announced a change of management, and a kitchen now run by "Chef Mier," formerly of Orlando, Florida. We do not know who Chef Mier was. The ad was headlined "Only Choice Foods" and said the Silver Dollar was "Famous for Mixed Drinks."[45]

A change of format came in 1966, possibly due to another ownership change: the Silver Dollar declared itself a "supper club." A week or so after the change, the *Evening Star*'s "After Dark" reporter, John Seagraves, paid a visit. It is clear from his review that he and the restaurant management had different definitions of "supper club."

According to Seagraves, the Silver Dollar had long been "a neighborhood restaurant where one could get a passable meal without leaving half of his pay check in the cash register on the way out."

Seagraves described the physical renovations: booths along one wall, banquette tables in the middle, and red-upholstered couches in the back, together with a small dance floor. There also was what Seagraves thought an incongruous touch for a supper club: small push-button juke boxes at each table.

The musical act selected for the reopening was an established New York singer named Lonnie Sattin, who performed standards like "Smoke Gets in Your Eyes" and "Around the World." There was a rock and roll trio that both performed on its own and accompanied Sattin, though apparently not well because they were unaccustomed to his style of music. There also was a female vocalist.

Seagraves was quite concerned about his fellow customers' apparel:

> *The other evening the place was inhabited mainly by women in slacks and other forms of attire a female might wear when she's doing the Monday wash. . . . Many men wore open sport shirts, unpressed pants, and the like . . .*
>
> *It only seems sensible that if one wants a supper club with the slightest amount of class he first sets down some ground rules, such as admitting only men with suits and keeping the gals out if they insist on wearing those hip-hugging slacks.*

Seagraves also took offense at the payment regime:

> *There is no cover or minimum at the Silver Dollar but if you want a mixed drink have $1.50 ready when the waitress arrives. The new policy apparently is a pay-as-you-drink one. More class.*

Despite Seagraves's misgivings, the Silver Dollar found a niche as a musical venue. An item in the *Evening Star* in 1970 included the Silver Dollar in a list of "area clubs that on any given night will have a decent rock band on hand as well as a pleasant atmosphere." The young crowds attracted by the music in turn attracted the attention of the Citizens Association of Georgetown, which at least once included the Silver Dollar Café in its campaign of opposition to liquor license renewals for bars that it found noisy or otherwise offensive (see chapter 23).[46]

The Silver Dollar closed in the early 1970s. The M Club restaurant occupied the space briefly, but by 1975, a French restaurant, Bistro Français, was there (see chapter 21).

The Shamrock

Longtime residents Philip and Richard Levy recalled that, during the 1950s, Georgetown was more southern, with "honky tonk bars and entertainment places on M Street, mostly west of Wisconsin Avenue." Among them was The Shamrock (at 3295 M Street). Philip remembered that prominent country artist Patsy Cline, who grew up in Winchester, Virginia, played at The Shamrock. Richard remembered bikers coming to The Shamrock on a Friday night and recalled that the noise and the leather jackets were intimidating.[47] Patrons' motorcycles could also be seen parked in front of B.J.'s Restaurant at 3236 M Street (future home of Clyde's).[48]

The Shamrock had opened in the 1940s. In the late 1940s, Roger Woodward and his brother Richard performed there as the Shamrock Trio. In 1953, Woodward bought The Shamrock. He later remembered that even in the 1940s The Shamrock had stood out among the several country music clubs in Georgetown. That reputation grew under Woodward, and acts that played The Shamrock included Patsy Cline, Jimmy Dean, George Jones, and Bobby Bare. The Country Gentlemen were the house band for fifteen years from 1957 to 1972. Woodward told a reporter, "I can remember when Roger Miller begged me for a job here." Woodward said he thought about switching to rock and roll but decided he just could not go through with it.[49]

Many of The Shamrock's customers were from the suburbs. The fear and higher crime rates after the 1968 riots, plus the advent of suburban competitors, made suburbanites less willing to come to Georgetown for the music, and business declined after that. The Shamrock closed in 1974, and Winston's, a bar aimed at "post-collegiate singles" took over the space.[50]

The Shadows

New Georgetown University graduates Bob Cavallo and Frank Weis (ages twenty-two and twenty-one, respectively) opened The Shadows in 1961 at 3125 M Street. Like The Shamrock, it hosted well-known acts as well as local groups and, in a few cases, local musicians who became well known. A group called the Mugwumps played there in the early 1960s. Two members of that group (Cass Elliot and Denny Doherty) went on to become part of the Mamas & the Papas. Two others (John Sebastian and Zal Yanovsky) became part of the Lovin' Spoonful. The bill varied. African singer Miriam Makeba appeared in February 1963. Later that year the bill featured the Journeymen and Bill Cosby. The lineup in August 1964 included Martin St. James, a "mentalist." Jazz acts played The Shadows as well, including vocalist Nina Simone.

The Shadows included a room called "The Dark Room." "Something always develops in The Dark Room!" said the ads.[51]

The Shadows succeeded wildly for a while. A *Washington Post* review described crowds of as many as 150 waiting to get in. Although The Shadows was gone by 1967, it and The Shamrock established Georgetown as a place to go for entertainment. Entrepreneurs saw an opportunity in that, and more bars and restaurants started opening in the mid-1960s.

The Crazy Horse

The Crazy Horse opened in 1964 in space at 3259 M Street that had long housed P. T. Moran's feed store and briefly was home to a bar called the French Quarter. The room was long and narrow, and the wood floors were worn. The music was live and loud and accompanied by flashing lights. The dance floor was small and always crowded. And as one reviewer noted, "not a fern in sight." In 1987, the manager told a reporter that he ordered three hundred cases of beer a week just from the Budweiser distributor. An article in 1978 described the line to get into the Crazy Horse: one hundred feet long on a twenty-five-degree evening.[52]

In earlier years, the Crazy Horse attracted a sometimes rowdy crowd. Later the owners tried to change that with a dress code (shirts with collars, no flannel shirts), music more dance oriented than the hard rock that had been customary, and an end to the wet T-shirt contests. They had a staff of eight bouncers.[53]

Washington Post columnist Bill Gold shadowed two police officers for an evening in Georgetown, starting out at the Crazy Horse. He described two doormen checking IDs and signs on each table reading "We are on the fringe of a residential area. Please observe quiet after leaving these premises." He

For thirty years, the Crazy Horse did business in this building at 3259 M Street. (*Photo by the author*)

said that "I judged from the sound [inside] that two locomotives had crashed head on and then backed off a few feet to have another go at it."[54]

The Crazy Horse remained in business for thirty years, finally closing in the late 1990s.

The Apple Pie

The Apple Pie occupied the most historic premises of any bar on "The Strip"—it was located in a house that two hundred years before had been home to Uriah Forrest, a Maryland revolutionary leader. Later it was the residence of William Marbury, who was the plaintiff in *Marbury v. Madison*, the 1803 U.S. Supreme Court case that established the court's authority to review the constitutionality of legislation. The house is now part of the Ukrainian embassy.

The room, with an allowed capacity of 199, had high ceilings that reduced the sense of crowding. A long bar took up most of one side. There was a balcony above. Both the balcony and main floor were a bit tilted toward the front of the room, like a theater, providing a better view for people at the back of the room. There was a Rock-Ola Ultra jukebox, which featured a graphic of a moving skyline and plenty of volume.[55]

Two reviewers five years apart said different things about the crowd at the Apple Pie. In 1969, shortly after the bar opened, one observed that the customers were mostly college age, and "one sees shirts open at the collar, overly long hair and desert boots." (He was comparing the Apple Pie to the more upscale Clyde's and Nathan's.) His comments on the food were more or less positive; of a $1.45 spaghetti and meatballs he said, "[f]or the price it wasn't bad."[56]

The Apple Pie occupied the building on the right in this 2025 photo. That building and those on either side of it now comprise the Ukrainian embassy. (*Photo by the author*)

In 1974, the author of a "Going Out" column said:

> *The clientele of the Apple Pie is generally attractive, pretty clean cut and collegiate. Long hair tends to belong to the waiters, the bands and the women players. . . . You can tell the regulars because they stick close together and make it hard for all but the most deserving to break into their circle. However, the atmosphere is generally friendly and conversations are struck up easily.*

Regarding the food, he said, "Prices are commensurate with the background status of the food and it's not a bad place to have lunch if you're in the area."[57]

The musical acts at the Apple Pie were local or regional. They had names like Itchy Brother, DC Dog, and the Dubonnettes. But it was a place one could go for live music at a low price. The cover charge was low, and in 1974, bottled beers were available for $1 as well as Budweiser on tap.[58]

The Apple Pie's end was unfortunate. Tax problems are common among restaurants, and the Apple Pie was one of those. In 1976 the IRS seized the bar's property and sold it at auction, including three cash registers, 36 tables, 81 chairs, 10 bar stools, 133 glasses, two speakers, a refrigerator, and the liquor license.[59]

Desperado's

By 1980, a bar called Desperado's had opened in the Apple Pie's former quarters. Desperado's featured decrepit decor and promising musical acts. A 1981 review of local music clubs said it "looks like a Western movie set—after it has been trashed in the big saloon brawl scene." In 1982, when Desperado's closed, owner Rich Ventig said,

> *"Joint" really is the word. . . . It sustained itself as a joint because of the physical nature of the building. No tenant here ever had the kind of lease with an incentive to do any genuine work on the building.*[60]

Desperado's was the first step up the ladder for some of the bands that appeared there, enabling them to move on to bigger venues. So many musical acts played clubs like Desperado's that it is impossible to briefly summarize the musical fare; we can only look at random examples. Spread over a week in 1980, Desperado's had a rhythm and blues festival. Acts included Double Trouble (Texas-style blues) and the Son Seals Blues Band. The Good Humor Band, which had played Desperado's at the beginning, was also the act on the last night.

The closing was driven by a new landlord who raised the monthly rent from $2,000 to $9,000, a familiar pattern as Georgetown's prestige grew. The space's two-hundred-person capacity limited its ability to compete for name musical acts with larger spaces like the Bayou, which could hold five hundred.[61]

Gunchers

Gunchers Saloon at 3403 M Street was one of Georgetown's most unusual bars. Started by Louis Calomaris when he was twenty-eight, it had the usual features of a bar but also had an array of penny-arcade machines scattered around the place. At Gunchers, customers could

- "Discover Your Personality," using a machine that assessed it based on your grip.
- For ten cents, have your fortune told by a "Cleveland Grandmother" prediction machine that had cost Calomaris $2,900.
- Ask a machine to tell you about your future husband or wife. One card said "your future husband will be a gigolo, and Oh! Boy! How he can juggle."
- Be tested by the Booze Barometer.
- Play a "Big Game" slot machine.
- Play any number of pinball machines.[62]

Children loved the place, and parents held birthday parties there. In a sense, it was a precursor to the late twentieth century's Chuck E. Cheese pizza restaurants, with arcade machines and video games to entertain children. In the evening, though, the customers were a typical Georgetown collegiate bar crowd.

Other bars that were part of "The Strip" at various times in the 1960s and 1970s included Mac's Pipe & Drum (3401 M Street, 1960–1981),

Gunchers Saloon was in the building on the left in this 2025 photo, and Mac's Pipe & Drum was in the building to the right. (*Photo by the author*)

Winston's (3295 M Street, 1977–1990 or later), the French Quarter (3263 M Street, 1964–1968), Paul Mall (3235 M Street, 1974–1990), and the Peppermint Lounge (1965).

THE BAR LICENSING WARS

Over-licensing of bars in Georgetown had been an issue before. At a 1798 meeting of the Georgetown Corporation, which governed the town, a committee reported that there were fourteen licensed taverns in the town. That led the corporation to adopt the following resolution:

> *In the opinion of this Corporation great injury and inconvenience arises to the citizens of this town from the indiscriminate manner in which Tavern licenses have been granted within its limits—that a number of the persons to whom granted do not possess the requisites to enable them to comply with the Terms of the Law upon that subject.*[63]

One hundred and seventy years later, Georgetown neighborhood organizations would make the same complaint.

Following the repeal of Prohibition, Congress in 1934 enacted an alcoholic beverage law for the District of Columbia. Two parts of that law would play a part in events thirty years later.

First, the law established twenty-one as the minimum drinking age, but an exception permitted the serving of beer and wine to anyone eighteen or over.

Second, while the law contemplated that any establishment serving alcohol would also have to serve food, it provided no enforcement mechanism. Applicants for a beverage license had to "satisfy" the Alcoholic Beverage Control (ABC) Board that food rather than beverages would be the prospective establishment's main source of revenue going forward, but there was no requirement that, in order to be eligible for renewal of its license, the owner actually operate as it had said it would. In 1968, Joy Simmons, the chair of the ABC, explained that this posture was based on an opinion from the city's lawyers, who said that it was impossible for a restaurant to compel customers to eat, and therefore the ABC must settle for evidence of the restaurant owners' intent.[64]

The Seabright Restaurant at 3267 M Street opened in 1948. One of the first signs of Georgetown neighborhood resistance to bars came at the 1952 ABC board hearing on Seabright's application to expand its existing license for beer and wine to also allow sales of hard liquor. At the hearing, a group of neighbors opposed renewal, saying that, as the *Evening Star* summarized, renewal "would depreciate property values in that re-developed [*sic*] area of Georgetown." The license was granted after seven police officers testified that the restaurant was run well and "they foresee no rowdyism."[65] This was a harbinger of hearings to come. The Seabright later would evolve into the Corral, a focus of neighbors' anger in the 1960s.

The year 1965 was when Georgetown's crowds and rowdy youth behavior became notorious. Both of the city's major newspapers ran long articles about the situation. In February, the *Evening Star*'s report was under the headline "Georgetown Now Updated, but It Didn't Expect This."

> *Off-beat and often frenetic bars and night clubs have been multiplying there, hundreds of young people gravitate to them to perform the frug, the jerk, the swim, the watusi and something called the oh-good-grief. These dances, the rites of a loosely-knit but athletic cult, are performed to the accompaniment of incredibly loud music. . . . The new clubs have been moving in, in recent months beside the quieter and more civilized places established during M Street's renaissance of the past 10 years. The new frug-watusi parlors also coexist with a few of the old hillbilly bars that have been there for years. . . . So the street is a juxtaposition of the chic, the seedy and the weird.*[66]

Residents complained about public urination and car antennas being snapped off, and they expressed fear that "our area is being propelled into a breeding place for crime."[67]

Neighborhood residents were not the only ones irritated by the crowds and noise—so were owners of more upscale bars and restaurants. Bill Bonbrest, a co-owner of the recently opened Clyde's, expressed concern about the noise and publicity, and Charley Hapsas, who owned the more upscale Charley's Restaurant at 3235 M Street, said "the influx of teenagers around here is becoming a problem."[68]

The *Washington Post* weighed in with its own article a few months later, under the headline "Old Georgetown Is Full of Young Sprouts." It described the plight of Mr. and Mrs. Eric Rendle, who lived on Potomac Street. They "try to enjoy their patio overlooking their pool. But from across the eight-foot alley thunders every booming beat of 'Take It, Take It, Baby' and 'Hey Little Girls.'" More than the noise, though, the Rendles objected to what happened when the bars closed at 2 a.m.—noisy groups of young people congregating on the street, who "double-park or communicate by horn." They also objected to the parking problems caused by the influx of suburbanites.[69]

BARS AND BAR WARS

The two sides saw the situation from very different vantage points. The residents saw their historic neighborhood and their lifestyle marred by mobs of young people attracted to a proliferation of bars, with attendant noise, parking shortages, nuisance behavior, and crime. The bar owners saw the Citizens Association as a small minority of residents who were trying to put them out of business for those residents' own selfish ends, interfering with the operation of free markets, and using the owners' businesses as scapegoats for neighborhood problems generally.

For decades, the neighborhood groups pushed for two things. First, they thought the number of bars was a problem in and of itself, and they wanted the number of licensed bars to be limited in some way. This proposition ran into a logical problem. The licensing process focused on one establishment at a time, and not on cumulative impacts. When neighborhood groups raised the proliferation issue in a license renewal hearing, the bar owner would actually concede the point, saying that, because there were so many bars, the neighborhood groups could not prove that patrons of *his* bar were the ones misbehaving. (Joseph Schladt, owner of the West Washington Hotel, had made the same argument in 1896 [see chapter 20].)[70]

Second, the groups wanted the Alcoholic Beverage Control (ABC) Board to hold a restaurant owner responsible at license renewal time if its business model had strayed from what it had represented when it first applied for its license. They felt that if an owner had said it would run a family restaurant but in fact was running a bar for undergraduates, its license should not be renewed. The obstacle to this was the opinion of the city's lawyers described earlier in the chapter.

In 1965, the Georgetown Citizens Association launched an all-out campaign opposing grants of new or renewal liquor licenses. They would challenge dozens of licenses over the next twenty-five years.

The different perspectives and their intensity were apparent at a November 1965 ABC board hearing about license renewals for the Peppermint Lounge (3263 M Street) and the Corral (3267 M Street). The Citizens Association referred to the establishments as "rotten apples" and called witnesses who described problems with parking, public urination, and crime. One witness reported having been threatened. The commander of the local police precinct said that arrests west of Wisconsin Avenue jumped 58 percent over two summer months compared with the same period a year earlier. The people arrested were both suburbanites and D.C. residents.

The bar owners argued that there was no evidence that it was customers of the Crazy Horse and the Corral in particular who caused the problems the witnesses described. (When one resident was asked how he could link the crime specifically to patrons of the two bars, he replied that "[i]f there are skunks in the neighborhood, I don't think it's necessary to differentiate between smells.")[71]

The president of the Restaurant Beverage Association issued a statement after the hearing saying that the opposition was "an overblown attack by a few determined agitators." A report issued by the Restaurant Beverage Association called the opposition "an enterprising real estate clique" that "now sought to preserve their investments by resisting and thwarting all natural change."[72]

After the ABC Board's January 1966 decision to deny license renewals for the Peppermint Lounge, the Corral, and the Roundtable (2813 M Street), events showed just how determined the two sides were. The denial was a victory for the neighborhood groups—it was the first time the board had required a licensee seeking renewal to actually have operated as it said it would when the license was first granted. The owners of all three bars appealed to the federal courts, where they lost in March.[73] The Corral and the Peppermint Lounge went out of business at that point.

The Roundtable's owners fought on until the U.S. Supreme Court refused review of their case in January 1967. The Roundtable owners did not give up easily, though, and in July 1967 they applied for a license for a new "Adams Restaurant" in the old Roundtable space, which they said would be "a fine family restaurant." After the Roundtable experience, the ABC Board was skeptical about that promise and refused the license.[74]

The two sides spent a great deal of time and money litigating. Between 1970 and 1976, disputes among the Citizens Association, bar owners, and the ABC Board wound up in the District of Columbia's highest court nine times.[75]

The residents made a little headway on the over-concentration argument in 1968 when the ABC Board refused by a 2–1 vote to grant a license for a proposed Ballot Box restaurant at 1079 Wisconsin Avenue. One of the board members voting against the license agreed that it indeed was possible to have too many bars in the area; that the crowds they attracted created problems of noise, traffic, vandalism, and crime; and that adding another bar "could not help but aggravate" those problems. She noted that there already were forty-one licensees in Georgetown, twenty-six of them within an eight-hundred-foot radius.[76]

Ultimately the residents' concentration argument would win out, but that would not happen for twenty more years.

Because the association viewed the problem as not just the wrong kind of bars but also too many bars, it opposed licenses for all restaurants, including ones that would not be expected to attract a rowdy crowd. When the ABC Board granted a license to Le Steak, for example, the Citizens Association litigated all the way to the U.S. Court of Appeals. Le Steak was what its name suggests—a restaurant serving primarily steak. Its bar seated only six people, and its prices were set high enough (with a $7.95 per person minimum) that, as the owner put it, Le Steak "will not attract the hippie element." There also was lengthy litigation over licenses for The Big Cheese (3139 M Street) and Café de Paris (3056 M Street). Some suggested that opposing these was a mistake, and that allowing more fine dining restaurants would attract a more mature crowd.[77]

A few bars kept away the rowdy crowd by setting drink prices higher or by refusing to serve anyone under age twenty-one. Carol Joynt said that when her husband ran Nathan's in the 1970s (at 3150 M Street) "he always priced the drinks at a price where the college kids wouldn't want to come drink there." Clyde's had a dress code requiring jackets after 8 p.m. on weekends.[78] The bars with such codes were a small minority.

The Crazy Horse took a variety of measures in 1966. Besides a dress code, they rented a parking lot, sound-proofed the doors, and assured the ABC Board that they did not allow "females of any kind in miniskirts or other abbreviated costumes." Their license was renewed despite opposition partly because the board recognized these steps as a good-faith effort to not be a nuisance.[79]

In 1982, yet another *Washington Post* article described the crowds that descended on Georgetown on weekend evenings. It sounded a lot like the article from seventeen years before.

> *Winston's is part of the cluster of bars in the 3200 block of M Street, which includes Crazy Horse, Desperado's, Beneath It All and Paul Mall. Area residents complain that loud music and rowdy patrons are the bane of their lives. They say customers park illegally, drink beer, urinate on sidewalks and in gardens, and vandalize property before driving away intoxicated.*[80]

The manager of Winston's, however, saw it differently, noting that nightclubs in Georgetown were a tradition, and that the students from area universities who came to Winston's were "very well-behaved." He felt that his and the other bars were "scapegoats" for every problem in Georgetown.[81]

In 1985, pressure built to increase the drinking age to twenty-one. Congress had passed legislation that would deny states (including D.C.) a portion of their federal highway funds if they did not increase their drinking age by October 1987. Both Maryland and Virginia already had repealed exceptions allowing eighteen-year-olds to drink beer and wine there. Opponents of an increase in D.C. complained that it would be unfair to young people and penalize businesses. They said the burden on D.C. bar owners would be particularly great because of the large student population. "It would probably put us out of business," said the owner of the 21st Amendment, a bar near George Washington University.[82] Highway funds are an overwhelming incentive, however, and in late 1986, the city council passed legislation raising the drinking age for beer and wine to twenty-one.[83]

Did the higher drinking age drive college bars on "The Strip" out of business? It seems not. Business may have fallen off, but between 1985 and 1990, the total number of restaurants on M Street west of Wisconsin Avenue decreased by only one, from thirty-five to thirty-four. The only student-oriented bar that disappeared by 1990 was Annie Oakley's at 3204 M Street. The Crazy Horse, Pall Mall (3295 M Street), Winston's, and the Saloon (3239 M Street) all survived. A cottage industry in fake ID cards did arise.[84]

In 1988, after previous unsuccessful attempts, neighborhood leaders finally convinced the ABC Board to recommend to the city council a moratorium on the issuance of new liquor licenses in Georgetown. To back up their argument that there were just too many bars in the neighborhood, they cited statistics: the number of alcohol licenses in Georgetown had grown from 13 in the late 1960s when residents began pressing their concerns to 134 in 1988. Proponents said that a moratorium would enable them to concentrate on policing existing bars rather than resisting new licenses, and predicted that "the perception of Georgetown as a playground would end if we had a moratorium."[85]

A three-year moratorium went into effect in 1989. It would be renewed several times, remaining in effect for twenty-five years.[86] But the moratorium ended only grants of new licenses. Tension with the existing licensees continued.

A new residents' group, Residents for a Safer Georgetown, emerged in the 1980s. Besides resisting license renewals, the group staked out bars to document underage drinking, crowding, and fights. Owners of some bars sought peace by signing agreements with Residents for a Safer Georgetown. The agreements were demanding, as illustrated by the one that the Saloon on M Street signed. It required that the Saloon maintain food sales at 15 percent of total sales, offer no happy hours, and establish a dress code for doormen. That the agreement included a ban on wet T-shirt contests shows the width of the cultural chasm.[87]

In the 1990s, some commentators began to suggest that Georgetown had calmed down. A *Washington Post* writer in 1992 observed that crowds on the streets were much smaller and attributed the change to higher bar prices and the negative side effects of a greater police presence, which responded to increased crime but also put off other customers.[88] By the second decade of the twenty-first century, things had changed enough that many leaders in Georgetown began to think the moratorium had outlived its usefulness. Changes in the city had contributed to calming in Georgetown, including an influx of affluent young citizens, a drop in crime rates elsewhere, and the growth of entertainment districts in other areas such as 14th Street NW, Penn Quarter, and H Street NE.

Some said the moratorium had had unintended consequences. They suggested that the limit on new licenses drove up the cost of buying an existing license, raising entry barriers for new competitors who might spur existing bars to spruce up. Lack of competition protected the bad actors and kept them in place.

Finally, in 2014, some Georgetown civic leaders (though not all) joined with the Georgetown Business Improvement District to urge the ABC Board to end the moratorium. It was allowed to expire in 2016.[89]

CHAPTER 24

Movie Theaters

ONLY ONE MOVIE THEATER DOES BUSINESS IN GEORGETOWN AS OF 2025 (a multiplex cinema on K Street), but at various times between 1914 and 1997, nine theaters operated in the neighborhood.

Early moviegoers saw films in locations other than theaters. In the Washington *Bee* of June 5, 1909, "Dr. Richardson, the religious king show of moving pictures," advertised his availability to show films in churches. Mr. G. R. F. Key recalled seeing movies shown by Richardson at the First Baptist Church of Georgetown at 27th and Dumbarton. He said that Richardson was African American and would be booked at least twice a year into each church in the neighborhood. He would provide dialogue and narration during the silent films.[1]

THE M STREET OPEN AIR THEATER

Outdoor theaters were popular in the early years of film, before air conditioning. In the heat of a Washington summer evening, an outdoor theater would be cooler than a crowded indoor one. Among the outdoor venues was the M Street Open Air Theater, also known as the Georgetown Open Air Theater, located on M Street just east of Bank Street. In 1911, two brothers named Davis built a high wooden fence around what had been a coal and wood yard, 138 feet along M Street and 80 feet up Bank Street. Bank Street slopes steeply up from M Street, so it is safe to assume that the 24-foot stage and the screen were against the fence along M Street and the customers sat, probably on benches, on the hill going up from there. By 1915, the theater had a roof and electric fans to provide a breeze.

MOVIE THEATERS

Detail from Baist's 1915 survey atlas, showing the M Street Open Air Theater. (Baist Real Estate Atlas Survey of Washington, *1915*)

On July 31, 1915, *Motion Picture News* described the weekly dance contest, which was a joint venture between the Davis brothers and the owner of a nearby country store:

> *When the storekeeper disposes of his stock of merchandise, the orchestra strikes up the dance music and the contest begins. The couples waltz, fox trot and hesitate to a finish for a prize of five dollars in gold for the best efforts of terpsichorean art. That this weekly prize may not be won continuously by the same couple, all prize winners are barred from making further entry until the wind-up night at the close of the season, when these alone may compete for a handsome silver trophy.*[2]

The theater closed in the early 1920s.[3]

THE BLUE MOUSE

The Blue Mouse Theater was located at 1206 26th Street just across the M Street Bridge at the east end of Georgetown. It was the one theater under African American ownership. George Martin opened the theater in 1914 and ran it for fourteen years, hosting both movies and vaudeville. One local resident recalled paying an admission charge of a nickel or a dime and staying for five or six hours, seeing the same movie over and over. The owners of the Republic and Lincoln Theaters on U Street later took over the Blue Mouse and renamed it the Mott. It closed in 1949.[4]

THE M STREET THEATER

A block away from the M Street Open Air Theater was the similarly named M Street Theater, at 3227 M Street, built in 1909 and initially operated by Crandal Mackey. In the 1930s, it was renamed the Lido Theater. When the theater opened, children were admitted free to view what signs said were "high grade moving pictures."[5] The theater closed in 1948, and the building was torn down and replaced in 1950.

THE SCENIC THEATER

Another early theater was the Scenic, opened in 1907 at 1303 Wisconsin Avenue. Joseph Morgan, who built it, furnished it with folding chairs that he bought from an undertaker. In 1909, the building was torn down and replaced, and in 1912 the new building was remodeled. The theater closed in 1917.[6] The building later was home to the Maison des Crepes restaurant (see chapter 21 for a photo of the building).

THE DUMBARTON/GEORGETOWN THEATER

The longest-running Georgetown theater was the Dumbarton, which operated at 1349 Wisconsin Avenue (between Dumbarton and O Streets) from 1913 to 1986. Henry Frain and William Marceron started the business and constructed the building, which featured an unusual, Gothic-arched facade.

In 1948, the theater became a center of controversy when it showed *Mom & Dad*, a film described by the Internet Movie Database as "the most successful exploitation/sex hygiene film ever made." "You'll laugh, cry . . . and learn facts," the ads said.

Photo of the Dumbarton Theater's original facade. The posters for the movies being shown tell us the photo was taken in 1913. (*Peabody Room, D.C. Public Library*)

GEORGETOWN'S RETAIL PAST

Rather than the theater booking the movie, the film's producer (Charles Mead, doing business as Hygienic Productions) would rent the entire theater, and his own staff would run the show. There was a break during the film when "Eminent Hygiene Commentator Elliot Forbes" would deliver a lecture titled "Secrets of Sensible Sex," including a sales pitch for a book available for purchase at the show. To add to the hype, there were separate showings for men and women, and ushers who distributed literature were dressed as nurses. Complaints about the show led the District of Columbia government to order the theater closed.[7]

George and Peter Heon, who ran a restaurant in Georgetown (see chapter 21), bought the theater in 1949, remodeled it, and renamed it the Georgetown.[8] Alas, the romantic facade was a casualty of the renovation, replaced by stone facing.

LEFT: Facade of the Georgetown (formerly Dumbarton) Theater in 2014, showing stone facing installed in 1949. (*Photo by the author*)
RIGHT: Facade of the Georgetown Theater after renovations in 2020. (*Photo by the author*)

MOVIE THEATERS

The film featured for the grand reopening was *Adam's Rib* starring Spencer Tracy and Katharine Hepburn. The Heons reverted for a few months to running the sort of "B pictures" that the theater had offered before they bought it, but they then converted to an "art theater" business model, showing a combination of foreign films and American classics. In the 1970s, the focus changed to films that were more profitable. Some ran for a long time, including *Annie Hall* for more than a year. In the mid-1970s, the theater began to run soft pornographic films.

Because of its location, the Georgetown in its later years had some well-known patrons, including Richard Nixon and John and Robert Kennedy. Caroline Kennedy had a childhood birthday party there.[9]

In the *Georgetowner* of September 26, 1986, longtime Georgetown resident Robert Sellers reminisced about going to the movies at the Dumbarton Theater:

> First would come the "comedy": Would it be Popeye or a Laurel and Hardy? The "Chapter" would follow—Buster Crabbe as Tarzan, or Zorro, maybe Tailspin Tommy or Crabbe again as Flash Gordon.
>
> At night the price went from a dime to fifteen cents, which wasn't that hard to hustle, even during the depression . . .
>
> We first saw "The Thin Man" at "The Dump" as we affectionately referred to our theater. We were entranced by "Lost Horizon," puzzled by "A Midsummer Night's Dream." We fell in love with Eleanor Powell there, and Ruby Keeler.

The Georgetown closed in 1986 and reopened as the National Jewel Center, a controversial jewelry mart. As of this writing in 2025, the building, with its iconic neon sign restored, houses a coffee shop.

In Georgetown, a few bars introduced an innovation in 1965: showing full-length movies, a business model called "Cinematheque." The association of local theater owners objected, telling the District Department of Licenses and Inspections that this was unfair competition for theaters and that the nightclubs should be required to get the same licenses as theaters.[10]

Except for the Foundry Theater in the basement of a new office building, the theaters that opened in Georgetown in the second half of the twentieth century were in older structures adapted to their new use—two car dealerships and a bowling alley. A theater required a large space, and historic preservation building controls in place from 1950 on made it difficult to demolish existing structures and build something bigger.[11]

THE BIOGRAPH THEATER

Movie buffs Alan Rubin, David Levy, Leonard Poryles, Paul Tauber, and Neil Cohen opened the Biograph Theater in 1967, in what had previously been the home of the Manhattan Auto dealership at 2819 M Street. Their motto was "crazy we may be, but stupid we're not." The Biograph was another "art theater," showing foreign films and revivals of classic American movies. It seated 280 customers in a wide but shallow auditorium. Instead of tickets, patrons bought brass tokens that they inserted into a turnstile to enter the theater, something like a subway station. Rubin later would describe the Biograph as a twenty-nine-year-long film festival. The theater never lost money, but it closed in 1996 when the building was sold to the CVS drugstore chain.[12]

A 1968 photo of the Biograph Theater at 2819 M Street. (*DC History Center*)

THE KEY THEATER

Don King started the Key Theater in 1969, remodeling a building at 1222–26 M Street that had been built in 1927–1928 as the Georgetown Recreation Center bowling alley (see chapter 25). Because the building had been constructed for a bowling alley, there were few structural pillars in the middle of the building, creating an open space suitable for a theater. A *Washington Post* reporter described the original auditorium as comfortable enough, but "strictly utilitarian, with molded plastic seats [and] undecorated plastic sheet walls." Carpets, sets, and drapes were all orange, a popular color at the time.[13]

In 1973, David Levy left the Biograph Theater partnership and bought the Key Theater on his own. The Levy family have run businesses in Georgetown for decades, including a clothing store on M Street and the still-operating Bridge Street Books (see chapters 5 and 27). Levy trained as a lawyer and practiced law for several years but left the profession for the Biograph opportunity.

David's brother Philip Levy later recalled that the Key

> was a nice commercial movie theater. He then turned it into what was similar to what the Biograph had been, but something even more . . . more advanced, in a sense. Rather than showing old movies—though they showed new movies, too, at the Biograph—it was a mix of a lot of things. The Key was basically showing new American independent films.[14]

For a year in 1983–1984, the Key ran a series of Alfred Hitchcock classics such as *Rear Window* and *Vertigo*. Particularly profitable for nine years were midnight weekend showings of the cult classic *The Rocky Picture Horror Show*, where many audience members showed up in costume. In 1985, Levy expanded by adding three auditoriums on the upper floors of the building, bringing the total seating capacity to 712.[15]

Levy finally closed the Key in 1997. He told a reporter that changes in the movie business had made the theater unprofitable. Films that once were shown exclusively at the Key now were released to multiple theaters at the same time, at higher prices. Newspaper ad rates had increased. Lack of parking was a competitive disadvantage.[16]

THE CEREBRUS THEATERS

The Cerebrus Theaters reused the former home of Parkway Dodge at M and Thomas Jefferson Streets. Martin Field and Harold Slate, who also owned the Janus Theaters on Connecticut Avenue, opened the Cerebrus I, II, and III in 1970. The three auditoriums were small, seating only 150 to 195 people. An affiliate of the KB Theaters chain bought the Cerebrus in 1974. In 1991, they lowered the admission price to $1; however, this move failed to revive the business, and the Cerebrus closed in 1993.[17]

CHAPTER 25

Bowling Alleys and Pool Halls

BOWLING AND BILLIARDS ARE COMBINED IN THIS CHAPTER BECAUSE THEY often have been combined in a single business. In the past, both were frequent adjuncts to saloons.

BOWLING

Bowling is an old game. In the Middle Ages, Germans engaged in *Kegling*, which involved tossing round stones at a group of standing clubs.

In Washington in the mid-nineteenth century, newspaper ads touted bowling lanes in two types of locations. One was excursion resorts. The Capitol Garden Pleasure Resort at 2nd Street and Maryland Avenue announced its plans to build "a splendid bowling alley" in 1854, and Blackistone's Pavilion and the White House Pavilion, both located downstream on the Potomac, advertised bowling as an option alongside dancing, fishing, and picnicking. The atmosphere may have been more wholesome at the YMCA, which in 1871–1872 advertised that it had bowling alleys.[1]

The other setting was saloons, where bowling alleys often were found in the basements or attics. Until Prohibition, bowling alleys remained firmly connected to alcohol consumption and consequently had an unsavory reputation. Their clientele was almost entirely men. Women were put off by the consumption of alcohol and tobacco (chewed and smoked) and by surly, no doubt profane exchanges between bowlers and the men who had low-paid and sometimes dangerous jobs as pin spotters.[2]

The only nineteenth-century bowling alley on Wisconsin Avenue or M Street was located in the 1860s and 1870s in the White House Restaurant at 33 High Street (today's Wisconsin Avenue) near the C&O Canal. Advertisements referred to it as the "White House Restaurant and bowling *saloon*" and noted that "The Bar is Stocked with Choice Wines Liquors and Cigars." For more on the White House Restaurant, see chapter 21.³

Georgetown Bowling Club/Potomac Alleys

The Georgetown Bowling Club opened in 1910 at 1219 Wisconsin Avenue. It soon was renamed the Potomac Bowling Club.

It really was a club. It ran a classified ad in 1911 seeking a "porter for club." A newspaper item about a bowling tournament said that R. E. Chapin

The building on the right in this 2025 photo was home to the Potomac Bowling Club and other bowling alleys from 1911 to 1928 and, later, was home to Britt's Cafeteria (see chapter 21). (*Photo by the author*)

BOWLING ALLEYS AND POOL HALLS

and W. E. Howser were "members of the Potomac Bowling Club of the District League."[4]

Today the building seems small for a bowling alley. Later in the twentieth century, bowling facilities became quite large, with sometimes dozens of lanes laid out side to side, but early in the century, bowling centers were smaller. This building was only 29 feet wide, but it was deep. In 1908–1909 an existing addition on the rear of the building was either further extended or replaced, making the depth of the first two floors 138 feet. This provided room for four or five bowling lanes.[5]

Frank Armstrong took over the bowling alley in 1915 and ran it through 1921, under the name "Potomac Alleys." He and his family lived in the

This photo taken between 1910 and 1926 shows bowling alleys in a narrow space at Washington's Jewish Community Center. This probably is similar to the interior of the Potomac Bowling Club. (*Library of Congress National Photo Co. Collection LC-F82-1484*)

building. Armstrong was a native Washingtonian, born in 1876, who had previously worked as a bowling alley manager.

Prohibition was a challenge for many bowling businesses because they had to make money from the bowling rather than making much of it from alcohol sales. Some bar owners converted their businesses into full-fledged bowling alleys, while others failed. This was the start of bowling's transition into an activity for all, including women and families.

We do not know if Prohibition contributed to the closing of Armstrong's business late in 1921, but it is possible. The space became vacant, though Armstrong and his family may have continued living in the building for a while. He went on to work as a dairy products salesman and died in 1944.[6]

Farley Veale bought the building sometime between 1917 and 1921. Veale's business was real estate rather than bowling, but he had a big impact on bowling in Georgetown. He was born in 1862 in Loudon County, Virginia, son of a farmer. From 1894 to 1900, he ran a livery stable at 1072 Wisconsin Avenue, just north of the C&O Canal. In 1900, he became a manager at the Parkway Livery Company, across the street at 1065 Wisconsin Avenue.[7] With the advent of the automobile, the owners of Parkway Livery transitioned to a new enterprise, Parkway Motor Co., focused on the automobile. Veale made the transition with them. For more about the horse-to-car transition generally, see chapter 4.

In 1924, Veale left Parkway Motor Co. and, with a partner, started Georgetown Realty and Insurance Company, of which Veale was the president. It had its offices at 1219 Wisconsin Avenue, the former home of the Potomac Bowling Club. The office must have been on one floor and the bowling lanes on another.

In 1923 and 1924, Veale leased space in the building to Charles Weinstein, who ran a pool hall there, after which the former bowling alley space was vacant. In 1927, Veale leased the space to Gerald R. Cooley, who ran a bowling alley there for one year.

Cooley was not a bowling expert either, but he wanted to be. He was born in Iowa in 1896, and by 1920, he had moved to Washington with his wife Pearl and was working as a clerk for the Department of Agriculture. He soon moved on to the Treasury Department, where he would have a long career interrupted by a four-year stint in the bowling business.

BOWLING ALLEYS AND POOL HALLS

The Georgetown Recreation Center

Two things led to the construction of Georgetown's only purpose-built bowling alley at 1226 Wisconsin Avenue.

One was the increasing popularity of duck pin bowling in Washington. In 1928, one hundred new duck pin lanes were opened in the city. The number of bowling establishments citywide grew from eight in 1925 to eleven in 1930. Commentators noted that the smaller, lighter duck pin ball made bowling more attractive to women and children.[8] Veale and Cooley no doubt were aware of this boomlet.

The other was visible from Veale's office and Cooley's bowling alley at 1219 Wisconsin Avenue: there was a large lot across the street at the corner of Wisconsin Avenue and Prospect Street (1226 Wisconsin Avenue). It had 56 feet of frontage on Wisconsin Avenue and was 130 feet deep, 7,280 square feet all told. On the lot were two buildings that had been vacant on

Georgetown's only building constructed for use as a bowling alley, at 1226 Wisconsin Avenue, later housed the Key Theater (see chapter 24). (*Photo by the author*)

and off for several years. Veale bought the lot in 1927 and quickly obtained a building permit to construct a two-story building, 130 feet by 56 feet, filling the entire lot. The permit was specific that a bowling alley was the intended use of the building.

The new building was almost twice as wide as 1219 Wisconsin. When the new bowling alley opened in February 1928, it had fifteen lanes (probably on two floors) as well as eight billiard tables. An ad at the time refers to Cooley as the proprietor; he presumably leased the building from Veale. At the same time, his bowling alley across the street at 1219 Wisconsin Avenue closed; it must have been temporary quarters while the new building was being constructed.[9]

Washington was a racially segregated city, and it is likely that the Georgetown Recreation Center was segregated. Despite the segregation of customers, however, pin setters often were African American.[10]

After ten years of Prohibition, things other than alcohol had to lure patrons. Bowling leagues were among those lures, and they proliferated.

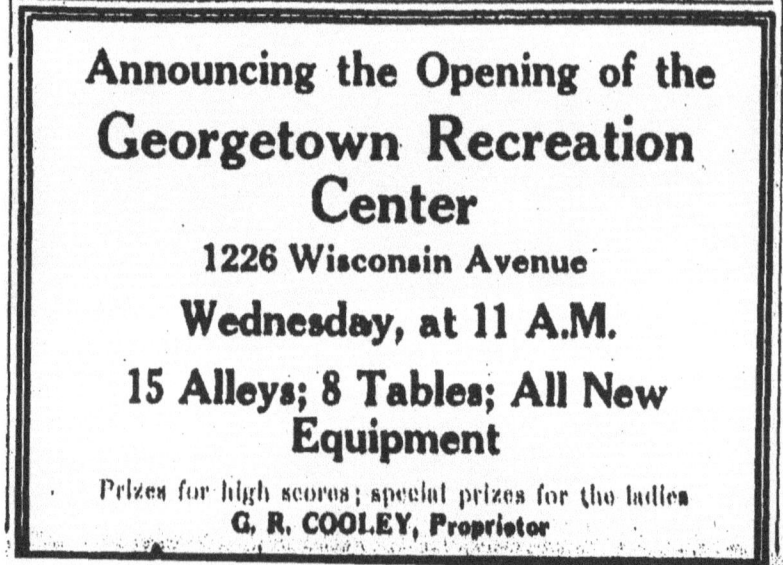

An ad appearing in the *Evening Star* announces the opening of the Georgetown Recreation Center in 1928. (Evening Star, *February 21, 1928, 29*)

BOWLING ALLEYS AND POOL HALLS

Sam Benson, a former streetcar motorman hired by Cooley to work at the Georgetown Recreation Center, was founder and president of the Georgetown Recreation League. The league's opening match was on September 21, 1928, between the teams of the center itself and the Potomac Savings Bank. Other teams in the league represented the Georgetown Gaslight Co., Blackman's Jewelry, the Georgetown Athletic Association, Georgetown Realty Co., and a number of other bowling facilities. A sign of the arrival of women on the bowling scene was a match in 1929 between Commercials Team of the Washington Ladies' League and Sam Benson's Recreation All Stars.[11]

An August 1940 ad sponsored by the Metropolitan Washington Duckpin Operators Association listed the association's members (including the Georgetown Recreation Center) and emphasized that all of their bowling alleys were air conditioned, a plus in a Washington August before residential air conditioning was common.[12]

At the time the Georgetown Recreation Center opened, Veale was in his late sixties and was phasing out of his business activities. Veale and his wife Emma had one child, a daughter named Louise, whose husband Edwin Schlegel worked for Veale's Georgetown Realty and Insurance Company in the second half of the 1920s. The Veales and the Schlegels were neighbors at times, living in two apartments upstairs at 1219 Wisconsin. In 1929 and 1930, Schlegel represented the company in Richmond, Virginia.

When Schlegel returned from Richmond, he took over the Georgetown Recreation Center. By 1932, Cooley was back at the Treasury Department, where he remained for more than twenty years.

In 1935, Veale sold 1219 Wisconsin Avenue to Joseph Wise. Georgetown Realty and Insurance Company continued to lease office space in the building.

When Veale died in 1938, Louise Schlegel inherited the building at 1226 Wisconsin. In 1941, she sold it and the bowling business to the same Joseph Wise and his wife Hilda. The Wises continued using the name "Georgetown Recreation Center" at least until 1942. In 1946, they closed the bowling alley and sold the building. Years later, the building's large space would lead to it becoming the Key Theater (see chapter 24).

BILLIARDS

Since 1914, there have been ten businesses on the neighborhood's two main streets that called themselves pool halls or billiard parlors. The Georgetown Recreation Center also offered billiards in addition to bowling, as did Frank Armstrong's Potomac Alleys.

There was a boom in billiards in Washington in the early twentieth century. Citywide, there were twenty-five pool halls in 1900, none of them located in Georgetown. The citywide number grew to forty-seven in 1905 and eighty-seven in 1910. Little of that growth was in Georgetown, where only three or four pool halls operated in those years.

Billiard parlors had shorter lives than other kinds of Georgetown businesses. While in most other classes of stores there were a few that operated for more than twenty years and sometimes twice that long, billiard parlors often lasted five years or less.

William Xander

William Xander came to the United States from Germany in 1898, at age sixteen. He started out as a bartender. By 1902, at the age of twenty, he had become a partner in a Bladensburg, Maryland, hotel.[13] In 1903, he married Margaret Niemann, born in Maryland to German parents. They would have six children.

In 1908, Xander opened a saloon on Louisiana Avenue NW, not far from the Capitol. In 1910, he relocated to Georgetown, opening a saloon at 3238 M Street NW, in space occupied as of this writing in 2025 by Clyde's Restaurant.

Perhaps Xander had noted the growing numbers of pool halls in Washington after 1905, or maybe he had a pool table in his saloon and just saw that it was popular. In 1913 he opened a pool hall next door to the saloon, at 3236 M Street (also occupied by Clyde's today). He may have cut a door between them.

The new pool hall was short-lived. Around midnight on June 28, 1915, firefighters responded to a report of a fire in the building at 3238 M Street. Smoke on the lower floors was so intense that four men who rented rooms on upper floors had to be brought down on ladders. The fire had originated in the saloon's kitchen and caused $700 in damage. The saloon was closed by early 1916, perhaps because Xander chose not to rebuild after the fire. The pool hall continued to do business for another year, and then it too disappeared. Xander ran a new saloon on 15th Street NW for a while, but he soon left the pool hall and saloon business and found work as a salesman. He died in 1932.

Abraham Mitchell

Abraham Mitchell, an African American born in Virginia, opened his first pool hall in 1905 on Marion Street NW. He moved it three times in the next four years, first to 7th Street NW and then to H Street NE. He moved his residence to Georgetown in 1910 and, a year later, opened another pool hall there. He closed the H Street location after a year or so.

Mitchell's Georgetown location was at 3256 M Street (a building since replaced by the Georgetown Park mall). This was only a few doors west of William Xander's pool hall. Mitchell and his wife Addie lived nearby, at 3006 and later 3008 M Street. In 1917, Mitchell also had a barbershop just a few doors farther up at 3272 M Street. After 1918, both businesses were gone. Mitchell relocated again, opening a pool hall on Georgia Avenue NW. Such frequent relocation was possible because a billiard parlor's income-producing assets (pool tables) are easily movable.

William N. Payne

William N. Payne ran a restaurant on M Street for twenty years before changing businesses and opening a pool hall. Payne was born in Falls Church, Virginia, in 1853, the son of a farmer. In 1891, he opened a restaurant at 3218 M Street (actually described in city directories as an "eating house" or "dining room"). Over the next few years, the restaurant occupied a series of spaces around the central intersection of Wisconsin Avenue and M Street. Sometime in 1900, the restaurant closed.

What Payne did for the next few years is a mystery. In 1906, though, he was back in the restaurant business, this time at 1209 Wisconsin Avenue, again near the intersection with M Street.

Payne remained at that address for twelve years overall, but in 1913, he replaced the restaurant with a pool room. We can only guess why he made this change. It seems likely he was responding to the new popularity of billiards and pool, discussed earlier in the chapter. He also was sixty-one years of age and may have thought a pool hall could be an escape from the toil of restaurant work.

Payne soon discovered that there were other challenges in the pool hall business. Police raided his business on January 31, 1914, and he and several customers were arrested. Payne was charged with permitting gambling on the premises. One can imagine how difficult it would be for a pool hall owner to keep customers from betting on their games, so perhaps he did not know about the gambling. There is no record of the case's outcome.[14]

Payne's pool hall disappeared after 1919. He died in 1921 at age sixty-eight.

CHAPTER 26

Bicycle Shops

THE BICYCLE WAS A LATE NINETEENTH-CENTURY INVENTION, AND THERE was a bicycle retailing and repair boom in Washington in the early twentieth century. The number of bike shops citywide grew from sixteen in 1895 to eighty-four in 1900, then tapered off to thirty-one in 1920. That boom passed Georgetown by, however. There was a smaller boom around 1975, when the number of bicycle shops on Wisconsin Avenue and M Street grew to four.

Today people think of Georgetown as a bicycling destination because of the C&O Canal towpath, the Capital Crescent Trail, and other bike trails that converge in the neighborhood. The presence of those trails has not greatly increased the number of bike shops, though. In 2025 as this is written, there are three bike shops on the two main streets, along with two on side streets.

RAY AND CHESTER COGSWELL

Brothers Ray and Chester Cogswell ran the first long-lasting bicycle shop in Georgetown. Their family moved to Georgetown between Ray's birth in Leavenworth, Kansas, in 1880 and Chester's birth in Washington in 1883. By 1900, the family had settled in Georgetown, and their father Fred was working as a printer. Chester began his career as an elevator operator and Ray as a typesetter, but they did not stick with those jobs for long.

In 1902, Ray opened a bicycle shop at 3054 M Street. The next year he moved it to 3019 M Street, where it would remain for the next seventeen years. Later, the building would house Meyer Levy's men's clothing store. For a photo of the building, see chapter 5.

The 1903 city directory said Chester was a machinist but did not say where he worked. Chances are good that he worked in Ray's shop—in these early days of bicycling, a repair shop no doubt had to make many of its own spare parts. In 1904, Ray took Chester into the business, renaming it Ray Cogswell & Co.

Then an odd gap occurred. The Cogswell bike shop disappeared after 1905 and reappeared in 1913. From 1909 to 1912, Houston Warren ran a bike shop at 3019 M Street. Warren was African American, from Tennessee, and ten years older than the Cogswell brothers. He was a machinist and, in 1907, had run a bike shop on 12th Street NW. He told the census taker in 1910 that he was a machinist in a bicycle shop. He did not say he owned the shop, even though at the time the store was listed under his name in the city directory.

Had Warren bought the business, or was he managing it for the Cogswell brothers? We do not know. We do know that in 1910 Ray told the census taker he was an electrician, so he was doing other things. Chester, on the other hand, said he was a salesman in a bike shop. Which shop? Warren's?

In 1913, Ray returned as proprietor of the shop. After that one year, Ray withdrew from the business and Chester carried on as the proprietor. Ray became an electrical contractor for the rest of his career, working at first out of the bicycle shop's space.

A 1919 ad for the shop listed the prices of some brands: Speeder, $7; Irvington, $10; Mitchell, $12; Flying Merkle, $30 to $50. Cogswell offered credit; one ad said an Adlake or Orient bicycle could be had for $1.25 a week. The shop also sold secondhand bikes.[1]

Chester ran the bicycle business through 1920; he then closed it and became a poultry farmer. We do not know whether the brothers changed careers because the bike shop was not profitable or because they just decided they would rather do something else. They did open the shop during the peak of the bicycle boom, though, and the number of bicycle shops in the city was gradually shrinking during the years they were in business, so they may have faced a declining market.

MELVIN YOUNG

Melvin T. Young was born in Wisconsin in 1908. His father, an electrician, moved the family to Washington when Melvin was a boy. Melvin attended the U.S. Naval Academy, graduating in 1932. He served in the D.C. Naval Reserve for several years, including training duty at sea. In 1934, he married Marie Duehring, a D.C. native, and the two of them settled in the Clarendon area of Arlington, Virginia.

In 1933, Young opened a business at 1611 Wisconsin Avenue (just above Q Street) selling electrical equipment and supplies, perhaps putting to use knowledge acquired from his electrician father. That did not last long, however, and the next year he had a bicycle repair shop at that address. He continued to call it a repair shop until 1941, but his advertising tells us he was selling bikes as well. A 1937 ad, for example, offered "BICYCLES—New display of Columbia, Colson Rollfast and Hercules."[2]

From 1941 on, Young called his store the "Georgetown Bicycle and Utility Shop." He had called his original electric supply business the "Utility Shop" and was still using the phrase "utility shop" in 1948 when he advertised a $39.95 special on Columbia bicycles for girls and boys. By the 1950s, he had dropped the word *utility*, and the name changed to "Georgetown Bicycle Store."[3] It is not clear exactly what "utility" meant, although Young did run ads in the summer of 1939 saying his store was a place to get lawn mower blades sharpened.

Young accepted trade-ins and offered rebuilt bicycles (probably the trade-ins, after he reconditioned them).[4] His ads emphasized service. "We Service What We Sell" was a slogan of the Bicycle Dealers Association of the Greater Washington Area. Young was an officer of the association, and newspaper ads appeared from time to time (probably run by the association) that listed Washington area bicycle dealers (including the Georgetown Bicycle Shop) and highlighted that phrase.[5]

Young himself advertised constantly but conservatively. There were occasional display ads, but most of Young's ads were smaller, in the classified section of the *Evening Star* under "bicycles."

In May 1951, Young opened a second shop in Arlington, at Lee Highway and Kirkwood Road, under the name Parkway Cycle and Hardware. (Perhaps "utility shop" had referred to hardware.) Ads that May said "introducing to the Washington Area a completely new bicycle store" and offered a 10 percent discount to customers who brought the ad to the store with them. Another ad that month offered a $5 discount at either store to anyone bringing in the ad. The two stores often advertised jointly during the 1950s.[6]

The two stores sold more than just bicycles—in 1956 they advertised a lawn mower clearance sale at both stores. One wonders how much demand there was for lawn mowers in Georgetown, where lawns are few and tiny. During the 1956 holiday season, the Arlington store advertised Lionel model trains as well as bicycles. A 1950 ad said the Georgetown store also sold toys and games.[7]

Young closed the Georgetown store in 1958. The Arlington store continued to operate until the mid-1970s. It was close to Young's home, and he may have decided it was just more convenient to concentrate on that location. Later on he may have sold the Arlington store, too. A 1975 newspaper story about the popularity of motorbikes included a quote from "Karen Schumacher of Parkway Cycle and Mower Co."[8]

Young was active in his community. Besides his work with the Bicycle Dealers Association, he was a member of the board of the Georgetown Lions Club and, at one point, was a candidate for appointment to the Arlington County School Board. Marie Young died in 1968, and Melvin married Marion Keane in 1970. He died in Arlington in 1993 at age eighty-five.[9]

CHAPTER 27

Bookstores and Record Stores

THIS CHAPTER CONSIDERS BOOKSTORES AND RECORD STORES TOGETHER because, over the years, many stores have sold both. We will use the term *record store* to refer to any store selling recorded music, whether on records, tape, or compact discs.

Wisconsin Avenue and M Street were home to only a handful of bookstores and record stores until the mid-1970s, when the number grew to six or seven. The 1980s and 1990s were the heyday of Georgetown bookstores and record shops, with thirteen to fifteen of them on the two main streets. More recently the number has shrunk due to online competition and the advent of music streaming services. As of this writing in 2025, there are no record stores in the neighborhood and only three bookstores selling new books, along with one selling used books.

DEBORAH AND MARY THOMAS

The earliest available Georgetown directory is from 1830. It lists three bookstores: one run by Richard Cruikshank near today's M and Thomas Jefferson Streets, one run by James Thomas at 31st and M Street, and one run by Deborah Thomas (no apparent relation to James) at Wisconsin Avenue and N Street.

Deborah Thomas's store was in business for more than thirty years. She was born in Albany, New York, in 1780 but had moved to Washington by 1820. Her husband, John V. Thomas, died in 1823. We do not know whether he started the bookstore and she continued running it after his death (as was common) or she herself founded the business.

Like some other early Georgetown booksellers, Deborah Thomas also sold stationery. Her son William, born when she was only sixteen, was a bookbinder. She had three other children.

Deborah died in 1852. Her youngest child, Mary, had been an art teacher but, with her mother's death, took over the business and continued it for another ten years. In 1862, it was listed in the Georgetown directory as selling "books and fancy goods." "Fancy goods" referred to notions, novelties, and accessories that were primarily ornamental.

The Thomas bookstore closed after 1862. William continued working as a bookbinder until his death in 1875, and he apparently prospered—in 1870 he told the census taker that his house on Prospect Street was worth $18,000.

JOHN LEARMONT

A store called the Record Changer did business briefly on Wisconsin Avenue in the late 1940s, but the first lasting record store was run by John Learmont. Learmont was a lieutenant colonel in the British army who served as a military attaché in Washington. He was a record collector, and when he left the army he remained in Washington and started a record shop at 1625 Wisconsin Avenue (near Q Street), opening on April 1, 1950.

The radio schedule in the *Evening Star* later that same month revealed that Learmont had a sideline:

> *John Learmont, former British lieutenant colonel and record collector turned record dealer, starts a new program of outstanding records of the week on WQQW at 11:30 a.m. today.*[1]

Learmont later found a second sideline. On October 25, 1953, the *Evening Star*'s radio schedule column noted that at 2:30 p.m. that day on WGMS

> *John Learmont, who writes the program notes for the National Symphony Orchestra, will discuss and play excerpts of music to be presented by the Symphony in Constitution Hall.*[2]

In 1954, RCA Victor suddenly reduced its record prices. Twelve-inch LP records that had been selling for $4.10 to $5.95 now were to sell for $3.98, and prices on ten-inch records and 45 rpm discs were cut as well. Learmont was one of two record dealers who criticized RCA's timing; the suddenness of the announcement consequently left them with an inventory of records purchased assuming resale at the old, higher prices that they now would be compelled to sell at the new, lower ones.[3]

By this time, Learmont had ventured into selling books as well as records. In 1956, Learmont moved the store to 1227 Wisconsin Avenue, just above M Street. He advertised an "inventory sale" at the new location, featuring "L.P.'s (Overstock and Cut-outs)" at 25–65 percent off; 45 rpm records were forty-five cents each.

Learmont made his last radio appearances in 1959, doing record reviews on WMAL-FM. In the early 1960s, though, he found yet another sideline: selling tickets for live events around the city. Examples of the artists for whose performances he sold tickets were the Opera Society of Washington, Joan Baez, Pete Seeger, the Clancy Brothers, Spanish pianist José Iturbi, and a multiartist "Greek Festival '65." Many of the event ads identifying Learmont's as a place to buy tickets also said tickets were available from the Talbot Ticket Agency in the Willard Hotel; perhaps Learmont had an arrangement with them. In any event, Learmont's shop was a source of tickets throughout the 1960s.[4]

In 1963 or 1964, Learmont moved again, to 3131 M Street, around the corner from his previous location. In 1967, he changed the store's name to the "Georgetown Record and Book Shop."

In 1976, Learmont moved his store again, this time to Frederick, Maryland. Both the *Evening Star* and the *Washington Post* ran articles, a month apart, exploring whether the closings of Learmont's store and a few others were signs of impending decline in Georgetown (a perennial theme in the press). Learmont and the others who were closing up shop said they were driven out by high rents, traffic, lack of parking, and "the press of the huge mobs that clog Georgetown on evenings and on weekends." These were reflections of the change that had occurred as Georgetown became a place for people from around the region (and tourists from around the country and the world) to shop and find restaurants and entertainment. At the same time, though, the shopkeepers' complaint was ironic: they were unhappy because there were too many potential customers on the streets.

Learmont's comment was this:

> It has changed so much. Businesswise, it's becoming a kind of downtown, a kind of Times Square in what was hitherto a kind of quiet community.[5]

He also noted that businesses like restaurants and hairdressers could pass rent increases on to their customers through higher prices, but he did not have that option—"if a book is marked $8.95 I have to sell it at that or less."[6]

Learmont's location was taken over by Horizon Book Shops, a chain. Joe McEvoy, Horizon's vice president, said of Learmont, "John is a beautiful man but he's not an aggressive businessman," contrasting Learmont's limited opening hours with Horizon's plan to be open 10 a.m. to 10 p.m. seven days a week.[7] McEvoy's criticism seems unfair. Learmont was nothing if not enterprising, and his radio appearances, National Symphony program notes, and ticket-selling operation all served to bolster his record business.

FRANCIS SCOTT KEY BOOK SHOP

Georgetown's longest-lasting bookstore was not on Wisconsin Avenue or M Street but, instead, in a residential neighborhood at 28th and O Streets: the Francis Scott Key Book Shop.

Elizabeth M. Barrett and Edith Foye started the business in 1934, at 1401 29th Street NW, at the corner with O Street. Barrett lived near the store at 29th and Q Streets. Foye, who later remarried and became Edith Jarvis, was the great-great-granddaughter of Francis Scott Key, and she named the store for him.[8]

The first mention of the shop in the press was a *Washington Post* item on February 28, 1934, saying that historian Grace Dunlop Ecker would be at the shop to read excerpts from her new book, *A Portrait of Old Georgetown*. A year later the shop was listed as a collection point for a drive to provide books for Coast Guardsmen and lighthouse keepers.[9] In 1937, an *Evening Star* article told of an exhibit of woodcuts to be held at

> that uniquely charming book shop in the old town, called the Francis Scott Key Book Shop. Except that it is very clean and tidy in some ways it makes one think of an old London book shop.[10]

BOOKSTORES AND RECORD STORES

In 1941, Doris Wagner Thompson and Martha Johnson bought the store, which by then had been open for seven years. Johnson had been working there since 1937 and thus knew when it became available for sale. Thompson was the manager of another bookshop.

The two new owners moved the business from the 29th Street location to a building at the other end of the block, on the corner of 28th and O Streets. The new location, while in a residential area, was not far from the Herring Hill commercial area on P Street between 26th and 28th. The building at that time had an "ample bay window" that no longer is there.[11]

This house was home to the Francis Scott Key Book Shop. During the bookshop's tenure, the center window in the photo was a bay window. (*Photo by the author*)

Doris Thompson was born in Washington in 1907. Thompson brought to the partnership a network of contacts in the diplomatic community and Washington society. She may have been aided in acquiring those contacts by the affluence of her husband Ross's family. In 1930, when Doris and Ross were twenty-three, they lived with Ross's mother in a house valued at $100,000, with five servants.

In 1940, the Thompson household included two individuals identified in the census as "lodgers" (in this case probably meaning house guests rather than paying boarders). One of them was Doris's soon-to-be business partner Martha Johnson, nicknamed "Marty." She was born in New York City in 1905. Her father was in the army, and she had lived in the Philippines and all over the United States. She brought to the partnership four years of bookshop experience and a persuasive, no-nonsense manner.[12]

Despite its residential surroundings, the building had housed stores for decades. Louis and Mary Hoelman had run a grocery store in the space from 1900 to 1916. Before that, since 1860 or before, the space had been the bakery of Mary Hoelman's father, Gottlieb Hurlebaus. The space had been residential since 1916. The building also had two apartments upstairs. The Hoelman family still owned the building and would be the bookshop's landlords for the next fifty years.[13] They leased to Thompson and Johnson not just the ground floor space, but the entire building, including the upstairs apartments.

Besides selling books, the store had a lending library, staffed sometimes by a part-time employee and sometimes by volunteers. Martha Johnson said one customer asked the shop to deliver to her a weekly selection of books from the lending library—but stressed she wanted none that included sex, war, or poor people.[14]

Like many long-running Georgetown businesses, the Francis Scott Key Book Shop had famous people among its customers, including Adlai Stevenson (who lived in one of the upstairs apartments during World War II), Dean Acheson (who lived around the corner), Caspar Weinberger, W. Averell Harriman and his wife, and Joseph Alsop. Every summer Alsop would purchase two boxes of books that the store would ship to his vacation home. Emily Durso, who started working in the store as a teenager in 1967 and was a part owner for a while in the 1970s, recalled years later that Alice Roosevelt Longworth would arrive at the store every Friday afternoon in a chauffeur-driven car. After chatting with the staff for a while, she would pick four or five books to read during the coming days. She was particularly interested in books about unidentified flying objects.[15]

Also like some other long-running Georgetown shops, the Key Book Shop provided extraordinary personal service. Thompson and Johnson watched neighbors' houses when they were away, let contractors into neighbors' houses, and accepted package deliveries for them. One customer would describe people to whom he wanted to send gifts, and the shop would select, wrap, and ship something. A customer could give the store a list of grandchildren with names and ages, and the store would choose, wrap, and mail an appropriate birthday gift to each. An author had the shop gift wrap and ship two hundred copies of his book even though he did not buy them from the shop—they came directly from his publisher. One embassy went from calling with questions about books to calling with questions about anything, such as where to buy a carpet or a crib. Diplomats leaving for overseas posts would arrange for the shop to send them periodic packages of books, which Johnson could select because she knew her customers' tastes. Johnson freely admitted that providing this service required over-staffing the store.

Every afternoon Marty Johnson served tea and homemade cookies to whomever happened to be in the store at 3 p.m., including customers and delivery drivers.

Thompson and Johnson refused to discount prices or sell paperbacks. There was no cash register. Johnson lived in one of the upstairs apartments, and Thompson lived a few doors up the street.[16]

Consistent income came from contracts to supply books to the libraries of the Central Intelligence Agency, the State Department, and the National Security Agency. Every week messengers would hand-deliver lists of books that those libraries wanted to purchase. The long relationship between the store and these agencies was due in part to discretion—the orders were kept confidential.[17]

Jean Waterhouse, who helped Johnson manage the store after Doris Thompson's death in 1970, described customers' tastes in books. Nonfiction outsold fiction three to one. The store sold lots of biographies and books about politics and global affairs. Spy novels, especially British ones, were also big sellers.[18]

Because their work running a bookstore brought them into contact with authors and publishers, Thompson and Johnson developed a sideline as literary agents. It began with customers who were aspiring authors asking Johnson to help them get their manuscripts looked at by publishers. After doing this as a favor for several customers, the two of them organized a separate literary agency that they ran from an office next to the bookshop.

One book that Johnson helped bring to publication was written by a ten-year-old. Virginia Cary Hudson wrote a series of essays for her teacher in 1904 that were lost in an attic for decades. The wife of the Episcopal bishop of Washington ran across them in the 1950s and found they were entertaining, often funny, and remarkably perceptive given the author's age. She convinced Johnson to show the essays to the Macmillan Company publishing house, which published them as *O Ye Jigs & Juleps* in 1962. As of 1971, 330,000 copies had been sold in twenty-one printings.

Another client of the agency was Harriet Vaughan Davis, the mother-in-law of Walt W. Rostow, a senior White House staffer in the Johnson administration. She wrote *Aboard the "Lizzie Ross"* about her life as a child on a clipper ship captained by her father, where she lived until she was fourteen.[19]

When Thompson died in 1970, Martha Johnson continued running the store. At the time of a *New York Times* profile in 1984, Martha was eighty years old and had been running the store for forty-three years. In the later years, her poodle Susan kept her company in the shop. Martha died in 1985.

The store continued to operate under the ownership of Martha Johnson's heirs and the management of Jean Waterhouse, who had been helping Martha manage it since 1979. In 1990, the heirs decided to sell. They instructed their lawyer, Mary Burnett Hatch of Roanoke, Virginia, to find a buyer, if possible, who would continue to run the store as it had been.

Among the forty-five answers that Hatch received from published advertisements was an inquiry from two women in their early thirties, the same age that Doris Thompson and Martha Johnson had been when they bought the store forty-nine years before. Vivian Brown and Jennifer Herman had met when they both worked for the same bookstore in Alexandria, Virginia, and for two years, they had been searching for a store of their own. Hatch was sold by their combination of desire to preserve the store's tradition with realism about the challenges doing that would entail. The

Hoelman heirs were impressed, too, and as their contribution to preserving the store, they agreed to a lease at the same modest rent Johnson had been paying: $2,100 a month.

Brown and Herman took over in August 1990. The one-month transition before Waterhouse's previously planned retirement proved difficult for everyone. Waterhouse was rankled by, among other things, Brown's and Herman's decision to do away with the lending library, which was unprofitable. Another challenge for the new owners may have been acceptance by staid neighborhood customers—having the store run by two casually dressed young women would be a change.

The store did indeed run much as it had before (absent the lending library). The new owners continued to help their neighbors by keeping keys and checking when burglar alarms went off.

The store finally had to close in early 1995. The Hoelman heirs decided to sell the building (sixty-four years after Mary Hoelman's death). Brown and Herman lost their lease and could not afford to relocate the store.[20]

BRIDGE STREET BOOKS

Philip Levy, who opened Bridge Street Books in June 1980, had a varied career before he went into the bookstore business. He worked as a messenger at one point, then was on the staff of Ralph Nader's Impeach Nixon organization in 1973, and also managed the Key Theater on M Street, which was owned at the time by his brother David.

According to Philip and his brother Richard, the genesis of the bookstore was a family trip to England, when, as Richard put it, all Philip wanted to do was go to plays and look in bookstores. He spent hours browsing in the famous and enormous Blackwell's Book Shop in Oxford. Philip and Richard's father, Sam, owned a clothing store on M Street (see chapter 5) and invested in Georgetown real estate. On the flight back from England, Sam told Philip he had a piece of retail space next to the future site of a hotel (today's Four Seasons) and suggested he open a bookstore in the space. Richard's version of the story differs—he says he (Richard) made the suggestion before the trip.

First, Philip had to learn the business, so he worked in a bookstore for two years before opening on his own.

The opening on June 27, 1980, hit a snag—the cash register would not work. Philip had to call someone to come and fix it, and he was unable to open the doors until 3:30.

Of the early years, Philip said "the thing that served me best when I first started was being stubborn and stupid. What I mean by that is if I had been smarter I would have given up within a year or two." He also took a particular piece of advice from his father: never spend money to save money. When a distributor offered a discount for buying extra copies of a book, the advice kept Philip from buying unneeded extra inventory.

The location next to the Four Seasons and near the headquarters of the World Bank and the International Monetary Fund was a plus. Philip Levy joked that "if you have an accent, you like us better than if you don't."[21]

Washington Post columnist George Will (who still frequents the store) wrote in 1989 that Bridge Street Books "is a small island of individuality where [Philip's] tastes and hunches are offered to the eclectic whims of bookstore browsers." When he opened, Philip wanted to specialize in works consistent with his left-leaning politics, but he soon faced a conundrum—should he carry Henry Kissinger's memoirs? He did. Years later, Will described him as "a 60s radical who has come to terms with commerce."[22]

The store is tiny. In 1995, Levy said it was about one thousand square feet, into which he crammed 15,000 volumes. The space is no larger today. By contrast, the Barnes & Noble store just up M Street had forty thousand square feet at the time, and 220,000 volumes. Despite Barnes & Noble's size, Levy claimed that half the books in his stock would not be found at Barnes & Noble.[23]

Philip Levy died in 2017. His death stirred local concern about what would become of the store. Today, however, the store is still in business, owned by members of the Levy family.[24]

CHAPTER 28

Toy Stores

SURPRISINGLY, IT WAS NOT UNTIL 1930 THAT A DEDICATED TOY STORE opened in Georgetown. In that year, Clayton B. Long, who had run a furniture store at 1251 Wisconsin Avenue since 1923, opened a toy store nearby at number 1267. The store closed after just two years, possibly a victim of the Depression.

Since Long opened, there generally have been only one or two (occasionally three) dedicated toy stores on Wisconsin Avenue and M Street. That is not the whole story, however, as some stores of other types have sold toys as a sideline. Ads by the Georgetown Bicycle Store in 1950 noted that it also had toys and games. The Kendrick-Harrison Furniture Store advertised itself in late 1923 as "headquarters for toys in Georgetown," no doubt to take advantage of the Christmas season demand for toys.[1]

It was not until 1975 that Georgetown really had toy stores. The specialized Kite Site on Wisconsin Avenue south of M Street opened in 1974 and operated until the early 1990s. The much-beloved Red Balloon opened just a couple of doors away in 1970 and remained until the late 1990s. When the Georgetown Park mall opened, it contained two toy stores: the Georgetown Zoo, which sold stuffed animals, and national chain FAO Schwartz. They both closed in the early 2000s.

THE RED BALLOON

The Red Balloon opened in November 1970 in a small space at 1208 31st Street, just north of M Street. A *Washington Post* article announcing the opening described the shop aptly as "a pre-school boutique." The owners were Susan and Dwight Olson, whose goal, the reporter said, was to create a store "where you could find young, kicky, often handmade clothing with an individual look." Susan was a dressmaker, and the store featured her designs as well as those of other local designers. Much of the clothing was hand-crocheted or otherwise handmade. Along one wall of the store, Dwight built a big train engine that children could play on while their mothers shopped.[2]

The clothes were beautiful, but they were not inexpensive. For example, in 1971 the store offered red knit pants for $13, a quilted bolero print skirt for $16, a $19 hand-crocheted dress with matching hat, and a four-piece pinafore outfit for $25. The same issue of the *Washington Post* that advertised these items contained ads for *adult* men's shirts for $15 and for an *adult* woman's skirt for $25 in one case and $12 in another.[3]

Although the store's focus was clothing, it also sold a few toys. In the 1971 Christmas season, it offered a four-foot-long wooden "train to end all trains," promising "it should last a lifetime and be an heirloom."[4]

The Olsons did not stay in the business for long. In 1972, they sold the business to the aptly named Robert A. Joy. In October of that year, a second Red Balloon store opened in Les Champs, an indoor specialty mall in the Watergate complex. A newspaper ad announcing the new store was captioned "Red Balloon—Announcing the Birth of a New Balloon."[5] While we do not know, it seems likely that Joy was behind the expansion; the Olsons would not have gone to the risk and expense of opening a second store if they were planning to sell. Joy was a Boston native who had spent eight years in the Peace Corps before buying the store. He also played amateur ice hockey.[6]

That announcement ad included this list of what shoppers could find in either store:

- Snugli Baby Carriers
- Vermont Wooden Toys
- Oshkosh B'Gosh overalls
- Hand Tailored Children's Clothes
- Infants Tie Dye T-Shirts
- Educational Toys[7]

In 1976, Joy bought a building at 1073 Wisconsin Avenue, just south of M Street, with an antique store as the ground floor tenant. The antique store remained there for a while, but by mid-1978, the Red Balloon had relocated to the new building. The first newspaper item referring to the new location described handmade sleeping bags available for $65 to $75, in the shapes of a banana, an ice cream cone, a football, or an apple core.[8]

Like the Olsons, Joy carefully selected what the store sold. In an interview, he said he refused to stock Mattel's He-Man and She-Ra action figures, calling them "merciless marketing" comparable to what "Chrysler commercials with beautiful blond girls" are to adults.[9]

Joy was killed tragically in a helicopter accident in August 1987. With the Olsons gone, the store's clothing inventory had shrunk so that by then it was primarily a toy store. Joy's obituary referred to it as such. His wife Linda continued the business until the late 1990s. She sold the building in 2001.[10]

THE KITE SITE

In 1975, Chuck Bernstein opened the Kite Site at 1075 Wisconsin Avenue, specializing, of course, in kites. His store was just across an alley from the Red Balloon, and there was a little bit of competition between the neighbors—the Red Balloon sold kites as well, though its inventory was less extensive. The Kite Site carried a similar a range of common, ready-made kites but also sold exotic models like the Ghost Clipper, which, in 1977, sold for $35 and looked like a tall ship under full sail.

Bernstein took his kites seriously. In 1977, he told a reporter

> *Americans tend to think of kites as frivolous, something kids fool with. Actually, kite building is an ancient art, and in Asia, particularly, whole cities get involved.*[11]

The annual Smithsonian Kite Festival brought crowds to the store every year. A customer seeking materials to build a kite for the festival would have to contend with crowds the week before and after the festival. Michael Chapman, who managed the store for a while, said in 1987 that he stayed open until midnight the night before the festival.[12]

Bernstein moved the Kite Site to 3101 M Street in 1979 and opened another business in its old space on Wisconsin Avenue, "In the Bag," which sold luggage, purses, briefcases, and myriad other kinds of bags. In 1985, he moved In the Bag to 3106 M Street, and in 1990, the Kite Site moved to that address as well. Both stores closed in the early 1990s.

Bernstein then became a freelance reporter, and his work frequently appeared in the *Washington Post*. One of his first pieces was "The Wind on a String" in 1995, about—what else—kites. It listed stores where kites or kite makings could be bought, but that list did not include the Kite Site, which already had closed. Bernstein sometimes wrote about recreational activities like white water rafting, but many of his articles were about food, with titles like "Love and the Art of Chopped Liver," "The Mechanics of Matzoh Balls," and "Nuts about Making Peanut Butter." *Washington Post* food reporter Phyllis Richman profiled Bernstein's early taste for pineapple on pizza.[13] One of Bernstein's pieces profiled Patsy Rankin, who had followed a similar career path, closing her kite store in Rehoboth Beach, Delaware, to teach cooking and later open a restaurant in nearby Bethany Beach (which still is in business in 2025).[14]

CHAPTER 29

Sporting Goods Stores

Sporting goods stores have not been numerous in Georgetown—only one or two on Wisconsin Avenue and M Street at most times.

JACOB SHAPPIRIO

Jacob Shappirio opened his sporting goods shop on M Street in 1921. He was fifty-seven years old when he opened the store, and he had had at least two careers before that.

Born in Russia in 1863, Shappirio came to the United States in 1880. He moved to Washington in 1890 and went into partnership with Joseph Sholsky to run a clothing store in downtown Washington. We know little about Joseph Sholsky, but in 1891, Shappirio married Mary Sholsky, who no doubt was Joseph's sister or daughter.[1]

Later in the 1890s, Shappirio was a tailor and ran his own clothing store, also downtown. In 1900, he went to work for J. M. Stein & Co., who called themselves "merchant tailors," yet he continued to run his own clothing store a few blocks away.

Shappirio stayed with Stein for fifteen years, but over that period the nature of his own store on the side changed. In 1905, his clothing store became a sporting goods store, which remained in business for five years. It closed around 1910, and Shappirio worked solely as a tailor for Stein after that.

Two newspaper stories suggest that Shappirio's store had a diverse inventory. In 1897, a man was sentenced to prison for "the larceny of a pair of opera glasses from Joseph Shappirio, a dealer at 905 D Street." In 1902, a "dink knife" allegedly used to commit a murder had been sold by Shappirio to someone who a few days later had sold it to the murderer.[2]

In 1916, Shappirio made a dramatic career change—he became a stockbroker, joining the firm of Lawrence J. Dietz & Co., members of the New York Stock Exchange (NYSE) with offices in the Woodward Building on 15th Street downtown. Shappirio was listed in that year's city directory as the manager of the firm. In 1918, the name of Shappirio's employer changed to O. H. Gore & Co., also a member of the NYSE. The partners in the Gore firm were Shappirio and Ollie H. Gore.

Things did not go well for the new firm. In January 1920, the firm became insolvent, and at the request of its creditors, a court appointed a receiver for the firm and its assets. The creditors claimed that the firm's indebtedness would approach $100,000, an enormous sum at that time. In December of that year, the receiver told the court that Shappirio and Gore had unlawfully concealed assets of the firm and had concealed or destroyed financial records. Curiously, there was no press coverage of the matter after that; either the receiver's allegations proved to be wrong or the matter was settled somehow.[3]

The insolvency, of course, ended Shappirio's career as a stockbroker. He then went back to something he knew—sporting goods. In 1921, he opened a sporting goods store in Georgetown, at 3060 M Street. He did not have any apparent prior connection to Georgetown, and why he chose to locate the new store there is a mystery.

In 1926, opportunity knocked in the form of a mortgage foreclosure sale of a property a few doors down from the store, at 3068 M Street. Jacob and Mary Shappirio seized the opportunity, bought the property, and moved the store there. They lived next door at 3070 M Street. Jacob was not on the deed; the property was titled in Mary's name only, possibly because of still-threatened claims against Jacob from the O. H. Gore & Co. bankruptcy.[4]

Jacob Shappirio died in 1932. Mary carried on the business for three more years, closing it in 1936. She lived on until 1958.[5]

HOOVER BROTHERS

Georgetown's other sporting goods store in the 1930s was Hoover Brothers at Wisconsin Avenue and Volta Place. In 1924, when he was twenty-five years of age, Elbert C. Hoover started out stringing tennis racquets from the family home near 1st and W Streets NW. He made his own strings, calling the business the Washington Racquet Stringing Co. In 1925, his younger brother Irwin joined the business, and they opened a store at 14th and F Streets downtown. They renamed the business "Hoover Brothers" and sold tennis supplies as well as stringing racquets.[6]

The two brothers grew up in a long-standing Washington family. Their grandfather, also named Elbert, had been a messenger. Their father James was at one time a dealer in butter and cheese, and he later sold real estate. When he was a child, Irwin was chosen by a local bakery as a model for their advertising, which dubbed him "Corby's Mother's Bread Boy." His picture appeared on the bakery's delivery trucks. Irwin later attended Johns Hopkins University.[7]

The brothers were big supporters of youth tennis. Newspapers in 1926–1928 carried multiple articles about tournaments in which they provided organizational assistance, accepting applications from potential entrants or conducting drawings to determine tournament pairings. They also donated racquets and trophies for prizes.[8]

In 1929, the brothers moved the business to 1519 Wisconsin Avenue. Though they now called it a sporting goods store, we can assume tennis-related products were their strong suit.

In 1931, Elbert died at the age of only thirty-two. Irwin continued the business for five more years, closing it in 1936. During World War II, he worked as an inspector at an aircraft manufacturing plant. After the war, he went into the real estate business in Northern Virginia. He died in 1970.

SPORTING GOODS AS A SIDELINE

In addition to the few dedicated sporting goods stores, some merchants of other products dabbled in sporting goods for brief periods. Agnes Albrecht and her son Harry owned a tobacco store on M Street. In 1910, they started selling sporting goods in the same store, a combination that would be laughable today. Their thinking may have been that the market for both products was primarily male. The store closed in 1915. For more on the Albrechts, see chapter 13.

Cavanagh and Kendrick Hardware did business in Georgetown from 1923 until the 1950s, but the proprietors tried a number of other businesses on the side, including a sporting goods store from 1921 to 1927. At one point, they combined the sporting goods business with their music and record store in a single space.[9]

CHAPTER 30
Georgetown's Own Banks

Georgetown today is home to branches of regional and nationwide banks. In the past, though, three significant banks were founded and headquartered in Georgetown. While many of their banking activities are beyond the scope of this book, the three institutions provided retail banking services to neighborhood residents, and two of them built landmark buildings that still stand today.

THE BANK OF COLUMBIA

Congress created the District of Columbia and appropriated funds for construction of the President's House, the Capitol, and a few other federal buildings, but it provided nothing for the development of the rest of the city. George Washington, the original owners of the city's site, and the commissioners charged with overseeing the city's development planned to pay the development costs from the sale of lots, thinking that investors would want to buy lots in a city that would boom as the government took root there. Investors by and large were not willing to bet on that, and demand for lots was very disappointing.

A variety of wheeler-dealers appeared on the scene, some offering schemes such as lotteries to raise money. Among them was Samuel Blodgett, who promoted the idea of a bank that would raise money by subscriptions and then would give priority in its lending business to projects that would develop the city. In 1793, when Georgetown still was part of Maryland, the Maryland legislature passed "An ACT to establish a bank in the District of Columbia."[1] The legislation said the new institution was to be known as

GEORGETOWN'S OWN BANKS

The Bank of Columbia operated in this building at 3210 M Street from 1796 to 1806. (*Photo by the author*)

the Bank of Columbia, and listed individuals who had agreed to initially subscribe for the bank's stock, including Blodgett and a dozen prominent Georgetown citizens. Blodgett would become the bank's first president.

In 1796, the Bank of Columbia constructed a building at 3210 M Street, which it occupied until 1806 and which still stands today.

The bank may have been doing business at that same location before it constructed the new building. A hand-drawn 1799 map shows an unidentified bank on the site, with a tavern next door. The tavern was the City Tavern.

GEORGETOWN'S RETAIL PAST

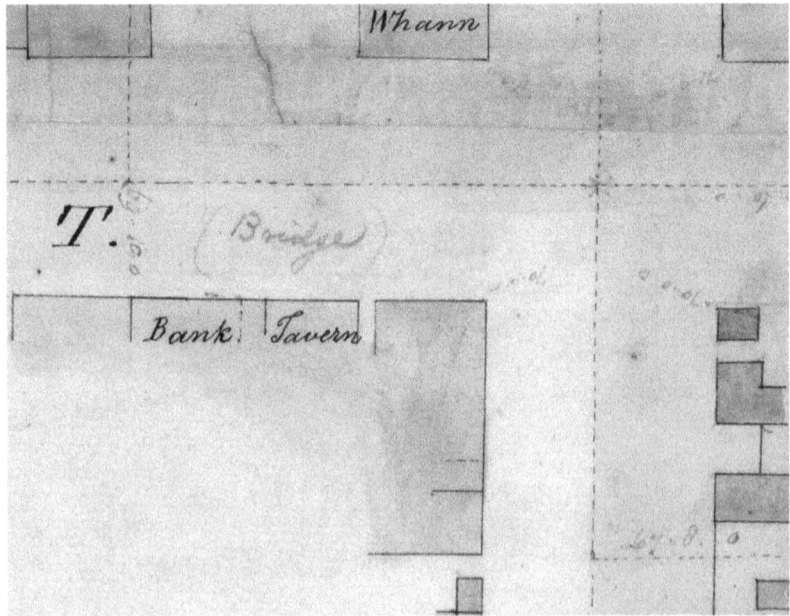

This excerpt from a 1799 map shows a bank on Bridge Street (now M Street) and the City Tavern next door. (*Library of Congress, 88693279*)

In the 1960s, workers renovating the old tavern building found a bricked-up connecting door between the tavern and the bank. The door may have facilitated withdrawals and deposits for those doing business in the tavern, although it may also have been created during a brief period later when the bank building served as a barroom for Lang's Hotel next door (see chapter 20 for more on the City Tavern and Lang's Hotel).[2]

In 1845, years after the bank had moved out, the building was leased by the Town of Georgetown, which used it as a town hall. In the 1880s, the building was turned into a fire station.

When the bank left 3210 M Street in 1806, it moved to a mansion-like building it had just constructed on the north side of M Street west of 33rd. It was among the largest buildings in Georgetown and cost the then-enormous sum of $200,000 to build, suggesting that these were not the stereotypically conservative, tight-fisted kinds of bankers. The street on the west side of the site was named Bank Street because of the bank's presence, not because of the street's steep incline.

This portion of an 1865 photograph shows how the Bank of Columbia building stood out on the Georgetown skyline. (*Library of Congress, 2018667022*)

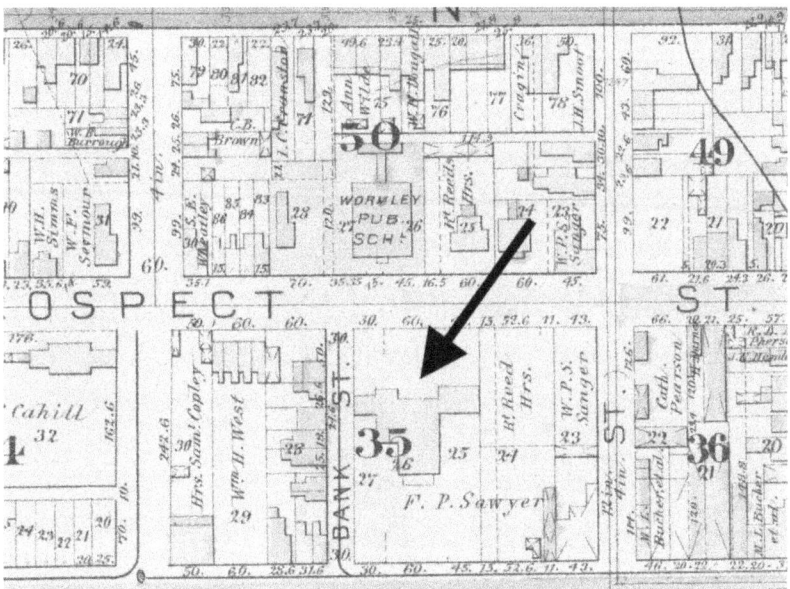

This 1887 survey map shows just how large the Bank of Columbia building was. (*Hopkins 1887 survey atlas of Washington*)

The Bank of Columbia served as a depository for the federal government's funds and as the government's agent for making public payments. It had a branch in the Treasury Department building. During the War of 1812, the Treasury lacked funds to pay the costs of moving Andrew Jackson's army to New Orleans. The Bank of Columbia provided a quick loan, requested and personally guaranteed by President James Madison.[3]

The bank was born amid the wheeling and dealing of the city's birth, and for the bank, the wheeling and dealing never really stopped. In 1836, the bank closed its doors and voluntarily went into liquidation. The building had previously been nicknamed "the White Cow," and when the bank closed, someone observed that "she was milked so hard by her owners that she died."[4]

The building became a private home (a big one) and remained one for more than sixty years, until it finally was demolished in 1900.[5]

FARMERS AND MECHANICS' NATIONAL BANK

The Farmers and Mechanics' Bank of Georgetown was founded in 1814 and initially was located in a house on the southeast corner of today's 31st and M Streets. Like the Bank of Columbia, the Farmers and Mechanics' Bank provided a loan to the federal government during the War of 1812, at the request of President James Madison, to finance an expedition transporting supplies down the Mississippi River.[6]

Around 1820, the bank replaced the house with a much larger building, which still stands today. The building's original red brick facade was renovated in 1911, adding a stucco finish and Greek revival features.[7]

In 1872, the bank became a national bank and was renamed the Farmers and Mechanics' *National* Bank of Georgetown.

In 1920, a hundred years after building its first home, the Farmers and Mechanics' Bank began acquiring several lots at the corner of Wisconsin Avenue and M Street for a new headquarters. The new stone building, today a Georgetown landmark, was completed in 1922.

This photo of the Farmers and Mechanics' National Bank Building at 31st and M Streets was taken before 1911. (*Allan B. Slauson,* A History of the City of Washington, Its Men, and Institutions *[Washington, D.C.: Washington Post Company, 1903], 177*)

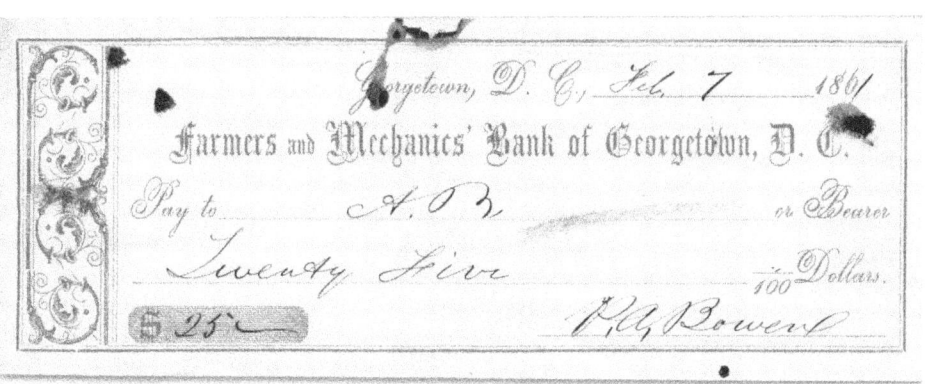

A check written in 1861 on the Farmers and Mechanics' Bank of Georgetown. (*Author's collection*)

GEORGETOWN'S RETAIL PAST

This building was constructed by the Farmers and Mechanics' National Bank in 1922. (*Photo by the author*)

A newspaper item about the bank's move into the new building in December 1922 included this commentary:

> *The Farmers and Mechanics' National has lived modestly. It is still housed where it has been for over a century: remodeled over and over again, but it had ceased to be up to the requirements of a modern banking home.*
>
> *After many frugal years, Harry V. Haynes, a modern up-to-date bank president, decided to throw off the old garb and follow trade to the new modern building on the Wisconsin Avenue corner.*[8]

After Farmers and Mechanics' National Bank moved into its new home, the old building was vacant for some years, then was home to Fidelity Building and Loan Association from 1933 to 1937. In 1940, Chambers funeral home took over the space, occupying it for thirty-five years. As of 2025 it serves as offices for a German television network.

Under Harry Haynes, the bank in the 1920s sought to expand beyond being a community bank for Georgetown to serving a bigger part of the Washington area. In 1927, it opened its one branch office, at Wisconsin Avenue and Warren Street NW.[9]

In 1928, that expansion stopped when Farmers and Mechanics' National Bank was merged into Riggs National Bank. To preserve the memory of Georgetown's bank, Riggs renamed the M Street building the "Farmers and Mechanics' *Branch*." Those words are still engraved on the building's wall just below the cornice.[10]

In the 1950s, as a sign of the growth of the automobile, Riggs bought property just north of the building site and created a parking lot for its customers. Today the building houses a branch of PNC Bank.

POTOMAC SAVINGS BANK

Like Farmers and Mechanics' National Bank, Potomac Savings Bank began as a local Georgetown institution. On May 3, 1903, the *Evening Star* reported that the Potomac Savings Bank had been organized and "will begin operations in the next few weeks." On May 18, the bank's first newspaper ad appeared, touting 3 percent rates on savings accounts and declaring that "One Dollar Opens an Account." The ad listed the thirteen members of the bank's board of directors, which included three Georgetown retailers: Alphonse M. Baer, who had a clothing store on M Street (see chapter 5); grocer George W. Offutt; and agricultural equipment dealer George Boteler (see chapter 2).[11]

The bank first opened for business at 1264 Wisconsin Avenue, in the building occupied today by Martin's Tavern. A year later, the bank bought a building at 1200 Wisconsin Avenue, on the northwest corner with Wisconsin Avenue, that had been built around 1850. The building was occupied by an existing tenant, however, and the bank would have to wait five years for that lease to expire before moving in. For the interim, the bank leased a building across Wisconsin Avenue at 3157 M Street, on part of the future site of the Farmers and Mechanics' Bank building.[12]

In 1909, just before moving across the street to its new building, the bank ran a classified ad offering to sell a bank safe measuring 5.6 by 7.2 by 3.3 feet—133 cubic feet.[13]

GEORGETOWN'S RETAIL PAST

Headquarters of the Potomac Savings Bank in the 1920s. (*Library of Congress National Photo Company Collection LC-F82-3132*)

The new building was a banking office by day but was a community meeting space by night. From the time the bank moved in, newspapers reported on meetings held in the building by organizations like the Georgetown Citizens Association, the Men's Club of Christ Church, Georgetown, and the Ancient Order of Hiberians. In 1914, the bank was the site of meetings of business leaders and citizens pondering the impact of the planned replacement of the Aqueduct Bridge to Virginia and deciding how to express the neighborhood's views about that.[14]

In 1923, the *Evening Star*, in an article titled "A Lively Youngster," reported that the bank was entering its twenty-first year. The connections to the Georgetown business community remained. George Offutt had died late in 1922, and his cousin, fellow grocer Henry Offutt, was now the president. Alphonse Baer still was on the board, and George Offutt's son George Jr. was the bank's attorney.

By 1933, the Great Depression had decimated the banking industry, with hundreds of banks closed. On March 5, 1933, the day after he was inaugurated, President Franklin Roosevelt declared a nationwide bank holiday from March 6 to March 9, temporarily closing nineteen thousand banks. Federal bank examiners would look at each of those banks and permit those that were sound to reopen when the bank holiday ended. In the District of Columbia, thirteen banks were not permitted to reopen, and one of those was Potomac Savings. Each of the thirteen was placed in the hands of a conservator who would manage it until it could reopen or had to be permanently closed. The conservator for Potomac Savings was George Offutt Jr.[15]

Initially, the bank sought to raise additional capital by selling new stock, but that effort was unsuccessful. This was a tense period for the depositors, who could not withdraw their funds and would lose their money if the bank could not reopen. In May, a different plan emerged, under which several of the closed banks would be merged into a single new one.

That plan bore fruit. Potomac Savings and three other banks were combined to create the Hamilton National Bank, which opened its doors on September 24, 1933. The new bank was managed by a combination of the people who had been managing the four banks before the merger. It would operate for twenty-one years in the building at Wisconsin Avenue and M Street, as well as in eight other locations around the city.[16]

In 1954, Hamilton National Bank was merged with the National Bank of Washington, which did business in the building at Wisconsin Avenue and M Street until the bank was closed in the early 1990s. After that, the former bank lobby became a clothing store.[17]

CHAPTER 31

Herring Hill Neighborhood Shops

There has long been a grouping of retail stores in the 2600 and 2700 blocks of P Street, at the eastern edge of Georgetown and away from the retail core along Wisconsin Avenue and M Street.

The neighborhood surrounding the two retail blocks was once known as Herring Hill. Legend says it got the name because of the plentiful herring once found in Rock Creek in the springtime.[1] The area was populated by African Americans even before the Civil War, some of them freed from slavery, some fleeing slavery, and some whose owners had not officially freed them but did not try to recover them, either. Some may also have been enslaved but permitted by their owners to "live out" in their own dwellings. In 1860, seven hundred African Americans lived in Herring Hill, with their own churches and other institutions. One resident told an 1860 census taker that the residents "lived like free."[2]

In *A Portrait of Old Georgetown*, Grace Dunlop Ecker quotes at length the reminiscences of William Gordon about life on Herring Hill, including this:

> *Christmas was the great time for the [African Americans]. Ordinarily, they were not allowed in the streets after the town bell rang, at nine o'clock at night, but at Christmas this restriction was removed.*[3]

The concentration of African Americans in Herring Hill continued until widespread renovation took place in Georgetown. Census records show that, in 1920, the overwhelming majority of people residing between 28th Street and Rock Creek, from Olive Street to P Street, were African American. The pattern in the 1940 census was similar.

Before World War II, as now, most of the stores on these two blocks of P Street were what today we call "convenience retail," serving nearby residents. In 1914, there were three grocers, a clothes cleaner, and a coal dealer, along with a photographer and a hardwood flooring dealer. Eleven years later in 1925, there were four grocers, two tailors, a shoemaker, an upholsterer, a notions shop, and a restaurant. Ten years later, in 1935, the mix was similar: three grocers, a tailor, a drugstore, an upholsterer, and a newsstand.

In 1987, the *Washington Post* published the recollections of Pauline Gaskins Mitchell, a longtime Georgetown resident and historian of the Mount Zion Methodist Church. She remembered that Herring Hill businesses owned by African Americans outnumbered those owned by whites.[4] That recollection is not quite correct. Herring Hill did contain a concentration of businesses owned by African Americans, but they were not a majority of the businesses there. As in the retail core, many businesses on P Street were owned by immigrants.

Herring Hill Ethnicity of Business Owners

Business Owner	1920	1930	1940
African American	2	5	0
U.S.-born white	3	2	0
Foreign born	3	6	2

The stores owned by African Americans were of different kinds than those owned by others. During the 1920–1940 period, African American businesses included dressmakers, barbershops, shoemakers, a news dealer, a milliner, and a drugstore. During that same period, however, the several grocery stores in Herring Hill were owned mostly by immigrants, and there were no African American grocers. Immigrants also owned a tailor shop and a dry cleaner.

AT-HOME BUSINESSES

Mitchell remembered that "[u]nhampered by zoning regulations, some residents opened little stores. Some were located in rooms that ordinarily would have served as parlors."[5]

GEORGETOWN'S RETAIL PAST

A number of those tiny businesses were on P Street.[6]

- Mrs. William L. Ragan worked as a dressmaker from her home at 2725 P Street in 1922.
- Mary Barnes was a dressmaker, at 2728 P Street from 1927 to 1929, and at 2725 P Street after that until 1937. Barnes was African American, born in Washington in 1875. At 2725 P Street, she actually was a lodger in the home of William and Mabel Andrews.[7]
- Alice Barton lived and ran her millinery business at 2804 M Street from 1917 to 1920.
- Edward Smith ran an upholstery business in his home at 2616 P Street, from 1919 through 1938.

Perhaps the most colorful Herring Hill business owner was Adaline Waters, who sold notions from homes at 2706 P Street and later 2702 P Street, from at least 1915 through 1930. Waters was born into slavery in Virginia in 1855. A few weeks before her death in 1937 at age eighty-two, she was charged with throwing a cup of hot water on a twelve-year-old neighbor. Waters claimed that she had thrown only cold water, and was provoked because the boy threw a brick through her window "and otherwise annoyed her." She said she was glad all of her children were dead because they "won't know I've been disgraced." After the trial, she showed court attendants a scar that she claimed had been caused by an overseer's whip when she was a child.[8]

DRUGSTORES

Walter Napper opened the Imperial Drugstore at 2624 P Street first in 1933 and continued to operate it until at least 1943. Napper was African American, born in Virginia in 1865. He had been in the drugstore business for a long time—the 1910 directory shows him running a drugstore on 7th Street NW. It probably was Napper's death or retirement that led to the P Street space being taken over by the Haviland Cleaners, which did business there for more than forty years, from some time before 1956 through 1998.

On the western edge of the two-block concentration of stores stood Pride's Pharmacy at 28th and P Streets. Armistead T. Pride, classified by the census as mulatto, was born in Lynchburg, Virginia, in 1873. His father, also named Armistead, was a barber. The son came to Washington in 1890 and studied pharmacy at Howard University, graduating in 1893.[9] The 1892 city directory listed him as a barber residing at Howard, so he may have worked his way through pharmacy school by cutting hair, a skill he no doubt learned from his father.

Pride opened his own drugstore in 1895, when he was only twenty-two. It originally was located at the corner of 28th and Dumbarton, but 1898 he moved the store to the corner of 28th and P Streets. He remained in business there for twenty-seven years, through 1925. In 1926, he sold the store building to Malcolm and Harold Morgan, the owners of the Morgan Brothers Pharmacy located two blocks away at Thirtieth and P Streets. In 1927, they leased the space to a delicatessen. As this is written in 2025, the space is home to Stachowski's Market, a butcher shop.

Pride retired in 1935, but five years later, he emerged from retirement and opened another drugstore at 22nd and M Streets; he ran that for ten years before retiring again. After World War II, Pride was instrumental in founding the Washington College of Pharmacy, and he served as its dean for ten years.[10]

GROCERY STORES

The little two-block retail stretch was awash in grocery stores—always at least three, and in some years four or five.

The building at 2701 P Street has been a store since 1910.

- In 1910, Saul Berman built a small warehouse at the back of the lot, probably as an adjunct to the opening of his grocery store.[11] Berman and his wife Gertrude came to the United States from Russia in 1904. In 1920, they were living above the store, with their three children and two lodgers. Berman ran the store until 1928.
- After the Bermans, Hyman Korn sold groceries at this location. Korn was from Austria, and he also lived above the store, with his wife, her brother, and his own brother.
- Morris and Beatrice Ginsburg, immigrants from Russia, took over the store after 1935 and did business there through at least 1943.
- Nathan Enzel opened the first liquor store in the building in the 1950s, and it has continued as a wine and liquor store since.

This building at 2701 P Street has been home to a series of stores since 1910. (*Photo by the author*)

In 1909, Jacques Heidenheimer, a musician, constructed three buildings at 2601–2605 P Street. Heidenheimer did not live in any of them, but a few years later 2601 P became home to a series of grocers:

- Shoub (first name unknown), 1914 (or earlier)–1919
- Jacob Rosenbloom, 1919–1921
- Jacob Bialek, 1922–1930

HERRING HILL NEIGHBORHOOD SHOPS

- Bella Goodman, 1931–1935
- Jacob Bialek again, 1937–1939
- Harold Brockman, mid-1940s
- Bernard Fishman, mid-1950s

Rosenbloom, Bialek, and Goodman all were immigrants. The national origins of the others are unknown. The building was a dog kennel later in the 1950s and a florist from 1969 to 1977.

In the first half of the twentieth century, seven different grocery stores occupied the retail space at 2601 P Street. (*Photo by the author*)

GEORGETOWN'S RETAIL PAST

Sanitary Grocery Co., a large chain of small groceries (see chapter 10), opened several stores in and around Herring Hill, including at 2531 P Street (1924–1937) and at 1417–19 28th Street (see more later in the chapter). There also was a Sanitary store for a while at 3003 P Street. The small independent grocers probably felt the competition from Sanitary, but they seemed to survive. The advent of supermarkets in the 1950s, however, reduced the market for neighborhood groceries on Herring Hill as elsewhere, and by 1956, Nathan Enzel ran the only grocery store in these two blocks. A 7-Eleven opened at 2617 P Street in the 1960s that continued as the only grocery store on P Street until it closed in 2022. A Streets Market grocery store is operating in the space in 2025.

2610 P STREET

The house at 2610 P Street was the site of a series of businesses, all owned by African Americans.

William Jackson ran a shoe repair shop there in 1919. Jackson was born in Virginia in 1887 and lived not far away at 28th and O Streets. In 1920, he teamed up with Lewin Veney, and the shop became "Jackson & Veney, shoemakers." Veney was born in Virginia in 1890. Jackson apparently moved on the next year, and Veney ran his own shoemaking business in the space until 1927.

There apparently was no store in the building from 1928 until 1937, when "The Nearly New Shop" opened. It was listed in directories as selling "general merchandise," which the store's name suggests was secondhand.

In the 1950s, the building again housed a shoe-related business, this time the shoeshine shop of Clarence Warren. Warren was a jack-of-all-trades who previously had been in several businesses in the neighborhood. He had run a "general transfer" business (trucking?) for a while, then a shoeshine business in 1929–1932, a delicatessen in 1934, and a newsstand in 1935–1938, all at 2540 P Street. After Warren closed his shoeshine business in the mid-1960s, 2610 P Street went back to being a residence.

1417 28TH STREET

Just south of Pride's Pharmacy, a building at 1417 28th Street was unusual for side street retail because it was built from the start to be a store rather than a home.

The building at 1417 28th Street NW is perhaps the only structure on a Georgetown residential street that was built to be a store. (*Photo by the author*)

Before 1923, there were two houses or a duplex on the lot. From 1900 to 1923, George Kent had his barbershop there. Kent was an African American native of Washington, born in 1867. After working for a couple of years as a porter, he opened his barbershop at 1417 28th Street. He continued giving haircuts there for twenty-seven years.

In April 1923, Leonard S. Nicholson bought the building where Kent rented the space for his shop. A Canadian-born physician, Nicholson was an active real estate investor. In the 1920s, he bought forty-three properties in Washington, many of them in Georgetown. In May 1923, he obtained a building permit to construct a brick store building on the site. The building contained two stores, numbered 1417 and 1419.[12]

We do not know whether George Kent had to close his barbershop in 1923 because he lost his lease, or whether his planned departure made the old vacant building an attractive development opportunity for Nicholson. Whichever it was, Kent made a career change at that point: he opened a delicatessen nearby at 2700 O Street, which he ran until at least 1939. In 1940, he was working as a janitor at the District Building (Washington's city hall). He was sixty-nine by then, so he may have closed the deli and taken the janitor's job in search of something less demanding.

Nicholson was a speculator, not a long-term investor. As soon as the new building at 1417–19 28th Street was completed, or possibly while it was still under construction, he sold it to Shoul and Dora Gladstone in January 1924. His investment may not have been profitable. He bought the building for $2,500. His building permit application estimated that the building would cost $3,500 to construct. If that estimate was accurate, he lost money when he sold to the Gladstones for $5,500, though perhaps construction was not yet complete when he sold or it cost less than originally projected.

The Gladstones, born in Russia, already ran a grocery store on 8th Street NW. Rather than moving that business, they leased both halves of the 28th Street building to the Sanitary Grocery chain, who combined the two stores into one. The new store opened in 1925.[13]

The Gladstones closed their store on 8th Street around this time. Shoul, who was sixty-four, may have been ready to retire, and the 28th Street building could have become part of their retirement nest egg. Shoul died in 1929. Sanitary closed their store in 1935, and Dora sold the building the next year.

Looking at the list of retail stores on this stretch of P Street, one is struck by how few businesses involved recreation. The big exception was just outside Georgetown to the east, the Blue Mouse Theater at 26th and M Streets, which had an African American owner (see chapter 24). There were only two restaurants, both short-lived, run by Sidney Sutton at 2712 P Street in 1925 and William King at 2603 P Street in 1934. Given the likely restrictions on African Americans' access to restaurants and other entertainments on Wisconsin Avenue and M Street, this is surprising.

CHAPTER 32
Changes in the 1980s
Georgetown Park and New Immigrant Entrepreneurs

The Georgetown retail district witnessed two big changes in the 1980s: the opening of the Georgetown Park mall and an evolution of the mix of stores on Wisconsin Avenue.

GEORGETOWN PARK

Large-scale commercial development was new to Georgetown—part of its charm always was the small-scale nineteenth- and early twentieth-century architecture. By the 1960s, the industrial uses that had dominated the hill from M Street down to the Potomac River were disappearing, and developers began to build on the properties that became available as a result. These were larger-scale projects than Georgetown had seen before, office buildings, and mixed-use developments.

There had been two previous attempts at an indoor mall in the neighborhood.

The Georgetown Mall

In the late 1960s, David Edin, the owner of a clothing store in New York's Greenwich Village, began exploring the idea of a branch in Georgetown. He was intrigued by a five-thousand-square-foot space above the Key Theater, which had been vacant for some time. Unsure whether people would walk up a flight of stairs to shop, he did a test run for a month using inventory brought from his New York shop. People must have walked up, because "The Georgetown Mall" opened in 1970, occupied by ten shops including Magus Leathers, Century Wig Fashion, Cloud 9 (selling antique furs and jackets), Henry Baby (a women's boutique), the Riga Gift Shop, the Far East Bazaar, Abacus Gallery, and a shop selling Spanish leather goods.

The Georgetown Mall struggled for a decade. Much of it was vacant by the mid-1970s. It made something of a comeback by 1981, when there were six tenants, but in 1985, the number fell to two, and the mall disappeared after that.[1]

THE FOUNDRY

While several of the first big waterfront projects included street front space for shops, only one provided indoor retail space. Inland Steel built the Foundry Building on the block between Thirtieth and Thomas Jefferson Streets, with its north side fronting on the C&O Canal. The project incorporated the restored Duvall foundry building that gave the project its name. Inside the new building was a two-level shopping arcade that opened in 1976. This was a much more ambitious, better-funded project than the Georgetown Mall. A year or so after the initial opening, a Rizzoli bookstore occupied the old foundry building, looking out on the canal through a large arched window on the second floor. In the early months, Inland sponsored promotional events like a jazz festival and a Fourth of July celebration.

Twenty-two stores appeared in a display ad in the *Washington Post* a few months after the opening (before Rizzoli's arrival). They were the sort of small, interesting shops for which Georgetown was known. Included were a custom macramé shop, an upscale audio dealer, a seller of fly-fishing equipment, the Canal Company antique shop, a plant store, an oriental rug dealer, and several boutiques.

The shops were successful at first, but as the years went by, vacancies increased. By May 1984, only eight years after the opening, enough space was vacant that K-B Theaters converted the entire lower level into a multiscreen movie theater. The theaters closed in 2002, and today there is no retail left in the building.[2]

The Foundry and Georgetown Park had in common the lack of an anchor tenant to attract shoppers inside. The Foundry had the additional challenge of getting shoppers to walk down the hill from M Street, toward

CHANGES IN THE 1980S

a waterfront that they were used to thinking of as dark and empty, not to say dangerous after sunset. Even as of this writing in 2025, retail other than restaurants does not seem to work south of the C&O Canal. Office buildings like Washington Harbor (on the waterfront) and Jefferson Court (neighboring the Foundry on the south) included ground-floor space for retail but never were able to lease much of the space.

DEVELOPMENT OF GEORGETOWN PARK

Georgetown Park occupied the former car barn of the Washington and Georgetown Railroad Company, a streetcar company that used cable cars driven by an underground cable. A second building across the canal on Grace Street was the powerhouse, where big motors pulled the underground cable.

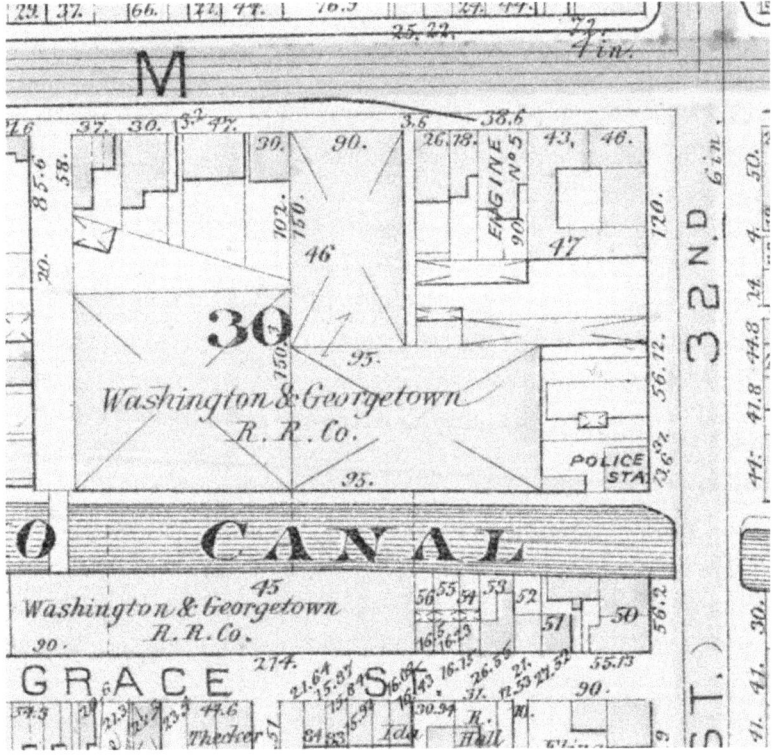

An 1887 survey shows the future Georgetown Park site. At that time, today's Wisconsin Avenue was called 32nd Street. (*Hopkins 1887 survey atlas of Washington*)

GEORGETOWN'S RETAIL PAST

In 1977, Western Development Corporation won approval from the U.S. Commission of Fine Arts to construct a mixed-use development on the site. A new building would be constructed behind the car barn, while preserving the historic M Street facade. (The powerhouse building would be restored.) The one proposed feature the commission did not approve was a pair of six-story office towers that would have been visible from Wisconsin Avenue, looming behind the historic car barn. The proposed project was to include 121 retail stores (totaling 210,000 square feet) and 155 condominium units.

Washington Post architecture critic Wolf Von Eckardt viewed the proposed project as the continuation of a trend that had begun with Ghirardelli Square (in a renovated chocolate factory in San Francisco) and continued with Faneuil Hall Marketplace in Boston: the renovation of a historic structure into retail, to which shoppers would be attracted by the combination of a historic architectural setting and unusual shops. Von Eckardt noted that, except for the two office buildings eliminated by the commission, the proposal had attracted much less opposition than other developments on the waterfront. He theorized that "the difference . . . is the snob appeal of Georgetown Park. It is the difference between a street vendor and a Garfinckel's sales person."[3]

Georgetown Park was complicated to build. The newly constructed parts of it were sandwiched between historic facades on M Street (that had to be propped up) and the 150-year-old walls of the C&O Canal. Existing structures, such as Clyde's Restaurant, had to be connected to the new building and protected from damage during construction. Financing also was a challenge during the late 1970s, a period of high inflation and very high interest rates.

When Georgetown Park opened in September 1981, Herbert Miller, the president of Western Development, told a reporter that "it's not a shopping mall, it's the world's first shopping park." Expensive finishes included wood-floored hallways instead of tile and elaborate cast-iron supports for the central skylight. The building combined two architectural styles: restored federal facades and a very Victorian interior. Miller resisted comparisons to other urban retail projects, saying, "Georgetown Park isn't like any of them. Nothing is the same; there's nothing like this anywhere. Georgetown Park is the only Georgetown Park in the world."[4]

Georgetown Park interior. (*Library of Congress, LC-HS503-5856*)

On opening day (September 27, 1981), seventy stores were open, and all but a few of the remaining thirty spaces were leased. Miller acknowledged that there was no anchor, which meant that, instead of small shops benefiting from traffic generated by the anchor, "you have to do it on your own."[5] He did point to a few larger stores that would generate traffic, particularly a Garfinckel's store. Garfinckel's was a long-standing, upscale Washington specialty store that did anchor a few suburban malls. This store, however, had limitations because it was smaller; it did not sell men's clothing, for example.

Almost all the stores in the mall were new to Georgetown; only a few came from existing locations elsewhere in the neighborhood. Ann Taylor (a Garfinckel's affiliate) and the Store for Pappagallo moved from Wisconsin Avenue, and modern furniture store Scan moved from Canal Square, a block away. Although spaces in Georgetown Park were larger than older Georgetown retail stores, most were smaller than in other malls, with less storage space.[6] The powerhouse building was the largest space, leased to Conran's furniture and home goods store.

Western Development had built the project in partnership with the Donohoe Construction Co., which did the actual construction. Historically high interest rates meant that Western and Donohoe could not afford to finance the entire property long term with just debt; they brought in the AT&T pension fund as a partner. A few years later, the pension fund became the mall's sole owner.

Georgetown Park was so successful that, in 1986, work began on a four-story, 118,000-square-foot addition that would provide room for sixty more stores. Next door to the mall, the historic Georgetown Market, in which Western had been leasing space to a number of small shops and restaurants, was to be converted to a gourmet food hall. A representative of Coldwell Banker Commercial Real Estate Services told a reporter around this time that the mall had been operating at 98 percent occupancy since it opened and was commanding rents of almost $400 per square foot.[7]

By 1998, that stellar economic performance was a thing of the past. The consensus in the real estate community was that the mall was suffering from its lack of both an anchor store and street-facing stores. Many felt it needed a renovation that would both make room for a full-size anchor and make the inside of the mall more visible to pedestrians outside. As one press report put it,

> a mall with small shops that face inward and no anchor or other traffic generator is not a formula for success. In Georgetown, any interior mall is an anomaly. The action is on the street.[8]

In 2006, Georgetown developer Anthony Lanier tried to buy the property, and former owner Western Development made a competing offer to buy it back. A lawsuit resulted, revolving around whether an old 1985 agreement between the AT&T pension fund and Western entitled Western to a chance to buy ahead of Lanier.

Western managed to acquire the property despite the ongoing lawsuit, but banks were unwilling to finance necessary renovations while the litigation was pending. The litigation also spooked potential tenants; as tenants moved out, replacements were hard to find. Negotiations with Bloomingdale's department store fell through. Ultimately, Western failed to make its mortgage payments, and the mall went into foreclosure in 2010. One article about the decline said vacancies had grown from 10 percent in early 2009 to 56 percent by spring 2010.[9]

Angelo, Gordon & Co. bought the property at the foreclosure sale and formed a partnership with Vornado Realty Trust to renovate the mall. They allowed most leases to expire so as to clear the space. The few tenants who remained included J. Crew, Anthropologie, and H&M, all of which fronted on the street. The new owners converted the mall to what one sees today—a grouping of larger retail stores with street frontage, and no interior mall. Another attempt at a deal with Bloomingdale's fell through, but other stores like T.J. Maxx signed leases, and the building returned to solid occupancy.[10]

GEORGETOWN PARK'S IMPACT

There is no question that the Georgetown retail sector changed after Georgetown Park opened. Among other things, upscale shops and chain stores became more numerous on M Street while on Wisconsin Avenue small, elegant shops were replaced by more prosaic ones. Landlords realized that chain stores were interested in coming to Georgetown and raised rents to levels that only chain stores could afford. As David Roffman, the editor of the *Georgetowner*, said in 1987, "[Georgetown] is turning into a mall, with one difference: we have no parking."[11]

In the mid-1980s, there were various theories as to just what impact the mall had had. One theory was that many stores had moved from Wisconsin Avenue to Georgetown Park or to M Street near Georgetown Park. John Latham of Clyde's was a proponent of this theory, saying, "The mall took a lot of the better shops all at once from Wisconsin Avenue."[12]

In fact, there does not appear to have been a mass migration to the mall and its vicinity from elsewhere in Georgetown. Between 1981 (the year Georgetown Park opened) and 2010, only five stores closed locations on Wisconsin Avenue and opened inside the mall: Ann Taylor, Pappagallo, Hess Shoes, Britches Great Outdoors, and Brass Boot. Only two of these had made the move in the 1980s. Scan Furniture also moved to the mall from the Canal Square development south of M Street. Only three stores moved from Wisconsin Avenue to street-front spaces on M Street near the mall (the Georgetown Frame Shop, Häagen-Dazs, and Up Against the Wall). Only one of those made that move during the 1980s.

A second theory was that the presence of Georgetown Park attracted chains and other upscale stores that were new to Georgetown, and those new stores chose to locate in the mall or on nearby M Street instead of on Wisconsin Avenue. This does seem to have happened. Most dramatic was the increase in clothing stores on M Street west of 30th from six in 1991 to nineteen in 1990 and sixteen in 1995. Shoe stores increased from two in 1981 to five in 1990 and four in 1995. More utilitarian stores disappeared from M Street, including Meenehan's Hardware (faced with a 400 percent rent increase—see chapter 17), a car lot, an auto repair business, a bakery, two decorators, an appliance store, and three galleries.

WISCONSIN AVENUE EVOLUTION

In the 1980s, some of the small, charming shops on Wisconsin Avenue closed. According to the owners of remaining Wisconsin Avenue stores, business dropped off because the formerly unique mix of stores was gone.

Some Georgetown institutions indeed did close, including the Design Store, The Gentleman's Jodhpur, Marimekko, Beyda's, The French Kitchen, Dorcas Hardin, and Johnson's Dress Shop, all of which had disappeared by 1985. Of the 159 stores listed on Wisconsin Avenue in 1970, 47 remained in 1985. Charming Georgetown shops were not entirely gone, however. Those 47 included the Georgetown Silver Shop, the Early American Shop, Lastrega, Powder & Smoke, The Phoenix, The French Market, Appalachian Spring, Little Caledonia, the Audubon Book Shop, and the French Shop Boutique. Within another two years, David's Village Shop and the Saint-Aubin de Paris dress shop also closed.

Some theorized that many shops were replaced by restaurants. The owner of David's Village Shop said, "There are more restaurants and bars than retail clothing and that's not enough draw on the Wisconsin Avenue side to draw people up to us, which would draw visitors in the evening but not during the day."[13] There was indeed an increase in restaurants, from fourteen on Wisconsin Avenue above M Street in 1970 to twenty in 1985; however, this was a period of dramatic increase in the number of Georgetown restaurants generally. Between 1970 and 1985, the total number of restaurants on M Street and Wisconsin Avenue grew from thirty-seven to eighty-seven.

Besides the perceived glut of restaurants, at least one business owner complained that too many shoe stores had moved into Wisconsin Avenue spaces vacated by more typical Georgetown shops. There is no question that shoe stores on Wisconsin Avenue multiplied, from four in 1970 to nine in 1975 and thirteen in 1985. Quantitatively, this does not seem like a world-changing increase—there were 158 retail businesses on Wisconsin Avenue in 1985.

As we have seen, immigrants have run stores in Georgetown for generations. In the 1980s, the pattern was repeated on Wisconsin Avenue. Some of the vacant space was taken over by immigrants from Iran, who had fled that country after the fall of the shah. A clash of cultures ensued, between an aggressive, Middle Eastern style of retailing and the more genteel approach that had characterized Wisconsin Avenue. In 1987, the *Washington Post* published a report by Marc Fisher about these changes, under the title "Street of Gold."[14] Fisher mentioned four of these stores, which had opened between 1981 and 1983. Three more followed in 1984 and 1985.[15]

The newcomers brought a different approach to retailing. Existing retailers complained about them bargaining on the price of merchandise; eating pizza at the cash register; displaying shirts in plastic bags; displaying shoes in manufacturers' boxes with dust on them; and standing in front of their stores (in one case with an open shirt) and calling to passersby to come in. One can understand the existing merchants' disapproval of bargaining—customers who found haggling acceptable in one of the newcomers' shops would come to the traditional retailers' stores and expect the same.

The existing merchants were concerned that the *style* of the newcomers' stores would repel their own customers and make them reluctant to walk up Wisconsin Avenue from M Street. In time, both the existing merchants and Georgetown residents became concerned about the customers that the new stores attracted. Several of the new stores began selling gold chains and other gold jewelry. Many of those who came in search of the jewelry were young people from other parts of Washington, often African American. There was much speculation about where young people got the money to buy pricey jewelry. The former Georgetown (Dumbarton) Theater was converted into a bazaar-like National Jewel Center (see photo in chapter 24). Even the Georgetown Pharmacy, a Georgetown institution that had been sold by "Doc" Dalinsky to one of the newcomers, began offering gold chains (to Dalinsky's horror).

One newcomer who Fisher interviewed had a different perspective:

> *People blame me because they see these guys with my gold. Where were these people when my business was for the area, when it was a gourmet shop? I went bankrupt. I designed it for them, good food for them—nothing. They want something free. They complain we bargain. In the whole Georgetown, everyone bargains.*[16]

Another newcomer said residents actually want no commerce other than a little grocery and dry cleaner.

A *Georgetowner* article in 1985 summed up the angst:

> *White Flint and Tyson's Corners [sic] have great stores. So does Columbia, Maryland and several other towns outlying D.C. Georgetown's best selling point is its ability to provide one truly great shopping street unmatched in vitality, variety and excitement. That used to describe Wisconsin Avenue and the nearby blocks. But what do we have today? Vendors and unruly kids. Panhandlers and tacky storefronts. Overflowing trash barrels and filthy sidewalks. And down on M Street a veritable Whiskey Gulch. The solution has to be a commitment to quality, "world class" retailing.*[17]

CHANGES IN THE 1980S

COMPETITION FROM SUBURBAN MALLS

Georgetown's retail businesses have to attract customers from elsewhere in the city and the metropolitan area—the neighborhood residents alone cannot support the amount of retail space that is in the neighborhood. In 2015, Georgetown had 227 square feet of retail space per resident. The average for the entire District of Columbia was 34 and for the United States was 53.[18]

A frequent lament in articles about Georgetown's retail challenges is competition from suburban malls where parking is easy. This competition intensified in the 1980s, particularly with the opening of a new Pentagon City mall in Arlington, which D.C. residents could easily reach by subway. A few stores that started in Georgetown opened outposts in suburban malls, like Georgetown Cotton and the various incarnations of the Britches men's clothing store.

Parking, of course, has long been a challenge in Georgetown. Merchants closing up shop often cite easier parking elsewhere as contributing to declines in customer traffic. At the same time, it is a measure of the attractiveness of the neighborhood that for decades shoppers and diners from outside have come and confronted that challenge.

In 1977, the *Georgetowner* ran this satirical item highlighting the absurdity of trying to match the parking facilities of suburban malls:

> *Enthusiasm has been running rampant in the past few weeks since final plans were released to raze the east side of Wisconsin Avenue between the Riggs parking lot and P Street to make way for the world's most continuous commercial mall. . . . Considerate of the parking problems which plague our area, the developers have planned Whitehurst Freeway-style ramps which will feed traffic from either side of M Street up over existing shops, the Old Stone House, etc. onto huge scenic rooftop parking lots overlooking the homes which are adjacent to the mall.*[19]

Any strategy to compete with malls has to avoid a paradox: if Georgetown becomes like a mall, why should any suburbanite shop in Georgetown? Moses Robbins, owner of Georgetown Cotton and other neighborhood businesses, lamented the trend he saw and summed up the paradox in 1985:

> *Georgetown will eventually become another sleepy mall, with the successful stores being the chains. [Without one-of-a-kind stores] it will turn into something*

sedate, without individual style—so that eventually there will no longer be a reason to come shopping here.[20]

Some of this effect became visible in the 2000s. Mall-like chain stores multiplied on M Street near Georgetown Park. Landlords, seeing that national chains were interested in Georgetown space, sought the high rents that the chains could afford, and smaller local stores that could not afford those rents had to move. Some storefronts remained vacant for years while their owners held out for a chain tenant.

An executive for the national clothing chain Esprit, interviewed by Fisher, put his finger on Georgetown's strong suit: "People really like to be on streets with real stores now. Look at Newberry Street in Boston or Madison Avenue in New York. People are mall-resistant now on the upwardly-mobile side."[21]

The COVID-19 pandemic in 2020–2022 devastated the Georgetown retail sector. As this is written in 2025, a strong comeback has taken place. Vacancy rates have dropped, and a variety of new stores have opened, some part of national chains and some independent. As has happened often in the past, the neighborhood appears to have defied predictions of its impending demise.

ACKNOWLEDGMENTS

Thanks are due to many people who gave me advice, support and assistance over the years it took to write this book. Jerry McCoy, librarian of the Peabody Room in the Georgetown Branch of the D.C. Public Library, and, after Jerry retired, his colleague Derek Gray, guided me through the Peabody Room's extensive files about Georgetown's stores and buildings. They and the staff of the Washingtoniana Room (now the People's Archive) at the main D.C. Public Library helped with research in photographic collections. The staff of the Kiplinger Library at the DC History Center helped with access to photographs in the Kiplinger collection, as well as city directories and survey atlases.

Hayley Wilkinson, archivist at the Tudor Place Historic House and Garden, devoted an afternoon to helping me find and examine receipts from the Peter family's business dealings with Georgetown retailers.

Over a long lunch at Martin's Tavern, Billy Martin filled me in on the history of his family, the tavern, and Billy Martin's Carriage House.

Dr. Sahar Kassem, the owner of Morgan's Pharmacy, kindly gave me access to mid-century photographs of the pharmacy that unfortunately we were not able to include in the book.

Paul Williams and Molly Doyle were great sources of advice about the publication process in general.

Special thanks to Jed Lyons and the staff at Globe Pequot, including Gene Brissie, Nicole Myers, and Nancy Syrett, as well as others who I never met or talked to but who I know worked on producing the book. Professionals all, they gave patient and reassuring guidance to a first-time author. I've read many books whose authors praised the assistance of their publishers. Now I know just what they meant.

And, of course, thanks to my wife, Ann Marie, for her constant support, her tolerance for my absorption in this project, and her willingness to listen to me drone on time and again about my latest discoveries in our neighborhood's history.

NOTES

Introduction

1. Susan Kriete, "How to Research a Family Business: City Directories," New York Public Library, n.d., https://libguides.nypl.org/familybusinessresearch/citydirectories; Melissa C. Tennant, "City Directories: More Than Basic Facts," Allen County Public Library, 2022, https://static.libnet.info/frontend-images/pdfs/acpl/Genealogy/City_Directories_handout_2022.pdf. (The Allen County Public Library in Fort Wayne, Indiana, has an extensive collection of genealogical references, including city directories.)

Chapter 1. A Brief History of Georgetown

1. *Proceedings and Acts of the General Assembly of Maryland* 44 (November 16, 1746–November 12, 1747): 595; *Proceedings and Acts of the General Assembly of Maryland* 64 (October 1773–April 1774): 151. *Maryland Session Laws*, 1785, v. 204, 77 (1785); v. 204, 392 (1789); and v. 558, 49 (1801). County boundary changes caused Georgetown to be part of Prince George's County, then Frederick County, and later Montgomery County.

2. Richard P. Jackson, *The Chronicles of Georgetown* (Polkinhorn, 1878), 3, 9.

3. Hugh Thomas Taggart, *Old Georgetown, District of Columbia* (Lancaster, PA: New Era Printing, 1908), 49.

4. Nicholas King, *Partial Cadastral Map of Southern Part of Georgetown, Washington D.C.*, map, 1799?, Library of Congress, https://www.loc.gov/item/88693279/.

5. David Mould and Missy Loewe, *Remembering Georgetown: A History of the Lost Port City* (Charleston, SC: History Press, 2009), 58; Jackson, *Chronicles of Georgetown*, 119.

6. Mould and Loewe, *Remembering Georgetown*, 65.

7. Mould and Loewe, *Remembering Georgetown*, 65.

8. Kathleen M. Lesko, Valerie Babb, and Carroll R. Gibbs, *Black Georgetown Remembered—a History of Its Black Community from the Founding of "The Town of George" in 1751 to the Present Day* (Washington, D.C.: Georgetown University Press, 1991), 3, 10, 16; Jackson, *Chronicles of Georgetown*, 68.

9. Kathryn Schneider Smith, *Port Town to Urban Neighborhood: The Georgetown Waterfront of Washington, D.C., 1880–1920* (Dubuque, IA: Kendall/Hunt, 1989), 10.

10. Smith, *Port Town to Urban Neighborhood*, 7.

11. 16 Stat. 419 (February 21, 1871).

12. John D. McGill, editor of the *Georgetown Courier*, quoted in Mary Mitchell, *Chronicles of Georgetown Life 1865–1900* (Cabin John, MD: Seven Locks, 1986), 43.

13. Mitchell, *Chronicles of Georgetown Life*, 44–45.
14. Jackson, *Chronicles of Georgetown*, 55–56.
15. 18 Stat. 116 (June 20, 1874).
16. *Annual Report of the Commissioners of the District of Columbia*, June 30, 1880, statistical map #3.
17. Order of October 4, 1880, in *Annual Report of the Commissioners of the District of Columbia*, 1880–1881.
18. Smith, *Port Town to Urban Neighborhood*, ch. 1; Mitchell, *Chronicles of Georgetown Life*, 81.
19. Mitchell, *Chronicles of Georgetown Life*, 85; Smith, *Port Town to Urban Neighborhood*, 31.
20. Mitchell, *Chronicles of Georgetown Life*, 87–89, 107; Smith, *Port Town to Urban Neighborhood*, 31.
21. Quoted in Smith, *Port Town to Urban Neighborhood*, 33, based on her 1984 and 1985 interviews with Nordlinger and an oral history interview with Kronheim conducted by the Jewish Historical Society in 1980–1981.
22. Lesko, Babb, and Gibbs, *Black Georgetown Remembered*, 42; quote from Mitchell, *Chronicles of Georgetown Life*, 110.
23. Grace Dunlop Ecker, *A Portrait of Old Georgetown* (Richmond, VA: Dietz, 1951), 155.
24. Smith, *Port Town to Urban Neighborhood*, 30.
25. Advertisements using the phrase can be found in the *Washington Post*, January 14, 1912, TM15; *Evening Star*, January 7, 1912, 28; and *Evening Star*, March 2, 1913, 26. Building permits for the obscuring buildings were number 5660, issued on January 1, 1926, for construction of 3108 M Street; and number 3770, issued April 19, 1926, for construction of 3110 M Street.
26. Lily Josephine Lewer, "Old Georgetown Will Have New Birth of Beauty and Dignity," *Evening Star*, March 25, 1928, 90.
27. Smith, *Port Town to Urban Neighborhood*, 119.
28. Scott Hart, *Washington at War 1914–1945* (Englewood Cliffs, NJ: Prentice Hall, 1970), 150, quoted in Dennis Earl Gale, "Restoration in Georgetown, Washington, D.C., 1915–1965" (PhD diss., George Washington University, September 30, 1982), 104.
29. Gale, "Restoration in Georgetown," 219.
30. Neville Waters Jr. identifies an earlier beginning in 1900–1910. Lesko, Babb, and Gibbs, *Black Georgetown Remembered*, 43.
31. *The WPA Guide to Washington, D.C.* (repr., New York: Pantheon, 1983), 276, 346.
32. Gale, "Restoration in Georgetown," 65–66, 71–76, 130, 135; Alison K. Hoagland, *The Row House in Washington, D.C.: A History* (Charlottesville: University Press of Virginia, 2023), 92–95.
33. Gale, "Restoration in Georgetown," 201–3.
34. Gale, "Restoration in Georgetown," 252; Emma Oxford, oral history interview with Richard and Philip Levy, Citizens Association of Georgetown, June 18, 2014, https://cagtown.org/2014/06/18/richard-phillip-levy/.
35. Gale, "Restoration in Georgetown," 252–54 (emphasis in original).
36. Old Georgetown Act, D.C. Code Section 5-801, 64 Stat. 903 (September 22, 1950).
37. Dorothea Andrews, "Georgetown Envisions M St. 'Williamsburg,'" *Washington Post*, April 2, 1950, B3.

NOTES

38. George Kennedy, "Georgetown Architecture Becomes a Matter of Law Instead of Builder's Choice," *Evening Star*, July 15, 1951, 33.

39. Jean M. White, "They Weren't Taken to the Cleaners but They Were Taken at Their Word," *Washington Post*, April 25, 1962, B1.

40. Lesko, Babb, and Gibbs, *Black Georgetown Remembered*, 95–97.

41. Zachary M. Schrag, *The Great Society Subway: A History of the Washington Metro* (Baltimore, MD: Johns Hopkins University Press, 2006), 155–56.

Chapter 2. Farm Supply and Feed Stores

1. Elmer Barton, ed., *Historical and Commercial Sketches of Washington and Environs: Our Capital City, "the Paris of America": Its Prominent Places and People . . . Its Improvements, Progress and Enterprise . . .* (Washington, D.C.: Barton, 1884), 190.

2. Notice of a bankruptcy sale, *Evening Star*, February 17, 1906, 16. Cropley's seed store was at 3213 M Street.

3. "Was Below the Average," *Evening Star*, September 5, 1900, 2; "Auspicious Opening," *Evening Star*, August 27, 1901, 2; "Montgomery Fair," *Evening Star*, August 22, 1905, 7.

4. "Bankruptcy Sale of Farming Implements, Hardware, Seed, Garden Tools, Wire Fencing, Fixtures, Iron Safe, Etc., Contained in No. 3147 M St. N.W.," *Evening Star*, November 11, 1922, 27 (capitalization in original). A harrow is a device used to smooth out plowed land by breaking up remaining clods.

5. *National Intelligencer*, March 20, 1845, 1.

6. *National Intelligencer*, August 16, 1848, 4.

7. *National Intelligencer*, March 20, 1845, 1; March 16, 1847, 3.

8. G. M. Hopkins, *A Complete Set of Surveys and Plats of Properties in the City of Washington, District of Columbia*, vol. 3 (Philadelphia: Hopkins, 1887), plate 38.

9. "Alfred Lee & William Lee, Father & Son Feed Dealers," obituary, *Weekly Freedman's Press*, July 18, 1868; Mary Mitchell, *Chronicles of Georgetown Life 1865–1900* (Cabin John, MD: Seven Locks, 1986), 91.

10. Will of Alfred Lee, dated March 1, 1866, probated in the District of Columbia, 1868 (exact date unknown), 1868-253.

11. Receipts in the archive of the Tudor Place Historic House and Garden in Georgetown, dated January 8, 1931, and November 19, 1936. The archive contains dozens of such receipts.

12. "Patrick T. Moran," obituary, *Evening Star*, February 23, 1923, 2.

13. "Dandelions? Weed and Feed," advertisement, *Evening Star*, April 15, 1977, 40. The Arlington store was at 5715 Lee Highway.

14. "Superstores Open, Catering to Man's Best Friend," *Washington Post*, September 20, 1993, OF05.

Chapter 3. The Horse-Based Economy

1. Richard Rhodes, *Energy: A Human History* (New York: Simon & Schuster, 2018), 207–12.

2. Rhodes, *Energy*, 229–34.

3. "Rare Chance," advertisement, *Evening Star*, October 20, 1881, 2.

4. Mary Mitchell, *Chronicles of Georgetown Life 1865–1900* (Cabin John, MD: Seven Locks, 1986), 93.

5. John DeFerrari, *Capital Streetcars: Early Mass Transit in Washington, D.C.* (Charleston, SC: History Press, 2015), 23.
6. "Lincoln's Bodyguard Dead," *Evening Star*, January 19, 1910, 11.
7. Elmer Barton, ed., *Historical and Commercial Sketches of Washington and Environs: Our Capital City, "the Paris of America": Its Prominent Places and People . . . Its Improvements, Progress and Enterprise . . .* (Washington, D.C.: Barton, 1884), xv, 223.
8. Building permit 1115, issued November 19, 1891, to R. H. Darne.
9. Fayette was in partnership for two years with Frank Offutt, who was part of a family of Georgetown entrepreneurs. For another two years, his partner was Frank Presgraves.
10. "Lincoln's Bodyguard Dead," 11.
11. Building permit 2552, issued June 26, 1890.
12. *Washington Times Herald*, December 20, 1953, 26; "Changes Force 'Boots and Saddles' for Stombock's of Georgetown," *Evening Star*, February 27, 1970, 45.
13. "Stombock's Rides into Sunset; Saddlery Closes after 95 Years of Serving 'VIPs,'" *Washington Post*, June 1, 1990, C1.

Chapter 4. Horses Exit; Cars Arrive

1. Display advertisement, *Evening Star*, January 23, 1914, 14.
2. "Entire Equipment of the Parkway Livery Company at Nos. 1065–1067 Wisconsin Avenue Northwest," advertisement, *Evening Star*, October 11, 1916, 19.
3. Advertisement, *Evening Star*, March 12, 1916, 27.
4. "Robert Golden Carter," obituary, *Washington Post*, December 4, 1956, B2.
5. "Building to House Auto Showroom," *Washington Post*, October 20, 1929, R1.
6. "Garage Rebuttal Set for Canal Residents," *Washington Post*, June 27, 1954, M6; "Motor Firm Must Vacate Old Stone House Lot," *Washington Post*, February 16, 1956, 23.

Chapter 5. Clothing Stores: From Immigrant Families to Boutiques

1. Robert J. Gordon, *The Rise and Fall of American Growth* (Princeton, NJ: Princeton University Press, 2016), 86.
2. The Georgetown population was 11,571 in 1878. Richard P. Jackson, *The Chronicles of Georgetown* (Polkinhorn, 1878), 68.
3. Robert Hendrickson, *The Great Emporiums: The Illustrated History of America's Great Department Stores* (New York: Stein and Day, 1980), 30.
4. Pierce's ad ran in the *Washington Post*, May 13, 1894, 5 (capitalization in original); Luttrell & Wine's ad appeared in the *Washington Post*, April 9, 1880, 2.
5. Grace Dunlop Ecker, *A Portrait of Old Georgetown* (Richmond, VA: Dietz, 1951), 165.
6. "Benjamin Mayfield," obituary, *Evening Star*, January 9, 1900, 8; "S. Thomas Brown," obituary, *Evening Star*, February 22, 1913, 13.
7. Gordon, *Rise and Fall of American Growth*, 87.
8. Building permit 7163, issued June 20, 1910, authorized construction of a dwelling with one store. Herman had purchased the property the year before. *Washington Post*, listing of real estate transfers, December 5, 1909, 10.
9. Herman Brodofsky had died in 1914. In 1930, Katie's household included her mother, Bessie Brodofsky. Bessie died in the early 1930s and left behind an unusual will, giving a half interest in the building at 2815 M Street to Katie and only $5 to each of her other children

NOTES

and her grandchildren. Katie settled the resulting dispute by buying the building from the others in 1933. Deed recorded in District of Columbia land records, September 6, 1933 (document 1933015506).

10. Building permits 1463 and 1464, both issued January 16, 1893. Hopkins's 1887 survey atlas shows a single structure on the site (G. M. Hopkins, *A Complete Set of Surveys and Plats of Properties in the City of Washington, District of Columbia*, vol. 3 [Philadelphia: Hopkins, 1887]). Baist's 1903 survey atlas shows two structures, both deeper than the single one had been (G. W. Baist, *Baist's Real Estate Atlas Surveys of Washington, District of Columbia*, vol. 3 [Philadelphia: Baist Surveyors, 1903]).

11. Deed from Baer to Brodofsky, recorded November 9, 1920, liber 4400 at folio 333.

12. Pat Lewis, "An Old-Time Business Finally Fades Away," *Washington Star-News*, February 2, 1975, 21.

13. Emma Oxford, oral history interview with Richard and Philip Levy, Citizens Association of Georgetown, June 18, 2014, https://cagtown.org/2014/06/18/richard-phillip-levy/.

14. Deed from Herman E. and Marie M. Gasch to Samuel and Gertrude Levy, recorded in District of Columbia land records, January 22, 1938 (document 1938001996); building permit 229445, issued to Samuel Levy, January 25, 1940; deed from Frederick J. and Morgan R. Goddard to Harry and Sara Meyers, recorded in District of Columbia land records, December 4, 1940 (document 1940039584).

15. *Evening Star*, June 15, 1943, 4. For examples of Hanes ads, see *Evening Star*, November 7, 1940; June 7, 1943, 17; May 28, 1944, 15; November 29, 1944, 3; and November 17, 1948, 9.

16. *Evening Star*, January 16, 1945, 7; January 9, 1946, 7; January 30, 1947, 2; February 6, 1947, 8; December 3, 1947, 9; and June 29, 1950, 2. The ad for the Northcool suit appeared in the *Evening Star*, June 21, 1950, 2.

17. *Evening Star*, February 17, 1950, 2.

18. "Samuel Levy," obituary, *Washington Post*, May 15, 1995, D5; "Men's Pin Tourney Card Tonight," *Evening Star*, April 29, 1940, 16.

19. Marc Fisher, "Street of Gold," *Washington Post Magazine*, November 8, 1987, 21.

20. Bart Barnes, "Bridge Street Books Founder and Proprietor," obituary of Philip Levy, *Washington Post*, October 24, 2017, B8.

21. Like the Brodofskys, the Baers were from a region that had its borders redrawn repeatedly—Alsace. In census listings, members of the family said they were born in Germany or France, depending on which country Alsace was part of in that year.

22. Mary Mitchell, *Chronicles of Georgetown Life 1865–1900* (Cabin John, MD: Seven Locks, 1986), 75–77. Information on Wolf Nordlinger's Civil War service is available at Ancestry, https://search.ancestry.com/cgi-bin/sse.dll?indiv=1&dbid=1138&h=1784995&ssrc=pt&tid=108117409&pid=370073873657&usePUB=tru.

23. Building permit 1463, issued January 6, 1893.

24. The mother of Adolphe, Alphonse, and Benoit Baer was Frederika Nordlinger, the sister of Wolf and Bernard Nordlinger.

25. "Alphonse M. Baer Funeral Is Today," *Evening Star*, May 7, 1937, 13.

26. "Mrs. Betsy Levy's Suit for Divorce," *Washington Post*, August 17, 1898, 10; "Real Estate Transfers," *Evening Star*, March 28, 1903, 3.

27. "Real Estate Transfers," *Evening Star*, July 10, 1906, 3.

28. "Real Estate Transfers," *Evening Star*, July 10, 1906, 3; "Real Estate Transfers," *Evening Star*, April 9, 1908, 3; "Real Estate Transfers," *Evening Star*, March 30, 1911, 16; "Real Estate Transfers," *Evening Star*, May 29, 1914, 16; "Real Estate Transfers," *Evening Star*, April 16, 1915, 19.
29. Building permit 3057, issued to Rebecca Levey [sic], January 14, 1916.
30. "Barnett Levy Expires," *Evening Star*, September 23, 1925, 17.
31. *Evening Star*, August 20, 1918, 5; June 5, 1920, 9; and September 23, 1925, 17.
32. "Barnett Levy Expires," 17.
33. "Mrs. Rebecca Levy Dies at Age of 68," *Evening Star*, December 22, 1931, 29. Deeds recorded in District of Columbia land records, July 7, 2003 (document 2003085696); and October 6, 2003 (document 2003128454).
34. Advertisements, *Washington Post*, January 1, 1950, S5; May 13, 1951, S10; and March 4, 1951, S12.
35. "Second Hand Rose: A Real Find," newspaper article found in the files of the Peabody Room of the D.C. Public Library, Georgetown branch (the copy of the article does not indicate what publication it is from); "Does Secondhand Rose Have an Imposter on Wisconsin Avenue?," *Georgetowner*, December 14, 2012, https://georgetowner.com/articles/2012/12/14/does-secondhand-rose-have-imposter-wisconsin-avenue/.
36. Winzola McLendon, "She's Found a Gold Rush in Dressing Wives of the New Frontier," *Washington Times Herald*, October 27, 1963, F3.
37. Matt Schudel, "Boutique Owner Dorcas Hardin," *Washington Post*, January 21, 2006, B5.
38. Nina S. Hyde, "Best Customer Buys Dorcas Hardin," *Washington Post*, January 14, 1975, B2; Bailey Morris, "Hurdles Passed, More to Come," *Evening Star*, August 3, 1976, 42.
39. Nina S. Hyde, "Twilight of a Boutique," *Washington Post*, January 14, 1977, B1.
40. 3214–18 P Street.
41. "G. U. Gridmen Awarded Letters," *Washington Post*, December 28, 1928, 13.
42. "36 and N Streets, Distinct Georgetown Community," *Georgetowner*, February 3, 1955, 2; "Georgetown University Shop Changes Ownership," *Georgetowner*, April 30, 1954; "Stephen Barabas, Founded Shop in Georgetown," *Washington Post*, November 6, 1980, C4.
43. Deeds recorded in District of Columbia land records, November 20, 1936 (document 1936034017); and May 20, 1940 (document 940015320).
44. District of Columbia Marriage Bureau listings, https://www.ancestry.com/search/collections/62797/records/655790?tid=&pid=&queryId=ea2cbe28-f4b2-411d-b7c8-87634336e443&_phsrc=RHt389&_phstart=successSource; U.S. Military Register, https://www.ancestry.com/search/collections/2345/records/5332919?tid=&pid=&queryId=144365c9-9c59-42b5-a088-1cb1c5e838b8&_phsrc=RHt391&_phstart=successSource.
45. Jean White, "Saltz Firm Will Open New Branch," *Washington Post*, May 1, 1955, B10; "Lewis Saltz, 60, Haberdasher," obituary, *Washington Post*, March 16, 1958, A22; Laurie Fineran, "Tradition Is Men's Shop's Trademark," *Evening Star*, September 21, 1978, 14.
46. White, "Saltz Firm Will Open New Branch," *Washington Post*, May 1, 1955, B10.
47. Caroline E. Mayer, "Saltz Co. to Close Last Store," *Washington Post*, May 6, 1986, D3.
48. Deed recorded in District of Columbia land records, April 20, 1964 (document 1964013053).
49. Jerry Knight, "Saltz Sells Georgetown Shops," *Washington Post*, October 29, 1980, D7.

NOTES

50. "Men's Shop Opens in Chevy Chase," *Washington Post*, June 22, 1979, C9; Laurie Fineran, "Tradition Is Men's Shop's Trademark," *Evening Star*, September 21, 1978, 14.

51. Robert Devaney, "Georgetown Men's Shop Hangs Its Last Pin Stripe," *Washington Post*, February 15, 1990, DC1.

52. Lix Barentzen, oral history interview with Betty Hayes, Citizens Association of Georgetown, August 3, 2014, https://cagtown.org/2014/08/03/betty-hays/; "The Phoenix at 50," *Georgetowner*, April 20, 2005, 10; "Phoenix Rises: Boutique Reopens after Overhaul," *Georgetown Current*, March 1, 2017; deed recorded in District of Columbia land records, April 18, 2000 (document 2000036801); building permit 1513, issued 1896 to James Keliher.

53. *Washington Post*, March 3, 1969, D6.

54. "History of Britches," Britches Bespoke, accessed March 6, 2025, https://britchesbespoke.com/britches-history.

55. Kara Swisher, "Making It Menswear at Britches," *Washington Post*, June 17, 1992, F1; Margaret Webb Pressler, "Britches Owner Puts Retailer Up for Sale," *Washington Post*, June 28, 1995, F1; Margaret Webb Pressler, "Britches' Expansion-Minded Owners Looking for a Good Fit," *Washington Post*, June 17, 1996, 11; Dina ElBoghdady, "Britches to Close Five Area Stores; Retailer Files for Bankruptcy Dec. 28," *Washington Post*, January 26, 2002, E3; Michael Barbaro, "Surprised Staff Bitter about Closing of Store; Shoppers Console Workers on Last Day," *Washington Post*, January 29, 2003, E6.

56. Robert Devaney, "Britches of Georgetowne Founder Plans to Revive Brand," *Georgetowner*, October 15, 2015.

Chapter 6. Shoe Stores and Shoe Repair

1. Tax records say that Chamberlain's heirs owned the building in 1917–1918, and Bredice told the census taker in 1920 that he owned it then.

2. Buttinelli's name is misspelled "Buddinelli" in the 1926–1928 directories. In 1910, he was listed as a shoemaker at 215 10th Street SW. In 1913, he was listed as a shoemaker at that address as well as at 1246 1st Street, NW. In 1921, he was working at 137 B Street SE.

3. One ad ran in the *Evening Star*, March 30, 1926, 44.

4. Passenger list of returning citizens for the SS *Conte Rosso*, Ancestry, October 26, 1926, https://www.ancestry.com/imageviewer/collections/7488/images/NYT715_3746-0557?queryId=f6173bae-3c65-448d-89b4-b7df33d35d1e&usePUB=true&_phsrc=RHt350&_phstart=successSource&pId=2001647136; passenger list of returning citizens for the SS *Roma*, Ancestry, December 7, 1927, https://www.ancestry.com/imageviewer/collections/7488/images/NYT715_4182-0083?queryId=e6594e86-5f70-4655-b913-456cc6b888d4&usePUB=true&_phsrc=RHt353&_phstart=successSource&pId=2004098428. Both arrived in New York. We know of the move to Eye Street because on both records they gave immigration officials that address.

5. Christina Del Sesto, "The Sole Proprietors," *Washington Post*, September 30, 1990, SM14; Stephen S. Rosenfeld, "Shop 'Cashes-In' on Uncashed Kennedy Checks," *Washington Post*, December 22, 1961, B16.

6. Del Sesto, "The Sole Proprietors," SM14.

7. The Speciales' shop was at 3112 and 3005 M Street.

8. "A. E. Felser, Businessman Here for 50 Years," *Evening Star*, September 13, 1961, 33.

9. *Evening Star*, March 23, 1945, 27.
10. *Evening Star*, November 3, 1946, 24.
11. *Washington Post*, March 3, 1950, B2. The article refers to Kaplan as the owner of the H Street store, but we can assume he owned the others that were doing business under the same name.
12. *Evening Star*, July 7, 1955, 47. A few months before, on December 15, 1944, another ad had urged Virginia residents to visit "our Alexandria store, The Family Shoe Mart," *Evening Star*, December 15, 1944, 32.
13. "Demetro" is the spelling used in the 1920 census. In some years, however, city directories spell it "Demetrio."

Chapter 7. Barbershops and Hair Salons

1. Ronald S. Barlow, *The Vanishing American Barber Shop: An Illustrated History of Tonsorial Art, 1860–1960* (St. Paul, MN: William Marvy, 1996), 109.
2. Barlow, *The Vanishing American Barber Shop*, 103.
3. Barlow, *The Vanishing American Barber Shop*, 19.
4. Mary Mitchell, *Chronicles of Georgetown Life 1865–1900* (Cabin John, MD: Seven Locks, 1986), 14.
5. Robert Sellers, "The Block," *Georgetowner*, February 13–26, 1987, 27.
6. Advertisement for Fink's Ideal Parlors (an ice cream parlor) at 2922 M Street NW, *Washington Post*, July 15, 1905, 10.
7. Barlow, *The Vanishing American Barber Shop*, 65.
8. John Kelly, "Having the Lives of Their Times," *Washington Post*, May 18, 2005, C.13.
9. Deeds recorded in District of Columbia land records, May 12, 1922 (document 192205120001); September 16, 1931 (document 1931027624); and October 20, 1948 (document 1948041785).
10. "Philip A. Coniglio, Ran Barber Shop," *Washington Post*, April 17, 1969, B10.
11. Passenger list for the SS *Trojan Prince*, arriving August 17, 1900, available at Ancestry, https://www.ancestry.com/search/collections/7488/records/4007062922?tid=&pid=&queryId=4510224a-d079-4a4d-addf-0562017e978f&_phsrc=RHt354&_phstart=successSource. Joseph's first name on the passenger list is Giuseppe.
12. New York marriage certificate 17891, July 14, 1910, reflecting marriage on June 25, 1910.
13. District of Columbia tax assessment records, 1917–1918.
14. "40 Persons Hurt When Tenleytown Car Jumps Track," *Washington Post*, November 26, 1925, 1.
15. *Washington Post*, February 19, 1939, B9; December 26, 1940, 6; and February 26, 1944, 8.
16. "Cutlery Stolen from Shop," *Evening Star*, October 31, 1914, 7.
17. "Hair Tonic Burns, Porter Is Injured," *Washington Post*, January 2, 1938, M4; Barlow, *The Vanishing American Barber Shop*, 128.
18. Deeds recorded in District of Columbia land records, June 6, 1952 (document 1952022468); and January 11, 1962 (document 1962001121).
19. Marilyn Butler, "Mapping Georgetown: Where Will Georgetown Take You?," *Georgetowner*, April 3, 2023, https://georgetowner.com/articles/2023/04/03/mapping-georgetown-25/; Marilyn Butler, "Mapping Georgetown: Emily Durso at the Francis Scott Key Book

NOTES

Shop (Part II)," *Georgetowner*, April 17, 2023, https://georgetowner.com/articles/2023/04/17/mapping-georgetown-emily-durso-at-the-francis-scott-key-bookstore-part-ii/.

20. *Washington Post*, April 7, 1937, 13; *Evening Star*, June 20, 1937, 64.

Chapter 8. Jewelers

1. Building permit 2025, issued to Benoit Baer Jr., September 23, 1909.
2. *Washington Post*, September 18, 1910, ES11.
3. "Milton Baer, Jeweler and Lifelong D.C. Resident," *Evening Star*, May 27, 1957, 15.
4. Advertisements in the *Evening Star*, September 15, 1919, 21; deed recorded in District of Columbia land records, July 3, 1924 (document 192407030149).
5. "The Work of 'Gophers': One of the Boldest Safe Robberies Ever Effected," *Washington Post*, November 27, 1886, 1.
6. "Thief's Punishment Swift," *Washington Post*, October 28, 1897, 2.
7. *Evening Star*, November 1, 1898, 5.
8. *Washington Post*, September 13, 1908, 7.
9. An example appears in the *Washington Post*, August 7, 1910, 6.
10. *Evening Star*, October 15, 1903, 5; December 19, 1903, 32.
11. "Say Claim Is Usurious," *Washington Post*, January 11, 1907, 16.
12. *Evening Star*, August 12, 1918, 5; April 25, 1936, 64 (capitalization and italics in the originals).
13. Deed recorded in District of Columbia land records, June 7, 1928 (document 192806070075).
14. Deed recorded in District of Columbia land records, April 18, 1940 (document 19400011423).
15. Advertisement, *Evening Star*, September 15, 1939, 64.
16. *Washington Post*, November 2, 1911, 2; "Chamber of Commerce Names Two Committees," *Washington Post*, February 13, 1924, 13; "1927 Committees Named by Chamber of Commerce Head," *Washington Post*, April 17, 1927, M26; "Chamber's Group on Parks Named," *Washington Post*, March 30, 1929, 20; "Chamber's Retail Group Announced," *Washington Post*, April 1, 1929, 18; "Stocks Being Offered by Federal American," *Washington Post*, May 12, 1926, 13.
17. Advertisement, *Washington Post*, November 28, 1918, 2; "Tribby Again Offers to Do Police Duty," *Washington Post*, September 27, 1941; a copy of Tribby's application to the Sons of the American Revolution is available at Ancestry, https://www.ancestry.com/search/collections/2204/records/1160280?tid=&pid=&queryId=340b2293-1f2b-4d6d-8d6e-df17a9cdc5cd&_phsrc=RHt367&_phstart=successSource.
18. Advertisements in the *Evening Star*, May 7, 1950, 82; June 11, 1950, 76; November 26, 1950, 67; October 28, 1951, 73; and November 22, 1951, 21.
19. Maureen Dowd, "Georgetown Loses J. Clinton Tribby," *Evening Star*, June 11, 1977.
20. "Georgetown Fights to Preserve Structure Near Old Stone House," *Evening Star*, May 5, 1958, 23.

Chapter 9. Laundries: The Evolution of Cleaning Clothes

1. Except where otherwise noted, information in this chapter about the general history of the laundry business comes from Anwen P. Mohun, *Steam Laundries—Gender, Technology*

GEORGETOWN'S RETAIL PAST

and Work in the United States and Great Britain, 1880–1940 (Baltimore, MD: Johns Hopkins University Press, 1999).

2. Deeds recorded in District of Columbia land records, September 3, 1948 (document 1948035598); and February 23, 1966 (document 19660065670).
3. Sing Lee did business at 3028 M Street and Sam Moy at 3029 M Street.
4. *Evening Star,* January 12, 1901, 17. Similar ads ran for the next several days, and in the *Washington Post.*
5. For example, *Evening Star,* February 9, 1901, 17.
6. *Washington Post,* December 2, 1901, 3.
7. "Laundry Sold," *Evening Star,* August 17, 1907, 10.
8. "Old Caps Ease Pain for Red," *Evening Star,* May 13, 1975, 19.
9. Advertisements in the *Evening Star,* May 24, 1916, 21; June 30, 1916, 24; October 31, 1916, 23; and June 16, 1917, 11. *Butler v. Frazee,* 211 U.S. 459 (1908).
10. Mohun, *Steam Laundries,* 259–65.
11. Mohun, *Steam Laundries,* 81.

Chapter 10. Grocery Stores: Corner Store to Supermarket

1. This narrative about the evolution of the retail grocery industry is based primarily on Robert J. Gordon, *The Rise and Fall of American Growth* (Princeton, NJ: Princeton University Press, 2016), and Paul P. Ellickson, "The Evolution of the Supermarket Industry: From A&P to Walmart," University of Rochester, March 15, 2015, http://paulellickson.com/SMEvolution.pdf. Ellickson actually identifies the advent of Walmart as a fourth phase.
2. Gordon, *The Rise and Fall of American Growth,* 78.
3. Ellickson, "The Evolution of the Supermarket Industry," 5.
4. Ellickson, "The Evolution of the Supermarket Industry," 8; Gordon, *The Rise and Fall of American Growth,* 334.
5. The population number is from an 1878 census; see Richard P. Jackson, *The Chronicles of Georgetown* (Polkinhorn, 1878), 68.
6. Alec MacKaye, oral history interview with Eugene T. Lyddane III, Citizens Association of Georgetown, March 10, 2014, https://cagtown.org/2014/03/10/eugene-lyddane/.
7. Information about improvements to the building comes from a history of 3101 M Street written by Michael J. Fine and Beth A. Phillips and dated December 22, 1981, found in the file about the building in the Peabody Room of the D.C. Public Library's Georgetown branch.
8. Emma Oxford, oral history interview with Richard and Philip Levy, Citizens Association of Georgetown, June 18, 2014, https://cagtown.org/2014/06/18/richard-phillip-levy/. Examples of former corner stores are at 1331 28th Street (now renumbered 2733 Dumbarton Street) and 1326 29th Street.
9. "A. M. Hilleary, Grocer, 85," *Evening Star,* August 13, 1962, 25.
10. Betty van Iersel, oral history interview with Tyler Abell, Citizens Association of Georgetown, July 21, 2011, https://cagtown.org/2011/07/21/abell-tyler/.
11. Helen Tangires, "Contested Space: The Life and Death of Center Market," *Washington History* 7, no. 1 (Spring/Summer 1995): 47–49, 54.
12. Jackson, *The Chronicles of Georgetown,* 102–8.
13. Jackson, *The Chronicles of Georgetown,* 102–3.

NOTES

14. "Sanitary Grocery in Huge Merger," *Evening Star*, September 27, 1928, 2.

15. Tom Birch, oral history interview with Judy Davis, Citizens Association of Georgetown, January 22, 2013, https://cagtown.org/2013/01/22/judy-davis/.

16. In the late nineteenth century, G. M. Hopkins of Philadelphia published atlases of maps of the District of Columbia and other cities showing the location of streets, houses, and other improvements based on actual surveys. From the early through mid-twentieth century, survey atlases for the District of Columbia were published by G. W. Baist's Sons, also of Philadelphia.

17. Interview with Donald Kernan, *Georgetowner*, April 6–19, 1978. Other former 1948 Safeway locations in this architectural style are at 2011 S Street NW, 2928 Georgia Avenue NW, 1611 Montello Street NE, 6203 3rd Street NW, and 2007 18th Street NW.

18. George W. Gray, "Industry Plans Recovery," *Evening Star*, March 19, 1933, 19.

19. Gray, "Industry Plans Recovery," 19.

20. *Georgetowner*, April 24, 2023, https://georgetowner.com/articles/2023/04/24/business-ins-outs-streets-market-dig-ever-body-fangyan/.

21. John McKelway, "The Rambler . . . Notes a Change," *Evening Star*, May 22, 1963, 23.

22. Bill from the Tudor Place archive dated August 1, 1911 (marked paid).

23. McKelway, "The Rambler . . . Notes a Change," 23.

24. "A Local Life: Jack Neam, 88," *Washington Post*, January 3, 2010, C6; "Neam's Upper Crusts—the Corner Grocery for the Hungry Rich," *Washington Post*, March 31, 1981, D1.

25. Catherine Habanananda, oral history interview with Elizabeth Jacob, Citizens Association of Georgetown, June 5, 2011, https://cagtown.org/2011/06/05/elizabeth-jacob/.

Chapter 11. Drugstores

1. Robert J. Gordon, *The Rise and Fall of American Growth* (Princeton, NJ: Princeton University Press, 2016), 222–24.

2. Mary Mitchell, *Chronicles of Georgetown Life 1865–1900* (Cabin John, MD: Seven Locks, 1986), 13–14.

3. Elmer Barton, ed., *Historical and Commercial Sketches of Washington and Environs: Our Capital City, "the Paris of America": Its Prominent Places and People . . . Its Improvements, Progress and Enterprise . . .* (Washington, D.C.: Barton, 1884), 224.

4. See also receipts from the Tudor Place Archive dated June 1, 1908; October 1, 1908; January 1, 1910; and January 1, 1911.

5. World War II Draft Card of Thomas E. O'Donnell, Ancestry, https://www.ancestry.com/interactive/6482/005205818_05094/23905648?backurl=https://www.ancestry.com/family-tree/person/tree/11585447/person/-436652399/facts.

6. Auction notice in the *Evening Star*, April 4, 1911, 17; mortgage foreclosure notice, *Evening Star*, October 3, 1911, 19; deed from O'Donnell to the Morgans recorded in District of Columbia land records, November 30, 1923 (document 192311300235).

7. "Gang of Five Youths to Be Arraigned in Robbery Case Today," *Evening Star*, May 29, 1941, 11.

8. The building permit from this work has been lost, but maps in Baist's survey atlases show the footprint of the building expanding sometime after 1924 but before 1931 to fill the entire lot. G. W. Baist, *Real Estate Atlas Survey of Washington, District of Columbia*, vol. 3 (Philadelphia: Baist Surveyors, 1924, 1931).

9. 4231 Wisconsin Avenue NW. The brothers bought the newly constructed building from James E. Douglass in June 1927. See District of Columbia building permit 5766, issued January 11, 1927; and deed from Douglass to the Morgans recorded June 7, 1927 (document 19270607189).

10. Obituaries of the parties give different dates for when the store changed hands. The best evidence of the transfer date, though, is a display ad in the *Evening Star* on September 6, 1942, 8, which refers to the store as "operated by Dr. Joseph Schenick."

11. Deed recorded July 13, 1944 (document 1944019721).

12. "Leah Dietz Schenick, Pharmacy Employee," *Washington Post*, February 28, 2001, B6. The headline probably is wrong about her being an employee, since the body of the obituary notes that her husband owned the pharmacy where she worked.

13. *Evening Star*, September 15, 1942, 30; July 31, 1943, 19 (capitalization as in the originals).

14. For an example of Schenick's advertising, see *Evening Star*, December 21, 1950, 44.

15. "J. Harold Morgan Dies; Georgetown Druggist," *Evening Star*, March 3, 1963, 51.

16. "National Security Agency Clerk Catherine Misner," *Washington Post*, June 14, 2005, B5.

17. Janet Bohlen, "Growing Up in Georgetown in the '40s: The Way It Was in Georgetown," *Washington Post*, May 15, 1986, DC1.

18. Betty van Iersel, oral history interview with Barry Deutschman, Citizens Association of Georgetown, March 26, 2010, https://cagtown.org/2010/03/26/barry-deutschman/; Robert Devaney, "Longtime Residents Make Georgetown History Come Alive," *Georgetowner*, January 25, 2012, https://georgetowner.com/articles/2012/01/25/longtime-residents-make-georgetown-history-come-alive/.

19. District of Columbia building permit 1573, issued November 12, 1878.

20. Barton, *Historical and Commercial Sketches*, 237. The building was constructed in 1887 according to the D.C. government's HistoryQuest DC website, https://dcgis.maps.arcgis.com/apps/webappviewer/index.html?id=2ab24bc3b6da4314b9f2c74b69190333.

21. "Affairs in Georgetown," *Evening Star*, May 3, 1897, 6; notice of dissolution of the Wrenn and Waters partnership in the *Evening Star*, February 17, 1892, 1. Wrenn and Waters was listed only in the 1892 city directory; there was no listing for it in 1890 or 1891. In 1891, Morris Waters was listed as a "drug clerk," suggesting that he was not yet in business for himself.

22. While Donahue does not appear to have done his own advertising, the name of the store appears in a number of newspaper ads run by product manufacturers that list the Washington area drugstores offering their products. For example, see the Parker Pen ad in the *Evening Star*, August 27, 1935, 6. Listings for the store in directories, however, merely say "Thomas F. Donahue, druggist."

23. Deed from Charles Wiltse to Thomas F. Donahue (document 8600000151).

24. List of building permits in the *Washington Post*, July 29, 1928, R1, includes the permit issued to Donahue for this work.

25. Dalinsky's obituary ("Harry Dalinsky, Georgetown Druggist, Dies," *Washington Post*, April 10, 1992, C5) says he bought the store in 1936, but directories continued to list Donahue there until 1938, which is more likely to be accurate than relatives' recollections many years later.

26. For example, an item in the *Georgetowner* of May 26–June 8, 1976, calls him "mayor." So do several other articles in the files of the Peabody Room of the Georgetown Branch of the D.C. Public Library.

NOTES

27. John Carmody, "Doc's Georgetown Pharmacy Isn't Just a Drugstore, It's a Family," *Washington Post*, May 10, 1970, A13.

28. "Far Out Pharmacist," *Evening Star*, May 8, 1979, 53.

29. "Far Out Pharmacist," 53.

30. The shop was at 1422 Wisconsin Avenue. The directory listings say it sold cosmetics, but the 1970 *Washington Post* profile says it was a gift shop.

31. A photo of the kit can be found in the Peabody Room of the Georgetown Branch, D.C. Public Library.

32. Linda Wheeler, "After 105 Years, Georgetown Pharmacy to Fill Its Last Prescription: Pharmacy Owner Cites High Rents," *Washington Post*, December 15, 1988, B1.

33. Constance Chatfield-Taylor, oral history interview with Harold Sugar, Citizens Association of Georgetown, April 5, 2010, https://cagtown.org/2010/04/15/harold-sugar/.

34. Joe Pichirallo, "6 City Drug Stores Refuse to Sell Life Issue with Welch Interview," *Washington Post*, January 27, 1981, C1.

Chapter 12. Candy Stores, Ice Cream Shops, and a Factory

1. Grant Quarternous, *A Georgetown Life—the Reminiscences of Brittania Wellington Peter Kennon* (Washington, D.C.: Georgetown University Press, 2020), 174 (emphasis in original). Brittania Peter was the great-granddaughter of Martha Washington and was the owner of the Tudor Place estate in Georgetown.

2. Grace Dunlop Ecker, *A Portrait of Old Georgetown* (Richmond, VA: Dietz, 1951), 108; Historic American Buildings Survey, DC-104.

3. Tom Birch, oral history interview with Judy Davis, Citizens Association of Georgetown, January 22, 2013, https://cagtown.org/2013/01/22/judy-davis/.

4. Ecker, *A Portrait of Old Georgetown*, 108; Mary Mitchell, *Chronicles of Georgetown Life 1865–1900* (Cabin John, MD: Seven Locks, 1986), 77; Dennis Earl Gale, "Restoration in Georgetown, Washington, D.C., 1915–1965" (PhD diss., George Washington University, September 30, 1982), 105; Pauline Gaskins Mitchell, "Growing Up Black in 'The Village' West of Rock Creek," *Washington Post*, July 23, 1987, J1.

5. "Georgetown Candy Store to Be Museum Exhibit," *Washington Post*, October 6, 1957, B8; Jean M. White, "Opening Day at New Museum Attracts Turnout of 8,000," *Washington Post*, January 24, 1964, C1.

6. Elizabeth Kytle, *Home on the Canal* (Cabin John, MD: Seven Locks, 1983), 104–95.

7. Kytle, *Home on the Canal*, 256.

8. Peter J. Chaconas had only one child, Theodore. The 1910 census shows him living with Theodore's family above the store, and says he immigrated to the United States in 1907. The 1901 and 1903 city directories list Peter J. Chaconas as Theodore's partner in the store. There is no other Peter Chaconas listed in directories. Given the middle initial "J," it seems likely the 1910 census got the immigration year wrong. The line above Peter Chaconas in the census is another relative also said to have immigrated in 1907, identified as "niece" though it is unclear whose niece. The 1930 census lists Peter's immigration year as 1893, the same year given for Theodore in 1910.

9. Photo by the author.

10. *Washington Post*, June 13, 1990, D7.

GEORGETOWN'S RETAIL PAST

11. Ad from the *Sligonian* 9, no. 3 (December 1924): 25, https://documents.adventistarchives.org/Periodicals/Sligo/Sligo19241201-V09-03.pdf.

12. Alcoholic Beverage Control Board, "Official Notice," *Washington Post*, March 10, 1934, 24.

13. Deed recorded in District of Columbia land records, April 13, 1934 (document 1934006518).

14. Paul Dickson, *The Great American Ice Cream Book* (New York: Atheneum, 1978), 29–30, 44–52; Elmer Barton, ed., *Historical and Commercial Sketches of Washington and Environs: Our Capital City, "the Paris of America": Its Prominent Places and People . . . Its Improvements, Progress and Enterprise . . .* (Washington, D.C.: Barton, 1884), 70; Henry Brown Floyd MacFarland, *District of Columbia: Concise Biographies of Its Prominent and Representative Contemporary Citizens and Valuable Statistical Data* (Washington, D.C.: Potomac Press, 1908), 168–69; "Enlarged Plant of Local Firm," *Evening Star*, March 28, 1931, 20; "Ford E. Young, 92, Dean of Ice Cream Industry Here," *Evening Star*, October 2, 1972, 42; "Melvern and Fussell-Young to Become Ice Cream 'Giant,'" *Evening Star*, October 1, 1953, 54; building permit 1865, issued January 3, 1919. The demolition date is based on advertisement for sale of building materials from the demolition; *Evening Star*, August 16, 1953, 37.

Chapter 13. Tobacco Shops

1. In 1875, the city directory listed both Peter May and John Albrecht as cigar makers at 81 Bridge Street. Given Peter's age at the time (twenty), it seems likely he worked for Albrecht, who was nine years older. That listing appeared only for a year, after which Peter's listing gave his family's home address, which had also been the case in 1874.

2. "Arrested on Charge of Libel," *Washington Post*, October 4, 1901, 12.

3. Elmer Barton, ed., *Historical and Commercial Sketches of Washington and Environs: Our Capital City, "the Paris of America": Its Prominent Places and People . . . Its Improvements, Progress and Enterprise . . .* (Washington, D.C.: Barton, 1884), 238.

4. *Evening Star*, December 21, 1869, 4 (capitalization in original).

5. *Evening Star*, July 18, 1882, 2. How Albrecht came to have a liquor license is a mystery. This was around the time the store had moved to the 3119 M Street space. The previous occupant might have been a bar or restaurant.

6. Examples in *Washington Post*, September 8, 1910, ES11; July 9, 1911, E2.

7. The store was at 3207 M Street.

8. "The Ear," *Evening Star*, May 9, 1980, 18.

9. Advertisements in the *Evening Star*, September 9, 1969, 59; January 13, 1970, 79; March 3, 1978, 5; and April 27, 1978, 16. "The Ear," 18.

10. "Georgetown Tobacco," Georgetown Tobacco, n.d., https://gttobacco.com/about/.

Chapter 14. Florists

1. Arlington County land records index.

2. "Lee Hwy. Rezoning Plea Stirs Neighbors' Protests," *Washington Post*, July 9, 1987, B3.

3. *Evening Star*, March 27, 1934, 63 (capitalization in original).

4. *Evening Star*, December 22, 1932, 3.

5. "Milton H. Comley, 71, Ex-Arlington Florist," *Evening Star*, November 7, 1971, 27. Examples of ads using the Milton Comley name can be found in the *Evening Star*, July 9, 1951, 13; August 5, 1968, 10.

NOTES

6. Deed recorded in District of Columbia land records, October 26, 1937 (document 1933032628).
7. "Dry Agent Fired for Courting Girl," *Evening Star*, September 6, 1925, 13.
8. Advertisement, *Evening Star*, November 27, 1949, 50.
9. "Three Quints Share Rec. League Lead," *Evening Star*, January 5, 1947, 28.
10. *Washington Post*, January 24, 1954, S10.
11. Death announcements in *Washington Post*, September 30, 1953, 18; and *Evening Star*, June 13, 1973, 69.

Chapter 15. Furniture and Home Furnishings Stores

1. Advertisements in the *Evening Star*, April 27, 1865, 2; July 2, 1856, 2; and March 25, 1864, 2.
2. "Georgetown Corporation Laws," *Evening Star*, January 7, 1864, 3.
3. "Georgetown," *Evening Star*, October 21, 1878, 4.
4. "Kept the Machine and Was Arrested," *Washington Post*, June 14, 1894, 1.
5. The arrival date is confirmed by a report in the *Evening Star* about jury selection in a court case involving Riggs bank ("Riggs Bank Case Called for Trial," *Evening Star*, May 8, 1916, 1, 4). William's son Charles was among the selected jurors, and the article included information about himself that Charles had provided to the court, including the date of his arrival in Washington as a child.
6. Will of William H. Schutt, probated in the District of Columbia on January 6, 1891; notice of dissolution of the partnership of Charles and William Schutt, *Evening Star*, January 21, 1893, 1.
7. *Evening Star*, May 8, 1939, 30 (capitalization in original).
8. *Evening Star*, May 3, 1922, 19; May 8, 1922, 19; September 11, 1922, 10; October 17, 1923, 23; October 6, 1924, 14; September 24, 1924, 24; October 1, 1924, 4; October 6, 1924, 14; November 23, 1925, 21; September 27, 1926, 17; September 26, 1928, 34; September 26, 1929, 45; and March 10, 1931, 29.
9. "Vestrymen and Delegates," *Washington Post*, April 21, 1897, 9; "Parish Elections by Episcopalians," *Washington Post*, March 30, 1921, 2; "Officers Elected by Episcopalians," *Washington Post*, April 18, 1922, 9; "6 Women Elected to Church Vestries, to First in Diocese," *Washington Post*, April 22, 1924, 2; "Episcopal Church Officials Elected in Capital Diocese," *Washington Post*, April 2, 1929, 22; "Episcopal Churches Elect Officers at 1932 Meeting," *Washington Post*, March 29, 1932, 5; "Episcopal Churches Elect New Officers and Delegates," *Washington Post*, April 18, 1933, 2.
10. "Hermann Had Notice," *Washington Post*, February 27, 1907, 12.
11. "New Business Building Planned for Georgetown," *Evening Star*, March 19, 1910, 14.
12. For information about the building interior, see Historic American Buildings Survey, DC-117, Library of Congress, https://www.loc.gov/item/dc0128/.
13. "All Get the Ballot," *Evening Star*, November 3, 1912, 19.
14. Will of George W. Wise, admitted to probate April 8, 1926.
15. World War I Draft Registration of William Kendrick, Ancestry, https://www.ancestry.com/search/collections/6482/records/23809560?tid=&pid=&queryId=8a46853b-0525-4a14-9b94-0c50044c6216&_phsrc=RHt371&_phstart=successSource.

16. *Washington Herald*, January 29, 1922.
17. Eileen Summers, "Doors Meet All Demands!," *Washington Post*, April 17, 1955, F19.
18. Mary L. Vaughan, "19 Unfinished Doors Turned into Profit," *Evening Star*, November 2, 1955, G57.
19. *Evening Star*, February 8, 1955, 11.
20. *Evening Star*, April 3, 1962, 5 (ellipses in original).
21. *Evening Star*, December 11, 1959, 9; January 13, 1960, 23; and April 3, 1962, 5. *Washington Post*, April 7, 1955, F19.
22. Summers, "Doors Meet All Demands!," F19.
23. *Evening Star*, January 9, 1966, 183; October 8, 1967, 19.
24. An ad in the *Evening Star* (April 29, 1956, 122), said the store was located at 3144 M Street. A later *Star* ad (August 19, 1956, 67) gave the location as 3140 M Street.
25. An ad in the *Washington Post* (March 18, 1969, A2) refers to "our new store" at 3146 M Street.
26. Lynn Dunson, "Flood Aid in District Mired in Paperwork," *Evening Star*, July 19, 1972, 48; "$100,000 Fire Hits Warehouse in Georgetown," *Evening Star*, December 1, 1972, 32.
27. Christina Del Sesto, "Public Figures," *Washington Post*, January 12, 1992, N9.
28. Lurma Rackley, "Street Vendors Defend Their Rights," *Evening Star*, April 20, 1973, 20.
29. Rudolph A. Pyatt, "Georgetown Retailers Bristle at Talk of Decline," *Evening Star*, August 15, 1976, 18.
30. David Segal, "Door Store Closing Its Own," *Washington Post*, May 10, 1996, F3; "Norman N. Tolkan, Furniture Merchant," *Washington Post*, January 9, 2014, B6.
31. *Evening Star*, June 29, 1924, 34.
32. Deed from Mary St. John to Kelly Furniture Co. Inc., recorded in District of Columbia land records, March 19, 1928 (document 192803190013).
33. *Evening Star*, October 27, 1926, 13; September 30, 1928, 94; October 13, 1929, 71; April 29, 1932, 13; and October 11, 1936, 98.
34. *Evening Star*, October 27, 1926, 13; September 30, 1928, 94; October 13, 1929, 71; April 29, 1932, 13; October 11, 1936, 98; and July 16, 1936, 11.
35. "Gifts for Employees of Beyda's Linen Shops and Kelly Furniture Co.," *Evening Star*, December 10, 1936, 17.
36. *Evening Star*, February 28, 1938, 13; March 5, 1938, 19.
37. *Evening Star*, April 1, 1940, 21.
38. "Husband Hit Her, She Says, and Asks Divorce and Alimony," *Evening Star*, September 21, 1935, 31; "Store Owner Is Jailed on Alimony Charge," *Evening Star*, August 3, 1940, 16.
39. *Evening Star*, October 29, 1942, 4.
40. *Evening Star*, February 27, 1943, 21; March 29, 1943, 31; and January 28, 1924, 10.
41. The prices are from an ad in the *Evening Star*, October 6, 1943, 2.
42. Deeds recorded in District of Columbia land records, February 20, 1943 (document 1943004078); January 6, 1944 (document 1944000392); and December 12, 1944 (document 1944000392). The January 1944 deed recited that Edmund and Elinor were residents of Miami.
43. "Little Caledonia: A Bastion of Civility," *Georgetowner*, December 18, 1992–January 7, 1993.

NOTES

44. "A Plan of Little Caledonia," *Georgetowner*, January 16–29, 1987, 20.
45. "Top Hats and Tiaras," *Evening Star*, May 29, 1938, 51.
46. *Evening Star*, December 4, 1938, 58.
47. Deeds recorded in District of Columbia land records, November 17, 1941 (document 1941039656); June 12, 1942 (document 1942017316); and April 5, 1945 (document 1945011301).
48. *Evening Star*, December 3, 1947, 24; January 23, 1948, 81; April 4, 1948, 25; July 18, 1948, 22; July 23, 1948, 22; April 2, 1950, 73; November 16, 1950, 40; December 21, 1950, 41; and April 19, 1951, 34.
49. Margaret Child, "Capital Careers," *Washington Post*, October 2, 1988, 70; Jura Koncius, "The Shop That Never Changes," *Washington Post*, December 21, 1995, T6; "Shops: The Little Caledonia That Could," *Washington Post*, October 9, 1997, 5; Annie Groer, "Goodbye to All That," *Washington Post*, February 7, 2002, H3.
50. Deeds recorded in District of Columbia land records, September 16, 1998 (document 199800072721); October 12, 2000 (document 20000958590); and January 2, 2001 (document 2001000118).

Chapter 16. Antique Dealers

1. *Evening Star*, June 21, 1957, 42, 55; October 28, 1964, 16.
2. *Washington Post*, July 18, 1944, 6.
3. *Washington Post*, February 20, 1958, 12.
4. "George Kernodle," obituary, *Evening Star*, March 3, 1957, 36.
5. Marriage announcement in the *Annapolis Evening Capital*, January 9, 1896, 1. There was another Lewis (or Louis) B. Jones born in New York in 1872, who was a naval officer. We know they were separate individuals because in the 1900 census there was a Lewis B. Jones working as a highway engineer in Albany, New York, and a Lieutenant Junior Grade Lewis B. Jones assigned to a naval installation in Brooklyn. Census records also indicate that the father of one Lewis was born in New Hampshire and the father of the other in New York. There also was another Isabella Jones who was a prominent children's rights advocate in Washington in the 1960s. An *Evening Star* item on December 17, 1971 (p. C-2) describes her as a "grandmother-to-be." At that time, the Isabella Jones who ran the antique store was an experienced grandmother aged ninety-three with sons in their seventies.
6. *Evening Star*, January 14, 1926, 53.
7. Deeds recorded in District of Columbia land records, April 19, 1946 (document 146016329); and November 14, 1946 (document 1946051182).
8. Solomon's store was at 1324 Wisconsin Avenue; *Evening Star*, December 27, 1942, 65; January 19, 1943, 29.
9. *Evening Star*, April 19, 1931, 71; February 7, 1932, 2.
10. "Isabella Jones," obituary, *Washington Post*, December 25, 1974, B6.
11. Photo from the Historic American Buildings Survey, DC-109, Library of Congress, https://www.loc.gov/item/dc0147/ .
12. U.S. Index to Naturalization Petitions filed in New York City, petition 126918, record 2670112.

13. District of Columbia Marriage Records, film 00239.
14. *Evening Star*, February 16, 1942, 67; March 24, 1943, 47.
15. Deeds recorded in District of Columbia land records, May 18, 1943 (document 1942014601); December 20, 1943 (document 1943032967); and August 3, 1945 (document 1945025975).
16. *Evening Star*, November 4, 1949, 32; June 7, 1945, 31.
17. World War I and World War II draft registrations available on Ancestry, https://www.ancestry.com/search/collections/6482/records/23902734?tid=&pid=&queryId=bd406367-0e73-47a4-a90b-9a3bb857336d&_phsrc=RHt283&_phstart=successSource and https://www.ancestry.com/search/collections/1002/records/17608395?tid=&pid=&queryId=7af1597f-9218-4ebe-8a8d-e6fee8aafe10&_phsrc=RHt285&_phstart=successSource; building permit 173977, issued to Esunas on August 29, 1934; drawing from a wall report in the office of the D.C. Surveyor. Deeds recorded in District of Columbia land records, January 9, 1925 (document 192501090098); November 8, 1926 (document 19261180003); March 28, 1928 (document 192803030013); October 5, 1928 (document 19281015029); March 17, 1945 (document 1945008783); and December 14, 1945 (document 1945043061). *Evening Star*, death announcement, July 30, 1962, 24; *Evening Star*, want ad, October 30, 1935, 36; *Washington Post* article about Prohibition violation, October 1, 1921, 2.
18. Sarah Booth Conroy, "Shopping for True Treasures at Consignment Shops," *Washington Post*, Washington Home section, November 23, 2015, 13.
19. History of the Christ Child Society, n.d., https://www.christchilddc.org/page.cfm?p=507.
20. *Evening Star*, February 17, 1935, 62; November 16, 1935, 30.
21. *Evening Star*, December 5, 1943, 71; December 12, 1944, 18.
22. "Bony Armadillo Newest Offering in Christ Child Opportunity Shop," *Evening Star*, May 6, 1951, 33.
23. "Opportunity Shop Receives Rare Articles," *Evening Star*, May 9, 1952, 41.
24. *Evening Star*, April 30, 1961, 63.
25. "Indictment in D.C. Burglary Is Linked to 'Skillful' Ring," *Washington Post*, December 22, 1976, 28.
26. Advertisements in the *Evening Star*, May 19, 1964, 48; September 25, 1964, 31; and September 19, 1965, F7. "The Uncommon Shopper," *Evening Star*, January 4, 1970, 177; Annie Gowen, "More Coming through the Door at Consignment Shops," *Washington Post*, February 26, 2009, H6; Jennifer Barger, "At the Op Shop, Customers Can Browse the Old-Fashioned Way, No Matter the Season," *Washington Post*, November 23, 2015.
27. "Seeking Pre-owned Bargains," *Washington Post*, March 1, 1970, G1.
28. *Washington Post*, April 12, 1970, H21.

Chapter 17. Hardware Stores

1. The 1850 numbers are from U.S. Census slave schedules available at Ancestry, https://www.ancestry.com/search/collections/7668/; the 1862 numbers are from Dorothy S. Provine, *Compensated Emancipation in the District of Columbia—Petitions under the Act of April 16, 1862* (Westminster, MD: Willow Bend Books, 2008), 176, petition 179.
2. Advertisement, *Evening Star*, October 6, 1930, 37.

NOTES

3. *The WPA Guide to Washington, D.C.* (repr., New York: Pantheon, 1983), 744; Richard P. Jackson, *The Chronicles of Georgetown* (Polkinhorn, 1878), 32, 238; Grace Dunlop Ecker, *A Portrait of Old Georgetown* (Richmond, VA: Dietz, 1951), 161–63; "G. Morris Steinbraker, Georgetown Builder, 81," *Evening Star*, January 6, 1975, 38; building permit 1266, issued November 12, 1886; deed from Linthicum Institute to Vestry of Christ Church recorded in District of Columbia land records, January 10, 1957 (document 1957000977).

4. An advertisement in the *Evening Star*, December 9, 1872, 1, describes the inventory.

5. "Sale of Steam Marble Works Machinery," *Evening Star*, August 13, 1870, 4.

6. "Real Estate Matters," *Evening Star*, September 9, 1893, 15; "Major Haines Reports Progress," *Evening Star*, October 10, 1883, 1.

7. "Georgetown," *Evening Star*, June 3, 1892, 10; "Four Percent Paid," *Evening Star*, May 23, 1903, 23.

8. "Altair Cycle Club," *Evening Star*, January 25, 1896, 17; "Affairs in West Washington," *Evening Star*, September 16, 1881, 4.

9. Arthur G. Peterson, "Retracing the Old Georgetown-Alexandria Canal," *Evening Star*, January 3, 1944, 37.

10. Kelly Richmond, oral history interview with Jim Weaver, Citizens Association of Georgetown, May 31, 2011, https://cagtown.org/2011/05/31/jim-weaver/.

11. "72-Year-Old Man Remembers When District Had 33 Thriving Harness-Making Shops," *Washington Post*, February 1, 1940, 19.

12. "Weaver Rites Set for Today," *Washington Post*, November 4, 1933, 4; "Weaver Bros. 42 Years in Business," *Washington Post*, August 24, 1930, R1.

13. *Evening Star*, November 9, 1962, 88 (emphasis and capitalization in original).

14. "Five-Alarmer Watched by Thousands," *Washington Post*, July 8, 1963, A1.

15. "Masons Dedicate Georgetown Site," *Evening Star*, November 14, 1964, 12; "Death Removes Business Leader," *Evening Star*, December 11, 1925, 26; "Masonic Hall Lays Cornerstone," *Washington Post*, November 15, 1964, B4.

16. Richmond, oral history interview with Jim Weaver.

17. "James B. Weaver Jr., President of Hardware Store," *Washington Post*, May 3, 2013.

18. Cathy Farrell, oral history interview with Patrick Meenehan, Citizens Association of Georgetown, September 11, 2019, https://cagtown.org/2019/09/11/patrick-meenehan/.

19. "Application for Registration—Naturalized Citizen, Filed September 18, 1878," Ancestry, https://www.ancestry.com/imageviewer/collections/2133/images/32734_620305173 _0256-00898?treeid=&personid=&hintid=&queryId=ae47856125f186501b58249fcae7aadc &usePUB=true&_phsrc=IHF2293&_phstart=successSource&usePUBJs=true&pId=36822.

20. Arriving passenger list for the SS *Cedric*, arriving New York, December 19, 1921, Ancestry, https://www.ancestry.com/imageviewer/collections/7488/images/NYT715_3063 -0503?treeid=&personid=&hintid=&queryId=d3ad42f22b7da003590c530d5cbe0 cd1&usePUB=true&_phsrc=IHF2297&_phstart=successSource&usePUBJs=true& _ga=2.262915020.134124062.1616021399-87164605.1608674116&pId=4026088373.

21. Catherine Farrell, oral history interview with Margaret Meenehan and Sharon Meenehan O'Brian, Citizens Association of Georgetown, August 3, 2015, https://cagtown .org/2015/08/03/margaret-meenehan-and-sharon-meenehan-obrian/.

22. *Evening Star*, April 12, 1951, 56.

GEORGETOWN'S RETAIL PAST

23. Farrell, oral history interview with Margaret Meenehan and Sharon Meenehan O'Brian; "Meenehan's Wake," *Washington Post*, January 24, 1980, D1.

Chapter 18. Paint and Glass Stores

1. *Evening Star*, April 30, 1916, 29; June 25, 1916, 23. *Washington Post*, May 15, 1921, 2.
2. Deed recorded in District of Columbia land records, March 25, 1927 (document 192703250087); advertisement, *Evening Star*, June 20, 1927, 5.
3. Deed from Craig & Hook Inc. to W. R. Winslow recorded in District of Columbia land records, December 8, 1928 (document 192812080052); deed of release of the mortgage recorded December 11, 1928 (document 192812110148).
4. Advertisement, *Washington Post*, November 19, 1922, 94; "William R. Winslow, 86, Founder of Paint Store," *Evening Star*, January 17, 1973, 37; "William R. Winslow, Paint Co. Founder," *Washington Post*, January 17, 1973, B6.
5. *Washington Post*, July 30, 1943, 13.
6. Help wanted ads that sought painters in 1968 and 1969 told those interested to apply at "Becker's Paint Store" at the Prospect Street address: *Evening Star*, September 25, 1968, 9; March 27, 1969, 48. Deeds recorded in District of Columbia land records, August 5, 1966 (documents 1966025867, 1966025937). The last ad in the *Washington Post* for Becker Paint & Glass appeared on June 9, 1971, D5.
7. *Washington Post*, August 31, 1986, G10.
8. "Guy Harper Is Named Boys Club Official," *Evening Star*, January 21, 1950, 20; "Winslow Foundation Gives Scholarships to Four University Students," *Evening Star*, August 3, 1950, 20.
9. "Charles W. DeMaine's Funeral," *Washington Post*, October 3, 1910, 2.
10. Tax records indicate that they owned the building by 1917. The deed recorded in District of Columbia land records on October 30, 1957 (document 1957033408), shows that Alice's estate sold the building in 1957.
11. U.S. Army Transport Service passenger list for the SS *Orizaba*, sailing from St. Nazarene, France, to Newport News, Virginia, May 2–June 11, 1919, Ancestry, https://www.ancestry.com/search/collections/61174/records/6909125?tid=&pid=&queryId=e5e97c2e-e07b-4402-9398-70bbffb05ab9&_phsrc=RHt373&_phstart=successSource.
12. *Washington Post*, February 25, 1917, 13; *Evening Star*, April 30, 1910, 8.
13. *Evening Star*, March 11, 1917, 7; April 1, 1917, 12. An example of the Goodyear ad is at *Washington Post*, June 29, 1919, 9.
14. We know the store was in business by March 17, 1948, when it ran a classified ad seeking a young man to learn the business, *Evening Star*, March 17, 1948, 40.
15. *Evening Star*, March 7, 1952, 37. The alley and the open area behind the building are visible on survey maps of the period, though it is impossible to know for sure if that area was the location of the "plentiful parking."
16. *Washington Post*, June 21, 1953, 56; June 24, 1953, 19.
17. Historic American Buildings Survey, DC-120, Library of Congress, https://www.loc.gov/item/dc0201/.

NOTES

Chapter 19. Appliance Stores: Keeping Up with Innovations

1. Robert J. Gordon, *The Rise and Fall of American Growth* (Princeton, NJ: Princeton University Press, 2016), 121; Anwen P. Mohun, *Steam Laundries—Gender, Technology and Work in the United States and Great Britain, 1880–1940* (Baltimore, MD: Johns Hopkins University Press, 1999), 249–60; Alison K. Hoagland, *The Row House in Washington, D.C.: A History* (Charlottesville: University Press of Virginia, 2023), 115.

2. "Electrical Display Begun," *Washington Post*, June 4, 1907, 16; "Lightning Twisters," *Evening Star*, June 4, 1907, 20; "Electric Refrigerator," *Washington Post*, December 3, 1905, E3.

3. *Evening Star*, September 25, 1922, 10; "Home Electrical Appliances Make Women's Life Easy," *Washington Post*, July 12, 1925, F5.

4. Actually, there were two categories: "electric refrigerators," with one listing, and "refrigerators, electric," with a single listing for a different store.

5. *Evening Star*, May 4, 1927, 10; *Washington Post*, December 11, 1986, A54.

6. *Washington Post*, June 26, 1928, 4; November 7, 1928, 16; and March 21, 1929, 4. *Evening Star*, July 11, 1927, 34.

7. *Washington Post*, June 24, 1934, S10; March 12, 1935, 7; and August 7, 1938, 17.

8. *Washington Post*, May 12, 1944, M3; December 18, 1947, 18.

9. *Washington Post*, March 1, 1957, A14; May 8, 1960, F31; and September 29, 1954, 20.

10. For example, see *Washington Post*, September 10, 1967, F12.

11. Advertisement, *Washington Post*, September 9, 1976, 118.

12. *Evening Star*, May 3, 1981, 115; July 11, 1927, 34; and May 4, 1927, 10.

13. *Washington Post*, December 11, 1986, A54.

Chapter 20. Staying Overnight: Early Taverns to Hotels

1. The principal sources for this chapter's discussion of Georgetown taverns are two articles by Oliver Wendell Holmes, "The City Tavern: A Century of Georgetown History 1796–1898," *Records of the Columbia Historical Society* 50 (1980): 1–35; and "The Colonial Taverns of Georgetown," *Records of the Columbia Historical Society* 51/52 (1989): 1–18.

2. *Evening Star*, November 14, 1909, 60.

3. Oliver Wendell Holmes, "Suter's Tavern: Birthplace of the Federal City," *Records of the Columbia Historical Society* 49 (1973–1974): 11–12.

4. The ad ran in the *Washington Federalist* of July 8, 1803, according to Holmes in "Suter's Tavern," 22. This history of Suter's Tavern also is based on Allen C. Clark, "Suter's Tavern," *Records of the Columbia Historical Society* 42/43 (1940–1941): 83–117.

5. Holmes, "Colonial Taverns," 23.

6. Abigail Adams to Mary Cranch, November 21, 1800, in *New Letters of Abigail Adams 1788–1801*, ed. Stewart Mitchell (New York: Houghton Mifflin, 1947), 257–60.

7. Jean White, "Historic Old Georgetown Tavern Is Being Restored," *Washington Post*, April 11, 1960, B1.

8. White, "Historic Old Georgetown Tavern Is Being Restored," B1.

9. Holmes, "The City Tavern," 25.

10. Dorothy S. Provine, *Compensated Emancipation in the District of Columbia—Petitions under the Act of April 16, 1862* (Westminster, MD: Willow Bend Books, 2008), 153, provides the

text of the petition for compensation. An actual image is available at "Petition," Ancestry, https://www.ancestry.com/imageviewer/collections/2159/images/31556_217985-00762?pId=2025.

11. David Mould and Missy Loewe, *Remembering Georgetown: A History of the Lost Port City* (Charleston, SC: History Press, 2009), 106.

12. White, "Historic Old Georgetown Tavern Is Being Restored," B1; "The City Tavern—a Restoration of Distinction," newspaper article found in the Peabody Room, D.C. Public Library. The newspaper from which the article appeared could not be determined, but it is not the *Evening Star* or the *Washington Post*.

13. Constance McLaughlin Green, *Washington—a History of the Capital* (Princeton, NJ: Princeton University Press, 1962), 1:17.

14. Green, *Washington—a History of the Capital*, 1:17; Holmes, "The City Tavern," 27.

15. *Evening Star*, November 15, 1854, 3.

16. "Georgetown Correspondence," *Evening Star*, October 16, 1855, 2. Advertisements in the *Evening Star*, December 3, 1855, 2; July 21, 1856, 3.

17. Notices of auction in the *Evening Star*, March 10, 1860, 3; April 19, 1860, 3.

18. "Military Hospital," *Evening Star*, May 10, 1861, 2.

19. Louisa May Alcott, *Hospital Sketches* (Boston, MA: Redpath, 1863), 25.

20. Mary Mitchell, *Divided Town* (Barre, MA: Barre, 1968), 45–46, 95; Margaret Leech, *Reveille in Washington* (New York: Harper Brothers, 1941), 223–24.

21. *Evening Star*, May 28, 1863, 3; June 15, 1864, 2.

22. *Evening Star*, November 8, 1866, 2.

23. *Evening Star*, November 28, 1862, 4; October 3, 1867, 3.

24. Mitchell, *Divided Town*, 13.

25. "Affairs of Georgetown," *Evening Star*, October 25, 1867, 3. *Evening Star*, November 28, 1867, 2; April 25, 1868, 2; and September 23, 1868, 2.

26. An advertisement announcing the sale appeared in the *Evening Star*, April 12, 1871, 2.

27. Mary Mitchell, *Chronicles of Georgetown Life 1865–1900* (Cabin John, MD: Seven Locks, 1986), 42.

28. The first reference to the West End Hotel in the *Evening Star* appeared on December 23, 1876, 7. The new name first appeared in a city directory in 1877.

29. Auction notice, *Evening Star*, April 2, 1880, 3.

30. Passenger list for the SS *America*, arrived New York, April 24, 1866, Ancestry, https://www.ancestry.com/search/collections/7488/records/6065635?tid=&pid=&queryId=6a611329-6efb-4b64-907e-320641763286&_phsrc=RHt377&_phstart=successSource.

31. Bremen State Archive records of German Desertions of Sailors 1855–1874, Ancestry, https://www.ancestry.com/imageviewer/collections/1271/images/DEUIMMCREWBREM_145675-00210?treeid=&personid=&hintid=&queryId=537f5784a4ddd075941fb2f0026f76ac&usePUB=true&_phsrc=IHF2332&_phstart=successSource&usePUBJs=true&_ga=2.36603045.426418239.1616881065-87164605.1608674116&pId=9058.

32. Historic American Buildings Survey, DC-103, about 1238 Wisconsin Avenue, Library of Congress, https://www.loc.gov/item/dc0294/. Schladt's obituary says that his father had constructed the building, but that seems unlikely. There is no sign of Schladt's father having been in Washington, and the first Schladt to own the site was Joseph himself, who bought it in 1883.

33. "Georgetown," *Evening Star*, April 14, 1891, 6.

NOTES

34. *Evening Star*, June 15, 1892, 10.

35. *Evening Star*, July 18, 1896, 2. The photo described appeared in the *Washington Post Magazine* on January 30, 2000. Examples of the ads were in the *Washington Post* of June 2, 1901, 36; and June 8, 1902, 29.

36. The census records are confusing as to John Kemp's age and date of immigration to the United States. The records are in error, or perhaps Schladt had two cousins named John Kemp. The accident was noted in the *Washington Post*, June 7, 1894, 6.

37. "Georgetown," *Evening Star*, May 3, 1893, 10; "Flying Carrier Pigeons," *Evening Star*, May 6, 1893, 3.

38. "A Poker Room Raided," *Evening Star*, December 5, 1891, 15.

39. "Coppers Disguised Themselves," *Evening Star*, June 27, 1894, 9.

40. "Tilt over a License," *Washington Post*, February 19, 1895, 9.

41. "Tilt over a License," 9.

42. "Work of the Excise Board," *Washington Post*, February 19, 1895, 10; "Tilt over a License," 9; "Schladt Is Shut Out," *Washington Post*, April 10, 1896, 10.

43. "Liquor License Granted, One Rejected," *Evening Star*, June 30, 1896, 8.

44. "Two Bullets Hit Him," *Evening Star*, October 13, 1896, 2.

45. "Denies Charge of Gas Tapping," *Washington Post*, January 6, 1901, 11; "Tapped a City Water Main," *Washington Post*, February 12, 1901, 12; *Evening Star*, March 2, 1901, 6; "Selling Liquor without License," *Evening Star*, April 24, 1908, 22.

46. "Victim of Explosion Reported Recovering," *Evening Star*, November 6, 1911, 5.

47. "Asks Writ to Stop Hotel Sale by U.S.," *Washington Post*, September 26, 1925, 16.

48. "Historic Wisconsin Avenue Hotel Yields Rum in Raid," *Washington Post*, September 23, 1932, 16; "Hosteler, 83, Freed after Night in Jail in Prohibition Case," *Washington Post*, December 9, 1932, 16.

49. "Luxury Georgetown Inn," *Washington Post*, July 8, 1961, C3; "Inn Geared to Elegance," *Washington Post*, March 31, 1962, D1; lease recorded in District of Columbia land records, November 3, 1961 (document 1961034057).

50. "The Court End of Town Lives Again in New Inn," advertising spread, *Evening Star*, May 20, 1962, 233; "Georgetown Inn Décor Is Lavish," *Evening Star*, May 6, 1962, 42; Myra McPherson, "Georgetown's New Inn Is Close in and 'Far Out' Too," *Evening Star*, May 13, 1962, E-10; "The Georgetown Inn Premieres Again," *Evening Star*, May 19, 1962, 16.

51. "The Georgetown Inn Premieres Again," 16.

52. *Washington Post*, December 5, 1963, A30; "Hotel Developer Collins Bird, 73, Dies," *Washington Post*, June 16, 2000, B7.

53. Deed recorded in District of Columbia land records, December 31, 1968 (document 1968027232).

54. Richard Lee, "In Pursuit of the Perfect Piano Bar," *Washington Post*, October 16, 1977, 344.

55. Donald Dresden, "The Four Georges: An Unfelicitous Foursome," *Washington Post*, March 25, 1973, PC38.

56. *Washington Post*, May 15, 1983, AD28.

57. Deed recorded in District of Columbia land records, January 16, 1980 (document 8000001670); Mary Bird, "The Georgetown Inn at 50 Celebrates Its History, Plans Reno-

vation," *Georgetowner*, June 18, 2012, https://georgetowner.com/articles/2012/06/18/georgetown-inn-50-celebrates-its-history-plans-renovation/.

Chapter 21. Restaurants

1. John DeFerrari, *Capital Streetcars: Early Mass Transit in Washington, D.C.* (Charleston, SC: History Press, 2015), 18–19.
2. Oliver Wendell Holmes, "The City Tavern: A Century of Georgetown History," *Records of the Columbia Historical Society* 50 (1980): 25.
3. "Elks Deplore C. A. Rodier's Death," *Washington Post*, February 21, 1901, 12; meeting announcement, *Washington Post*, February 1901, 3.
4. "Steakhouse Gave Owner Entrée into Investments," *Washington Post*, November 29, 2004, B1.
5. Robert Sellers, "The Block," *Georgetowner*, February 13–26, 1987, 27. For more in general about the numbers game and the gang who ran it in Foggy Bottom and Georgetown, see Leo Warring, *The Foggy Bottom Gang—the Story of the Warring Brothers of Washington, D.C.* (Cleveland, OH: Parafine, 2020).
6. In 1918, Britt and Weaver dissolved a small D.C. corporation called Columbia Lunch Company, of which both were directors. "Legal Notices," *Evening Star*, March 30, 1918, 17.
7. "Affairs in Georgetown," *Evening Star*, November 7, 1900, 8.
8. "Britt's Is Sold—but Will It Stay," *Evening Star*, May 26, 1966, 57.
9. "Britt's Is Sold," 57.
10. "Britt's Is Sold," 57.
11. "Britt's Is Sold," 57.
12. "Britt's Is Sold," 57.
13. District of Columbia land records show Pete as the grantee under several deeds in the area.
14. *Georgetowner*, July 11, 1964.
15. Among the sources for discussion that follows of the Martin family restaurants is an interview by the author of William Martin IV (William 4), the current proprietor of Martin's Tavern, on April 29, 2024.
16. Fritz Hahn, "Martin's One for the Ages," *Washington Post*, June 11, 2004, H5; "Billy Martin Georgetown Restaurateur," *Washington Post*, December 2, 2004, B6.
17. Richard Slusser, "Waiters Mellowing at Martin's Tavern," *Evening Star*, August 5, 1971, 17.
18. Warring, *Foggy Bottom Gang*, 116.
19. *Washington Examiner*, February 20, 1939; Hahn, "Martin's One for the Ages," H5; *Georgetowner*, July 1, 2015; *Georgetowner*, September 11, 2023; Margaret Truman, *Murder in Georgetown* (n.p.: Arbor House, 1986).
20. Slusser, "Waiters Mellowing at Martin's Tavern," 17.
21. Deeds recorded in District of Columbia land records, March 5, 1941 (documents 1941006840, 841).
22. Joyce Lowenstein, oral history interview with Billy Martin (William 4), Citizens Association of Georgetown, July 8, 2010, https://cagtown.org/2010/07/08/billy-martin/.
23. *Washington Post*, January 22, 1956, H9 (emphasis in original).

NOTES

24. Advertisement, *Georgetowner*, June 23–July 6, 1976 (capitalization in original); "Martin Will Open New Restaurant in Georgetown," *Evening Star*, March 28, 1953, 28; Emily Davies, "A D.C. Piano Man, Left Behind by Pandemic Recovery," *Washington Post*, B1.
25. "Martin Will Open New Restaurant in Georgetown," 28.
26. Lowenstein, oral history interview with Billy Martin (William 4).
27. Michele Jacobson, oral history interview with Al Wheeler, Citizens Association of Georgetown, August 4, 2011, https://cagtown.org/2011/08/04/al-wheeler/.
28. Lowenstein, oral history interview with Billy Martin (William 4).
29. "Billy Martin's Carriage House to Become Expanded Tramps," *Washington Post*, November 21, 1978, D13; "Night of the Disco," *Washington Post*, July 26, 1976, D10.
30. *Washington Post*, January 4, 1982, C1.
31. *Washington Post*, November 21, 1978, D13.
32. "Death of a Disco," *Washington Post*, January 4, 1982, C1. Jacobson, oral history interview with Al Wheeler; author interview with Billy Martin (William 4), April 29, 2014.
33. Author interview with Billy Martin (William 4).
34. Author interview with Billy Martin (William 4).
35. DeFerrari, *Capital Streetcars*, 177.
36. *Evening Star*, May 12, 1957, 39. The earlier ads ran between April 18 and April 21, for example, April 18, 1957, 8.
37. "Restaurant Can't Bar Rival's Use of Soufflé King," *Washington Post*, December 24, 1959, A1; Milton Vierst, "Many a Good Chef Is Lost Betwixt Gaul, Georgetown," *Washington Post*, June 5, 1960, A3.
38. Sally Quinn, "C'est tout en famille: The Discreet Charm of the Charcuterie," *Washington Post*, April 8, 1973, K1.
39. Quinn, "C'est tout en famille," K1; Donald Dresden, "Rive Gauche Deserves Good Marks," *Washington Post*, September 7, 1969, 7.
40. Quinn, "C'est tout en famille," K1.
41. Quinn, "C'est tout en famille," K1; William Rice, "The Passing of the Culinary Godfather," *Washington Post*, November 28, 1973, B1.
42. John Rosson, "It's Expensive but Worth It," *Evening Star*, November 13, 1969, 54; Dresden, "Rive Gauche Deserves Good Marks," 7.
43. Rice, "The Passing of the Culinary Godfather," B1.
44. DeFerrari, *Capital Streetcars*, 179.
45. John Rosson, "Dine with Cezanne," *Evening Star*, January 8, 1974, 13.
46. Quinn, "C'est tout en famille," K1; February 19, 1978, B12. DeFerrari, *Capital Streetcars*, 179.
47. John Rosson, "Place Vendome's Reborn as a High-Style Brasserie," *Evening Star*, April 17, 1981, 17; Phyllis Richman, "Richman on Restaurants: Place Vendome," *Washington Post*, June 28, 1981, SM36.
48. Walter Nicholls, "What's Cooking, Neighbor? Gerard Cabrol, Bistro Français," *Georgetowner*, January 16, 2015, https://georgetowner.com/articles/2015/01/16/whats-cooking-neighbor-gerard-cabrol-bistro-francais/; Robert Devaney, "Bon Anniversaire! 40 années de Bistro Français," *Georgetowner*, October 7, 2015, 10.

49. John Rosson, "For These Numbing Days of Winter, a Special Selection of Hearty Meals," *Evening Star*, January 22, 1978, 90.
50. John Rosson, "Fine Ambiance, Superb Flavors," *Evening Star*, October 9, 1975, E-8; Donald Dresden, "Bistro Français," *Washington Post*, February 29, 1976, 32.
51. Tom Sietsema, "Right Place, Right Time," *Washington Post*, October 21, 2001, SMG12.
52. Deed recorded in District of Columbia land records, August 27, 1985 (document 8500031459); "The Month of May in Restaurant Openings and Closings," *Washington Post*, May 31, 2016, https://www.proquest.com/docview/1792671062/57200EB08FAD445EPQ/2?accountid=46320&sourcetype=Blogs,%20Podcasts,%20&%20Websites.
53. John M. Rosson, "Taste for Crepes Burgeons among Gourmets," *Evening Star*, June 1, 1968, 32.
54. Rosson, "Taste for Crepes," 32.
55. Donald Dresden, "Maison des Crepes Probably Won't Remind You of Your Last Trip to Paris," *Washington Post*, June 7, 1970, 46.
56. Rosson, "Taste for Crepes," 32; John M. Rosson, "Crepes in Alexandria," *Evening Star*, August 4, 1973, 43.
57. John Rosson, "Dining: Brasserie Breton," *Evening Star*, June 17, 1979, 31.
58. Emerson Beauchamp, "The Old and the New," *Evening Star*, July 14, 1960, 54.
59. John Rosson, "Truly, Truly French," *Evening Star*, June 6, 1961, 33.
60. John Rosson, "Chez Odette Remains a Dining Bargain," *Evening Star*, January 28, 1971, D-4; John Rosson, "Chez Odette—Paris à la Mode," *Evening Star*, February 5, 1972, 12.
61. Tanya Lervik, oral history interview with Tom Birch, Citizens Association of Georgetown, May 12, 2012, https://cagtown.org/2012/05/12/tom-birch/.

Chapter 22. Prohibition in Georgetown

1. Sheppard Act, P.L. 64–383, enacted March 3, 1917; Volstead Act, P.L. 66-65, enacted October 25, 1919; Garrett Peck, *Prohibition in Washington, D.C.—How Dry We Weren't* (Charleston, SC: History Press, 2011), 33.
2. National Prohibition Act (aka The Volstead Act), P.L. 66-65 (1919), Title I.
3. "Bookmaking Raids Net Six Arrests," *Evening Star*, November 30, 1924, 4.
4. "Punished for Sale of Liquor at Court," *Evening Star*, June 14, 1918, 2.
5. The map is reproduced in Peck, *Prohibition in Washington, D.C.*, 138.
6. Peck, *Prohibition in Washington, D.C.*, 143; 3.2 percent beer was legalized by the Cullen-Harrison Act, Public Law 73-3.
7. "After Years of Hope, Bar Owner Quits Few Days Too Soon," *Washington Post*, September 16, 1933.

Chapter 23. Bars and Bar Wars

1. Public Law 87-470, 76 Stat. 89, May 31, 1962; "Senate Approves Stand-Up Drinking at D.C. Bars (but behind Screens)," *Washington Post*, May 18, 1962, A1; John Pagones, "Clyde's Leads Comeback of Saloons," *Washington Post*, September 13, 1963, B13.
2. "Clyde's Owner Says Copying Success Is Key," *Current*, December 29, 1999; *Georgetowner*, August 5–25, 1983; July 15–28, 1985.
3. "Clyde's: A Recipe for Success," *Washington Post*, August 1, 1988, BF24; "Clyde's Leads Comeback of Saloons," *Washington Post*, September 13, 1963, B13.

NOTES

4. Lance Morrow, "Georgetown Now Updated but It Didn't Expect This," *Evening Star*, February 1, 1965, 23.

5. Morrow, "Georgetown Now Updated," 23; *Washington Post*, September 13, 1963, B13.

6. Bart Barnes, "Dishwasher Rose to CEO, Helped Clyde's Restaurants Prosper," *Washington Post*, January 29, 2019, B6; Michael Kernan, "Old Ebbitt Auction: Auction of the Old Ebbitt Grill's Potpourri," *Washington Post*, June 17, 1970, C1.

7. Kernan, "Old Ebbitt Auction," C1.

8. Deeds recorded in District of Columbia land records, August 21, 1973 (document 7300020748); July 12, 1974 (document 7400015715); and June 11, 1976 (document 7600015202).

9. Donald Dresden, "The 1975 Guide to Dining Out," *Washington Post*, May 18, 1975, 28.

10. Blaine Harden Washington, "New Clyde's to Be Built at Tyson's," *Washington Post*, July 28, 1978, D11.

11. Timothy Robinson, "Clyde's Sued by 3 over Dress Code Rule," *Washington Post*, August 24, 1976, C1; "A Tempest in a Tee Shirt," *Washington Post*, August 28, 1976, A10.

12. "Restaurateur Catered to Georgetown Crowd," *Washington Post*, August 24, 2014, C8.

13. Debbi Wilgoren and Andrew DeMillo, "Boaters in a Row with Clyde's over Eatery," *Washington Post*, June 8, 2001, B3.

14. Carol Joynt, *Innocent Spouse* (Portland, OR: Broadway Books, 2011), 86. The following discussion of Nathan's is based on Carol Joynt's recollections in an interview (Linda Greenan and Cathy Farrell, oral history interview with Caroll Joynt, Citizens Association of Georgetown, July 9, 2016, https://cagtown.org/2016/07/09/carol-joynt/), as well as *Innocent Spouse* and a *Washington Post* profile headlined "Without Reservations" (July 15, 1999, C1).

15. The new menu received a generally positive review in "Change of Course," *Washington Post*, April 26, 1998, 381.

16. Greenan and Farrell, oral history interview with Carol Joynt.

17. Joynt, *Innocent Spouse*, 16, 68.

18. Joynt, *Innocent Spouse*, 137.

19. Joynt, *Innocent Spouse*, 235.

20. Joynt, *Innocent Spouse*, 235.

21. Joynt, *Innocent Spouse*, 235.

22. Joynt, *Innocent Spouse*, 247; for current and recent Q&A Café events, see www.caroljoynt.com.

23. Leslie Berger, "Georgetown after Dark: Loud, Lively and Preppy, Too," *Washington Post*, August 25, 1982, DC1.

24. Bill Peterson, "Potomac Journal: Al Harvey: 'All the Inspiration I Need Is My Guitar and Someone to Listen,'" *Washington Post*, July 24, 1975, DC1; Robert Devaney, "Mr. Smith's on M Street to Close by September," *Georgetowner*, September 10, 2014, https://georgetowner.com/articles/2014/09/10/mr-smiths-m-street-close-september/; Peter Murray, "Mr. Smith's Items to Be Auctioned Off," *Georgetowner*, September 15, 2014, https://georgetowner.com/articles/2014/09/15/mr-smith-be-auctioned/; Anders Kristofer Ohm, "A New Piano Bar Coming to M Street," *Georgetowner*, September 29, 2014; John Rosson, "Another New One and It's a Beaut," *Evening Star*, August 1, 1963, 32; Fritz Hahn, "A New Georgetown Home for Piano Fans," *Washington Post*, September 26, 2014, 12; Eve Zibart, "Mr. Smith's in Tysons," *Washington Post*, November 9, 1990, 19; Robert Devaney, "Chadwick's to Close; to

Be Replaced by Mr. Smith's," *Georgetowner*, September 10, 2014, https://georgetowner.com/articles/2014/09/10/chadwicks-close-be-replaced-mr-smiths/.

25. Berger, "Georgetown after Dark," DC1.
26. "Music Room," *Washington Post*, March 17, 1972, B3.
27. "Henry Yaffe, 88; Owner of Mr. Henry's Pubs," *Washington Post*, March 28, 2006, DCB5.
28. Donald Dresden, "Low Prices and Plain Fare at the Third Edition and Jamie Gore's Steak Pub," *Washington Post*, October 3, 1971, 54.
29. "The Fascinating History of 70s and 80s Fern Bars," Things Boomers Like, January 13, 2023, https://thingsboomerslike.com/get-ready-to-feel-nostalgic-the-fascinating-history-of-70s-and-80s-fern-bars/; Tom Sietsema, "Third Edition," *Washington Post*, November 26, 1983, 186; Allan Lengal, "At Nightspots, They Keep the Peace," *Washington Post*, December 30, 2004, 8; Eric Brace and Fritz Hahn, "Movers and Shakers," *Washington Post*, March 29, 2002, 11. The author experienced the second floor's ambience when he dined there from time to time in the 1970s and 1980s.
30. Robert Devaney, "Last Edition of This Third Edition," *Georgetowner*, January 16, 2013, https://georgetowner.com/articles/2013/01/16/last-edition-third-edition/; Robert Devaney, "Third Edition to Become El Centro," *Georgetowner*, April 25, 2013, https://georgetowner.com/?s=third+edition+to+become+el+centro; Juliana Zovak, "Open This Week: The Sovereign and Beard Papa's," *Georgetowner*, March 30, 2016, https://georgetowner.com/articles/2016/03/30/open-week-sovereign-and-beard-papas/.
31. Donald Dresden, "Low Prices and Plain Fare at the Third Edition and Jamie Gore's Steak Pub," *Washington Post*, October 3, 1971, 54.
32. Dresden, "The 1975 Guide to Dining Out," 281; Phyllis Richman, "Ringside Seats at Hawthorne's," *Washington Post*, September 18, 1992, 35.
33. Linda Wheeler, "Georgetown Girds with Floodgates, Car Rental Bargains," *Washington Post*, November 7, 1985, A40; Michael Specter, "Flood Watch's Scenes of Fun and Disaster," *Washington Post*, November 8, 1985, 25.
34. "Tom Russo, Owner of Chadwick's, Dies," *Georgetowner*, January 31, 2014; Devaney, "Chadwick's to Close."
35. Wall's Grill never appeared in the city directory—the Publick House, probably its predecessor in the space, appears consistently from 1974 through 1982. We know that Wall's Grill was there because Phyllis Richman wrote a review of it: "Wall's Grill," *Washington Post*, October 10, 1981, SM46.
36. Sharon Warrant Walsh, "Dishing Up Popular Eateries," *Washington Post*, January 11, 1988, BF1; Barbara Blechman, "J. Paul's Preppy Pub," *Washington Post*, September 9, 1983, WK21.
37. Blechman, "J. Paul's Preppy Pub," WK21; Tom Sietsema, "J Paul's," *Washington Post*, April 17, 1986, DC3.
38. "Georgetown Fumes over Firehouse Burger King," *Washington Post*, September 15, 1983, DC1.
39. Robert Devaney, "J. Paul's Founder Paul Cohn Bids Farewell to His Restaurant Group," *Georgetowner*, February 17, 2014, https://georgetowner.com/articles/2014/02/17/j-pauls-founder-paul-cohn-bids-farewell-his-restaurant-group/; "J. Paul's to Close by Year-End," *Georgetowner*, November 19, 2018, https://georgetowner.com/articles/2018/11/19/j-pauls-close-years-end/.

NOTES

40. Sources for this history of the Cellar Door were Bart Barnes, "Promotor Dave Williams," *Washington Post*, January 29, 1999, B5; William C. Woods, "'Good Vibes' behind the Cellar Door," *Washington Post*, October 12, 1970, B1; "Neil Young's 'Live at the Cellar Door' Is a Window into D.C.'s Musical Past," *Washington Post*, December 10, 1973, C1; Richard Harrlington, "2 from D.C. Buy the Cellar Door," *Washington Post*, January 31, 1981, G4; Judy Bachrach, "Boyle: A Rock Empire above the Cellar Door," *Washington Post*, June 10, 1975, B1; William Rice, "1968 Was the Year of the Cellar Door," *Washington Post*, December 27, 1968, D9; Tom Zito, "Going Out the Cellar Door," *Washington Post*, December 18, 1973, C1; Richard Harrington, "The Door Closes in Georgetown," *Washington Post*, January 9, 1982, C1; Richard Harrington, "Cellar Door Joins the Band," *Washington Post*, August 14, 1998, G1.

41. Larry Rohter, "Bayou: New Name and New Faces," *Washington Post*, December 21, 1974, D3; Richard Harrington, "Last Call at the Bayou," *Washington Post*, December 30, 1998, D1.

42. "Tom McCarthy: The *Post*'s Roving Reporter Roves Washington, after Dark," *Washington Post*, September 20, 1937, 7.

43. "Legal Notices," *Washington Post*, March 13, 1943, B10; Frese draft card, Ancestry, https://www.ancestry.com/imageviewer/collections/1002/images/44467_11_00005-00057?use PUB=true&_phsrc=IHF2158&_phstart=successSource&usePUBJs=true&pId=17726345.

44. "Court Penalizes Nine More in Crusade for Cleanliness," *Washington Post*, August 18, 1943, B10; "Two OPA Price Cases Settled by Agreement," *Evening Star*, December 10, 1944, 29.

45. *Evening Star*, December 9, 1950, 10.

46. John Seagraves, "A Supper Club? Not This One," *Evening Star*, March 31, 1966, 35; "On the Town," *Evening Star*, October 18, 1970, 160–61; "Georgetowners Sue on Liquor License," *Washington Post*, June 3, 1968, C12.

47. Emma Oxford, oral history interview with Philip and Richard Levy, Citizens Association of Georgetown, June 18, 2014, https://cagtown.org/2014/06/18/richard-phillip-levy/.

48. *Georgetowner*, August 5–25, 1983.

49. For examples of groups playing The Shamrock, see advertisement in the April 1, 1971 *Evening Star*, 40.

50. Larry Rohter, "This Is the End, Roger, Isn't It?," *Washington Post*, December 16, 1974, B1.

51. John Pagones, "Success Story Develops in Georgetown Shadows," *Washington Post*, December 23, 1962, F15. Display advertisements, *Washington Post*, February 17, 1963, G4; July 7, 1963, G3; and April 21, 1964, A16. The Nina Simone ad is from the *Evening Star*, May 27, 1964, 95.

52. Tim Warren, "Still 'Crazy' after All These Years," *Washington Post*, May 10, 1987, W7; Morrow, "Georgetown Now Updated," 23.

53. Morrow, "Georgetown Now Updated," 23; Warren, "Still Crazy after All These Years," W7.

54. Bill Gold, "The Real Inside Story on Beer Joints," *Washington Post*, January 24, 1966, C6.

55. Photo caption in the *Evening Star*, March 1, 1970, 148; John Rosson, "Two Newcomers on the Scene," *Evening Star*, April 12, 1969, 34; Richard Harrington, "Apple Pie Is as American As," *Evening Star*, July 20, 1974, 51.

56. Rosson, "Two Newcomers on the Scene," 34.

57. Harrington, "Apple Pie Is as American," 51.

58. Rosson, "Two Newcomers on the Scene," 51; Harrington, "Apple Pie Is as American," 51.
59. Notice in the *Evening Star*, May 20, 1976, 40.
60. Richard Harrington, "Playing a Final Refrain," *Washington Post*, September 18, 1982, C1.
61. Charles McCollum, "A Selective Swing through the Music Clubs," *Evening Star*, February 20, 1981, 23; Richard Harrington, "Playing a Final Refrain," *Washington Post*, September 18, 1982, C1; Richard Harrington, "Pop Notes," *Washington Post*, February 12, 1980, B6.
62. Diana McLellan, "The Gunch on the Barroom Floor," *Washington Post*, March 25, 1975, 36; Penelope Lemov, "Family Out," *Washington Post*, June 9, 1977, DC10; "Try It!," *Washington Post*, November 17, 1974, PO17.
63. Oliver Wendell Holmes, "The City Tavern: A Century of Georgetown History 1796–1898," *Records of the Columbia Historical Society* 50 (1980): 6.
64. P.L. 73–85, January 24, 1934; "Hazy ABC Regulation Is a Threat to Washington Night Life," *Washington Post*, January 19, 1968, B12.
65. "Georgetown Café License Weighed after Hearing," *Evening Star*, September 17, 1952, 34.
66. Morrow, "Georgetown Now Updated," 23.
67. Morrow, "Georgetown Now Updated," 23.
68. Morrow, "Georgetown Now Updated," 23.
69. Robert L. Asher, "Old Georgetown Is Full of Young Sprouts," *Washington Post*, July 11, 1965, E5.
70. Palace Restaurant, Inc. v. Alcoholic Beverage Control Board, 271 A. 2d 561 (D.C. Court of Appeals, 1970); "M Street Spots Called City's 'Cancer,'" *Washington Post*, August 19, 1965, D18.
71. Berger, "Georgetown after Dark," DC1.
72. Thomas Dimond, "Georgetown Charges Aired on M Street Liquor Licenses," *Evening Star*, November 27, 1965, A1; George Lardner Jr., "Georgetowners Planning Rocky Road for Rock 'n' Roll Strip on M Street," *Washington Post*, November 29, 1965, A18.
73. Paul W. Valentine, "Court Backs ABC on M Street Bars," *Washington Post*, March 30, 1966, B1.
74. "Roundtable Loses Permit; ABC Grants 2 Renewals," *Washington Post*, January 30, 1966, B1; *Evening Star*, January 30, 1966, 19; "M Street Café License Bid Protested," *Evening Star*, July 13, 1967, 19; "Georgetown Witnesses Back License for Café," *Evening Star*, September 7, 1967, 29.
75. Citizens Association of Georgetown, Inc. v. Alcoholic Beverage Control Board, 268 A. 2d 801 (1970); Citizens Association of Georgetown, Inc. v. District of Columbia Alcoholic Beverage Control Board, 280 A. 2d 309 (1971); Citizens Association of Georgetown, Inc. v. District of Columbia Alcoholic Beverage Control Board, 316 A. 2d 865 (1974); Citizens Association of Georgetown, Inc. v. District of Columbia Alcoholic Beverage Control Board, 288 A. 2d 666 (1972); Palace Restaurant, Inc. v. Alcoholic Beverage Control Board, 271 A. 2d 561 (1970); Citizens Association of Georgetown, Inc. v. District of Columbia Alcoholic Beverage Control Board, 287 A. 2d 87 (1972); Citizens Association of Georgetown, Inc. v. District of Columbia Alcoholic Beverage Control Board, 305 A. 2d 861 (1973); Citizens Association of Georgetown, Inc. v. District of Columbia Alcoholic Beverage Control Board, 323 A. 2d 715 (1974); Citizens Association of Georgetown, Inc. v. District of Columbia Alcoholic Beverage Control Board, 359 A. 2d 295 (1976).

NOTES

76. "Liquor License Is Denied to Georgetown Café," *Evening Star*, August 13, 1968, 23.

77. "Georgetown Citizens Group Is in Court Again," *Evening Star*, July 18, 1970, 18; Citizens Association of Georgetown, Inc. v. Alcoholic Beverage Control Board, 268 A. 2d 801 (1970) and 280 A. 2d 309 (1971); Citizens Association of Georgetown, Inc. v. Alcoholic Beverage Control Board, 316 A. 2d 865 (1974).

78. Greenan and Farrell, oral history interview with Carol Joynt. *Washington Post*, September 13, 1963, B13; August 28, 1976, A10.

79. "M Street Night Spot Defended by Police," *Washington Post*, December 8, 1966, C1.

80. Berger, "Georgetown after Dark," DC1.

81. Berger, "Georgetown after Dark," DC1.

82. "D.C. Drinking Age Criticized," *Washington Post*, May 14, 1985, A1.

83. D.C. Act 6-229, November 25, 1986.

84. Jose Antonio Vargas, "21-Wannabes Practice the Art of Faking It," *Washington Post*, August 31, 2003, C5.

85. Linda Wheeler, "Too Many Bars, Say Residents: License Moratorium Urged in Georgetown," *Washington Post*, December 22, 1988, DC1.

86. Linda Wheeler, "Liquor Moratorium Urged for Georgetown," *Washington Post*, June 8, 1989, DC3.

87. Shaun Sutner, "Residents Pressure Bar Owners," *Washington Post*, January 9, 1992, DC1.

88. Eve Zibart, "Uneasy Quiet in Georgetown," *Washington Post*, May 22, 1992, N13.

89. Marua Judkin, "Will Trump Era Make Georgetown Rate Again?," *Washington Post*, November 19, 2016, C1.

Chapter 24. Movie Theaters

1. Robert K. Headley, *Motion Picture Exhibition in Washington, D.C.* (Jefferson, NC: McFarland, 1999), 33.

2. Headley, *Motion Picture Exhibition in Washington, D.C.*, 290. The map is from the survey atlas for 1919, G. W. Baist, *Baist's Real Estate Atlas Surveys of Washington, District of Columbia*, vol. 3 (Philadelphia: Baist Surveyors, 1919).

3. Headley says the theater operated from 1911 to 1915, but a Baist survey map for 1921 shows it still in place, perhaps abandoned. The 1924 Baist map shows that by then the theater was gone and new buildings had been constructed in its place. The theater was not listed in city directories, perhaps because of its seasonal nature and insubstantial physical plant. G. W. Baist, *Baist's Real Estate Atlas Surveys of Washington, District of Columbia*, vol. 3 (Philadelphia: Baist Surveyors, 1921, 1924).

4. Kathleen M. Lesko, Valerie Babb, and Carroll R. Gibbs, *Black Georgetown Remembered—a History of Its Black Community from the Founding of "The Town of George" in 1751 to the Present Day* (Washington, D.C.: Georgetown University Press, 1991), 56.

5. Headley, *Motion Picture Exhibition in Washington, D.C.*, 290.

6. Headley, *Motion Picture Exhibition in Washington, D.C.*, 316.

7. "Steps Taken to Issue Temporary License to Dumbarton Theater," *Evening Star*, September 2, 1948, 28. Details about how the film was booked, the contents of the lecture, and such are from "*Mom and Dad*," Internet Movie Database, https://www.imdb.com/title/tt0040603/?ref_=mv_close.

8. Deed recorded in District of Columbia land records, March 4, 1949 (document 1949006979).
9. District Line (column), *City Paper*, September 12, 1986; *Georgetowner*, September 12, 1986.
10. "Theater Owners Become Critics of Cinematheque," *Washington Post*, August 28, 1965, B1; "Liquor Board Plans Food Crackdown," *Washington Post*, September 11, 1965, B4.
11. The Old Georgetown Act, which began historic architectural controls in Georgetown, was enacted by Congress in 1950, D.C. Code Section 5-801, 64 Stat. 903 (September 22, 1950).
12. Adam Bernstein, "S. David Levy, 67; Owner of Biograph, Key Theaters," *Washington Post*, September 17, 2004, D6; Michael S. Rosenwald, "Alan Rubin, Co-founder of the Biograph Theater, Dies at 85," *Washington Post*, November 11, 2022, https://www.proquest.com/docview/2735411167/BD85FCCCD07F4D5EPQ/1?accountid=46320&sourcetype=Blogs,%20Podcasts,%20&%20Websites; Headley, *Motion Picture Exhibition in Washington, D.C.*, 235.
13. Headley, *Motion Picture Exhibition in Washington, D.C.*, 278; District of Columbia building permit 2977, issued October 7, 1927.
14. Headley, *Motion Picture Exhibition in Washington, D.C.*, 235; Richard L. Coe, "New Biograph Adds to M Street Action," *Washington Post*, September 15, 1967, 29; Emma Oxford, oral history interview with Philip and Richard Levy, Citizens Association of Georgetown, June 18, 2014, https://cagtown.org/2014/06/18/richard-phillip-levy/.
15. Bernstein, "S. David Levy, 67," D6; Chip Crews, "Key Theatre Locking Up at Year's End," *Washington Post*, November 6, 1997, C1.
16. Crews, "Key Theatre Locking Up at Year's End," C1.
17. Headley, *Motion Picture Exhibition in Washington, D.C.*, 207, 243.

Chapter 25. Bowling Alleys and Pool Halls

1. Advertisements in the *Evening Star*, September 2, 1854, 3; May 9, 1857, 3; and July 17, 1857, 1. An example of the YMCA's advertising is in the *Evening Star*, February 13, 1871, 1. Ads like it ran periodically into late 1872.
2. Andrew Hurley, *Diners, Bowling Alleys, and Trailer Parks: Chasing the American Dream in the Postwar Consumer Culture* (New York: Basic Books, 2002), 110, 113–15, 135–36.
3. One such ad appeared immediately after Rodier's listing in the 1874 city directory.
4. *Evening Star*, July 12, 1911, 13; February 12, 1911, 52. Photo by the author.
5. The change in the building's footprint can be seen by comparing maps of the site from Hopkins's 1887 survey atlas (G. M. Hopkins, *A Complete Set of Surveys and Plats of Properties in the City of Washington, District of Columbia*, vol. 3 [Philadelphia: Hopkins, 1887]) and from Baist survey atlases for 1903, 1907, and 1909 (G. W. Baist, *Baist's Real Estate Atlas Surveys of Washington, District of Columbia*, vol. 3 [Philadelphia: Baist Surveyors, 1903, 1907, 1909]). Regarding bowling lane dimensions, see Kira Byrd, "What Are the Official USBC Bowling Lane Dimensions?," Bowling for Beginners, March 14, 2024, https://bowlingforbeginners.com/bowling-lane-dimensions/; and "What Are the Bowling Lane Dimensions?," Bowling Knowledge, https://www.bowlingknowledge.com/bowling-lane-dimensions/.
6. Armstrong's World War I draft card, available at Ancestry, www.ancestry.com/imageviewer/collections16482/images/005205818_00152?pld=23900756; advertisement, *Washington Post*, November 27, 1913, 8, shows the name "Potomac Alleys."

NOTES

7. District of Columbia property tax records for 1917 and 1918 identify the Potomac Insurance Company as owner of the property. Records for 1930–1931 identify Veale as the owner. District of Columbia land records, which are available online for 1921 and after, include the deed by which Veale later sold the property but do not include a deed by which he acquired it, indicating that the acquisition was before 1921.

8. *Evening Star*, December 3, 1928, 66; *Washington Post*, December 30, 1928, M19.

9. Deed recorded in District of Columbia land records, October 3, 1927 (document 192710030086); building permit 2977, issued October 7, 1927. Advertisement announcing the opening of the Georgetown Recreation Center, *Evening Star*, February 21, 1928, 29.

10. Hurley, *Diners, Bowling Alleys, and Trailer Parks*, 185.

11. *Evening Star*, September 21, 1928, 17, 33; December 3, 1928, 35; and January 24, 1929, 42.

12. *Evening Star*, August 21, 1940, 14. *Washington Post*, January 18, 1942, L6; November 2, 1941, L8.

13. *Washington Post*, August 19, 1902, 4; July 7, 1898, 9.

14. *Evening Star*, February 1, 1914, 17.

Chapter 26. Bicycle Shops

1. *Evening Star*, April 30, 1903, 16; August 9, 1914, 64; and April 20, 1918, 16.
2. *Evening Star*, December 19, 1937, 76.
3. *Evening Star*, May 24, 1939, 31; November 11, 1948, 51.
4. *Evening Star*, March 29, 1940, 44; April 6, 1941, 71.
5. *Evening Star*, October 19, 1947, 43.
6. *Evening Star*, May 6, 1951, 102; May 29, 1951, 23; and December 15, 1956, 71.
7. *Evening Star*, October 26, 1950, 40; September 9, 1956, 40.
8. Barbara Palmer, "Virginia for Motorbikes," *Evening Star*, September 27, 1975, 34.
9. "26 Are Selected for Nomination to School Board," *Evening Star*, August 6, 1947, 25; "Georgetown Lions Club to Induct New Officers," *Evening Star*, June 10, 1949, 25.

Chapter 27. Bookstores and Record Stores

1. *Evening Star*, April 30, 1950, 61. Learmont identified the store's opening date in a newspaper interview in 1976, *Washington Post*, July 16, 1976, C1.

2. *Evening Star*, October 25, 1953, 109 (emphasis added).

3. "RCA Record Price Cut Viewed as Slap at Discount Houses," *Evening Star*, December 28, 1954, 24.

4. Examples of ads for events for which Learmont sold tickets can be found in the *Evening Star*, April 16, 1963, 39; November 10, 1963, 153; October 21, 1964, 75; May 8, 1965, 27; April 29, 1966, 42; and March 26, 1969, 42.

5. Joe Ritchie, "Some Shops Closing in Georgetown," *Washington Post*, July 16, 1976, C1.

6. Ritchie, "Some Shops Closing in Georgetown," C1.

7. Ritchie, "Some Shops Closing in Georgetown," C1; Rudolph A. Pyatt Jr., "Georgetown Retailers Bristle at Talk of Decline," *Evening Star*, August 15, 1976, 18.

8. Barbara Gamarekian, "Writing the Book on Bookshops," *New York Times*, December 11, 1984, B12. Martha Johnson talked about the origin of the name in the interview on which

the profile was based. An obituary of Edith Foye's father, Herbert Claude ("Chevy Chase Rites Held for Claude," *Evening Star*, May 4, 1933, 9) confirms that he was the great-grandson of Francis Scott Key.

9. "Mrs. Ecker to Read at Bookshop Tonight," *Washington Post*, February 28, 1934, 14; "Drive Will Start Soon to Collect Seamen Books," *Washington Post*, February 11, 1935, 70.

10. "Georgetown Garden Pilgrimage Saturday," *Evening Star*, May 16, 1937, 57.

11. Kenneth Turan and Layton McCartney, "You Are What You Read," *Washington Post*, November 12, 1972, 262.

12. Walter Nicholls, "Key Exchange," *Washington Post*, April 8, 1990, BW6.

13. Mary Hoelman's descendants finally sold the building in 1995; deed recorded in District of Columbia land records, May 17, 1995 (document 9500030620).

14. The lending library is first referred to in an *Evening Star* ad on December 10, 1950, 138. It still was operating in 1984. Gamarekian, "Writing the Book on Bookshops," B12.

15. Marilyn Butler, "Mapping Georgetown: Emily Durso at the Francis Scott Key Book Shop (Part II)," *Georgetowner*, April 17, 2023, https://georgetowner.com/articles/2023/04/17/mapping-georgetown-emily-durso-at-the-francis-scott-key-bookstore-part-ii/.

16. Nicholls, "Key Exchange," BW6.

17. Butler, "Mapping Georgetown."

18. Gamarekian, "Writing the Book on Bookshops," B12; Nicholls, "Key Exchange," BW6; "Martha Johnson, Owner of Key Bookstore, Dies at 85," *Washington Post*, October 19, 1988, D7.

19. Betty Beale, "Congressmen Are Models," *Evening Star*, May 20, 1966, 79, 86; "Matchmakers of the Marketplace," *Evening Star*, July 4, 1971, 99; Gamarekian, "Writing the Book on Bookshops," B12.

20. Nicholls, "Key Exchange," BW6; "End of an Era," *Washington Post*, January 22, 1995, 15.

21. Emma Oxford, oral history interview with Philip and Richard Levy, Citizens Association of Georgetown, June 18, 2014, https://cagtown.org/2014/06/18/richard-phillip-levy/.

22. George Will, "The Scribner's Bookstore Spirit Lives On," *Washington Post*, January 15, 1989, 9.

23. Oxford, oral history interview with Philip and Richard Levy.

24. Oxford, oral history interview with Philip and Richard Levy; "Philip Levy," obituary, *Washington Post*, October 24, 2017. *Washington Post*, November 20, 1995, F5; January 15, 1989, C7. Rod Smith, conversation with the author, May 13, 2021.

Chapter 28. Toy Stores

1. The first such ad by Kendrick-Harrison ran in the *Washington Post* of November 26, 1923, 10, and the final one ran on February 18, 1924, 13. An example of the Georgetown Bicycle Store ad appeared in the *Evening Star*, October 26, 1950, 40.

2. Cindy Harsley, "A Pre-school Boutique," *Washington Post*, November 22, 1970, H6.

3. *Washington Post*, April 4, 1971, 16, 27, 37, K13.

4. *Washington Post*, November 28, 1971, 12.

5. *Washington Post*, October 1, 1971, PO17; October 21, 1972, D22.

6. "Robert A. Joy, 45, Victim of Helicopter Crash," *Washington Post*, August 14, 1987, B4.

7. *Washington Post*, October 1, 1971, PO17; October 21, 1972, D22.

NOTES

8. Deed recorded in District of Columbia land records, August 3, 1976 (document 7600020417); Phyllis C. Richman, "I Can't Hear You, My Ear's in a Banana," *Washington Post*, June 4, 1978, SM63.

9. Victoria Dawson, "He-Mania: The Heroes' Welcome; The Cartoons Come Alive on the 'Masters of the Universe' Tour," *Washington Post*, February 27, 1987, C01.

10. "Robert A. Joy, 45, Victim of Helicopter Crash," B4; deed recorded in District of Columbia land records, June 19, 2001 (document 2001054472).

11. Hank Burchard, "Now the Real Kite Aficionados Get Their Day in the Skies," *Washington Post*, March 24, 1977, B9.

12. Patricia Brennan, "The Annual Ball on the Mall," *Washington Post*, March 27, 1987, n39.

13. Articles by Chuck Bernstein in the *Washington Post*: "Love and the Art of Chopped Liver," April 26, 1995, E1; "The Mechanics of Matzoh Balls," March 27, 1996, E1; "Nuts about Making Peanut Butter," September 11, 1996, E1; and "Rapids Transit," June 23, 1995, 7.

14. Phyllis Richman, "Turning Tables," *Washington Post*, March 28, 1978, SM38.

Chapter 29. Sporting Goods Stores

1. District of Columbia marriage record, film 002079253.

2. "The Jordan Murder," *Evening Star*, December 27, 1902, 2; "Liquor License Decision," *Evening Star*, July 2, 1897, 3.

3. "Receiver Named Here for Brokerage Firm," *Evening Star*, January 31, 1920, 1; "Accuses Bankrupt Brokers," *Washington Post*, December 31, 1920, 14.

4. Deed recorded in District of Columbia land records, April 14, 1926 (document 192604140082).

5. "Jacob Shappirio," obituary, *Washington Post*, October 4, 1932, 10. The obituary says that, after leaving the brokerage business, Shappirio opened a sporting goods store on E Street NW and later moved it to Georgetown. That does not square with all the other evidence; obituaries, being based on family recollections, sometimes contain such errors. As described earlier, Shappirio had a sporting goods store on D Street (not E), later went into the brokerage business, and after that opened the sporting goods store in Georgetown.

6. "Irwin C. Hoover, Ex-Realty Man, of Old D.C. Family," *Evening Star*, July 16, 1970, 27.

7. "Irwin C. Hoover," 27.

8. "Western High Athletes Are Awarded Insignia," *Evening Star*, June 16, 1926, 38; Corinne Frasier, "Woman in Sports," *Evening Star*, August 19, 1926, 39.

9. Advertisements in the *Evening Star*, July 18, 1919, 6; September 20, 1920, 10.

Chapter 30. Georgetown's Own Banks

1. "An Act to establish a bank in the district of Columbia," Laws of Maryland, chapter XXX (1793) (capitalization in original).

2. Historic American Buildings Survey, DC-119, on 3210 M Street, Library of Congress, https://www.loc.gov/item/dc0018/; Jean White, "Historic Old Georgetown Tavern Is Being Restored," *Washington Post*, April 11, 1960, B1. Washington's torturous financing and early development has been the subject of several books, including Fergus Bordewich, *Washington: The Making of the American Capital* (New York: Amistad, 2008); and Bob Arnebeck, *Through a*

GEORGETOWN'S RETAIL PAST

Fiery Trial: Building Washington 1790–1800 (Lanham, MD: Madison Books, 1991); Nicholas King, *Partial Cadastral Map of Southern Part of Georgetown, Washington D.C.*, map, 1799?, Library of Congress, https://www.loc.gov/item/88693279/.

3. "Georgetown," *Evening Star*, October 29, 1869, 2; *Washington Post*, December 26, 1928, SM3.

4. "Georgetown," 2.

5. The building appears in the 1887 edition of the Hopkins survey atlas of Washington but was gone by the time of the 1894 edition. Townhouses now on the northern part of the site were built in 1890, under building permit 1275, issued January 9, 1990.

6. "107 Years' History of Bank Recalled," *Washington Post*, October 2, 1921, 47.

7. "Building Remodeled," *Evening Star*, May 20, 1911, 17.

8. Building permit 4710, issued December 18, 1921; Y. E. Booker Jr., "Georgetown Bank Plans New Home," *Washington Post*, February 4, 1920, 12; "107 Years' History of Bank Recalled," 47.

9. Building permit 27, issued July 1, 1927; F. W. Patterson, "Old Bank Is to Open Branch in Northwest," *Washington Post*, December 29, 1927, 11.

10. *Washington Post*, October 4, 1928, 4.

11. "Affairs in Georgetown," *Evening Star*, March 3, 1903, 3; advertisement, *Evening Star*, May 18, 1903, 3.

12. "Affairs in Georgetown," *Evening Star*, October 15, 1904, 5; "Bank's New Home," *Evening Star*, October 20, 1904, 11.

13. *Evening Star*, July 16, 1909, 16.

14. For examples of items about community meetings, see "Urged for Postmastership," *Evening Star*, November 2, 1909, 52; "Care of Navy's Sick," March 16, 1910, 22; and "New Officers in Charge," January 6, 1913, 18. The meetings about the bridge were reported in "Want Bridge to Stay," *Evening Star*, July 11, 1914, 8; and "Advised to Drop Bridge Agitation," *Evening Star*, July 15, 1914, 6.

15. Edward Robb Ellis, *Nation in Torment* (New York: Capricorn Books, 1971), 286–87.

16. "New Bank Plans Meeting Approval of Stockholders," *Evening Star*, March 23, 1933, 17; "Many New Moves Seen in Banking," *Evening Star*, April 8, 1933, 15; "Three More Banks Join Spokane Plan," *Evening Star*, May 11, 1933, 14; "Northeast Bank to Join Merger," *Evening Star*, May 17, 1933, 1; "U.S. Savings Group Hoping for Merger," *Evening Star*, May 23, 1933, 15; advertisement, *Evening Star*, May 27, 1933, 3; "Hamilton to Open Doors Tomorrow," *Evening Star*, September 24, 1933, 1.

17. "Special Notices," *Washington Post*, August 31, 1954, 38; "Hamilton Quits AS&T Merger Plan," *Washington Post*, June 3, 1954, 36. "Lewis Expands Banking Realm," *Washington Post*, September 15, 1954, 35; "New Riggs Officers," *Washington Post*, October 2, 1954, 10.

Chapter 31. Herring Hill Neighborhood Shops

1. Grace Dunlop Ecker, *A Portrait of Old Georgetown* (Richmond, VA: Dietz, 1951), 180.
2. Mary Mitchell, *Divided Town* (Barre, MA: Barre, 1968), 63.
3. Ecker, *A Portrait of Old Georgetown*, 180,
4. *Washington Post*, July 23, 1987, J1.

NOTES

5. Pauline Gaskins Mitchell, "Growing up to See the Transformation of 'The Village,'" *Washington Post*, July 23, 1987, D.C.1.

6. Census records tell us that these people lived at the addresses listed for them in city directories, while the fact that they also listed themselves in the classified portion of the directories tells us that they were running businesses from their homes.

7. This was her status according to the 1940 census. She had stopped listing herself in directories as a dressmaker by then.

8. *Washington Post*, March 25, 1937, 7; May 4, 1937, 3.

9. "Armistead T. Pride, Pharmacist Here since '90s," *Evening Star*, September 7, 1960, 24.

10. *Washington Post*, September 7, 1960, C6.

11. Berman was issued a permit to build an eighteen-by-fifty-foot warehouse on June 30, 1910 (permit 7389). He was issued another permit to build a forty-four-by-fifty-five-foot warehouse on March 6, 1915 (permit 3418).

12. Building permit 10823, issued May 22, 1923.

13. Deed from Douglass Mackall to Leonard Nicholson recorded in District of Columbia land records, April 23, 1923 (document 192304230246). Deed from Leonard Nicholson to Shoul and Dora Gladstone recorded in District of Columbia land records, January 9, 1924 (document 19240109015). Building permit 10823, issued May 22, 1923.

Chapter 32. Changes in the 1980s: Georgetown Park and New Immigrant Entrepreneurs

1. Heidi Sinick, "Not One but Ten New Boutiques on a Georgetown Mini-Mall," *Washington Post*, August 23, 1970, H3; display advertisements, *Washington Post*, October 11, 1969, D8; December 11, 1970, A19.

2. Advertisements in the *Evening Star*, June 11, 1976, 59; June 27, 1976, 86. "K-B to Construct 7 New Theaters in Foundry Mall," *Washington Post*, May 28, 1984, WB3. The display ad was in the *Washington Post*, May 6, 1977, D9.

3. Wolf Von Eckardt, "Colossus on the Canal: $45 Million for Georgetown Housing, Shopping Mall, New Chic, Old Buildings," *Washington Post*, May 19, 1979, B1.

4. Jerry Knight, "Georgetown Gets a 'Shopping Park,'" *Washington Post*, September 27, 1981, H1.

5. Knight, "Georgetown Gets a 'Shopping Park,'" H1.

6. Knight, "Georgetown Gets a 'Shopping Park,'" H1.

7. M. B. Regan, "Ground Broken on Georgetown Park Addition," *Washington Post*, January 27, 1986, WB42.

8. "Miller Eyes Mall," *Washington Business Journal*, May 11, 1998, https://www.bizjournals.com/washington/stories/1998/05/11/story8.html; "Shopping in Georgetown," *Washington Business Journal*, September 10, 2001, https://www.bizjournals.com/washington/stories/2001/09/10/story1.html; and "Developers Duke It Out over Georgetown Mall," *Washington Business Journal*, November 27, 2006, updated July 28, 2009, https://www.bizjournals.com/washington/stories/2006/11/27/story7.html.

9. Lisa Rein and Jonathan O'Connell, "Georgetown Park up for Auction in May," *Washington Post*, April 14, 2010, A-15.

10. "Georgetown Park to Be Auctioned May 5," *Washington Business Journal*, April 14, 2010, https://www.bizjournals.com/washington/blog/breaking_ground/2010/04/georgetown_park_to_be_auctioned_may_5.html; "G'Town Park Litigation Could Set Precedent," *Washington Business Journal*, August 6, 2009, updated October 16, 2010, https://www.bizjournals.com/washington/blog/breaking_ground/2009/08/gtown_park_litigation_could_set_precedent.html; "Shops at Georgetown Park Poised for Makeover," *Washington Business Journal*, March 20, 2012, https://www.bizjournals.com/washington/blog/2012/03/shops-at-georgetown-park-poised-for.html; "Vornado Realty Trust Headed for the Exit at the Shops at Georgetown Park," *Washington Business Journal*, May 7, 2014, updated May 8, 2014, https://www.bizjournals.com/washington/breaking_ground/2014/05/vornado-seeking-buyers-for-georgetown-park.html. "The Decline and Fall of Georgetown Park," *Georgetowner*, January 23, 2012, https://georgetowner.com/articles/2012/01/23/decline-and-fall-georgetown-park/.

11. Caroline Mayer, "Georgetown Mall Opening a New Wing; Like Other Retailers There, It Faces Problems," *Washington Post*, November 5, 1987, E1.

12. Caroline Mayer, ". . . While More and More Georgetown Stores Go Away: Changes Worry Georgetown Retailers," *Washington Post*, October 7, 1985, WB1; Marc Fisher, "Street of Gold," *Washington Post Magazine*, November 8, 1987, W21.

13. Mayer, "While More and More Georgetown Stores Go Away," WB1.

14. Fisher, "Street of Gold," W21.

15. Fisher mentioned: Moda, 1510 Wisconsin Avenue, 1982; Maison de Fay, 1424 Wisconsin Avenue, 1981; Prince and Princess, 1400 Wisconsin Avenue, 1983; and L'Armoire, 1332 Wisconsin Avenue, 1981. Other new arrivals were Lizard Shoes, 1340 Wisconsin Avenue, 1984; Guccini Shoes, 1313 Wisconsin Avenue, 1985; and Ladies & Gentlemen, 1251 Wisconsin Avenue, 1985.

16. Fisher, "Street of Gold," W22.

17. "Wisconsin Avenue: Surviving against All Odds," *Georgetowner*, May 10–23, 1985.

18. Data provided by Joseph Sternlieb of the Georgetown Business Improvement District, quoted in "Without Upgrades, Georgetown's Commercial Future Will Be in Peril," *Georgetowner*, February 7, 2015, https://georgetowner.com/articles/2015/02/07/without-upgrades-georgetowns-commercial-future-could-be-peril/.

19. *Georgetowner*, May 18, 1977.

20. Mayer, "While More and More Stores Go Away," WB1.

21. Fisher, *Street of Gold*, W24.

BIBLIOGRAPHY

Adams, Abigail. *New Letters of Abigail Adams 1788–1801*. Edited by Stewart Mitchell. New York: Houghton Mifflin, 1947.
Alcott, Louisa May. *Hospital Sketches*. Boston, MA: Redpath, 1863.
Baist, G. W. *Baist's Real Estate Atlas Surveys of Washington, District of Columbia*. Vol. 3. Philadelphia: Baist Surveyors, 1903, 1907, 1909, 1913, 1919, 1921, 1924, 1931.
Barlow, Ronald S. *The Vanishing American Barber Shop: An Illustrated History of Tonsorial Art, 1860–1960*. St. Paul, MN: William Marvy, 1996.
Barton, Elmer, ed. *Historical and Commercial Sketches of Washington and Environs: Our Capital City, "the Paris of America": Its Prominent Places and People . . . Its Improvements, Progress and Enterprise . . .* Washington, D.C.: Barton, 1884.
Carter, Charles Carroll, William C. DiGiacomantonio, and Pamela Scott. *Creating Capitol Hill—Place, Proprietors and People*. Washington, D.C.: United States Capitol Historical Society, 2018.
Clark, Allen C. "Suter's Tavern." *Records of the Columbia Historical Society* 42/43 (1940–1941): 83–117.
DeFerrari, John. *Capital Streetcars: Early Mass Transit in Washington, D.C.* Charleston, SC: History Press, 2015.
———. *Historic Restaurants of Washington, D.C.* Charleston, SC: History Press, 2013.
Dickson, Paul. *The Great American Ice Cream Book*. New York: Atheneum, 1978.
Ecker, Grace Dunlop. *A Portrait of Old Georgetown*. Richmond, VA: Dietz, 1951.
Ellickson, Paul P. "The Evolution of the Supermarket Industry: From A&P to Walmart." University of Rochester, March 15, 2015. http://paulellickson.com/SMEvolution.pdf.
Ellis, Edward Robb. *Nation in Torment*. New York: Capricorn Books, 1971.
Gale, Dennis Earl. "Restoration in Georgetown, Washington, D.C., 1915–1965." PhD diss., George Washington University, September 30, 1982.
Gordon, Robert J. *The Rise and Fall of American Growth*. Princeton, NJ: Princeton University Press, 2016.
Green, Constance McLaughlin. *Washington—a History of the Capital*. 2 vols. Princeton, NJ: Princeton University Press, 1962.
Headley, Robert K. *Motion Picture Exhibition in Washington, D.C.* Jefferson, NC: McFarland, 1999.
Hendrickson, Robert. *The Great Emporiums: The Illustrated History of America's Great Department Stores*. New York: Stein and Day, 1980.

Hoagland, Alison K. *The Row House in Washington, D.C.: A History*. Charlottesville: University Press of Virginia, 2023.
Holmes, Oliver Wendell. "The City Tavern: A Century of Georgetown History 1796–1898." *Records of the Columbia Historical Society* 50 (1980): 1–35.
———. "The Colonial Taverns of Georgetown." *Records of the Columbia Historical Society* 51/52 (1989): 1–18.
———. "Suter's Tavern: Birthplace of the Federal City." *Records of the Columbia Historical Society* 49 (1973/1974): 1–34.
Honans, Benjamin. *The Georgetown Directory for the Year 1830*. Reprint, Westminster, MD: Willow Bend Books, 2004.
Hopkins, G. M. *A Complete Set of Surveys and Plats of Properties in the City of Washington, District of Columbia*. Vol. 3. Philadelphia: Hopkins, 1887.
Hurley, Andrew. *Diners, Bowling Alleys, and Trailer Parks: Chasing the American Dream in the Postwar Consumer Culture*. New York: Basic Books, 2002.
Jackson, Richard P. *The Chronicles of Georgetown*. Polkinhorn, 1878.
Joynt, Carol. *Innocent Spouse*. Portland, OR: Broadway Books, 2011.
Kytle, Elizabeth. *Home on the Canal*. Cabin John, MD: Seven Locks, 1983.
Leech, Margaret. *Reveille in Washington*. New York: Harper Brothers, 1941.
Lesko, Kathleen M., Valerie Babb, and Carroll R. Gibbs. *Black Georgetown Remembered—a History of Its Black Community from the Founding of "The Town of George" in 1751 to the Present Day*. Washington, D.C.: Georgetown University Press, 1991.
McFarland, Henry Brown Floyd. *District of Columbia: Concise Biographies of Its Prominent and Representative Contemporary Citizens and Valuable Statistical Data*. Washington, D.C.: Potomac Press, 1908.
McMaster, Richard K. "Georgetown and the Tobacco Trade 1751–1783." *Records of the Columbia Historical Society* 66/68 (1966/1968).
Mitchell, Mary. *Chronicles of Georgetown Life 1865–1900*. Cabin John, MD: Seven Locks, 1986.
———. *Divided Town*. Barre, MA: Barre, 1968.
Mohun, Anwen P. *Steam Laundries—Gender, Technology and Work in the United States and Great Britain, 1880–1940*. Baltimore, MD: Johns Hopkins University Press, 1999.
Mould, David, and Missy Loewe. *Remembering Georgetown: A History of the Lost Port City*. Charleston, SC: History Press, 2009.
Peck, Garrett. *Prohibition in Washington, D.C.—How Dry We Weren't*. Charleston, SC: History Press, 2011.
Provine, Dorothy S. *Compensated Emancipation in the District of Columbia—Petitions under the Act of April 16, 1862*. Westminster, MD: Willow Bend Books, 2008.
Quarternous, Grant. *A Georgetown Life—the Reminiscences of Brittania Wellington Peter Kennon*. Washington, D.C.: Georgetown University Press, 2020.
Rhodes, Richard. *Energy: A Human History*. New York: Simon & Schuster, 2018.
Schrag, Zachary M. *The Great Society Subway: A History of the Washington Metro*. Baltimore, MD: Johns Hopkins University Press, 2006.
Smith, Kathryn Schneider. *Port Town to Urban Neighborhood: The Georgetown Waterfront of Washington, D.C., 1880–1920*. Dubuque, IA: Kendall/Hunt, 1989.

BIBLIOGRAPHY

Taggart, Hugh Thomas. *Old Georgetown, District of Columbia.* Lancaster, PA: New Era Printing, 1908.

Tangires, Helen. "Contested Space: The Life and Death of Center Market." *Washington History* 7, no. 1 (Spring/Summer 1995): 46–67.

Warring, Leo. *The Foggy Bottom Gang—the Story of the Warring Brothers of Washington, D.C.* Cleveland, OH: Parafine, 2020.

Williams, Ames W. *Washington & Old Dominion Railroad 1847–1968.* Arlington, MA: Arlington Historical Society, 1989.

The WPA Guide to Washington, D.C. Reprint, New York: Pantheon, 1983.

INDEX

ABC (Alcoholic Beverage Control) Board, 283
Adams, Wilhemena, 55
Adam's Restaurant, 286
advertisements: banks, 337; barbershops and salons, 71, 76; bicycles, 311; billboards, 8; bookstores and record stores, 315, 350; bowling alleys, 304, 305; clothing and shoes, 37, 45–46, 52, 63, 324; drugstores, 116; feed stores, 8; jewelers, 79, 82, 83; laundries, 91; overnight lodging, 208, 212, 213, 217, 220–21, 224, 226; restaurants, 218, 238, 240–41
African Americans: as Blue Mouse owner, 292, 348; displacement of, 14; in Herring Hill area, 340–41; Lee family, 17–20; population of, 4, 12; small businesses of, VIII, 68–69, 72–75, 307, 310. *See also* enslaved people; Herring Hill area
agricultural implements businesses, 15–17
Albrecht family businesses, 139, 140–41, 329, 374n1
Alcoholic Beverage Control (ABC) Board, 283
Anchor Inn, 210
Angelo, Gordon & Co., 355
animal transport, 149
Ansell, Hilda, 272–74
antique dealers: about, 168–69; Christ Child Opportunity Shop, 177–80; Esunas (Joseph), 175–76; Kasab (Jacob), 174–75; Little Caledonia, 177; McCoy (Isabella), 171–72; Meggs (Caroline D.), 172–73
A&P, 96–97, 99, 107–8, 109
Apex Chocolates, 134
apothecaries. *See* drugstores
Apple Pie bar, 278–80
appliance stores, 202–6
Aqueduct Bridge, 4, 7, 29
arcade machines, 281
Arden Farms Co., 137
Arlington Livery Stable, 24–25
Armstrong, Frank, 301–2
Arney, Joseph, 128–29
Arnold's Bakery, 129
Atohl, George, 112
auctions, 216, 217–18
Auger family businesses, 229–31, 233–34
automobiles. *See* car-related businesses

B. A. Cove & Co., 202
Baer family businesses, 43, 47–49, 77–79, 83, 339, 365n21
Baker, Benjamin, 99
bakeries. *See* confectioners
Baltimore & Ohio Railroad, 4
banks: Bank of Columbia, 211–12, 268, 330–34; Farmers and Mechanics' Bank, 334–37; Hamilton National Bank, 339; National Bank of Washington, 339; Potomac Savings Bank, 337–39
Barabas, Stephen and Helen, 56, 58

404

INDEX

barbers and hair salons: about, 67–69; African American businesses, 72–75; Coniglio family, 69–70; Fabrizio (Frank), 70–72; hair salons, 67, 71, 75–76; Kent (George), 347–48; Starke (Albert), 69
Bardt, Arthur, 93–94
bargaining in retail, 357–58
Barnard, George B., 99
Barnes, William, 184
Barrett, Elizabeth M., 316
bars: ABC Board and, 283–89; bowling alleys in saloons, 299; challenges of, 259; Cinematheque business model, 295; complaints about, 282–85; moratorium on new licenses, 288–89; neighborhood groups opposing, 285–89; Seabright Restaurant, 283–84; on Wisconsin Avenue and M Street, 249. *See also* liquor businesses; Prohibition; "The Strip"; upscale saloons
Barton, Alice, 342
Bayou nightclub, 266, 271–72
Beattle, Henry, 120–21
Beck, Christian, 129
Becker Paint & Glass, 193–98
Belt's Tavern, 207–8
Berkobile, David, 141–42
Berman, Saul and Gertrude, 343
Bernstein, Chuck, 325–26
Berryman, William, 114
bicycle shops, 309–12
billiards, 306–8
Billy Martin's Carriage House, 238–39
Biograph Theater, 47, 296
Bird, Collins, 224, 226
Bistro Français, 243–44, 276
Blackie's House of Beef, 231
blacksmiths, 22–23, 26
Blodgett, Samuel, 330–31
Blue Mouse Theater, 292, 348
Bomstein, Howard, 271
Bonbrest, Bill, 284
Bond, Joan, 52–53

bookstores and record stores: about, 313; Bridge Street Books, 321–22; Francis Scott Key Book Shop, 316–21; Horizon Book Shop, 316; Learmont's, 314–16; Rizzolli's, 350; Thomas family, 313–14
Boroukhim, Jacky, 126
Boschke, A., 4
Boteler, George, 15–16
bottling plants, 217–18
boutiques, 53–55
bowling alleys, 299–305
Bowman, J. D., 124
boycotts, 127
Boyd, Robert, 202
Boyle, Jack, 269–71
Boynton, Lynn, 53
Brace's Pharmacy, 117–18
Brasserie-Bretonne, 246
Bredice, Don, 63–64
Bridges, Benjamin, Jr., 25
Bridge Street, 2, 3. *See also* M Street
Bridge Street Books, 47, 321–22
Britches stores, 60, 359
Britt's Cafeteria, 231, 232–34, 300
Brodofsky/Levy family, 38–39, 41–47, 48–49, 50, 243, 364–65n9. *See also* Levy family
Broidie, Nathan, 102
Brown, Stephen T., 16, 37–38
Brown, Vivian, 320–21
Brown, William T., 16–17
Brumbaugh, Carol, 52–53
Bunns, Edward B., 257
Burnett, Simon, 72
Buscher, Bernard, 34–35
Buttinelli, Sam, 62, 367n2

Cabrol, Gerard, 243–44
Cafritz, Conrad, 226
Calomaris, Louis, 281
Calza, Louis, 246
canals, 2, 4, 7
Candy Kitchen, 132–35

405

candy stores. *See* confectioners
Capital Restaurant Concept, 268
carpenters, 155–57. *See also* furniture dealers and home furnishings stores
car-related businesses: dealers, 30–34; growth of, 22, 302, 337; parts, 35; repairs, 34–35; service stations, 35; tire sales, 34; on Wisconsin Avenue and M Street, 29
Carter brothers (Robert, Fred, Walter, and William), 31
Cavallo, Bob, 276–77
Cavanagh and Kendrick Hardware, 329
Cellar Door, 269–71
Center Market, 105, 106, 143
Cerebrus Theater, 298
Chaconas family businesses, 132–34, 373n8
Chadwick's bar, 261, 263, 265–66
Chain Bridge, 29, 211
chain stores: drugstores, 126–27; grocers, 96–97, 99, 107–8, 109, 346, 348; indoor malls, 360
Chamberlain, James, 62, 367n1
Chambers funeral home, 336
Charles Schwartz & Son, 79
Charley's Restaurant, 284
Chesapeake & Ohio (C&O) Canal, 2, 4
Chez Odette, 246–47
Christ Child Opportunity Shop, 166, 177–80
Cinematheque business model, 295
Citizens Association of Georgetown, 275
city directories, VIII–IX
City Tavern, 210–15
Claire Florist, 145–47
Clark, P.J., 258
clothing stores: boutiques, 53–55; Britches, 60, 359; Brodofsky/Levy businesses, 38–39, 41–47, 48–49, 309; consignment stores, 51, 52–53, 179–80; dressmakers and tailors, 38; dry goods stores, 36, 37–38; Georgetown University Shop, 55–59; immigrants running, 38–40; Nordlinger/Baer businesses, 38, 40, 43, 47–49; ready-made clothing, 36; Red Balloon, 324–25; second Levy family business (Bernard and Rebecca), 49–52; Shappirio's store, 327–28, 395n5

Clyde's Restaurant, 284, 306
coal shipments, 4
C&O (Chesapeake & Ohio) Canal, 2, 4
Cogswell brothers, 309–10
Cohn, Paul, 267–68
Cohn (or Cole), Edmund M., 161–64
Collins, John, 223
Columbia Glass & Mirror Co., 193, 199–201
Columbia Lunch, 232–33, 240
Columbian Inn, 210, 212
Columbia Wholesale Confectionary Co., 134–35
Comley family businesses, 143–45
confectioners: about, 128–29; Apex Chocolates, 134; Candy Kitchen, 132–35; Columbia Wholesale Confectionary Co., 134–35; Fussell-Young Ice Cream Company, 135–37; Heon family, 234; Nielson's business, 134; Stohlman's, 129–32
Coniglio family businesses, 69–70
consignment stores, 51, 52–53, 179–80
convenience retail, 341
Cook, Patrick, 250
Cook, Val, 54–55
Cooley, Gerald R., 302–5
Corcoran, W. W., 37
Corral events, 286
COVID-19 pandemic, 360
Craig & Hook, Inc., 196
Crampton, John, 15–16
Crawford's Hotel, 216
Crazy Horse bar, 277–78, 287
Cropley family businesses: agricultural implements, 15–16; drugstores, 99, 116–17, 193; grocery stores, 99–100, 101, 116

INDEX

Cruit family businesses, 23
Cusson, Jannine, 241, 242

Dalinsky, Harry "Doc" and Marion, 123, 125–27
Daly, Eugene, 135
dance contests, 291
Darcey, John F., 154–55
Darne family businesses, 23–25m 34
David Richard store, 45
Davidson, Stuart, 254–56
Davis, Harriet Vaughan, 320
Davis, William C., 219
Davril, Paul, 60
DeMaine & Co., 193, 198–99
Desperado's bar, 280–81
Detroit, Nathan, 258
Deutschman, Barry, 123
DeVoe paints, 195
disco fad, 239
Dobbins, Daniel, 139
Dodge, Harry, 135
Donahue's Pharmacy, 124–25, 126
Donaldson, Arthur, 102
donations, 178–80
Door Store, 157–60
dress codes, 254, 256, 258, 275, 277, 287, 289
dressmakers, 38, 54
Dreyfuss clothing stores, 48–49
drugstores: about, 114–16; Brace's Pharmacy, 117–18; chains arriving, 126–27; Cropley as partner in, 116–17; Dumbarton Pharmacy, 126, 127; Georgetown Pharmacy, 123–27; in Herring Hill, 342–43; Morgan's Pharmacy, 120–23, 127; O'Donnell family, 118–21, 126; paint sold in, 193, 194
dry cleaners, 56, 93–95
dry goods stores, 36, 37–38. *See also* clothing stores
Dugan, John, 25–26, 33
Dumbarton/Georgetown theater, 292–96, 358

Dumbarton Pharmacy, 126–27
Durso, Emily, 76, 318–19
"dyers and scourers," 93

Eastern Market, 105
Edin, David, 349–50
electric appliances, 202–6
Elliott, Abraham, 64–66
Emery, Erika, 167
enslaved people, 181, 208, 209, 212–13, 340
Enzel, Nathan, 343, 346
Epstein, Julius, 224
Esunas, Joseph, 175–76
Expert Lunch, 229–31

Fabrizio, Joseph, 70–72
FAO Schwartz, 323
Farmers and Mechanics' Bank, 37, 334–37
Farmers & Butchers Marketing Company, 107
feed business, 17–21, 277
Felser, Joseph, 64–65
fern bars, 263–64
fertilizer manufacturing business, 15–16
Fichman, Charlie, 270
Fidelity Building and Loan Association, 336
Field, Martin, 298
fires, 187
First Cooperative Building Association of Georgetown, 183
Fisher's Market, 109–11, 187
Fitzgerald's, 257
floating restaurant proposal, 258
florists, 143–47
Food Mart, 109
Fountain Inn, 209–10
14th Street Bridge, 29
Foye, Edith, 316
Frain, Henry, 292
Francis Scott Key Parkway, 8–9, 10
Frazee, John D., 90–93
Fregnan, Hugo, 244–46
French Market, 112–13
Frese, Danny, 274

F. Scott's bar, 257
furniture dealers and home furnishings stores: about, 148; Door Store, 157–60; J.F. Darcey & Co., 154–55; Kelly Furniture Company, 161–64; Kendrick-Harrison Furniture Co., 155–57; Little Caledonia, 164–67; May family, 148–50; Schutts family, 155; 3140 M Street, 153–60; William E. Miller store, 157. *See also* antique dealers
Fussell-Young Ice Cream Company, 135–37, 224

Gale, Dennis, 11
Gannon, Sue, 52–53
Gantz, Edward, 93–94
Garfinckel's store, 354
gas stations, 35
Gem Lunch, 231–32, 233–34
George Bernard & Co. drugstore, 116
Georgetown Art and Craft Shop, 174–75
Georgetown Bowling Club, 300–302
Georgetown Bridge Company, 211
Georgetown Citizens Association, VIII, 285–89
Georgetown Corporation, 211
Georgetown Cotton, 359–60
Georgetown Electric, 202, 203–6
Georgetown history: decline in 1800s, 4–7, 364n2; forces affecting, VII–IX; government, 6–7; incorporation, 2; maps, 3, 5; as port for tobacco crops, 1, 2; as regional marketplace, 7–8; renaming effort, 6, 218; rental housing, 7–8; restoration in early 1900s, 11–12; street names, IX, 7, 124
Georgetown Hotel, 212
Georgetown Market, 35, 97, 105, 106
Georgetown Park, 349–56
Georgetown Pharmacy, 123–27
Georgetown Realty and Insurance Company, 302, 305
Georgetown Recreation Center, 303–5, 306

Georgetown Redevelopment Corporation, 213–14
Georgetown Slack Shoppe, 60
Georgetown Tobacco, 141–42
Georgetown University Shop (GU Shop), 55–59
Georgetown Zoo, 323
Gherardi, Blaise, 240–42
Giant Food, 109
gift shops, 126
Gilbert, Henry P., 182–84, 185
Gilbert Paint & Glass, 193
Ginsburg, Morris and Beatrice, 343
Gissel, Benjamin, 129
Gladstone, Shoul and Dora, 348
glass antiques, 170
Good Old Days Parade, 188–89
Gore, Ollie H., 328
Grady, J. William, 142
Griffith, Eleanor Cox, 83
grocery stores: A&P, 96–97, 99, 107–8, 109; evolution of, 96–97; Herring Hill, 343–46; public markets, 105–7; Sanitary Grocery, 99, 107, 346, 348; on side streets, 100–105; small stores, 96, 97–100; supermarkets, 97, 109; surviving businesses, 109–13
Gunchers Saloon, 281–82
Gushner, Samantha, 59

hair salons. *See* barbers and hair salons
Hamilton National Bank, 339
Hapsas, Charley, 284
Hardin, Dorcas, 54
hardware stores: about, 181; Cavanagh and Kendrick Hardware, 329; Gilbert, Henry P., 182–84, 185; Kentucky Hardware, 250; Linthicum, Edward, 181–82; Meenehan family, 189–92; Meenehan's Hardware, 356; Molloy (Thomas J.), 189–90; W. T. Weaver & Sons, 184–89
harness makers, 26–28
Harris, Daniel, 102

408

INDEX

Harrison, William W., 155–57
Hayes, Bill and Betty, 59
Hayes, John and Sharon, 59
Haynes, Harry, 337
Haynes electric cars, 30
Haywood, Hazzard, 75
Heatwold, John, 233
Heidenheimer, Jacques, 344
Helig, Philip, 141
Heon family businesses, 234–36, 294–95
Heritage House, 236
Herman, Jennifer, 320–21
Herr, A. H., 124
Herring Hill area: about, 340–41; at-home businesses, 341–42, 397n6; barbershops, 75; drugstores, 342–43; 1417 28th Street, 346–47; grocery stores, 343–46; restaurants, 348; 2610 P Street, 346
Hesselberger, George, 221, 223
High Street, 2, 3. *See also* Wisconsin Avenue
Hilleary, Albert and Flora, 103–4
Hindin, Richard, 60
history of Georgetown. *See* Georgetown history
Hitt, Rose Raynor, 75–76
Hoelman family businesses, 318–21
Holiday magazine, 12
Holohan, Mary, 250
home furnishings. *See* antique dealers; furniture dealers and home furnishings stores
Homeward store, 160
homing pigeons, 221
Hook, Elkanah M., 194–96
Hoover Brothers, 328–29
Horizon Book Shop, 316
horse-related businesses: blacksmiths, 22–23; harness makers, 26–28; history of, 22–23; stables, 23–26, 302
hospitals, 217
hotels. *See* overnight lodging
Howard's Odorless Cleaners, 95
Hudson, Virginia Cary, 320

Hunt, John W., 195
Huntsfeld Paint, 195

ice cream parlors. *See* confectioners
illegal numbers game, 232
immigrants: clothing stores and, 38–40; in Herring Hill, 341, 344–45; laundries and, 88–90, 93; small businesses of, vii–viii; on Wisconsin Avenue, 357–58
indoor malls: chain stores, 360; Foundry, 350–51; Georgetown Mall, 349–50; Georgetown Park, 349–56; suburban competition, 359–60
Inland Steel, 350
In the Bag, 326

Jackson, D. B., 20
Jackson & Veney shoemakers, 346
Jacob, George, 112–13
Jacobsen, Charles, 92
James O'Donnell & Bro pharmacies, 119
Jarvis, Edith, 316
jewelers: about, 77; Baer (Milton), 77–79; Krick (Harris), 85–86; newcomers buying, 358; Schwartz (Charles), 79, 83; Tribby brothers, 79–85
J. F. Darcey & Co., 154–55
J. M. Stein & Co., 327
John Glassford & Co., 2
Johnson, James H., 23
Johnson, Martha, 317–20
Jones, Isabella (née McCoy), 171–72
Jones Paint Store, 193
Joy, Robert A. and Linda, 324–25
Joynt, Howard and Carol, 258–60, 287
J. Paul's bar, 267–68
J. T. Lee & Co., 20

Kaplan, Albert, 65–66
Kasab, Jacob and Lydia, 174–75
Kelly, Cathie, 52–53
Kelly Furniture Company, 161–64
Kemp, John, 221
Kendrick-Harrison Furniture Co., 155–57

Kennedy, John F., 12
Kent, George, 75, 347–48
Kentucky Hardware, 190, 250
Kernodle, George H., 169–70
Key Bridge, 29
Key Theater, 47, 297, 303, 305, 321, 349–50
Killeen, John, 250
Kirby, Michael, 263–66
Kite Store, 323, 325–26
Korn, Hyman, 343
Krick, Harris, 85–86
Kronheim, Milton, 7
Kurtz, Paul, 271

Lang's Hotel, 212–13, 332
Lanier, Anthony, 355
Larsen's Harper Method Beauty Salon, 76
Laudier, Michel, 242
laundries: about, 87–88; Chinese immigrants running, 88–90, 93; dry cleaners, 93–95; industrial, 90–93
Lawson, Alice, 75
Laytham, John, 255–56
Lear, William, 202
Learmont, John, 314–16
Lee family feed business, 17–20
Lee family laundry business, 88–90
Lenehan, Donald F., 199–200
Le Steak restaurant, 287
Levy, Bernard ("Barney") and Rebecca, 49–52, 64
Levy, Louis, 92
Levy family: David, 45–47, 297, 321; Meyer and Lillie, 43–44, 48–49, 309; Philip, 12, 47, 297, 321–22; Richard, 12, 45–47; Samuel, 44–46, 49. *See also* Brodofsky/Levy family
Lewis, William V., 37
Lewis & Thos. Saltz clothing store, 57–58
libraries, 319
Lido Theater, 292
Lillian's Beauty Shop, 75, 76
Linthicum, Edward, 181–82
Linthicum Otho, 114–15

liquor businesses: beer sales, 248–50; in grocery stores, 343; historical perspective, 252; laws for, 253–54, 288; Molloy and Meenehan, 190–91; Schladt's license, 222–23. *See also* bars; Prohibition; "The Strip"; upscale saloons
literary agencies, 320
Little Caledonia, 164–67, 177
Lockhart, George B., 124
lodging. *See* overnight lodging; taverns
London Cleaners, 13
Long, Clayton B., 323
Long Bridge (14th Street bridge), 4
lunch counters, 229–34
Luttrell & Wine dry goods, 37
luxury in hotels, 225–26
Lyddane, Eugene T., 98–99
Lyons, Tom, 270

Mackey, Crandal, 292
Maison des Crepes restaurant, 244–46, 292
Malone, Newton A., 231–32
Mansfield, William M., 195
Mantzuranis, Henry, 234–36
Marceron, William, 292
Marshall's Palace Laundry, 92
Martin, George, 292
Martin's Tavern, 337
masons, 186, 187–88
Mason Waters dress shop, 55
May family businesses, 138–39, 374n1
Mayfield, Benjamin, 16, 37–38
Mayfield, William P., 16–17
"Mayor of Georgetown," 125
McCooey, Richard, 256
McFarland, William, 25
McGuinness, Joe, 266
McLaughlin, Charles, 211
Meenehan family businesses, 187, 189–92, 356
Meggs, Caroline D., 172–73
Merrick, Mary Virginia, 177
Merritt family businesses, 72

INDEX

Metro rapid transit system, 14
Meyers family businesses, 43–46, 49
Michael, Monroe, 272–74
Miller, Herbert, 352–54
Miller, William E., 157
Mitchell, Abraham, 307
Molloy family businesses, 189–92, 250
Molony, Michael and Mary Claire, 21
Mom & Dad (film), 292–94
Moore, Frederick L., 16
Moran, Michael V. and Michael F., 250, 251
Moran, Patrick T., 21, 277
Morgan Brothers Pharmacy, 120–23, 343
Morgan House, 213
movie theaters: Biograph, 296; Blue Mouse, 292; Cerebrus, 298; churches as, 290; Dumbarton/Georgetown, 292–96; in Foundry space, 350; Key, 297, 303, 305; M Street, 292; M Street Open Air, 290–91; Scenic, 292
Moy, Sam, 90
Mr. Henry's bar, 262–63
Mr. Smith's bar, 260–61, 266
M Street: bar businesses, 249; car-related businesses, 29; clothing and shoe stores, 48–49; formerly Bridge Street, IX, 2, 3; impact of Georgetown Park on, 355–58; market house, 6; residential and office buildings, 8. *See also specific businesses*
M Street Open Air Theater, 290–91, 391n3
M Street Theater, 292
musical venues. *See* bars

Nammour, Bechara, 268
Napper, Walter, 342
Nathan's restaurant, 258–60, 287
National Bank of Washington, 339
National Jewel Center, 295
Nazarian family businesses, 174
Neam's Market, 111–12
near beer, 248–50
Nearly New Shop, 346
Newman, Stephen B., 160

Nicholson, Leonard S., 347–48
Nielson, Adolphe, 134
Niemetz, Burnett, 94–95
nightclubs, 269–72. *See also* "The Strip"
Nordlinger/Baer family businesses, 7, 38, 40, 43, 47–49, 64

O'Donnell family businesses, 119–21, 126, 193
Offutt, Artaxerxes, 99–100
Offutt family businesses (George, Henry and George, Jr.), 81–83, 338–39
O'Harro, Michael, 239
Old Ebbit Grill, 255
"Old Georgetown" (horse), 27–28
Old Georgetown Act, 12–14, 146
Old Georgetown Shop, 171–72
Olson, Susan and Dwight, 324–25
Opportunity Shop, 166, 177–80
outdoor theaters, 290–91
overnight lodging: Belt's Tavern, 207–8; City Tavern, 210–15; Georgetown Inn, 224–26; Suter's Tavern, 208, 209–10, 224; Union Hotel, 216–19; West Washington Hotel, 219–24, 238, 250, 285; White Horse Inn, 208–9

paint stores: about, 120, 193; Becker Paint & Glass, 193–98; Columbia Glass & Mirror Co., 193, 199–201; DeMaine & Co., 193, 198–99; Gilbert Paint & Glass, 193; Jones Paint Store, 193
Palace Laundry, 90–93
Pantelich family's restaurants, 246–47
parking issues, 359
Parkway Cycle and Hardware, 311–12
Parkway Livery, 26, 30, 302
Parkway Motors, 30–32, 302
Pasqual, Joseph, 274
Paul, Marguerite ("Madam Paul"), 53
Payne, William N., 307–8
Payson, Anne, 166
Pennington, George A., 196
Pensky, David, 60

GEORGETOWN'S RETAIL PAST

Peoples drugstore chain, 115–16
People's Store, 42, 43, 243
Peppermint Lounge, 286
Peter, Robert, 2
Peters, Sally, 13, 145–47
pet food stores, 21
Phoenix clothing store, 59
piano bars, 260–61
Place Vendome, 240, 241
Place Vendome–Rive Droite, 242–43
pool halls, 306–8
Potomac Bowling Club, 300–302, 306
Potomac Laundry, 92
Potomac Pharmacy, 126
Potomac Savings Bank, 48, 337–39
Powder and Smoke gift shop, 126
Presgraves, Thomas L., 25
Prichard, Marian (née Wells), 164–67
Pride, Armistead T., 342–43
Professor Goodall's Floral Festival, 217
Prohibition: about, 248–50; bootleggers, 236; bowling businesses and, 302, 304; end of, 135, 190, 250–52; laws after repeal of, 283; police raids on hotels, 223
public markets, 105–7
Pure Food and Drug Act, 114

Q&A Café, 260
Quaker Oats Company, 8, 9

Ragan, Mrs. William L., 342
Randall family's hair salon, 75, 76
real estate, 49, 82, 145, 235, 347–48
record stores, 314–16
Red Balloon, 323–25
Reliable Cleaners and Dyers, 94–95
Residents for a Safer Georgetown, 289
Restaurant Beverage Association, 286
restaurants: Adam's, 286; Bistro Français, 243–44, 276; Britt's Cafeteria, 231, 232–34, 300; Chez Odette, 246–47; Clyde's, 306; floating, 258; Four Georges, 225–26; growth of,

227; Heon's Restaurant, 234–36; in Herring Hill, 348; lunch counters, 229–34, 240; Maison des Crepes, 244–46, 292; Martin family, 236–40, 337; Nathan's, 258–60, 287; replacing shops, 357; Rive Gauche, 240–43; Rodier family, 228–29; taverns, 227–29; White House Restaurant and Bowling Salon, 299–300
Reuwer, Harry and Henry "Duke," 203–6
Riggs National Bank, 37, 337
Rizzolli bookstore, 350
Rodier family businesses, 228–29
Rosendorf, Joseph and Katie (Brodofsky), 42–43, 48–49
Rose Raynor's Beauty Salon, 76
Roundtable events, 286
Rubin, Warren, 157
Russo, Michael, 266

Safeway, 107–8
Saint-Aubin de Paris, 53
saloons. *See* bars; liquor businesses; Prohibition; "The Strip"; upscale saloons
Saltz, Samuel Lewis ("Lewis"), 56–59
Saltz, Thomas and Julia, 56–59
Sam's Men's Shop, 44–46, 49
Samuel S. Cropley & Sons, 100
Sandoval, Richard, 265
Sanitary Grocery, 99, 107, 346, 348
Sansone, Frank, 64
Sansone, Libberante, 64
Scenic Theater, 292
Scheele's Market, 104–5
Schenick, Joseph & Leah, 121–22
Schladt, Joseph, 219–24, 285, 382n32
Schlegel, Edwin and Louise, 305
Schmidt, Vilma, 165
Schutts family businesses, 150–53, 155
Schutze, John, 139–40
Schwartz, Charles, 79, 83
Scott's Smart Shoes, 64
sculptures, 159–60

INDEX

Seabright Restaurant, 283–84
Seawall, Clement, 210
Second Hand Rose, 52–53
seed stores, 16
Semmes, Joseph, 211
service stations, 35
SFX Entertainment, 271
Shadows nightclubs, 269, 276–77
Shamrock bar, 276
Shappirio, Jacob and Mary, 327–28, 395n5
Shearer, Lewis N., 185–87
Sheffield, Simon W. and Viola, 72–74
Shenk, Linden and Lillian, 144–45
Shepherd, Alexander "Boss," 6
Shinn brothers, 217
shoe businesses, 51, 61–66, 346
Shugrue, Timothy, 24
Siedenberg, Norman, 83, 84–85
signage, 13
The Silver Dollar restaurant, 243, 244, 272–76
Silverman, Barry, 267
Simpson, Ellsworth T., 26, 30–31
1620 Shop, 52
Slate, Harold, 298
Smith, Edward, 342
Smith, George, 202
Smith, Robert H., 74–75
Smithsonian Institution, 131–32
Smoot, John, Jr., 58–59
soft drink stores, 248–50
Sosnitsky, Pierre, 242
Southern Auto Parts, 106
speakeasy raids, 250
Speciale, Joseph, 64
sporting goods stores, 327–29, 395n5
stables, 23–26
Stachowski's Market, 343
Starke, Albert, 69
Stohlman Chevrolet, 33–34
Stohlman's sweets store, 129–32
Stombock family businesses, 26–28
stone and gravel businesses, 183–84

"The Strip": about, 272; Apple Pie, 278–80; Crazy Horse, 277–78, 287; Desperado's, 280–81; drinking age and, 288; Gunchers Saloon, 281–82; others in 1960s and 1970s, 281–82; Shadows, 276–77; Shamrock, 276; Silver Dollar, 272–76
suburban malls, 359–60
Sugar, Harold, 126–27
supermarkets, 97
Suter's Tavern, 208, 209–10, 224
Swensen's Ice Cream, 132

tailors, 38
Talcott, Greg, 265
taverns, 227–28. *See also* overnight lodging
Taylor, Harry W., 196
tennis-related products, 328–29
theaters: Biograph, 47, 296; Blue Mouse, 292, 348; Cerebrus, 298; Dumbarton/Georgetown, 292–96, 358; Key, 47, 297, 303, 305, 321, 349–50; M Street, 292; M Street Open Air, 290–91, 391n3; Scenic, 292
theft, 149, 150
Third Edition bar, 263–65, 266
Thomas, Deborah, 313–14
Thompson, Doris Wagner, 317–20
3140 M Street, 153–60
Tillson, Ludie, 75
tobacco, 1, 2, 138–42
Tolkan family's Door Store, 157–60
Tombs rathskeller, 257
Tompkins, Gwynne, 223
toy stores, 156, 323–26
trails for biking, 309
Tramonte, Vincent, 271
Tramps disco, 239
Tribby brothers, 79–85
Tuberville, W. H., 203
2610 P Street, 346

Union Tavern (Union Hotel), 210, 216–19
upholstering business, 175–76

413

upscale saloons: about, 253–54; Chadwick's, 261, 263, 265–66; Clyde's, 254–58, 284; J. Paul's, 267–68; Mr. Henry's, 262–63; Mr. Smith's, 260–61, 266; Nathan's, 258–60, 287; Third Edition, 263–65, 266

Veale, Farley, 302–5
Veney, Lewin, 346
Vivien, Jacques, 244–46
volunteers, 178, 180
voting rights, 155

Wall's Grill, 267, 388n35
Warren, Clarence, 346
Warren, Houston, 310
Washington, D.C.: creation of, 209–10, 211; government, 6–7, 216; port, 6; during WWI, 11. *See also* Georgetown history
Waterhouse, Jean, 319, 320
Waters, Adaline, 342
Waters, John, 216–17
Waters, Morris, 124
Waugh, Albert, 138
Wear-Ever Company, 152
Weaver family's hardware store, 184–89, 232
Webster, Sally, 52–53
Weinstein, Charles, 302
Weis, Frank, 276–77
Wells, J. B., 202
Wells sisters' business, 164–67
West End Hotel, 218
Western Development Corporation, 352–55
West Washington Hotel, 219–24, 238, 250, 285

West Washington Market, 107
White Horse Inn, 208–9
White House Hotel and Billiard Parlor, 228
White House Restaurant and Bowling Salon, 228–29, 299–300
Wick, Nellie, 171
William E. Miller furniture store, 157
William H. Lee feed store, 20
William H. Stombock & Son, 27–28
Williams, Dave, 270–71
Winslow, William R., 196–98
Winston's nightclub, 288
Wisconsin Avenue: bars, 249; car-related businesses, 29; formerly High Street, IX, 2; immigrant businesses, 357–58; impact of Georgetown Park on, 355–58; residential and office buildings, 8. *See also specific businesses*
Wise, George W., 23, 154–55, 159
Wise, Joseph and Hilda, 305
Woodward & Lothrop department store, 157
Wrenn, Robert, 124
Wrenn, Theophilis, 141
W. R. Winslow Company, 196–98
W. T. Weaver & Sons, 184–89

Xander, William, 306–7

Yaffe, Henry, 262–63
Yockelson, Louis and Lillian, 52, 64
Young, Ford E., 136–37
Young, Melvin, 310–12

www.ingramcontent.com/pod-product-compliance
Lightning Source LLC
LaVergne TN
LVHW051218070526
838200LV00064B/4953